IMAGINATION

OTHER BOOKS BY HAROLD RUGG

The Teacher of Teachers

Foundations for American Education

American Life and the School Curriculum

Culture and Education in America

The Child-Centered School (with Ann Shumaker)

Imagination

Harold Rugg

LATE PROFESSOR OF EDUCATION,
TEACHERS COLLEGE, COLUMBIA UNIVERSITY

With a Foreword and Editorial Comments
by KENNETH D. BENNE

HARPER & ROW, PUBLISHERS

NEW YORK, EVANSTON, AND LONDON

Contents

Part III. TOWARD A THEORY OF THE CREATIVE IMAGINATION

Foreword

On May 17, 1960, Harold Rugg died suddenly while walking in the garden of his home at Woodstock, New York. All that morning he had been revising the manuscript of this book. The task of revision had become clear to him during the preparation of a paper which appears here, in an edited version, as the final chapter.

The form which the paper took was a series of theorems, with supporting evidence and argument for each. His plan of revision was to reorganize the voluminous body of evidence, which he had gathered in his years of study, around these theorems. Only a small part of this plan had been accomplished by May 17, 1960.

When Elizabeth Rugg asked me early in 1961 to put her husband's manuscript into shape for publication, I did not hesitate long before accepting. In part, my reasons for acceptance were personal. Harold Rugg had been my esteemed friend and colleague for twenty-five years. I was eager to help bring his final work to the reading audience which it deserved.

But, more fundamentally, my decision was based on a conviction that his work is crucially important for people in our time. Actually, my convictions about its importance are two not one.

The perpetuity, even the survival, of our civilization depends, in some large measure, upon finding a valid solution to the problem which he was struggling to clarify and to solve. What is the nature of man's power to create new and valid conceptions, forms and patterns of thought and relationship? And how can this power be disciplined and released? This problem is fundamentally important to modern man.

Harold Rugg brought an unexcelled breadth of scholarship, a scholarship seasoned by forty years of thought and study, to bear upon his chosen problem. What he has to say on the subject is worth pondering and understanding. Let me speak, in turn, of the importance of his problem and of Rugg's contribution to it.

An increasing number of people in American and Western civilization have grown anxious about the possible impotence of our culture to create the ideas and forms necessary to insure its adaptive continuity under radically changed and changing conditions of life. And the anxiety is justified. The threat of powerful traditions alien to our own tends to drive us into a conservative posture with respect to the values of our beleaguered heritage. Yet, even as we seek to conserve the core values of that heritage, our intelligence counsels us that effective conservation today requires creation of new ideas, new practices, new forms that are continuous with but not identical with the ideas, practices, and forms of the past.

The central wisdom of our tradition leads us to look to the individual person as the source of the new knowledge and new wisdom which collectively we require. But, as we examine the thought patterns of the individuals which contemporary enculturation and education are producing, we grow anxious. We find much evidence that these patterns are marked by conformity rather than creativity, retreat rather than advance, caution rather than daring in the very areas of life and experience where innovation is most needed.

And as we examine this evidence seriously, we find that we do not know very much about the process and conditions of human creativity. We have depended upon chance rather than design for creative break-through in the past. Creative individuality has developed, where it has developed, through processes and conditions not of our own deliberate making. Can we afford to depend upon chance in the future? If not, we must seek to understand creative processes, their nature, and their nurture, drawing help from every area of knowledge and wisdom available to us.

Of course, Rugg was not the only recent student concerned with the understanding and fostering of creative processes in men and women. In fact, concern with creativity has become fashionable in many circles in America during the past decade—reflecting the anxiety about ourselves and our civilization already noted. Santayana once observed, in discussing American character, that to be obsessed with vitality may be a symptom not of health but of anemia. Our growing obsession with "creativity" is in part a symptom of alarmed but fundamentally unaltered and uncreative activism. This symptom is most evident in efforts to find a gimmick or device which will enable American industry or politics or education immediately to mass-produce "creativity" without any need to reconstruct its ideologies and institutions or to understand fundamentally the conditions and processes of creative response.

Rugg's efforts were not at all of this sort. He recognized the depth and difficulty of the problem he was tackling. He was certain that clues to the clarification and ultimate solution of the problem lay widely scattered in the contemporary arts and sciences and in the practices and disciplines of wisdom, old and new, Eastern and Western. It was a task of exploration and synthesis that he undertook. His explorations took him into many fields of research and study, fields academically respectable and fields not so academically respectable. The range of his explorations and his attempts at synthesis are unusual in our age of specialization. And always, as he worked, he sought a synthesis, not an easy one, but one that was valid and, of necessity, creative.

When I decided to accept Elizabeth Rugg's request to edit this manuscript, I was not unaware of the broad construction its author had put upon his problem or of the vast scope of his efforts at synthesis. I had several extended conversations with Harold Rugg about the problems and progress of his work during the eight years after his retirement when it was his almost exclusive preoccupation. We always agreed upon the importance of the problem and upon the need for an integrative, multi-disciplinary approach to its clarification. We didn't always agree upon the weighting or evaluation of the knowledge or the ideas which might prove most fruitful in understanding the processes of individual creation. Some of the sources which I find most illuminating are still relatively unworked in the present treatment—the psychology of groups and interpersonal relations, the American pragmatic tradition (apart from James), and the study of human conflict and conflict resolution.

But the sources which Rugg had worked are rich and varied indeed. The task of reshaping his manuscripts into this book has been both challenging and arduous. I have sought always to realize his intention more fully, as I reordered and reworked his material. I mentioned previously his plan to rebuild his earlier material around the theorems presented in the final chapter. Since so little of this plan of revision was accomplished before his death, I found it easier to use his earlier versions—even of the parts that he had revised. Yet, knowing of his hope, I have added notes at several places in the text to point up material to the ideas most systematically enunciated in his theorems. Some may prefer to read the last chapter immediately after the author's introduction and then return to the rich and variegated assembly of ideas, wisdom, information, and argument which the earlier chapters provide.

In my efforts to realize the author's intention more fully and accurately through cutting, revising, and reordering his materials, the advice of Elizabeth Rugg has been indispensable. Her knowledge of the author's hopes and intentions had been built through continual conversations with him throughout the course of his study. She has verified the extensive quotations in the text and has put its many pages of bibliographical references into shape.

A sympathetic yet critical reading of my first revision of the manuscript by Professor Theodore Brameld helped me greatly in preparing the final draft.

It is my first hope that Harold Rugg would approve of what I have done with his work. It is my further hope that readers will find in the work a masterful contribution to the clarification of a most baffling and a most crucial problem of contemporary man.

KENNETH D. BENNE

Boston University
February 1963

Preface

For eight years I have searched for the answer to a single baffling question. What is the nature of the act of thought when, in one brilliant moment, there is a sudden veering of attention, a consequent grasp of new dimensions, and a new idea is born? Some autonomous forming process sweeps like a magnet across the chaotic elements of the threshold state, picking up the significant segments and, in a welding flash, precipitates the meaningful response. What is this magical force that forms the bits and pieces of the stuff of mind?

Over the centuries the creative flash has been given many names: Galileo's *il lume naturale;* Goethe's *Dæmonic voice;* Coleridge's *imagination creatrix;* Whitehead's *prehension;* the exclamatory "Ah ha!" of all men. The sudden accurate leaping of mind across barriers and into new fields is perhaps best described as a "flash of insight" and it is an experience of all of us. But what it is that explodes the perceptual flash, the incipient motor tendencies, and the fantasia of imagery into the scientific discovery or the radiant beauty of art is still the unexplained miracle of the creative act.

We have lived a hundred years into the second intellectual revolution of the modern West. We have seen man's imaginative achievements in atomics and his electronic powering and control of the machine to free human labor. We have witnessed his gains in the control of disease, his creation of high-speed automatic patterns for society. Each of these modern miracles had, as its initial germ, a flash of insight exploding in the mind of man. We know it happens, we partake of its fruits, but we do not understand the process, the leap of the mind by which this incredible thing occurs. We still continue to ask: What was the complete act of feeling and thought that gave us the magnificent ceiling of the Sistine Chapel? That lighted the first atomic fire? That stated the Declaration of the Rights of Man or the Sermon on the Mount? What was the source of Einstein's sudden imaginative grasp of the simultaneous factors of time and space? The body-mind process that took place in Cezanne as, standing before his canvas, in the off-conscious posture of concentration, he juxtaposed in imagination alternative lines, planes, colors, masses, textures—*then suddenly knew,* and painted? Each of these acts, whether of art, of morals or of science, is a creative act, an act of imagination.

One fact of major importance is known: only man can create. Neither the other animals nor man's astonishing computing machines can think creatively. As Ernst Cassirer, in an act which was itself creative, named him, man is *animale symbolicum.* In industrial societies of the West, controlled power and automation have now liberated man from his long bondage to habit and problem-solving, have freed him to do what he alone can do. That is to create. The high-speed computers of communication-control have mechanized part of problem-solving thought and all of habit. But, lest we gloat too soon, cast up mechanization's total account: The machine can "solve" any problem the data of which have been built into it. It can answer a question but it cannot ask it. It can "think" logically, but not creatively. *Only men can create, for only men have the capacity to turn signals into symbols.* The higher animals and such clever machines as Grey Walter's "Speculatrix" can turn signals into movements, and some animals can turn signals into gestural signs. But neither higher animals nor machines can achieve symbolic transformation. To know that is important, but that fact alone does not illuminate the nature of the creative flash of insight.

And so a strange paradox confronts us. While modern man has, by his own creative acts, brought civilization to the very verge of the abundant life and to the verge of its total destruction, he does not know *how* he has done it. His psychologists have mastered the psychology of habit, his philosophers have worked over, I think overworked, the logic of problem-solving and the scientific method of inquiry. The academicians continue to debate what they call the "body-mind" problem, and continue to argue as to whether thought may occur in any way other than in the conscious, logical, problem-solving state. But what takes place in the creative act is still unknown.

For many years I had been preoccupied with this problem and had been engaged in preliminary studies. Then in 1952, retired from academic duties and burdens at Teachers College, Columbia University, I settled down at my home in Woodstock to devote myself to the study of this great unknown. During the preceding thirty years I had searched many sources and tried several methods of building in myself an understanding of the creative process. The sympathetic observing of creative work in schools was one way— watching, questioning, appraising the development of children under the guidance of genuine artist-teachers. From that experience I was able to observe and describe how such teachers work. I gained, moreover, a first glimpse of some of the conditions of children's creative work in the arts and the sciences. But even from the most searching conversations with the teachers and the children, I got little light on the inner nature of the imagination.

During these thirty years I had lived in the midst of some two hundred painters, sculptors, writers, critics, designers, illustrators, composers, theatre directors, museum directors, and artist-teachers. I studied their works and asked them what they thought took place in the creative experience. As their answers came, rudiments of an "autobiography of the creative act" took shape. Slowly the vista widened, partly through my study of the products of these artists and even more through talking with them. But the results, while stimulating, fell far short of what I needed. I did find confirmation of my accumulating generalizations about *how* the creative man works, but little on the inner nature of the flash of insight itself. In most of the fine expressional artists neither mastery of concept nor capacity to communicate kept pace with their own art of expression; naturally so, for they were exemplifying Goethe's dictum that the graphic artist should paint and not talk.

In these years I also extended the examination of the creative autobiography through the printed retrospections of a few who were speculative and articulate as well as expressive. This included, in addition to the records of artists, the documents of men of the sciences, philosophy, and technology.

During this long period I worked largely with esthetic data from the works and lives of artists and scientists. Altogether, I examined the autobiographical retrospections of a hundred eminent members of the world's academies—Nobel prize winners, creative men of modern science and art. Their statements produced a tentative consensus of how productive men work and a few rare speculative hints concerning the creative process. I have set down that record here in Chapter I. In that consensus there is unanimity on the general characteristics of the imaginative act of discovery, the conscious preparation which precedes it, and the chief stages through which it moves. Creative activities, irrespective of medium, exemplify a common pattern. There was also considerable agreement on the conditions that favor the flash of insight. Some, as will be shown in Chapter I, were obvious and well known. But still the sum total of all that had been done in these ways threw little light on the hidden nature of the creative act.

During World War II the urgency of defense needs resulted in major discoveries and inventions of an original and creative sort. Since the war, industry, through a nation-wide talent hunt, has been gathering "the best of American youth into the technological laboratories and training them quickly for positions of imagination and decision-making." The national press has been editorializing about the "yearly forays of company scouts into our colleges in search of 'promising material.'" The Carnegie Corporation has announced its decision that "the field in which the bulk of the Corporation's income will be spent" is to be that of *creative* higher education. The pronouncements of these institutions call for a "new kind of young man . . . possessing the bubbling energy to bring about a dynamic society."

The significance of the creative process had been particularly sensed by the engineers and industrial designers and vigorous, well-financed attempts to study it by the group process had been carried on.[1] Since World War I the trend called "industrial design," meaning design for an industrial civilization, has become a major cultural phenomenon. It has already applied creative invention to the entire range of physical products of our society, and is beginning to have an effect in leavening the public taste. It is these industrial designers, with their roots in engineering and mathematics, who have experimented most successfully with the group invention of new products.

The chief center of stimulation has been John Arnold's work at the Massachusetts Institute of Technology, especially his annual seminars in Creative Engineering, held since 1954 and attended by industrial designers and corporation executives. Far from offering popularization of superficial psychological ideas, this seminar has provided basic instruction in the findings of psychology and creative design by university psychologists and such renowned and original designers as Buckminster Fuller.

The most impressive use of group invention among engineers and industrial designers discovered through my search is that of William J. J. Gordon's inventive design unit called Operational Creativity, in the A. D. Little Company of Cambridge, Massachusetts.[2] Now some fifteen years old, it was developed as an attempt to solve the problem of invention of ideas through group stimulation, criticism, and discussion. The procedure is to have a group of six to nine trained engineers invent theories, designs and working models of new products for the clients of the company; it is emphasized that no single designer can possibly meet the demands. In sharp opposition to the high-tension, off-the-top-of-the-head, quantity brain-storming of Osborn, Gordon creates a quiet, relaxed, permissive group climate conducive to free natural expression.

For the purposes of this study, group invention of products served in two ways: first, it supported the conception of the need for the quiet, relaxed, off-conscious mind, which was to become a guiding concept of the study; second, it pointed to possible differences between impulsive *perceptual invention* and deeper levels of the creative imagination. There was no question that the flash of insight was constantly involved in the process, and that one would do well to master the findings that were coming from this work. Nevertheless, while the group process literature offered convincing evidence that a collaborative team of competent minds should be used for stimulation, criticism, and corroboration or refutation, it became increasingly doubtful that it can take the place of the single creative mind. I became convinced that we should not expect much deeply original scientific or esthetic discovery to emerge from the group process; in fact, I find in history no example of such discovery. Every idea that has moved the world has been created by one imaginative mind or by a succession of them. This means that enough of the factual minutiae to guarantee understanding of the key concepts must be passed through a single organism, if the spark, the flash of meaning, is to jump across the barrier.

I could not escape the feeling, as I reviewed the earlier studies, that even the trained students working on the problem of the creative process were ignoring many of the indispensable archives of man's wisdom and scientific knowledge, and were approaching the unknown with an orientation so restricted that it barred off any possibility of reaching the hidden depths of the imaginative flash.

A preliminary study of the scientific and esthetic literature confirmed both feelings. I found that, in spite of the astonishing second revolution in the behavioral sciences and the arts, no more than a small fraction of their available results had been used. No one in the behavioral sciences had undertaken the encyclopedic task of integrating with their physiological and psychological concepts, either the vastly illuminating findings concurrently established in the philology, mythology and philosophy of the symbol, or the data from the work on symbol-formation by various psychiatrists.

In short, the problem of the creative process, even in the mid-twentieth century, was being investigated with only half of a bio-social psychology and with a thoroughly atomistic view of man's nature and behavior. For a generation we have given lip service to ideas of "the whole man" and "the complete act of thought," but few of us have put the full scope of the available and essential concepts to work. We have used only half of mind and dealt with less than half of man.

The conclusion became inescapable, therefore, that if we are to dispel the mystery of the creative act, we must draw upon all the sources of knowledge and approaches to knowing. But to do this requires that we liberate ourselves from two perennial and ensnaring dichotomies of thought. The first is the perpetuation of the historic dichotomy over mechanistic versus organic explanations of the universe, the earth, its living creatures, and man's life and behavior. The second is the dichotomy between the inside-outside ways of knowing. The two are, of course, phases of one basic cleavage.

There are two great sources of knowledge, not one, despite the claims of the pragmatists and the positivists. One is the tested, intuitive wisdom of the ages, both of East and West. The other is the profound conceptual consensus and the tested theories of what today we are calling the behavioral sciences. Unless one is sensitively alert to the two ways of knowing, he will not use both great sources of knowledge, and his discoveries will be correspondingly stinted. If he is a devotee only of the scientific way of inquiry, he will search the behavioral sciences, but nothing else. If he believes only in the intuitive way, he will devote himself to the speculative wisdom of the ages and ignore the vital findings of the human sciences. But if he believes in both, he will search and use the findings of both.

The resources of the two approaches, the intuitive and the scientific, so far as they bear on the imagination, must be brought together. Not their factual and technical minutiae, but their conceptual essence. This called for a careful study of the great discoveries of both. During the past five centuries the West has produced the scientific method of tested observation, profiting greatly by the Near East's successes in mathematical thinking. This was thinking of a special kind—logical in orientation. Thus, to the East's intuitive keys to discovery, the West had added its own invention, the symbolic logic of verification. Together (neither one alone could have done so), they produced our modern scientific revolution and are now transforming technology and social institutions over the entire earth. In the great books of the West, therefore, one should also find new clues, especially in its human sciences. What have its scientific method of inquiry and its empirical making-and-doing contributed to understanding and mastery of our ways of knowing and imagining?

It appeared that in order to produce more than statements of consensus and hypothesis from the study of the West's way of objective observation, it would be equally necessary to make oneself a student of the concepts of the relevant philosophic and scientific disciplines. I undertook, therefore, to parallel the study of the contemplative way with a conceptual synthesis of recent contributions of the behavioral sciences to understanding the creative imagination.

One difficulty was the lack of consensus on the boundaries of knowledge and research comprehended by the term "behavioral science." Psychology had been vaguely "behavioral" for seventy years since the study of the act by Brentano and Külpe in Europe, and by James, Baldwin, and others in the United States. Between 1910 and 1920, John B. Watson, a devotee of rigorous scientific methods, had called emphatic attention to body-movement, on the ground that only what the subject *did* could be observed and measured. In succeeding decades, varieties of this form of "behaviorism" reappeared recurringly in psychology and physiology, the conspicuous current example being cybernetics.

The emphasis on behavior as observable movement has done one serious disservice; this has led me to question the value of the current nation-wide acclaim of the human sciences as "behavioral." The blanket nature of the concept was obscuring important factors of knowing (and imagining, expressing and communicating) in the act of response. More especially, it was complicating the task of cultivating the inside way of knowing. I became convinced of the need for a comprehensive label for those sciences of man that embrace the foundations of his behaving and his knowing, his imagining, expressing and communicating. But that need has not yet been satisfactorily met, and the term "behavioral sciences" seems to be fastened upon us.

Keeping in mind this confusion over the term, I use it to embrace *all the fields of scientific study that bear on both human knowing and behaving.* These include the several branches and brands of psychology, including the social; related divisions of physiology, including neurophysiology and its biochemistry and biophysics; psychiatry and psychopathology, including psychoanalysis; the schools of philosophic thought currently dealing with the symbol, and their background studies of language and myth; and the current integration of neurophysiology, associational and conditioning psychology, electronics, and mathematics known as cybernetics; some workers would add economics, government, sociology, anthropology, and other social sciences and, because of my long contacts with the social sciences, I have done that.

In the course of my conferring with colleagues, some have urged that it is premature to undertake such a vast integration of conceptual knowledge; not enough is known, they have said. Others have protested that to undertake such an encyclopedic study was pretentious. Perhaps in meeting the first of these criticisms we shall dispose also of the second.

At the beginning of this century, one might properly have protested the state of our ignorance, but not today. The intellectual revolution has gathered such momentum that even now the annual accretions of measured knowledge are staggering. This expansion in the volume and scope of scientific knowledge has already created a new imperative. The art of conceptual synthesis has become an indispensable partner of the science of analysis. The solution of an unknown now depends upon two conditions. First, it depends on the assembling in one place, which means in one organism, of all the key concepts of the known data that might conceivably bear upon it. This is an adaptation of Peirce's beautiful concept of the "unlimited community" of ideas. Second, to facilitate the firing process, the flash of discovery waits on the optimal organization and integration of such concepts. Thus the scattered materials must not only be gathered; they must be formed. This principle of the unlimited community of concepts is partially conveyed by the current emphasis on encyclopedism in multi-disciplinary and inter-disciplinary researches. Multi-disciplinary theory must generalize in pace with objective experiment and fact-finding, anticipating the logic of the theory and making possible its demonstration.

In attempting to develop a sound theory of knowing or imagining, therefore, we have no recourse but to make ourselves conceptual encyclopedists. We must know the essence of all knowledge relevant to our problem, and this is a gargantuan task. We must, for example, know our civilization, its development, current changes and problems, and the current knowledge of human behavior, growth, learning, and creative expression. To master the essence of all the material bearing on the nature of the imagination, we must gather, almost continuously, the basic concepts from the sciences and arts of man.

Because of the present accelerating accumulation of measured knowledge this has become a multi-disciplinary task. Competent laymen do not need the technical knowledge or skill required to derive theories and invent experiments and formulae in mathematics, physics, technology, physiology, psychology, esthetics, and philosophy. But they can understand the key concepts of these fields; even become able to criticize them and suggest new ones, and to use them in their own fields where they do have technical competence. I repeat, they must have comprehensive conceptual understanding of all those optimal regroupings of knowledge that might conceivably bear on their problem. The present book is my personal documentation of this generalization.

These prolegomena should, perhaps, supply some anticipatory illustrations of the new conception of mind that emerged from my multi-disciplinary and organic approach. In the search for the ingredients of the creative flash, no task was more difficult than to rid myself of traditional stereotypes and to reorient the study in terms of new psychological dimensions. I have already spoken of the dichotomies concerning knowing and the sources of knowledge, and have emphasized the limited half-mind with which pragmatic and positivistic students have approached their problems. Another handicapping preconception is the almost universal emphasis on thinking as purely verbal with corresponding neglect of feeling and non-verbal symbolization. Most of us in the Western academic world have been brought up to pay attention only to what can be sensed through the eyes, ears, and other obvious organs of perception. Our world was the circumscribed one of traditional linguistics. The problems of mind could be approached and thinking could be done only through words. All thinking must be rational, must "make sense," and its most intelligent forms were logical, verbal propositions; in fact, normal mental life was logical thinking. All else—including feeling—was "nonsense," irrational, on a par with fantasy, hallucination, illusion.

Moreover, the conventional academic psychologies—connectionist, Gestalt, and experimental—have, for a long time, dealt only with *conscious* knowing and behaving. To this day most of our philosophic students, both the positivists and the typical followers of Dewey, have scorned or neglected the theories of nonconscious life. They have attended only to the reality-oriented mind of the sensory world, ignoring the strange but actual autistic phenomena which occurred in their own minds—dreams and other off-conscious phenomena. They stoutly maintained that attributing value to trance states was the act of crackpots and charlatans. Thus the philosophers and psychologists theorized about life and knowing on the basis of less than half of life—the conscious linguistic half—and ignored or ridiculed the unconscious and the nonverbal.

In my study and its new appraisal of the behavioral sciences, such shackling stereotypes were steadily pushed back as I sorted and sifted the scientific samplings brought up from the human conscious-nonconscious. A different conception of mind evolved: one that lets things happen as well as makes things happen; is autistic as well as realistic; is marked by relaxed control; and yet, at the same time, is actively dynamic. I began to see mind as functioning along one unbroken conscious-nonconscious continuum.

My changing conceptual synthesis and reorientation about man and his knowing and behaving advanced as discoveries in one field spotlighted dark corners in others. For example, some of the mystery of memory and the storage of the unconscious was dispersed when the psychologists' new findings on hypermnesia under deep hypnotic trance were bracketed, first, with the evoking of specific memories by the neuro-surgeon's electrode, and, second, with the proved facts of age regression by the psychiatrists' combined use of drugs, hypnosis, and psychoanalysis. The artist's well-known concept of "significant form" made new sense when the phenomenon of an autonomous forming process was found to be universal throughout all of the natural sciences, in cybernetics, in the philosophy of the symbol, in the experimental psychology of perception and in the history of ideas.

Fresh doubts were cast on conventional approaches to both the problem of meaning and the so-called body-mind problem when concepts were juxtaposed from such diverse fields as these: the psychologists' "responding with meaning"; the genetic development of meaning via the motor responses of childhood and youth; the motor-attitude theory of emotion; the several psychological theories of memory, set, and the incompleted act; and "directive state" theories of perception. A new view of concept-formation appeared when the symbolic data of philology and mythology were associated with those of cybernetics, itself a union of several disciplines.

In my multi-disciplinary search, the critical question I asked myself at each step in conceptual synthesis was, Does it throw new light on the mystery of creative imagination? At first I was rewarded only on rare occasions, but with increasing frequency new understanding came as data-gathering and organizing went on. Finally, I have been able to set down in a single record for the use of competent students of behavioral theory many concepts on the nature of imagination, which have had their origins in separate scientific disciplines. As far as I can ascertain it is the first time this has been done. I hoped, of course, to go far toward solving the great unknown myself, but I felt that if I failed, at least the new integration of data would facilitate a creative break-through in other minds.

This principle of juxtaposing concepts and theories which hitherto had been isolated from one another not only guided my search for the unknown factors of the creative imagination. It also set the conceptual structure of this book.

HAROLD RUGG

Part I

THE CREATIVE ACT:

DESCRIPTIONS

AND

DISTINCTIONS

1

Autobiography of the Creative Act

ONE way to explore the nature of the creative act is to ask the creative person: "How is a poem made—a house, a bridge, a motor designed—a scientific hypothesis drawn?" Many times creative men have been asked that question. Their answers have varied widely. Some, happily few in number, have said with C. G. Jung: "The creative act will forever elude the human understanding." But such iconoclasts have been countered by a host of eminent members of the world's academies, Nobel prize winners, representatives of both the sciences and the arts. Their statements constitute a distinguished autobiography of the creative process.[1]

POINCARÉ ON MATHEMATICAL CREATION

It is a fortunate circumstance that some of our men of genius were both curious and articulate about their processes of creation. One classic example was a lecture on "Mathematical Creation" given before the Parisian Société de Psychologie at the turn of the century by Henri Poincaré. I quote from it because it accents several of the conspicuous phases of the creative process. It is a retrospective account of the events that led to his discovery of Fuchsian functions which, throughout many baffled days, Poincaré had sought to prove could not exist. I find in it four episodes illustrating the cycle of the creative process. The first episode breaks down into several steps.

3

First came a long, conscious, and unsuccessful struggle to put together a coherent, logical body of ideas. Usually on these days, he says,

I seated myself at my work table, stayed an hour or two, tried a great number of combinations and reached no results. [After two weeks of such conscious struggle came the first flash of insight.] One evening, contrary to my custom, I drank black coffee and could not sleep. Ideas rose in crowds; I felt them collide until pairs interlocked, so to speak, making a stable combination. By the next morning I had established the existence of a class of Fuchsian functions, those which come from the hypergeometric series; I had only to write out the results, which took but a few hours.[2]

A second episode followed somewhat later, involving a new and diverting type of work. "I left Caen, where I was then living, to go on a geological excursion. . . . The incidents of the travel made me forget my mathematical work." He put his problem out of mind. Nevertheless it was in his mind, for one day while taking an omnibus, "At the moment when I put my foot on the step, the idea came to me, without anything in my former thoughts seeming to have paved the way for it, that the transformations I had used to define the Fuchsian functions were identical with those of non-Euclidean geometry. I did not verify the idea; I went on with a conversation already commenced, but I felt a perfect certainty. On my return to Caen, for conscience' sake, I verified the result at my leisure."

Then came a third episode dealing with a different problem, one involving arithmetical questions. This went through the same cycle of conscious struggle, but again with no success; it was dropped and Poincaré went on a vacation. Several days later, "while walking on the bluff, the idea came to me with just the same characteristics of brevity, suddenness and immediate certainty." There was another postponement of conscious verification which again was successful.

Finally, a fourth episode followed: first came another long, unsuccessful conscious struggle with an obstreperous remaining mathematical function; then, compulsory military service forced Poincaré to drop the problem out of mind for a period of time. Again, the solution appeared to him as unexpectedly, as unpreparedly as in the other instances, while he was serving his time in the army.

This, then, is the cyclic course of the complete act of original thought in mathematics, in which the work is specifically defined by a certain problem.

HOUSMAN ON THE PRODUCTION OF THE POEM

I turn, for my second example, to the arts. What happens to the poet, gripped by the urge to write, but with no problem or theme defined, no formulated but unanswered questions baffling his mind? I take an excerpt from A. E. Housman's *The Name and Nature of Poetry*.[3]

Having drunk a pint of beer at luncheon—beer is a sedative to the brain, and my afternoons are the least intellectual portion of my life—I would go out for a walk of two or three hours. As I went along, thinking of nothing in particular, only looking at things around me and following the progress of the seasons, there would flow into my mind, with sudden and unaccountable emotion, sometimes a line or two of verse, sometimes a whole stanza at once, accompanied, not preceded, by a vague notion of the poem which they were destined to form part of.

Then there would usually be a lull of an hour or so, then perhaps the spring would bubble up again. I say bubble up, because, so far as I could make out, the source of the suggestions thus profferred to the brain was an abyss which I have already had occasion to mention, the pit of the stomach.

When I got home I wrote them down, leaving gaps, and hoping that further inspiration might be forthcoming another day. Sometimes it was, if I took my walks in a receptive and expectant frame of mind; but sometimes the poem had to be taken in hand and completed by the brain, which was apt to be a matter of trouble and anxiety, involving trial and disappointment, and sometimes ending in failure.

The steps in the cycle of the artist's creative work, although the problem is a very different one, are essentially the same as those of the scientist: first, a relaxed condition of body and mind furthered by a two- or three-hour walk and a special stimulus; second, a "flowing into the mind [of verses] . . . with sudden and unaccountable emotion . . . accompanied . . . by a vague notion of the poem";

third, a lull, then a "bubbling up" of lines, even whole stanzas from an "abyss"; fourth, writing of the verses on arrival home, "leaving gaps" and "hoping for further inspiration."

But often the brain had to fill in the gaps—a matter of conscious struggle, disappointment, and failure. Housman speaks of one such episode which involved writing a single stanza thirteen times over a period of a year:

I happen to remember distinctly the genesis of the piece which stands last in my first volume. Two of the stanzas, I do not say which, came into my head, just as they are printed, while I was crossing the corner of Hampstead Heath between the Spaniard's Inn and the footpath to Temple Fortune. A third stanza came with a little coaxing after tea. One more was needed, but it did not come; I had to turn to and compose it myself, and that was a laborious business. I wrote it thirteen times, and it was more than a twelvemonth before I got it right.[4]

TWO VITAL CHARACTERISTICS

Agreement on several stages, generally four in prolonged creative work, is suggested by the examples previously mentioned: first, a preparatory conscious period of baffled struggle; second, an interlude in which the worker apparently gives up, pushes the problem back or down or "out of mind"—more properly into another compartment of "mind"—leaving it for the unconscious to work upon; third, a sudden and unexpected "flash of insight," coming with such certitude that a logical statement of it can be immediately prepared; fourth, a period of verification, critical testing, and reconstruction. I can find no essential disagreement with this sequence.

Turning from the stages of creative work to characteristics of the complete act, there is an equally clear agreement on two distinguishing features: an indispensable preparatory period, marked by conscious effort and intense concentration; and then the sudden and unexpected flash of illumination marked by a feeling of certitude.

While the imaginative flash cannot be brought forth by sheer force of will, prolonged conscious preparation is, nevertheless, indispensable. One must immerse himself deeply in the problem, excluding all else during a long period of time. Manifold instances can be cited from the autobiographical record. Helmholtz, Poincaré, and many others insist that the two great stages of incubation and the illuminating flash occur only if the way has been rigorously prepared. Poincaré's comment was: "A period of preliminary conscious work . . . always precedes fruitful unconscious work."[5] We do not merely apprehend the conditions and premises of a problem, drop it conveniently into the well of the unconscious, go to bed, sleep, and wake up the next morning with the problem solved. It is not that easy. Newton, when asked how he came to his discovery of the law of universal attraction, replied: "By constantly thinking it over." Delacroix's phrase for it was "a voluntary faithfulness to an idea"; Hadamard's is "a tenacious continuity of attention."[6]

To Darwin, Buffon, and many others patient persistence is the desideratum—untiring, plodding, uninterrupted continuity of thought. Malcolm Cowley reported that Hart Crane meditated over a particular poem for months or even years, scribbling verses on pieces of paper that he carried in his pockets, meanwhile waiting for the moment of pure inspiration when they would go together. Chekhov confirms the importance of concentrated thought: ". . . to deny that artistic creation involves problems and purposes would be to admit that an artist creates without premeditation, without design, under a spell. Therefore if an artist boasted to me of having written a story without a previously settled design, but by inspiration, I should call him a lunatic."[7] Another student reports that "sudden inspirations" never occurred except after some days of voluntary effort which had appeared absolutely fruitless. "But actually they have not been as sterile as one thinks [for] they have set going the unconscious machine and without them it would not have been moved." My experience agrees; to produce original results I must saturate myself with my problem and exclude all else, allow myself no other major concern for weeks, months, without end. As Ghiselin summed it up: "Production by a process of purely conscious calculation seems never to occur."[8]

The flash, when it finally comes, follows a long and disheartening period of confusion. Whitehead describes this period in his work of philosophical analysis, as "the state of imaginative muddled suspense which precedes successful inductive generalization."[9] Isadora Duncan, first American of the modern dance, expressed it in almost identical words—"a state of complete suspense."[10] British poet

Stephen Spender expresses it as "a dim cloud of an idea which I feel must be condensed into a shower of words."[11] Ghiselin emphasizes the "necessity for patience. The development desired may have to be waited for, even though its character has been clearly intimated. After the first suggestion . . . a long gestation may be required."[12]

John Livingston Lowes reports finding the same two characteristics of the creative act in his study of Coleridge's imagination, and also in an analysis of two historic scientific discoveries—Darwin's theory of evolution and Newton's principle of gravitation. Lowes speaks of the conjunction of the "larger factors of [Coleridge's] creative process, the storing of the Well [the unconscious], the Vision, and the concurrent operation of the Will," then adds that the flash comes to the scientist as to the man of art, and the factors are much the same. Lowes tells how Darwin had gathered his data on evolution over many years of conscious struggle; then one day the flash came, as Darwin records in his autobiography: " 'I can remember the very spot in the road, whilst in my carriage, when to my joy the solution occurred to me.' " "And then," adds Lowes, "and only then, with the infinite toil of exposition, was slowly framed from the obdurate facts the great statement of the theory of evolution."[13]

He cites the example of Newton's sudden flash about gravitation:

The leap of the imagination, in a garden at Woolsthorpe on a day in 1665, from the fall of an apple to an architectonic conception cosmic in its scope and grandeur is one of the dramatic moments in the history of human thought. But in that pregnant moment there flashed together the profound and daring observations and conjectures of a long period of years; and upon the instant of illumination followed other years of rigorous and protracted labour, before the *Principia* appeared. Once more there was the long, slow storing of the well; once more the flash of amazing vision through a fortuitous suggestion; once more the exacting task of translating the vision into actuality.[14]

Bertrand Russell tells of "the fruitless effort" he expended in trying to push his creative mathematics to completion by sheer force of will, before he discovered the necessity of "waiting for it to find its own subconscious development." Goethe's last phrase, says

Cocteau, was "More light," which "assumes meaning when one considers the struggle of Goethe against the shadow."[15] Paul Valéry, speaking to the French Philosophical Society, points to the first stage of poetic invention as "a kind of flash . . . a gleam of light . . . dazzling." It is "a special sensitization; soon you will go into the dark-room and the picture will be seen to emerge."[16]

Jacques Hadamard, French mathematician, says of his own creative processes: "On being very abruptly awakened by an external noise, a solution long searched for appeared to me at once without the slightest instant of reflection on my part—the fact was remarkable enough to have struck me unforgettably—and in a quite different direction from any of those which I had previously tried to follow." He adds that

the same character of suddenness and spontaneousness had been pointed out, some years earlier . . . Helmholtz reported it in an important speech delivered in 1896. Since Helmholtz and Poincaré, it has been recognized by psychologists as being very general in every kind of invention. Graham Wallas, in his *Art of Thought,* suggested calling it "illumination," this illumination being generally preceded by an "incubation" stage wherein the study seems to be completely interrupted and the subject dropped. Such an illumination is even mentioned in several replies on the inquiry of *L'Enseignement Mathématique.* Other physicists like Langevin, chemists like Ostwald, tell us of having experienced it.[17]

In summary, I conclude that the muddled suspense stage is inevitable and indispensable to the creative worker. If he works and waits, with incredible patience, eventually *il lume naturale* breaks through the fog.

Autobiographers of the intuitive act are equally in agreement that the flash is sudden, unexpected, and has certitude. When it comes, the discoverer knows he is right, before he verifies it logically. Gauss, referring to an arithmetical theorem which he had unsuccessfully tried to prove for years, writes: "Finally, two days ago, I succeeded, not on account of my painful efforts, but by the grace of God. Like a sudden flash of lightning, the riddle happened to be solved. I myself cannot say what was the conducting thread which connected what I previously knew with what made my success possible."[18]

An inventor reports: "Ideas come when I least expect them, often when I'm half asleep or daydreaming." Of another it is said that he "wakes with a new idea, suddenly and quite unexpectedly . . . in a flash . . . either in a period of relaxation or when the inventor himself is engaged in a different kind of work." A third "when the need for a certain invention arises," puts it out of the "objective side" of his mind: "I cease to labor over it and assign it to the subjective side . . . there it evolves, ripens, and finally spontaneously 'comes out.' "

From the statements of creative teachers in the schools come frequent references to the "intuitive flashes of insight" which mark the expressive work of young people. One of the most striking came from the Dewey School.

There are occasional flashes of insight, like those of the laboratory worker, when he intuitively knows how to do what he wants to do or what he should choose, although he cannot explain why. This realization that he has both impulses to action and insights for action make him sensitive to similar processes in others. He also becomes conscious of resources outside of himself in the achievements of other persons, in values that already exist—the values of the stored knowledge of the race, of customs and traditions. It was a fundamental principle of the school to await the dawning of these directive insights, to trust their arrival, and to provide the conditions that foster their awakening.[19]

Such examples could be multiplied n-fold if there were need, but these should suffice. They reveal the universality of the suddenness, unexpectedness, and certitude of the flash of insight that finally crowns the creative effort.

In the creative work of scientists, artists, and technologists, the flash is revealed. In science, it is revealed in the statement of the hypothesis; in the art of disciplined conversation, in the asking of the right question; in logic, in the drawing of the premise; in problem-solving, in the recognition or statement of the problem; in poetry, in the definitive word or phrase, long sought; in painting or sculpture, in the inevitably right distortion; in all, in the counterpoint of significant relation.

It is well-named—"the flash of insight"! It is like a flash of lightning across the black night sky, or the instantaneous electrical illumination of an enormous room.

FAVORABLE CONDITIONS AND FORCES

What favors the flash? The tense matrix of conscious problem-solving? On the contrary, it comes when the mind is off-guard, receptive. My consensus agrees with Ghiselin's: "Production by . . . purely conscious calculation seems never to occur."

The Quiet Mind of Relaxed Concentration

A chorus of voices from my file confirms this advice to the original thinker. After effortful conscious preparation, put the problem "out of mind," let go, sleep on it, do something else, go on a vacation trip or take another job. That was Poincaré's experience. Recall his "Changes in travel made me forget my mathematical work." Later, while talking casually to his friend, "the moment I put my foot on the step, the idea came to me." Still later he spent "a few days at the seaside and thought of something else, [when] walking on the bluff, the idea came to me." Months after that he entered military service and "one day . . . going along the street, the solution appeared before me." Housman found that on an afternoon walk, "as I went along, thinking of nothing in particular . . . [lines of verse] would flow into my mind." Mozart composed well, he said, "When I feel well and in a good humor, or when I am taking a drive or walking after a good meal. . . ."[20]

There is emphatic agreement that the flash comes when the person is in a state of relaxed tension; being off-guard seems to be a central condition. It is as though successive closed doors barred off a passageway of dark antechambers which ranged from the deep unconscious through several sub-, fore-, or pre-conscious rooms, into the light of conscious day. We forget our problem, sleep on it, let go, relax. In one way or another, we get the conscious mind off guard so that contacts on the fringe of consciousness can be established. Then, the spark explodes the meaning.

Prolonged Preparation

A few investigators of the psychology of invention, Nicolle and Souriau, for example, have seen in the processes of incubation only the play of chance. Although the history of discovery abounds in examples of apparently chancelike happenings, it is doubtful if chance alone can bring about an original idea. As has been clearly indicated, conscious and prolonged focusing of the direction of thought is necessary if the new idea is to explode.

The Pertinent, Ordered Storage of the Unconscious

No man, be he artist or scientist, technologist or philosopher, will be successful either in thinking directly or in "thinking aside" in his search for an unknown, unless his mind is equipped with all the needed materials with which to think: with that multitude of facts, principles, theories, that might contain the one stimulus needed to precipitate the new idea. He must know a vast deal about the right things. Not just know a lot, but know the specially related things required to set off the particular spark. It is conscious preparation by deliberate manipulation of concepts into close juxtaposition that gives the greatest promise of permitting the spark of recognition to be ignited.

We must not overlook the contributions of our predecessors to the problem at hand, both the facts in all their full ramifications, and the full range of theories that have been advanced to account for the unknown. And this includes the most daring theories, for one cannot predict what such hypotheses may do to another mind. And a decent humility should be the handmaiden of the principle, not forgetting Claude Bernard's dictum: "Those who have an excessive faith in their ideas are not well fitted to make discoveries."[21]

That James Joyce understood this necessity of encyclopedic, ordered knowledge is borne out by the erudition of his *Finnegan's Wake*. Amy Lowell wrote a generation ago: "I do believe that a poet should know all he can. No subject is alien to him, and the profounder his knowledge in any direction, the more depth will there be to his poetry."[22]

The creative record of history supports these contemporaries. Consider the encyclopedism of Leonardo da Vinci, of Newton and Goethe, and of the great synthesizers of the nineteenth century—the psycho-physics of Comte, Darwin in his documentation of organic evolution, Helmholtz's covering of the arts as well as the sciences, the vast scope of Wundt's twenty volumes, the two thousand footnotes of James's *Psychology*. In the days of Newton and

Leibniz it was not too difficult to achieve a mastery of the conceptual essence of what men knew. Today we live in an age of extreme and accelerating specialization. But this does not relieve us of the obligation to know the conceptual essence of our contemporary problems.

I say, therefore, that the flash will not occur unless the mind, conscious and unconscious, has been stored with a rich body of percepts, images, motor adjustments and concepts that are pertinent to the new concept struggling to be born.

The Perceptive and Alert Observer

The history of science is packed with discoveries resulting from the precisely needed juxtaposition of events and the presence of a curious observer, whose mind is organized with tightly related concepts. Köhler's learning experiments on chimpanzees supplied examples of the facilitation of the flash when favorable conditions of perception were juxtaposed. As Lawrence Cole said about it:

Very slight transformations in the spatial arrangements transform a difficult problem to a soluble one. The stick which is out of the line of sight when the animal is looking at the food is only a single isolated element in the total objective situation; alone, its use cannot be imagined. But when it is placed close beside the food, or directly in the line of sight *so that food and stick are easily seen together,* the learner quickly seizes the stick and uses it correctly. . . . The perceived relationship is the essential factor.[23]

Recall how Luigi and Lucia Galvani discovered the electrical aspects of nervous stimulation by tying a dead frog to an iron balustrade with a copper wire and "happening" to observe its behavior in an electrical storm. Or consider Oersted's discovery (1819) of the relation between magnetism and electricity by noticing that whenever he moved a wire carrying a current of electricity over a magnetic needle, the needle was deflected at right angles to the wire.

Historic cases of near hits and near misses in scientific discovery are another enlightening source on the point in question. Claparède reports how De la Rive just failed to invent the galvanoplastic method; and how "Freud missed finding the application of cocaine to the surgery of the eye."[24] Hadamard, translating and interpreting Claparède, says:

The most striking instance which he gives, concerns the invention of the ophthalmoscope. The physiologist Brücke had investigated the means of illuminating the back part of the eye and succeeded in doing so; but it was Helmholtz who, while preparing a lecture on that result of Brücke, conceived the idea that optical images could be generated by the rays thus reflected by the retina: an almost obvious idea, which as it seems, Brücke could hardly have overlooked. In that case, most evidently—at least to me—Brücke's mind was too narrowly directed toward his problem.[25]

The conscious combining of Walpole's notion of serendipity* with informed and alert curiosity in young minds has certainly brought undreamed-of gains in twentieth-century research. Since Willis R. Whitney's first General Electric Laboratory (1900), the great corporations have capitalized on the imaginative acuity and curiosity of youth. As Woodbury said: "It was a prime example of serendipity when Alexander Fleming discovered penicillin; . . . an unknown mold blew in through his laboratory window and upset a painstaking experiment. He dropped the experiment and investigated the mold instead. . . . Roentgen went through the same process with X-rays. So did Bell with the germ of the telephone. Edison was doing it all the time—in outstanding fashion when he discovered the principle of the photoelectric cell." [26] Witnessing the success of the modern electric light, X-rays for medical and industrial uses, diathermy, basic discoveries in plastics, the electronics men got the idea of financing serendipity. "Today, no large company dares to be without it and countless small ones are formed simply to exploit it."[27] For example, as a result of the invention of the transistor which serendipity turned up at the Bell Telephone Laboratories, we have today better telephones, hearing aids, radios, television sets, electric computers, military defense—in short, better automation.

---

* The current use of this term was inspired by Horace Walpole's fairy tale (1754), "The Three Princes of Serendip," who, it is said, were always making discoveries, by accident and sagacity, of things extraneous to their main quest.

Curious Quirks to Aid Concentration

Many years ago T. S. Knowlson gathered examples of various stimulating sensory conditions with which the creative workers provide themselves. Some of these seem bizarre indeed: "Dr. Johnson needed to have a purring cat, orange peel and plenty of tea to drink. Balzac wrote all night stimulated by constant cups of very strong black coffee. Zola pulled down the blinds at midday because he found more stimulus for his thought in artificial light. Carlyle was forever trying to construct a sound-proof room, while Proust achieved one. Schiller seems to have depended on the smell of decomposing apples which he habitually kept concealed in his desk."[28] Poincaré agreed about black coffee. Stephen Spender cites his reliance on tea and notes that Auden must have coffee and tobacco "when composing verse." In my own case, coffee four or five times during writing hours supplies the energy needed to lift me over the blockages. I've tried cocktails and beer over the years; a single one of either often duplicates Poincaré's "crowd of ideas," but more than one is useless.

Kipling had his pet quirks: he could produce creatively only with a pen, and the ink had to be really black, blue-blacks were an "abomination to his dæmon." My predilection is exactly the opposite, I must have blue-black, and quick-drying ink. Concentration is destroyed, moreover, if I have to move out of my horse-shoe-shaped desk to which I have become habituated. McKellar agrees: "The act of working in a place one finds congenial for work provides for a sensory input of cues that have in the past provoked thought, sustained endurance, or perhaps been fruitful in evoking original ideas. The effect of such stimuli cannot be ignored, particularly in any explanation of *sustained* creative thinking."[29]

Basic to concentration and the role of stimulating conditions for creative work is the general emotional mood for working. E. B. Holt's studies of the role of annoying stimuli in establishing moods apply here. "The rumble of a waterfall, the din and odour of factories and cities, and other 'mild annoyers' contribute unsuspectedly yet demonstrably to the organic tone of persons who have lived long in their vicinity."[30] McKellar agrees with Spender that original thinking and writing are extremely hard work and must be carefully provided for. "The philosopher Kant organized his life into a system whose rigour and austerity approached that of a well-planned military campaign. At certain precise times of the day Kant worked in bed. There he may well have had some intellectual dependence upon the tactile stimulation provided by the blankets, which were arranged round him in a highly original way invented by himself. He appears to have been greatly disturbed when some trees grew up and hid the tower which he used as a mental focus when thinking out his *Critique of Pure Reason.*"[31]

Malcolm Cowley, the historian of wild youth and the jazz age, tells how Hart Crane, the roaring boy of the twenties, used to write his poems.

There would be a Sunday afternoon party . . . in Slater Brown's unpainted and unremodeled farmhouse. . . . Hart would be laughing twice as hard as the rest of us in the big, low-ceilinged kitchen; he would be drinking twice as much hard cider and contributing more than his share of the crazy metaphors and overblown epithets. Gradually he would fall silent and a little later we would find that he had disappeared. In lulls that began to interrupt the laughter, now Hart was gone, we would hear a new hubbub through the walls of the next room—the phonograph playing a Cuban rumba, the typewriter clacking simultaneously; . . . Sometimes [Hart] stamped across the room, declaiming to the four walls and the slow rain of spring.

An hour later, after the rain had stopped, he would appear in the kitchen or on the croquet court, his face brick-red, his eyes burning, his already iron-gray hair bristling straight up from his skull. . . . In his hands would be two or three sheets of typewritten manuscript, with words crossed out and new lines scrawled in. 'Read that,' he would say, 'Isn't that the *grrrea*test poem ever written!'[32]

The Disciplinary Effect of Form

The flash is favored by a disciplined grasp of, and an intense concern for, the characteristic forms of working in a chosen medium. Long ago John Dryden, in the dedication of his *Rival Ladies,* endorsed such disciplined efforts by a paragraph devoted to the superiority of rhyme over blank verse. ". . . Imagination in a poet is a faculty so wild and lawless, that, like an high-ranging spaniel, it must have clogs tied to it, lest it outrun the judgment. The great easiness of blank verse renders the poet too luxuriant;

he is tempted to say many things, which might better be omitted, or at least shut up in fewer words; but when the difficulty of artful rhyming is interposed, where the poet commonly confines his sense to his couplet, and must contrive that sense into such words, that the rhyme shall naturally follow them, not they the rhyme; the fancy then gives leisure to the judgment to come in, which, seeing so heavy a tax imposed, is ready to cut off all unnecessary expenses."[33]

Critical students of letters have frequently commented on the disciplinary effects of writing under the compulsion of rigorous poetic forms.

Passion and the Creative Act

Even though all these favoring conditions be present, the flash is not likely to occur unless the work is carried forward under the white heat of enthusiasm and to the neglect of all else. Lowes, in his study of Coleridge's Notebooks, speaks of the "magical synthesis brought about by the shaping spirit of the imagination"; of "the charged and electrical atmospheric background of a poet's mind" and of "that heaving and phosphorescent sea below the verge of consciousness from which [his poems] have emerged."[34] And again: "Working at high tension, the imaginative energy assimilates and transmutes."[35] All of which shows ". . . that amazing discrepancy between the stuff of poetry and poetry itself. . . ."[36]

What moves us? "It is emotion that 'moves' us, hence the word," said Sherrington, and this is the stock answer of men of art and science alike. Lowes seems to agree that it is emotion that shapes the imagination. Roger Sessions, American composer and critic, says that the "gestures of the spirit, musical impulses . . . primitive movements" are "the very conditions of our existence." These energize our emotions; they are the "essence of musical expression." Speaking of the carefully modeled and scientifically tested passages of the last movement of Beethoven's Hammerklavier Sonata, he says, inspiration marks the "irresistible and titanic energy of expression already present in the theme. . . . Inspiration then, is the impulse which sets creation in movement; it is also the energy which keeps it going."[37] To recapture this passionate drive is the artist's problem, to bring sufficient energy to bear on the work. This produces the great conception, the vision of the whole. This is the source of power in the forming process. Under its influence the artist is not so much conscious of his ideas as possessed by them. Often the completed work is incomprehensible to him immediately after it is finished. Why is this? Because the experience of creating the work is incalculably more intense than any later experience he can have of it.

And the poet Jean Cocteau says that inspiration does not fall from heaven, rather that it is "the result of a profound indolence and of our incapacity to put to work certain forces in ourselves. These . . . work deep within us, with the aid of the elements of daily life, its scenes and passions, and . . . when the work that makes itself in us . . . demands to be born, we can believe that this work comes to us from beyond and is offered us by the gods." The writing that comes out of this deep passionate drive is, he says, a "visitation."[38]

In every excerpt I have taken from the dramatic autobiography of the illuminating flash, I find polarity between deep emotion and austere design. Julian Levi, American painter, says that his own plastic images are stirred by "certain geometrical relationships, certain rectangular forms and arabesques out of which grow particular harmonies and rhythms." The problem is to turn these into a painting which will "communicate the emotional content or exaltation of life." He quotes Georges Rouault: " 'I have painted by opening my eyes day and night on the perceptible world, and also by closing them from time to time that I might better see the vision blossom and submit itself to orderly arrangement.' "[39]

Some have seriously insisted that creative workers—poets, artists, even pure scientists—are a race of madmen. Housman, quoting Plato, comes close to it: "He who, without the Muse's madness in his soul comes knocking at the door of poesy and thinks that art will make him anything fit to be called a poet, finds that the poetry which he indites in his sober senses is beaten hollow by the poetry of madmen."[40]

As passion rises and concentration on the problem grows, the appearance of madness increases. As Jung said of Goethe's way of working: "It is not Goethe who creates *Faust,* but *Faust* which creates Goethe."[41] The mood reveals itself in manifold ways; for example, in profound emotional dissatisfaction with things as they are, or with one's own inability to bring forth a truly creative production. Blocked in his drive for full expression, Vincent van Gogh wrote to his brother Theo of his constant frustration, saying that he was one of the "prisoners in an I-don't-know-what-for horrible, horrible, utterly horrible cage . . . [He was] the man who is doomed to remain idle, whose heart is eaten out by anguish for work, but who does nothing because . . . he hasn't got just that which he needs in order to be creative. . . . Something is alive in me: what can it be?"[42] Again the men of science agree. Pavlov constantly adjured his students: "Remember that science demands from a man all his life. If you had two lives, that would not be enough for you."

These are the conditions, then, that favor the act of discovery: the quiet mind of relaxed concentration, prolonged conscious preparation, pertinent and ordered storage in the nonconscious mind, a perceptive and alert observer, the stimulation of curious aids to concentration, the disciplinary effect of the form of the medium and finally the compelling and passionate drive. But one mood pervades them all—the mood of quiet intuitive concentration.

Some synthesizing had been done before my study and some degree of consensus had already been achieved. Several of these stages and conditions favoring the flash of insight have long been recognized. But most of the earlier studies were based on a few cases, while the present synthesis has been drawn from a comprehensive sample of the world's distinguished autobiographies and hence, I think, has produced a more convincing consensus.

2

Creative Discovery and Logical Verification

IF a machine can be said to "think" at all, it thinks logically but not creatively. This is also true of many men. An important distinction is involved here between creative and logical thought, although men of exclusively logical interests may deny any distinction. There is, they say, only one kind of thinking; there is reasoning or reflective thought, problem-solving. Thus many philosophers and psychologists have tended to blur the distinction between creative and logical thought. Because of this tendency, teachers have never had a theory on which they could develop creative teaching, and because of the general lack of understanding of the problem, our homes, schools, and colleges have been denuded of the creative life they might have fostered and developed.

Since this distinction between the creative and the logical aspects of human behavior is basic to my whole book, I have made it the special theme of this chapter. I begin by embracing both phases in the complete act of thought, as Dewey did in his now classical analysis.[1] The term, "complete act," is employed to include many varieties of thought; the entire range from the scientist's questioning of the validity of established concepts, to the artist's seeking the appropriate form to organize his inner experience, to the short-term, practical problems which confront us in everyday life.

The creative aspect of the act of thought I shall call "discovery," using the term as meaning to find out, or to bring to light that which was previously unknown. My use of it will include all forms of discovery—physical objects and human subjects, their movements, the forces which govern their movements, and the relationships in which the latter are expressed. I shall use "create," "discover," "invent," and "originate" as synonymous, for they all suggest bringing to light something previously unknown.

DISCOVERY AND LOGIC IN THE COMPLETE ACT OF THOUGHT

My interpretation of the relative roles of discovery and verification runs somewhat counter to current pragmatic views. The standard interpretation in the schools and colleges is still a mixture of Dewey and the traditional logicians, but largely Dewey. Its brief re-examination here will be placed, therefore, against the background of two historic approaches.* The first is the traditional-logical approach which began with Aristotle's *Organon,* received important impetus in the twelfth- and thirteenth-century Renaissance, and was perpetuated in modern times by the academic professors of philosophy. The second is associationism, which was born in the seventeenth and eighteenth centuries from the work of Hobbes, Locke, Berkeley, and Hume in laying the foundations for the empirical science of modern psychology and for one kind of inductive logic.

The contemporary absorption of schools and colleges in problem-solving and their neglect of creative discovery has been brought about by an uncritical acceptance of Dewey's work on the scientific method of inquiry which actually sought to bridge the gulf between the two approaches to thinking noted above.

To illustrate his approach, Dewey quotes three examples of problem-solving: first, a simple case of practical deliberation submitted by a student of his and reported in *How We Think;* second, a

---

* I have found special help in Max Wertheimer's *Productive Thinking,* and shall build on it here. I disagree, however, with his naming of Dewey's empirical problem-solving approach as merely a development of the traditional logic, calling it "inductive and empirical." I prefer to treat it as an autonomous third approach.

"simple case of reflection upon observation"; and third, a case of scientific analysis. He breaks down the reasoning involved in solving each of these three problems into "five logically distinct steps":

1. a felt difficulty;
2. its location and definition;
3. suggestions of possible solutions;
4. development by reasoning of the meanings of the suggestions;
5. further observation and experiment leading to acceptance or rejection; that is, the conclusion of belief or disbelief.

His first three steps taken together are my "act of discovery"; the last two are my "verification," his "problem-solving." But Dewey subsumes discovery—which is recognition and forming of the problem (the flash of insight)—in the steps of his logical solution. Thus he leads us to minimize the clear difference between recognizing a problem and solving it. Dewey's five logically distinct steps of thinking, in my construction of the complete act of thought, become two. The first is the flash that reorients the imagining, that brings new dimensions, hitherto neglected factors, into the structure. While these appear in Dewey's analysis as the third step—"suggestions of possible solutions"—yet all are involved in the first two—"location and definition" of the problem. The complete act of thought, therefore, has two major phases: processes involved in creative or productive thought and processes of verification by logic and experiment.

My second phase—logical verification—is illustrated by Dewey's fourth and fifth steps. Logic now appears for the first time, confirming what Einstein said as reported by Wertheimer, namely, that the statement of hypothetical propositions "did not grow out of any manipulation of axioms"; it did not precede the exploratory productive thinking. "The way the two triple sets of axioms are contrasted in the Einstein-Infeld book," he said, "is not at all the way things happened in the process of actual thinking. This was merely a later formulation of the subject matter. . . . The axioms express essentials in a condensed form." Speaking of his ways of working at the problem, Einstein added: "These thought did not come in any verbal formulation. I very rarely think in words at all." Then he adds what seems to me to be the most significant. "A thought comes, and I may try to express it in words afterward."[2]

With respect to the priority of discovery over logic, Wertheimer shows that if one were to try to solve the problem by traditional logic, he would have to "state numerous operations, like making abstractions, stating syllogisms, formulating axioms and general formulas, stating contradictions, deriving consequences by combining axioms, confronting facts with these consequences, and so forth." [3] He adds that all we get out of such a logical analysis is "a concatenation of a large number of operations, syllogisms, etc." But that is not an adequate picture of what happens in creative thinking. By analogy, according to logic, a man can understand a piece of architecture by scrutinizing the bricks of which the building is made; but this gives him only a "survey of the bricks" and not of the building. He adds: "The technique of axioms is a very useful tool . . . one can deal with a gigantic sum of facts, with huge numbers of propositions, by substituting for them a few sentences which in a formal sense are equivalent to all that knowledge." [4] In Einstein's work axioms served as a kind of dressing-up of the data; they contributed to his sense of orderly organization and would, of course, appeal to academicians at large who are addicted to traditional logic. But axioms were employed after creative discovery, an approach which closely resembles that of the expressional artist.

There is a great moment in the complete act of thought when a sudden veering of attention brings an unexpected flash of understanding. In the endeavor to explain this process I shall re-examine the nature of thinking. First, let me give several examples.

A SIMPLE CASE OF PRACTICAL THINKING

Consider the well-known parlor game: "Given six sticks; arrange them so they will make four triangles." How do most people work at this problem? They try one arrangement, then another and still others, but each arrangement produces only two triangles, leaving one stick unused. There is a period of baffled trial and error; some persons succeed very quickly, some do not succeed for a long time, others never succeed. For those who solve the problem, the solution comes suddenly, as a "flash of insight," a hunch, a new idea. "Of course! Use three dimensions, not two!" Instead of laying all the sticks in one plane, leave three there as the base of the triangle and bring the other three up to meet above it, thus giving four triangles with six sticks. One verifies the insight by trying it out. What was the key to the solution? A complete reorientation in the way of looking at the problem, thinking in a new dimension. In this case it is actually a physical third dimension, but in the case of a nongeometrical problem it means thinking along a new line, getting out of an old rut, releasing oneself from an old stereotype.

A MOMENTOUS SCIENTIFIC DISCOVERY

Nothing in my study of the autobiography of creative thought has been more illuminating than the account I have pieced together of Einstein's long groping for the concept of relativity. The best single report of his creative and logical work is that written by Max Wertheimer from notes made during conversations with Einstein in Zurich in 1916. I have supplemented my study of that account by reading Einstein's published comments about his ways of working, and have put Wertheimer's interpretation in the wider setting of the contributions made by Einstein to the revolutionary developments of twentieth-century physics.[5]

My first example of practical thinking was a simple case in which the thinker started with the problem either clearly defined or on the verge of definition. But the Einstein example illustrates a different situation and one common to creative efforts both in science and in art. With him the location and definition of a problem involved six years of puzzlement and failure to grasp fully the conditions of the problem. This period was somewhat relieved from time to time by minor bits of insight concerning specific factors. Part of this confusion was due to the fact that, while brought up in the Gymnasium and University on the Galilean-Newtonian mechanistic explanations of the laws of motion, he had also been introduced to the conflicting explanations of Faraday and Maxwell in their field theory of electromagnetism. From that moment to the end of his life, he, like other persistently inquiring modern students, was confronted by one of the most perplexing unknowns of science and art. This is the relationship between corpuscle and wave, thing and force, mechanism and organism.

The first years of work were marked by Einstein's inability to make the Maxwell equations, describing the organic, electromagnetic field, fit Galilean-Newtonian mechanical explanations. The key was the concept of motion—motion of objects on the earth's surface, the movement of the earth itself, the movement of bodies in our universe, and motions of those in other universes. When Einstein was asked: "Was there conviction during these years about the concept of movement?" he answered: "No, not conviction, just curiosity, wanting to be sure." Although he could not state his problem clearly, he was driven by a deep feeling that he was moving in the right direction, he was "getting warm." The success of minor flashes contributed to this. For example, "Light is the key"; months later, "One cannot tell whether or not he is in a moving system." As the struggle went on, alternatives emerged. For example, "the conflict between the view that light velocity seems to presuppose a state of 'absolute rest' and the absence of this possibility in the other physical processes." Puzzling questions arose. "If one were to run after a beam of light, or ride on one, what then would be the nature of the situation with respect to the velocity of light? If you could run fast enough after a beam of light, would you reach a point where it would not move at all?" "The same light ray for another man would have another velocity."

Thus, for several years, a feeling of "uneasiness" about such unresolved issues marked his daily life, relieved from time to time by the flashing-up from the unconscious of new cues, new concepts, new queries. What is the velocity of light? And what does the motion of the observer have to do with it? Specific points became clear. For example, while the earth is moving, the planets of the earth's universe are also moving. This whole system of movements bears in some way on the problem of the velocity of light. One important cue came when he asked: "Would the Maxwell equations fit the facts if the velocity of light were assumed to depend on the motion of the source of light?" In the Galilean-Newtonian view there was no evidence, for example, that the velocity of light was constant. Recurringly, Einstein confronted questions of absolute movement. "Does light determine a state of absolute rest?" "What is the relation of the movement of light to movement in our system and movement in another system?" The difficulty seemed to center in the thought that one cannot tell whether or not he and his system are moving.

In the midst of Einstein's search, two important events occurred in mathematical physics. Michelson, at the University of Chicago, measured the velocity of light traveling in two pipes at right angles to each other (one pipe lying in the direction of the earth's movement) and reported that the velocity of light was the same in the two pipes. Even though this contradicted the traditional concept, scientists generally accepted the validity of the Michelson report. But Einstein was still puzzled, unable to reconcile the new findings with his data. Shortly after that the Lorentz-Fitzgerald hypothesis was offered to account for the uncertainties brought about by Michelson's experiment. The Lorentz-Fitzgerald hypothesis states that the two pipes had contracted by the exact amount "needed to compensate for the effect of the earth's motion on the velocity of light"; the entire apparatus contracted in the direction of the earth's motion—in one pipe by its length; in the other, at right angles to it, by its width. This satisfied the profession, but not Einstein. Here we have an illustration of the divine discontent of the creative man —the persistence of doubt, the unwillingness to accept hypothesis or logic until the most perfect and general body of conditions has been satisfied. Einstein could not accept the Lorentz-Fitzgerald hypothesis until he could confirm it by the logic of mathematical proof and experiment.

During the six years that had passed, Einstein had become reoriented in the direction that eventually led to success. Each minor redirecting situation was, in fact, an instance of feedback. Feedback in human behavior is that process by which brain and mind, on undergoing new experience, pick over the old organismic experience stored in the unconscious, transform it by integration with current stimuli, and produce the new idea or movement. One of my basic postulates is that the complete act of thought is studded with a succession of corrective feedbacks. In Einstein's case each of these recurring processes reoriented him toward seeing the whole structure of his problem in a new light.

Suddenly, in the seventh year of work, came the *recentering* imagined conception. This was the recognition of time as a new dimension. It reset the total problem and turned him to the new and successful path. From that moment his development of mathematical proof and his creation of thought models in the form of proposed experiments moved so rapidly that in five weeks' time the work was done. Up to this time, like his predecessors, he had worked only in the traditional Galilean-Newtonian three-dimensional space. Now he added time, popularly called the fourth dimension.

Other minor concepts succeeded the all-encompassing one, the most important of these latter concepts being that of simultaneity. Einstein had been clear about the simultaneity of events occurring at a single point, but what about the simultaneity of events occurring in two different places? The key was "the problem of the measurement of speed during the crucial movement." He said to himself at some point: ". . . if simultaneity in distant places is to have real meaning, I must explicitly take into account the question of movement, and in comparing my judgments with those of another observer, I have to take into account the relative movement between him and me." And in another place he added: "Every system has its special time and space values. A time or space judgment has sense only if we know the system with reference to which the judgment was made."[6]

The third and final stage of his work was to provide mathematical proof of the validity of his hypothesis and to propose a plan for experimental demonstration. His imagined conceptions needed verification by both of these methods and these he provided. The basis of this work was his axiomatic statement that the velocity of light, the invariant, is "the greatest possible." This concept proved to be the key on which were built "fundamental propositions from which we can derive conclusions that fit the facts." This conceptual flash, supplementing the major one of the dimensionality of time, not only illustrates how the approach to the problem is reoriented; it also establishes that, while logical thought is indispensable, it is employed only after creative, imaginative thought has produced the hypothesis. Einstein himself said: "The only virtue in axioms is to furnish the fundamental propositions from which one can derive conclusions to fit the facts." Needing to validate his basic axiom concerning the velocity of light, he developed new "transformation formulas for distances in time and space" which answer affirmatively the question— "Can a relation between the place and time of events in systems which move linearly to each other be so conceived that the velocity of light becomes a constant?" It could; the "derivations . . . reached from his transformation formulas showed mathematical coincidence with the Lorenz transformation." The latter was no longer *ad hoc;* it had logical verification.

Finally, Einstein proposed an experimental demonstration of the validity of his hypothesis, which was later carried out successfully by others. Now, at last, Einstein had both logical and experimental verification.*

Einstein's experience seems to fit the generalizations which Koestler formulated in his study of Kepler's discoveries concerning the laws of planetary motion.

Most geniuses responsible for the major mutations in the history of thought seem to have certain features in common; on the one hand scepticism, often carried to the point of iconoclasm, in their attitude towards traditional ideas, axioms and dogmas, towards everything that is taken for granted; on the other hand, an open-mindedness that verges on naïve credulity towards new concepts which seem to hold out some promise to their instinctive gropings. Out of this combination results that crucial capacity of perceiving a familiar object, situation, problem or collection of data, in a sudden new light or new context: of seeing a branch not as part of a tree, but as a potential weapon or tool; of associating the fall of an apple not with its ripeness, but with the motion of the moon. The discoverer perceives relational patterns or functional analogies where nobody saw them before, as the poet perceives the image of a camel in a drifting cloud.

This act of wrenching away an object or concept from its habitual associative context and seeing it in a new context is, as I have tried to show, an essential part of the creative process. It is an act both of destruction and of creation, for it demands the breaking up of a mental habit, the melting down, with the blow-lamp of Cartesian doubt, of the frozen structure of accepted theory, to enable the new fusion to take

---

* Although at this point the problem of Special Relativity had been solved, the search for a theory of General Relativity continued. It persisted, indeed, throughout Einstein's life as he repeated the steps of the original seven-year search.

place. This perhaps explains the strange combination of scepticism and credulity in the creative genius. Every creative act—in science, art or religion—involves a regression to a more primitive level, a new innocence of perception liberated from the cataract of accepted beliefs. It is a process of *reculer pour mieux sauter,* of disintegration preceding the new synthesis, comparable to the dark night of the soul through which the mystic must pass.[7]

DISCOVERY IN ARTISTIC EXPRESSION

I turn from science to art, especially to its nonverbal forms—the graphic and plastic arts, dance, music, and architecture. Here good autobiographical descriptions of the creative process are difficult to find. The painters' written record is private—letters to fellow-artists, informal table talk, notebooks, journals, diaries, conversations recorded by friends or relatives. Samples of these are listed in the notes to this chapter.[8] In general, they threw very little light on the place of the flash of insight in creative expression.

Then I was brought* a rare excerpt from Joachim Gasquet's account of dialogues with Paul Cezanne.[9] These conversations were carried on over years of friendship, in the studio, in the Paris Louvre, and with the painter in the fields in southern France, near Aix. I use a bit recorded by Gasquet in a luncheon interlude while observing Cezanne at work on a landscape of the Valley of Arc, before Mont Sainte Victoire. It is from that section devoted to what Cezanne called his "motif." He speaks of the transitory moods that governed him during weeks of painting, of feeling his way, exposing himself to the land and the air, looking, absorbing, waiting for nature to free his eyes from their camera habits of photographing the surface landscape. At length, he said:

I have grasped my motif. I lose myself in it. I reflect, I ramble about. The sun penetrates me obscurely, like a distant friend, warms my indolence, makes it fertile. . . . As the night descends it seems to me that I shall never paint, that I have never painted, I must have the night, in order that I may free my eyes from the earth, from this corner of the earth with which I am fused.

---

* By Frieda Schutze, to whom I am indebted for the translation from the German of pieces from Gasquet's *Cezanne,* pp. 104-105.

Gasquet asks: "Why, then, this brooding over the landscape?" He answers:

Because I am no longer innocent. We are civilized human beings. The longing for the classic is in us. . . . There is a sort of barbarism, more detestable than that of the academies, in the false primitives. It is no longer possible to be primitive today. We bring our skilled dexterities with us at birth; we breathe our craft with birth. This is the death of art and must be destroyed.

Then came a day of clear seeing. "On certain days," he said, "it seems to me that I paint naïvely. I am the primitive of my own development."

As the sun penetrated him, made his indolence fertile, the intuitive mood of inside identification is established, the quiet seeing becomes perception-in-depth. Blake called it "cleansing the doors of perception." When that is done, "everything would appear to man as it is, infinite." Cezanne comments on the climactic event.

One fine morning, the following day, gradually the geological foundations appear, the strata shape themselves, the great planes of my landscape. In my mind I draw the stony skeleton, I see the rocks glistening beneath the water, the sky acquiring weight. Everything is perpendicular. A pallid vibration conceals the outlines. The red earth rises from an abyss. I begin to separate myself from the landscape to see it. I detach myself from the landscape by this first sketch, these geological lines. The geometry, the measure of the earth.

In this moment he was "completely one with the valley." He, too, like Edward Carpenter, had glided below the landscape into the "quiet sense of his own identity with the self of other things." The stony geological strata shape themselves before him.

A tender excitement grips me. From the roots of this excitement rises the sap, color. A sort of liberation. The radiation of the soul, the vision, the mysterious becoming external, reciprocal action between the earth and the sun, the ideal and the real, the colors. An air-permeated, colored logic suddenly takes the place of somber, stubborn geometry. Everything falls into place, trees, fields, houses. I see. In spots. The geological foundations, the labor of preparation, the world of drawing collapses, has crashed as in a catastrophe. A tidal wave has swept them all away and caused them to rearrange themselves.

"Everything falls into place . . . I see." Again and again perception gives way to the metaphor-image. "A sort of liberation . . . the mysterious becoming external." Then the moment of true union is inaugurated. Blake has described a similar experience.

Trembling I sit day and night, my friends are astonished at me,
Yet they forgive my wanderings, I rest not from my great task!
To open the Eternal Worlds, to open the immortal Eyes
Of man inward into the Worlds of Thought, into Eternity
Ever expanding in the Bosom of God, the Human Imagination.[10]

The complete act of expression has the three major phases: deep feeling, a long period of looking and absorbing, preparing, gathering of self and task; a period of perception-in-depth, cutting through and under conventional ways of seeing, which in the creative imagination becomes concept; finally, putting down what the artist sees, striving to make his statement equivalent to his created forms of feeling.

CREATIVE DISCOVERY IN SCIENCE AND IN ART

Both experiences are dominated by a common esthetic quality of feeling. Both Cezanne and Einstein were stimulated by natural phenomena: Cezanne by landscape, sky and earth; Einstein by light and its velocity and by movement—the motion of objects on the earth's surface, of planets and stars, of our universe and perhaps of other universes.

There was also in both men a perplexed search for the problem, a feeling of one's way. Cezanne said, "I am confronted with my motif, I lose myself in it . . . it seems to me that I shall never paint, that I have never painted." Einstein, for years unable to locate or to state his problem, simply "knew something was wrong" with the explanations he had been taught. For both men there was a puzzling stage and an end of puzzlement. In Cezanne's words,

A new era begins. The true one! The one in which nothing eludes me, in which everything is dense and fluid at the same time, in accord with nature. Now there are only colors left and in them light, the being who thinks them, this ascension of the earth to the sun, this effusion of the depths toward love. It is the part of genius to capture this upward flight in one moment of equilibrium and yet to make its élan perceptible. I have the will to master this idea, this movement, this vapor of being above the glow of the universe.

Cezanne, like John Marin, responds to the natural weights and balances of nature's forces. Marin says: "As my body exerts a downward pressure on the floor, the floor in turn exerts an upward pressure on my body. Too, the pressure of the air against my body, my body against the air, all this I have to recognize when building the picture."[11] Cezanne speaks in the same vein.

My picture acquires weight, a weight presses upon my brush. Everything begins to fall. Everything sinks beneath the horizon, from my brain upon my picture, from my picture to the earth. Weighing heavily. Where is the air, the dense lightness?

It is the part of genius to release the friendship of all these things to the wide air in the same upsurge, in the same desire. . . . A minute of the world passes. To paint that in its reality! And forget everything else. To become that. Then to be the light-sensitive plate. To give the facsimile of what we see, to forget everything that appeared before us.[12]

"To give the facsimile of what we see!" Perhaps never did a plastic artist articulate purpose more perfectly, unless it was William Blake whose life-purpose was that stated in Cezanne's closing lines.

Both Cezanne and Einstein sought concentration in a quiet mind of intuition. Both worked and waited for the letting-things-happen mood to take over. In Einstein, as in Cezanne, the process was one of feeling rather than of verbalized thinking; a feeling that he was on the right track, long before the problem could be defined. In this respect also is revealed the common esthetic mood governing the work of both scientist and artist. At this point both men worked as intuitive artists.

Eventually the intense concentration of the quiet mind bears fruit. Cezanne's perception-in-depth brings in its train the imagined conception. So the artist, in the grip of intense concentration, strives to objectify what he sees in imagination, inside the earth, beyond the sky, inside the apple, inside the living man or woman. This is the inside way of knowing, the artist's way of identification with the object.

The man of science works in much the same way, for he, too,

puts himself inside the situation. His felt-thought, for example, tells him that the mechanical Galilean concepts of movements are not explained by the terms of the new organic concepts of electromagnetic fields. The feeling is little more than vague doubt, and for a long time Maxwell's equations do not "come out right." Then, after six years of struggle, comes the flash—the concept of simultaneity in the new dimension of time. The feeling that the velocity of light is absolute turned into a precise verbalized axiom.

Hence, it is certain that in the discovery phase of the complete act of thought, the ways of working of artist and of scientist have much in common.

VERIFICATION IN SCIENCE AND IN ART

In the verification phase, however, there are clear differences—differences in the nature of the problem, in general orientation and in methods of work, but above all in the nature of the goal.

There is a first distinction in the nature of the problem and the corresponding adjustment of the individual. The daily problems of every man and the technical problems of scientist or technologist are all given. They are stated, set in advance. The practical problem that we considered earlier was prescribed by the external world, and the problem-solver must orient himself precisely to its stated conditions.

Man working as artist, on the contrary, sets his own problems internally. In the act of expressional statement the orienting attitude is created by the artist's drives and personal experience. Expression is compelled by urges to objectify meanings, moods, imagined conceptions. The drive may be to write a poetic line, or to portray with brush or pencil, with tones or bodily movements. But in this initial stage of the creative act the attitude is molded by the artist's subjective experience. The only external references are to the corresponding stages of the artist's product. The contrast, then, is caused by differences in the precision and fixity of the scientist's objective problem and the continually shifting character of the artist's subjective vision and imagined conception.

There is a similar contrast in the methods of work. In the Dewey analysis of the complete act of thought, the initial creative step of recognizing the problem consists of the flashing-up of suggestions. These are formed, we know today, from the feedback data of percept and concept—facts and generalizations that have been registered in the nervous system, stored in the unconscious, and are drawn up either as memory or reconstructed imagination. The practical or scientific problem-solver gathers facts which have been measured against scales of approximately equal units. He analyses, classifies, and summarizes from the facts of the external world— facts which have been obtained under conditions of measured observation. They are generalizations, hypotheses which are accepted only when, under scrutiny, they fit the facts of the external world.

In the expressional act the artist also works from the data of earlier experience, but his "facts" are the words or images that well up out of the unconscious; the "tentative" modeling movements in which the sensitive hands of the sculptor or painter objectify their vision; the imagined arrangements of light and shade, color and materials, in the stage-set and costuming of the scenic designer; or the interpretive movements of the dancer. They are not measured against external standardized norms, but against the artist's unique sense of the words and movements which are necessary to his statement. The data are a succession of changing, unique organizations, each of which depends primarily upon his constantly changing imagined conceptions. The work consists essentially in objectifying moods and slowly defined images. Hence, the expressional artist is governed very little by externally set conditions.

These distinctions in orientation and method are clear, but we find an even more important difference in the goal of the two workers. From the moment that the problem-solving scientist or technologist has located and stated his problem, he knows his goal and the governing conditions under which it can be reached. The very statement of the problem fixes it precisely and it is unchanging throughout the work. But in the expressional act of the artist, the goal is the objectification of his imagined conceptions; he strives to say what he sees, his way. Moment by moment the goal changes because both vision and product change. The nature of the expressional process is basically tentative and experimental. There are constant interlineations, erasures, giving-up old organizations, adopting new ones, the entire process marked by a "divine discontent." In this respect Western artists are far less mature than the Eastern artists of the Tao and Zen traditions.

The basic difference between problem-solving and expression lies in the nature of "verification" in the two processes, not in the discovery phase of their thinking processes. While the scientist's solution of his problem must be susceptible to precise and public confirmation or refutation, the artist's product cannot be verified by another. There is only one correct solution to the scientist's problem, one right answer to the problem-solver's question. There is, after all, only one possible value of π. The technician's statement of his findings are verifiable by another who adopts the same orientation, uses the same data, employs the same instruments and aids in interpretation. Within a few days of each other, in 1845, the British astronomer, John Couch Adams and the French U.J.J. Leverrier, independently predicted the position of the then unknown planet Neptune, by working from a common body of observations and universal star maps, and by brilliantly conceiving the same hypotheses and making the same computations. Thus the scientific method is characterized by recurrence and uniformity, identity of data, standards, instruments and techniques and by verifiability.

Exactly the opposite is true of the expressional act. The goal being the objectification of the imagined conception of a unique personality, the product too must be a unique thing. The artist affirms, "I say what I see, my way—with form," in making his painting, his poem, his house. That is art, the formed expression of imagined conceptions. It is inconceivable, except by the remotest operation of the law of probability, that the special fusion of feeling-import, meaning and bodily understanding attained by one artist could be attained by another. If by rare chance it were so achieved, the second product would not be a confirmation of the original artist's generalizations; it would either be sheer imitation or a new original product. It would be measured against the second artist's personal vision, not against that of the first artist.

The contrasts we are making between the processes of science and art give a prevision of the role of logic in the inside-outside problem of knowing. As we have already seen, the intuitive, inside identifying way of the quiet mind of concentration is the true way of the creative act of discovery, either of man working as artist or of his hypothesizing brother of science and technology. But the outside way of scientific observation and analysis, utilizing modern man's best instruments of measurement and interpretation, is the way of scientific verification, and scientific verification has no place in expression.

That does not mean that there is no place for a logic in the artist's expressional work. One of our insistent needs is the development of an adequate symbolism for the nonverbal activities of life, for a logic of esthetics, comparable in rigor to the symbolic logic of Russell, Wittgenstein, Carnap, and the language philosophers. But that is a question of great subtlety and difficulty, the answer to which can only be briefly introduced in this chapter. There is no question, for example, of the important role of order in the statement-making of the artist. The formed statement of his imagined conceptions is the principle of his expressional act. Hence his responses must carry a nonverbal logic which can be discovered and stated. But its criteria will be found in the degree to which they objectify what he sees, feels, intends; not in the extent to which they measure up to any external norm.

It has been made clear that while there is only one human act of response, this act is governed by two very different moods, two orientations, the intuitive mood of discovery and the logical mood of verification. Both are indispensable to productive living, but the act of discovery is our special concern.

This brings us to an important idea: Imagination is the instrument of discovery. The poet and the scientist agree. Discovery is conceiving in imagination, or, more succinctly, discovery *is* imagined conception. The process of imagining, then, becomes the key to our problem.

The term imagination can be clarified by distinguishing it from perception and memory. Perception is formally defined as the "awareness of external objects, qualities of relations which ensue directly upon sensory processes." I have a percept of each of the lamps in my room. But I have an imagined concept of lamp and its function. The key to the contrast is that perception involves sensory experiences, awareness of present data, whether external or intraorganic, or awareness of the truth of a proposition. But imagination, says the Oxford Dictionary, is "forming a mental concept of what is not actually present to the senses . . . the power which the mind has of forming concepts beyond those derived from external objects." This is called the productive or creative imagination. In contrast, the "reproductive imagination" is "that faculty of the mind [including memory] by which are formed images or concepts of external objects not present to the senses, and of their relations to each other or to the subject." Thus memory images are vague holdovers from perceptual experience. I look at the skyline of New York from the New Jersey palisades, close my eyes and have a memory image. I read a descriptive account of Chengtu, which I have never seen, try to imagine what it looks like, and I have an imagination image. These are reality images, because they are both the product of and are verified (or verifiable) by experience.

Imagination is the universal and indispensable instrument of all levels of living in the human world. Our daily lives are dependent on it. All day long we imagine our way around the house or the community; visualizing alternative courses and alternative consequences of action. In fact, the principal function of the imagination is to enable the human being constantly to build thought models of the real world. The inventor conceives in imagination new arrangements of his machine-parts to bring about described movements. The creative dancer conceives in imagination the right movements for the objectification of his or her imagined conception. The mathematician imagines alternative hierarchies of symbols of relationship. Recall Einstein's never-ending task of imagining "what would happen if . . . one were to run after a beam of light or ride on one . . . if you could run fast enough . . . would you reach a point where it would not move at all?" Or the imaginative work in Cezanne's perception-in-depth of the strong hidden skeleton beneath the surface of his valley landscape.

The steps involved in thinking point to the crucial role of the imagination: the capacity to delay responses; to manipulate symbols in imagination; to sense and hold the direction dictated by perception and recall; and to generalize, that is, to form and use concepts. Much of our thinking is done by imagined body movements. A little boy in Lincoln School's first grade said, "I can't say it, but I can draw it." A four-year-old girl said, "Mummy, I'll dance it, you write it." The chief distinction between men and animals is this capacity to work out solutions to problems symbolically, in imagination. We say that the human thinker "runs ahead in thought." His contemplation of a situation may be merely implicit anticipatory body movements; or he expresses imagined, alternative courses of action—if I do that, then such and such will follow.

Thus imagining is building models of a miniature world. Few moments of life, sleeping or waking, are devoid of it. Dream imagery is a rich source of creativeness, as is the kaleidoscopic imagery of the autistic, hypnoidal mind on the borderline between the conscious and the unconscious states. And imagination is a major instrument of both phases of the complete act of thought— discovery and verification. To use Koestler's phrasing, "Artists treat facts as stimuli for imagination, whereas scientists use imagination to coordinate facts."

3

The Magic Threshold

I T is my thesis that the illuminating flash of insight occurs at a critical threshold of the conscious-nonconscious continuum on which all of life is lived. The true locus of the creative imagination is the border state that marks off the conscious from the nonconscious. This is the stage between conscious alert awareness, about which Dewey wrote for fifty years, and the deep nonconscious in which Freud was intensely absorbed. James was aware of it, calling it "the fringe," the "waking trance." Others spotted it long ago. Galton named it "antechamber"; Varendonck, "foreconscious"; Schelling, "preconscious"; Freud, "subconscious"; more recently Kubie, "preconscious"; and Tauber and Green, "pre-logical." This is the Taoists' state of "letting things happen," where daydreaming and reveries go on, where Whitehead's prehension and Wild's intuition, as primal awareness, function; where we know before we know we know. My hypothesis makes it the true creative center.

A convincing body of requisites of the flash of insight is present in what I call the threshold state. This is a conscious state, yet has antechamber access to the unconscious. This state of mind is off guard, relaxed, receptive to messages, but it is also magnetic, with a dynamic forming power. I think of it as "off-conscious," not unconscious, for the organism is awake, alert, and in control. It is hypnoidal, resembling the light trance of hypnosis, although not hypnotically induced or controlled. It partakes of both the hypnagogic, marking the drowsy state between waking and sleeping, and the hypnopompic, the corresponding state between sleeping and waking. It satisfies the criteria of the intuitive, receptive, identifying mind of intense concentration.

I have never succeeded in finding an adequate name for it. I have tried many: intuitive, autistic, quiet, relaxed, permissive, accessible, hospitable. The state is certainly permissive, yet it is more than that. It is actively magnetic, attracting materials out of the nonconscious into the vestibule of the conscious mind. *Such across-the-threshold power suggests the name which I have given it: the transliminal mind.*

I know no better description of the transliminal mind than that of Edward Carpenter, who was both scientist and poet. In one of his books he said: "The Man at last lets Thought go. . . . He leans back in silence on that inner being, and bars off for a time every thought, every movement of the mind, every impulse to action, or whatever in the faintest degree may stand between him and That; and so there comes to him a sense of absolute repose, a consciousness of immense and universal power, such as completely transforms the world for him."[1]

THE CHAMBERS OF THE MIND

Seventy years ago Francis Galton described the "chambers of the mind" in which "the ideas that lie at any moment within my full consciousness seem to attract of their own accord the most appropriate out of a number of other ideas that are lying close at hand, but imperfectly within the range of my consciousness." He speaks of a presence-chamber "where full consciousness holds court . . . and an ante-chamber full of more or less allied ideas, which is situated just beyond the full ken of consciousness. Out of this ante-chamber the ideas most nearly allied to those in the presence-chamber appear to be summoned in a mechanically logical way, and to have their turn of audience."[2]

Two generations before Galton, Coleridge, first modern student of the imagination, had pointed to the image as one of the chief materials of the flash of insight, saying that "ideas and images exist" in "that nascent existence . . . just on the vestibule of consciousness." Of this much we can be reasonably sure. In the vestibule which Coleridge called the "confluence of our recollections," we "establish a center, a sort of nucleus in [this] reservoir of the soul." We have here my center of creative energy, the transliminal state.

H. A. Taine compared the human mind "to the stage of a theatre, very narrow at the footlights . . . [where] there is hardly room for more than one actor . . . further away . . . there are other figures less and less distinct. . . . And beyond . . . in the wings and altogether in the background, are innumerable obscure shapes that a sudden call may bring forward."[3] Graham Wallas, in his *Art of Thought,* used the analogy of the two-phased vision of our eyes, a foveal center surrounded by a peripheral region, vague and blurred. "One reason," he says, "why we tend to ignore the mental events in our 'peripheral' consciousness is that we have a strong tendency to bring them into 'focal' consciousness as soon as they are interesting to us . . . we can sometimes by a severe effort keep them in the periphery of consciousness, and there observe them."[4] Herbert Read pictures the regions of the mind as three superimposed strata in which a phenomenon comparable to a fault in geology takes place.

Read is one of those who accepts Jung's concept of "the collective unconscious" as a great memory stored in the "genes" of the race. This memory, according to Jung, is a "seething caldron" of "instinctive associations of words, images, sounds" and from it somehow are generated "the archetypal forms . . . which constitute the basis of art." But Erich Fromm says the unconscious "is neither Jung's mythical realm of racially inherited experience nor Freud's seat of irrational libidinal forces." He has a conception of it much closer to my own: "It must be understood in terms of the principle: 'What we think and feel is influenced by what we do.' Consciousness is the mental activity in our state of being preoccupied with external reality—with acting. The unconscious is the mental experience . . . in which we have shut off communications with the outer world, are no longer preoccupied with action but with our self-experience. . . . Both conscious and unconscious are only different states of mind referring to different states of existence."[5]

Morton Prince denied the basic Freudian conception of "a wild, unbridled, conscienceless subconscious mind . . . ready to take advantage of an unguarded moment to strike down, to drown, to kill, after the manner of an evil genii." On the contrary, he regarded it "as a great mental mechanism which takes part in an orderly, logical way in all the processes of daily life but which under certain conditions involving particularly the emotion-instincts, becomes disordered or perverted. We think that in everyday life we consciously do the whole of our thinking; but I am inclined to think that our unconscious self does most of our thinking, and that we simply select from the ideas furnished by the unconscious those which we believe are best adapted to the situation; that our problems are much more solved by the unconscious than by the conscious."[6]

These are the bare bones of my guiding theorem, but it needs a broader-based setting. To point to a threshold mind as the place to search raises the question: Threshold to what, from what?

THE CONSCIOUS-UNCONSCIOUS CONTINUUM

The threshold state is that dynamic antechamber which connects the conscious and the unconscious. Since Galton's time much knowledge has been assembled concerning the antechamber and the unconscious. Both the end points and the central threshold of the scale can now be more closely fixed. At one end, normal conscious behavior is marked by alert concentration on a task or an idea. At the other end, the deep unconscious is characterized by the oblivion of the third and fourth hour of sleep, the long dream in its full kaleidoscope, or the deepest levels of the hypnotic trance. Students agree on the two end-points of the conscious-unconscious scale, and on a layer-like structure of the mind, even though they use varied words and figures of speech in dramatizing the opening of the doors of imagined conception.

I have come to think of life as lived on a conscious-nonconscious continuum. Six different ways of conceiving human behavior may be brought together on a single continuum. Behavior may be conceived as reaching from unconscious to conscious, from sleeping to waking, from trance state to normal state, from autism to reality, from fantasy to symbol, from inattention to hyper-alert attention.

Imagine the creative task we have considered in earlier chapters —the practical problem, the more extended scientific problems of an Einstein, a Poincaré, or a Dewey, the quandaries of Cezanne, Housman, or another artist—distributed along the scale of the conscious-unconscious. If we should emphasize Dewey's theory of problem-solving thinking or that of the logical positivists, we would visualize thinking as focused at the extreme conscious end of the scale. The calm thinker, alertly aware, consciously and tensely strives to focus attention on the problem. There is no reference to the unconscious, to the intuitive quiet mind. The stress, on the contrary, is on the active conscious mind. If we should follow Freud's interpretation, we would picture the person moved unwittingly by the unconscious, shaped in his thinking and action by long-forgotten, perhaps repressed, experiences of early childhood. I prefer to locate the creative worker at the critical threshold of the conscious-unconscious border, the transliminal state. In linear terms this is between Dewey and Freud. The conditions of working under these three states will be described and compared in succeeding chapters. Here I merely anticipate findings that establish the transliminal mind as the center for the exercise of creative energy.

CRITICAL TESTIMONY ON A PRECONSCIOUS STATE

The Waking Trance

Twenty years after the founding of the British Society for Psychical Research, the problem of the waking trance as a preconscious state was called to the attention of psychologists, philosophers and theologians by William James's now famous Gifford Lectures at Edinburgh (1901–1902).[7] When James reached Lecture 16, he generalized the many illustrations of "subconscious" states he had previously discussed, saying that "they form a distinct region of consciousness," which has certain characteristics. "The handiest of the marks by which I classify a state of mind as mystical is negative . . . it defies expression . . . no adequate report of its contents can be given in words . . . its quality must be directly experienced; it cannot be imparted or transferred to others . . . [such] states are more like states of feeling than like states of intellect."

The second mark, called "noetic" to describe its content of cognition as well as feeling, is of great importance in our search for the ways to open the doors of conceptualizing. While such states reflect qualities of feeling, James said, they "seem to those who experience them to be also states of knowledge. They are states of insight into depths of truth unplumbed by the discursive intellect. They are illuminations, revelations, full of significance and importance, all inarticulate, though they remain; and as a rule they carry with them a curious sense of authority for aftertime."[8] This is significant buttressing of my basic theory that every human act is felt as well as thought. It embraces both feeling and thinking. Every creative act is noetic and each carries a "sense of authority."

Since James's time, the library of episodes variously called "dreamy," "streamy," "subconscious," or "subliminal" has grown until it now comprises hundreds, perhaps thousands, of documents. They range from the universally expressed conviction of everyman that "I have been here before," and statistical studies of personal experiences, to the scientific accounts of psychologists and the autobiographical records of spiritual conversion.

The French psychologists, encountering the I-have-been-here-before experience, gave it a succinct name, "déjà vu." According to McKellar, 69 per cent of his 182 students in Aberdeen University reported that they had experienced it. It is, indeed, common. Many people say, "I feel I know what is going to happen a moment before it actually does—also what a person is going to say." It is easy to distort reports of such experiences. As McKellar says, "Déjà-vu experiences make good stories and . . . often improve in the telling." They are interpreted in a great variety of ways—as evidence of supernatural powers, telepathy or clairvoyance, of similarity in the content of the experience with previous ones, and of similarity in vocabulary and background.

The Flash and the Poet's Dæmon

The suggestion, frequently heard, of someone else carrying on, of "a man's attendant spirit," reminds me of Socrates and his "personal dæmon," of Goethe and his "Dæmonic powers," of poets hearing "voices speaking." Amy Lowell commented, "Some poets speak of hearing a voice speaking to them, and say that they write almost to dictation. . . . I do not hear a voice, but I do hear words pronounced." She defines the poet as "a man of an extraordinarily sensitive and active subconscious personality, fed by, and feeding, a non-resistant consciousness. A common phrase among poets is, 'It came to me.' "[9] Kipling, sitting "bewildered among other notions," struggling unsuccessfully to get the theme of one of his books, learned to relax and rely upon his personal dæmon. Time after time, the dæmon would finally say to Kipling, " 'Take this and no other.' " "I obeyed," he says, "and was rewarded. . . . After that I learned to lean upon him." He would put his problem away and wait: "Then said my dæmon—and I was meditating something else at the time—'Treat it thus and so.' " Kipling sums up the process in his autobiography, "When your Dæmon is in charge do not try to think consciously. Drift, wait and obey. . . . Walk delicately, lest he should withdraw."[10]

In Eckermann's *Conversations with Goethe,* there are many references to a "Dæmonic power." When Goethe's conscious writing gave more trouble than he expected, "something dæmonic prevailed, which was not to be resisted." Eckermann agreed that Goethe should yield to "such influences, for the dæmonic seems to be so powerful, that it is sure to carry its point at last."[11] One evening they "came upon the subject of the Dæmonic before we were aware. 'In poetry,' said Goethe, 'especially in what is unconscious, before which reason and understanding fall short, and which therefore produces effects far surpassing all conception, there is always something dæmonic. So it is with music, in the highest degree; for it stands so high that no understanding can reach it . . . religious worship cannot dispense with it; it is one of the chief means of working upon men miraculously. Thus the Dæmonic loves to throw itself into significant individuals, especially when they are in high places, like Frederick and Peter the Great.' "[12]

Off-Conscious Composing

The directed thinking that goes on in this fringe state, while definitely masterful, has also a curiously extra-personal quality. The creative mind behaves as though propelled, carried along in the grip of an other-worldly being. One of Galton's normal subjects described the off-conscious nature of this withdrawn mood, "I feel as if I were a mere spectator at a diorama of a very eccentric kind." The worker, fully conscious, aware of what is going on in the workaday world, even carrying on skills of great complexity, seems to himself to be composing in another and independent realm.

I can perhaps make myself clear by a personal example of such "off-conscious" composing. One autumn weekend in the midst of the great depression, I was scheduled to speak for one hour at Huntington, West Virginia, before the annual convention of the State Teachers Association. Before I rose to speak, the chairman asked if I would be willing to go to the radio station on the roof of the theatre, immediately at the close of the address, and broadcast it in a condensed fifteen-minute form. I agreed, on condition that I could speak to a small live audience assembled from the larger one in the theatre.

The experience that followed the hour-long address was an example of the operation of what I call the off-conscious, fringe state. From the instant the warning red and green lights came on I felt as if I had been taken over and put to work as the agent of some extra-worldly force. On the fringe of consciousness I was perfectly aware of what was going on around me, but in the sharp focus I felt utterly aloof, as if standing to one side, hearing myself speak to countless homes in West Virginia. Technically the speech seemed to be given on a dreamlike intuitive level. I heard myself speaking, I felt myself improvising, step by step, the bigger concepts of the hour-long speech, condensing them into the shortened form. Finally, I began to summarize as the warning light appeared before me, and stopped precisely on time with a sense of having missed no essential points of the longer address. The consensus of the 200 listeners bore me out that the fifteen-minute broadcast was the hour-long auditorium address in miniature. Yet, as Harold Rugg, I seemed to take part as an onlooker; I felt as though both mind and speech mechanism were being directed, manipulated by someone else.

This experience was repeated many times in my years of lecturing. Often as I sat on the platform during the chairman's introduction, there would come a moment when I would find myself leaning back, as Edward Carpenter had taught, on that "inner voice," concentrating on a point high up in the gallery, putting aside manuscript, outline, red-penciled notes, to let myself be taken over, it seemed, by some other guiding force. And I would rise in a kind of intuitive off-conscious state and speak and hold the people for an hour or more. There was no hocus-pocus, extra-worldliness about this, nothing supernatural. My long years of conscious preparation were tapped, the deep layers of the unconscious storage were drawn upon, organized by intellect and dramatized by feeling.

SCIENTIFIC SUPPORT OF THE THRESHOLD STATE

The Peculiar State of Hypnosis

That the transliminal mind is the creative center I have no doubt, but whether it is identical with, or merely related to, various trance states is open to further question and study. Of their existence and importance we have confirmation from hundreds of scientific studies of hypnosis, narcosis, sleep, and the pathology of thought. That the transliminal mind has much in common with them there can no longer be any doubt.

The scientific evidence on the hypnotic trance, for example, supplies one of the most fruitful single bodies of confirming fact. It also provides provocative neurophysiological and psychosomatic theories concerning the nature of the act of response. The evidence, to be sampled later, opens many hitherto closed doors on the flash of insight. Many investigators of hypnosis have recognized a "peculiar state" on the hypnoidal borderline of the unconscious that appears to have very much in common with the creative transliminal mind. Weitzenhoffer calls it, from his studies into hypnosis, a "borderline state"; Kleitman, Schneck, Brenman, Gill and Hackner, Darrow, and Ravitz, to name only a few, have all come upon it independently. Kleitman describes it as a "peculiar state," neither sleep nor wakefulness, which "is accompanied by characteristic subjective phenomena observed in hypnosis and particularly during the induction of hypnosis." Weitzenhoffer adds that most students of hypnosis regard these phenomena as "psycho dynamic manifestations. . . . They include . . . changes in body awareness, changes in modes of thought, release of emotion, and motor expression. Similar manifestations are also observed during the induction of narcosis. It may be that a common neuromuscular state is involved here."[13]

It is *possible* that there may be several threshold states, each one somewhat similar to, yet in some respects different from, the others. One may be the light trance of hypnosis; another the trance state of drug-narcosis; another may connect the autistic mind with the reality-oriented thinking of alert consciousness; another, the pre-conscious of Varendonck and Kubie; and still another might be an antechamber from the reality world into the psychotic world.

It is equally possible that all of these may be varieties of one common autistic, hypnoidal mind. From my studies the conviction has grown that all of these forms of "trance" state are closely re-lated to what I now call the transliminal mind. They all lend some support to the hypothesis of a threshold state which has access to the unconscious. Their study throws light on the unconscious sources of the creative mind.

Clear Psychiatric Evidence

Far more conclusive support for the thesis of a creative threshold mind comes from certain types of recent psychiatric research. Out-standing among these is the work of Lawrence Kubie.[14] His Porter Lectures at the University of Kansas (1958) interpreted twenty-seven technical studies which he had published over a period of twenty-five years, bearing on the relation between unconscious, preconscious, and conscious processes. In addition, they drew on fifty other published reports. His postulate that all life is lived on a "nearly continuous spectrum" of three concurrent systems agrees with my conception of the conscious-nonconscious continuum. The extreme three bands of his spectrum are the conscious system of symbolic function, the unconscious level of symbolic function, and, between them, the preconscious process. He says that three facts are clear about them. The first is that they all operate concurrently and in constantly varying patterns. The second posits that behavior is to be called "normal" when the conscious and preconscious proc-esses, in alliance, are dominant. Third, "we operate in the shadow of illness whenever unconscious processes are dominant." Kubie's report rests firmly on a large array of experimental and clinical data. While Freud creatively guessed at the conscious-unconscious spectrum, Kubie ignores many of the guesses and reiterations of Freud's followers. He uses six types of studies, examples of which are listed below: "(1) the experimental induction of neurotic states under hypnosis; (2) experimental work with differentiated preconscious perceptions during sleep; (3) experiments on the preconscious reactions to fleeting images on the tachistoscope of Charles Fisher, Lindley, Marsh and Worden; (4) experiments under hypnosis on the symbolic representation of repressed amnesic material; (5) the self-translating data of childhood during those phases in which language symbols are being formed; (6) data from schizophrenics with simultaneous multiple levels of meaning in symptoms, speech, action, and posture. . . ."[15]

Kubie formulates a thesis concerning creativity that appears to confirm mine very closely. "A type of mental function, which we call technically 'the preconscious system,' is the essential implement of all creative activity; and . . . unless preconscious processes can flow freely there can be no true creativity." I regard this as mutual corroboration concerning the operation of the preconscious and my transliminal mind. He, too, stresses the fact that life is never lived solely in the transliminal mind, saying "preconscious processes . . . never operate alone. They are under the continuous and often conflicting and distorting or obstructing influence of two other concurrent systems of symbolic functions, each of which is relatively anchored and rigid. Together the three systems constitute a spectrum with certain continuities, and at least one partial but critical discontinuity."[16]

I can find, after a thorough study of Kubie's work, only two possible differences between us. These refer to the creative nature of the conscious, unconscious, and preconscious. My evidence points to the definite presence of *some creative, imaginative capacities in all sectors of the continuum*. Kubie seems to ascribe creative ability *only* to the preconscious. He rules out all fully conscious imaginative work and also asserts that the unconscious is so completely rigid as to make the creative act impossible. This seems to me to deny the proved creativeness of dream and other unconscious states.

As for conscious processes, they are "flexible, adaptable, satiable, capable of learning from experience, admonition, exhortation,

and instruction." But unconscious processes are "rigid, stereotyped, and insatiable, unmodifiable by the experience of success or
failure, by rewards and punishments, by admonition or exhortation." Speaking as a psychiatrist, he concludes that in the conscious
processes we have "the essence of normal behavior," in the unconscious processes "the essence of sick behavior."[17] (Every human
act, he says, is a mark of being either well or sick.) The conscious
system is predominantly verbal, although not exclusively so, for
gestures, postures, movements are involved. Its primary purpose
is communication. The conscious level is a "relatively slow vehicle
of mentation." It is slow "precisely because its primary purpose is
not for thinking but for that slow-motion sampling of preconscious
thought processes which we call communication ('speech'). We
can *think* of many things at a time 'preconsciously,' (indeed at that
level, it is not possible to think of only one thing at a time): but
we can *communicate* only one meaning at a time."[18] He seems to
rest his case on this argument. While there is much to agree with in
this statement, it seems to me to ignore the vast current of imaginative relation-seeing and reconstruction which goes on only in
alert consciousness.

As for the "rigid and insatiable" inflexibility of the unconscious,
he is in clear opposition to the classical psychoanalytic interpretation, which makes the unconscious the source of the creative act
and ascribes to it escape and defense mechanisms caused by accumulating experiences of repression. He speaks of "unconscious
processes," but says, "This is a misleading bit of technical jargon;
because it is not the symbol that we employ which is unconscious,
but only that which it represents . . . all such hieroglyphics represent complex patterns of several concurrent unconscious meanings, superimposed one upon another."[19]

To clarify his meaning, he presents a diagram of mind drawn as
though it were made up only of the conscious and the unconscious
—no preconscious.

In order to clarify how and where creative functions operate between
these two poles, we must interpose another type of mental process between the Conscious and Unconscious process. It is so important to be
clear about this that, at the risk of repeating myself, I will paraphrase
what I have said elsewhere about the nature and function of these

"levels," or "systems" or "bands" in the more or less continuous spectrum which constitutes our symbolic functions.

There is the realistic form of symbolic thinking in which we are clearly aware of the relationship of the symbols of language to that which we intend to represent. Here the function of the symbol is to communicate the hard core, the bare bones of thought and purpose. This is conscious symbolic function.

At the other end of our spectrum is the symbolic process in which the relationship between the symbol and what it represents has been either distorted or completely ruptured by an active process which is technically called "repression." As a consequence, the symbol here is a disguised and disguising representative of unconscious levels of psychological processes. In this area the function of the symbolic process is not to communicate but to hide, not deliberately but automatically, and not only from others but even more urgently from ourselves. This is the unconscious symbolic process as it occurs in dreaming and in psychological illness.[20]

THE REQUISITES FOR THE ILLUMINATING FLASH

This consensus on the autistic characteristics of the transliminal mind led to my systematic exploration of it as the generating source of the flash of insight. Several definite requisites had to be satisfied. Was there evidence that sufficient potential ingredients were present to account satisfactorily for the flash? Were these ingredients dynamic, in such a state of movement as to guarantee that the explosive spark of meaning could jump across? Was power available to explode the meaning? Was a magnetizing, welding force present? Positive answers to these questions may provide a solid basis for my theorem of the creative threshold.

Availability of the Constituents

I found four definite constituents of the creative act. *First:* a continuous flow of perceptual experience. This is what the layman refers to as something being "in his mind." This is largely what we see, hear, smell, touch, and to which we relate ourselves in space and time. *Second:* a continuing flux of imagery pervading the entire conscious-nonconscious continuum. While visual, motor, and auditory imagery seem to be most prevalent, actually all the senses are involved. *Third:* motor adjustments, incipient movement, ideo-motor action, and sets or attitudes of expectancy. These produce one of the most important bodies of imagery—namely, motor imagery. This appears to be the initiating and indispensable requi-site for every act of response. No other factor is more important in my theory of behavior and of creative imagination. *Fourth:* the ordered, conceptual content of the mind; concept becomes synon-ymous with symbol and with metaphor image, and involves Gestalts or figure-ground relationships. It is the key to thinking and judging. These four constituents—percept, motor adjustment, image, and concept—are traced on the nervous system and preserved in the unconscious. They are the stuff of mind.

The Dynamics of Autistic Mind

That the second criterion of the flash, readiness to fire the mean-ing, is satisfied by the threshold state has already been suggested; recall the foregoing phrases: "a continual flow of perceptual ex-perience . . . ," "an unbroken flux of imagery . . . of incipient movement, ideomotor action and of sets of expectancy." All this spells movement, action. Thus the threshold mind is not only per-missive; it is at the same time potentially dynamic. Actually, the most overt feature of human life is movement. From conception to death we move; trillions of cells, firing steadily in electrochemical action, billions of unconscious, incipient movements of the body. As a single example, I quote a bit from a classic description by Sherrington of the round-the-clock electrical fireworks of the cere-bral cortex. He gives first a graphic record of its display during sleep (with a score of electrodes attached to the sleeper's scalp) while the brain is "superintending the beating of the heart and the state of the arteries so that while we sleep the circulation of the blood is what it should be." Some of the lights flash, he says, "pur-suing a mystic and recurrent manoeuvre as if of some incantational dance."

The great knotted headpiece of the whole sleeping system lies for the most part dark, and quite especially so the roof-brain. Occasionally at places in it lighted points flash or move but soon subside. Such lighted points and moving trains of light are mainly far in the outskirts, and wink slowly and travel slowly. At intervals even a gush of sparks wells up and sends a train down the spinal cord, only to fail to arouse it. Where however the stalk joins the headpiece, there goes forward in a limited field a remarkable display. A dense constellation of some thousands of nodal points burst out every few seconds into a short phase of rhythmical flashing. At first a few lights, then more, increasing in rate and number with a deliberate crescendo to a climax, then to decline and die away. After due pause, the efflorescence is repeated. With each such rhythmic outburst goes a discharge of trains of travelling lights along the stalk and out of it altogether into a number of nerve-branches. What is this doing? It manages the taking of our breath the while we sleep.

Then we "awaken" and the brain with us and

. . . we should observe after a time an impressive change which suddenly accrues. In the great head-end which has been mostly darkness spring up myriads of twinkling stationary lights and myriads of trains of moving lights of many different directions. . . . Swiftly the head-mass becomes an enchanted loom where millions of flashing shuttles weave a dissolving pattern, always a meaningful pattern though never an abiding one; a shifting harmony of subpatterns. Now as the waking body rouses, subpatterns of this great harmony of activity stretch down into the unlit tracks of the stalk-piece of the scheme. Strings of flashing and travelling sparks engage the lengths of it. This means that the body is up and rises to meet its waking day.[21]

Sherrington's picture of incessant cortical activity suggests that the entire organism is a mass of electrochemical dynamics. The corresponding activity of the imagery of the hypnoidal mind suggests that the unconscious storage (whichever physiological theory we accept) is also marked by unceasing internal movement. Each new bit of perception is built into an organism with a history, and one which is in ceaseless movement. Each accretion produces a new motor adjustment called attitude or set of anticipation, predetermining not only the next perception but also the augmenting storage. Since no human situation is ever perceived apart from an attitude which predisposes response to stimulus, meaning and orientation evolve through the fashioning of hierarchies of attitudes. The hypnoidal flux of perceptual fragments, shifting images and movements restructures sets, fuses sets upon sets. Moods form from the total changing storage and its usage, moods operating as orienting sets. The second criterion of the creative threshold readiness to fire the meaning is satisfied.

The Powering of the Imagination

Certainly the structural contents of the imagination are not only available in the transliminal mind, they are alive there. But is there also present a power plant with which to "fire" the flash of imagined conception? This important and subtle bio-psychological question has been largely answered by our picture of a body-mind organism pulsing with movement, centering attention on the "energetics" of creative power. Tension is perhaps the most meaningful and comprehensive concept. In using it, I shall imply both physiological and psychological connotations. The tension-system of the organism is the key to the energy of creative imagination. The sparking concept is movement. Revealing itself in the irritability of protoplasm, it is as basic to the science of behavior as is the concept of motion to the physical sciences. It is its biological correlate.

But movement is the product of the transformation of potential energy into kinetic energy. It is a truism that the source of human motive power is the energy in the sun's rays which gets into the body through the food we eat, the air we breathe and the light that surrounds us. The body is the energy-producing machine and its energy is both potential and kinetic. For truly creative work to be done, the drive of passion must be produced.

There is solid consensus on the necessity for inspiration, drive, the white heat of enthusiasm, for sustained creative production. To reach great creative heights, titanic energy seems to be a requisite. But does "emotion" supply this or does something deeper provide the emotion? Men of art do not, perhaps cannot, tell us. The archives of mid-century behavioral science do supply an impressive body of facts about certain forms of emotion and their physiological constitution. Yakovlev, American physiologist, discussing creative behavior and the brain, says without qualification that "emotional energy is the matrix and source of all human achievement through which man frees energy from matter."[22] It is in this sense that the artist, on the verge of discovery, tingles with excitement, is energized to work at high tension. This is the source of the scientist's obsession with discovery.

To say that for truly creative work to be done the drive of passion must be produced is to say in physiological terms that potential energy must be transformed into kinetic energy. This is as true of the powering of creative production as it is of physical work. The facts of drive have chemical and physiological explanations, including the enormous differences in the rate of metabolism between individuals; between childhood, youth, middle age, and old age; and the differences at various times in the day and the year. The changes in motive power are functions of body chemistry.

William James in a famous essay, *The Energies of Men,* dealt at length with examples of these hidden emotional resources, giving them the now familiar name, "reservoirs of individual power."[23] Charles Darwin said he "has occasionally recognized the full truth of the concept," citing "instances of jaded men mentally inventing imaginary attacks upon themselves and thereby building up passions for the sake of re-invigorating themselves"; these, he said, were "proof of the exciting nature of anger."[24]

Walter Cannon's researches on the adrenal glands showed between 1910 and 1930 that body movement

is made more efficient because of emotional disturbances of the viscera . . . the cessation of processes in the alimentary canal (thus freeing the energy supply for other parts); the shifting of blood from the abdominal organs . . . to the organs immediately essential to muscular exertion (the lungs, the heart, the central nervous system); the increased vigor of contraction of the heart; the quick abolition of the effects of muscular fatigue; the mobilizing of energy-giving sugar in the circulation.[25]

Cannon (1912) developed the emergency theory of the supreme role of the secretion of adrenin (and sugar) in the blood, in explaining the conditions of such strong excitement as that of fear and anger. He postulates that, under conditions of calm and quiet, "adrenin secretion is in abeyance. But in time of special stress under the influence of pain or its emotional equivalent, fear or anger, adrenin is discharged and serves to adapt the animal to the demands of the stressful occasion." In his reports of experimental results, Cannon cites a wide range of examples in which emotional excitement is associated with increased physical power and resistance to fatigue. He measured the vastly increased deposits of sugar in the urine of both college football players and of stadium spectators during the excitement of competitive sports. "In the dressing room before a critical contest," he says, "I have seen a 'gridiron warrior' . . . sitting grimly on a bench, his fists clenched, his jaws tight, and his face the color of clay. He performed wonderfully when the game began, and after it was over there was a large percentage of sugar in his urine!"[26] He adds examples from racing, running, rowing, and includes both contestants and spectators.

Stanley Cobb who worked with Cannon at Harvard, says: "These observations of Cannon have stood the test of time; his main theories of emergency adjustment and homeostasis are epoch-making contributions. Recent work has, of course, added new data and elaborated the concepts of emotional expression." Cannon's pioneering ended a quarter-century ago and those he taught have brought much new light on the physiology of the emotions. For example, Cobb adds, "Cannon dealt only with adrenalin (epinephrine or adrenin) which is the internal secretion of the adrenal medulla. The discovery and description of the various hormones of the adrenal cortex came after Cannon's main work was done." Cannon worked primarily on the adrenal medulla and largely missed the critical role of the adrenal cortex. Cobb postulates "that the adrenal cortex takes over where the medulla leaves off."[27]

Since Cannon broke the first trails in studying the endocrines, more than twenty hormones have been discovered in the adrenal cortex. These are regulators, concerned, for example, with the conversion of protein to sugar, maintenance of salt and water balance in the body fluids, and are directly connected to the anterior pituitary.

Equally important with the adrenals in the control of energy, is the action of the thyroid and the anterior pituitary. Cobb says of it: "An understanding of the way in which the anterior pituitary is controlled by the nervous system is essential."

The body is thus conceived as an energy-producing machine; for psychological work to be done, potential energy must be transformed into kinetic energy, as it is in purely physical production.

The basic energy postulate is that of a multi-trillion-celled organism continuously pulsating, from birth to death, with electrochemical movement; a ceaselessly active, integrated, energy system. It is known that this system autonomously renews itself through a never-finished tension-release-tension cycle. At every pulsation, as long as life endures, a difference in electrical potential always remains left over, an imbalance of surplus tension. "Molecular instability," says Gardner Murphy, "is a feature of nerve cells, just as it is of muscles and glands. Thus every cell in the body is an initiator of motivation; there are no sharply defined 'motive spots,' there are simply *degrees* of motivation—tension gradients—throughout the living system."[28] The basis of the drive dynamics, then, is a fusion of physiological and psychic tensions. What we call mind is a heaving sea of rhythmical electrochemical impulses and motor imagery, focused momentarily in consciousness as meaningful percepts and concepts.

The basis of drive-dynamics seems to lie, therefore, in tension. As the irritability of protoplasm, it is as basic to the science of behavior as the concept of motion is to the physical sciences. But tension is both of body and mind, bio-psychological. Body tensions are the source of physical energy; psychological tensions, of psychological energy. Both tensions are also called needs, for tension is the need to act. They also are twofold: physiological needs or drives, and psychological needs or motives. The two are never separated; tension, need, and motive are synonymous. Thus, bio-psychology stresses the integrative unity of physiological drive and psychological motive.

The foregoing is no more than a précis of the physiological record of the organism-as-a-whole reacting in its two interdependent environments. While structure and dynamics are sensitive and unstable throughout, there is evidence that the act is marked by the dominance-relations of distinctive regions. Certainly for searching analysis and critique it is proper to think of the contributions of the great regional systems in the organism to the flash of insight as well as to perception. Current behavioral opinion seems to recognize four such systems:

Tensions of the visceral system. These include hunger, thirst, excretion, oxygen-deprivation, vasomotor adjustments (responses to temperature changes), sexual drive (gonad and other endocrine tensions), maternal needs (endocrine and lactation tensions). All of these, of course, are culturally affected and also subject to cyclic periodicities of the day, month, and season.

Tensions of overt and inner movements, the action system. "Tension of a muscle group lowers thresholds for another contraction. . . . Muscle tone is constantly changing and causing new activity. . . . So, too, are the direct and indirect effects of any keyed-up condition (excitement) or any relaxed condition. Thus the muscles both guide and initiate action."[29] The entire body is a continuous power plant of physical explosion. The infant's incessant movement depends upon the synergy of environmental factors, visceral, and muscular factors. Because of many imbalances, muscular inactivity becomes unbearable, hence the apparently aimless movement of the young child.

Brain dynamics. The third important regional tension is that of cerebral cortex ("roof-brain") and interconnections with the midbrain ("visceral brain"). Electrochemical activity is going on continuously throughout the higher central nervous system. "There are, in a literal sense, centrally initiated motive patterns. The nervous system does not wait to be 'stimulated'; it is active even under general anesthesia."[30] The tensions of the nervous system are as important as activity and visceral tensions. Moreover, the integrated character of the process is revealed in the fact that successive increases in drive can arise either from tensions in a local function or indirectly through the increasing of other tensions in related regions.

Tensions of the endothalamic and autonomic systems. Finally, there is the emotional powerhouse which functions primarily through endocrine and mid-brain cooperation.

It can no longer be doubted that the autistic antechamber is a dynamic flux of potential ingredients of the creative flash. It involves not only a world of images but an organism tense with incipient movements and anticipatory attitudes, continuously set for response. These are the origins of the creative act. But, as James said, "origins alone prove nothing."

The Magical Welding Force

What causes the spark of meaning to explode? Chaotic bits and pieces went into the unconscious storage—perceptual snapshots, inadvertent body movements, twitches, and incipient tendencies, and a fantasia of kaleidoscopic imagery. But the floating images of reveries came out as ordered beauty. What was the shaping spirit that "saw and seized upon a hint of form" in Coleridge's twilight of the imagination, and "through the miracle of conscious art . . . moulded a radiant and ordered whole"? This is the astonishing magic of all great imaginative creations. Lowes illustrates from his studies of Chaucer:

It so happens that for the last twenty-odd years I have been more or less occupied with Chaucer. I have tracked him . . . into almost every section of eight floors of a great library. It is a perpetual adventure among uncharted Ophirs and Golcondas to read after him—or Coleridge. And every conceivable sort of thing which Chaucer knew went into his alembic. It went in a waif of travel-lore from the mysterious Orient, a curious bit of primitive psychiatry, a racy morsel from Jerome against Jovinian, alchemy, astrology, medicine, geomancy, physiognomy, Heaven only knows what not, all vivid with the relish of the reading—it went in stark fact, "nude and crude," and it came out pure Chaucer.[31]

Men have been asking, ever since Lucretius first put the words in Dryden's mouth, what is it moves "the sleeping images . . . toward the light."[32] Actually they are not inert, for their most obvious characteristic is surging movement, electrochemical as well as imagistic. But they have not yet come alive with meaning; they have not been fired by being juxtaposed with the appropriate mating material. Lowes illustrates it perfectly. He tells how in Chaucer, in Dante, and much later, in Coleridge, "through a flash of association by way of a common phrase, two objects have telescoped into a third. And at moments of high imaginative tension associations, not merely in pairs but in battalions, are apt in similar fashion to stream together and coalesce."[33]

The miracle of the creative act is that out of the utter chaos of the bio-psychological unconscious can be precipitated the ordered wholes that we know as conceptual thought; and yet it happens myriad times. The subliminal world is not architectonic. Its function is to supply the materials of constructive design. But some autonomous forming process sweeps like a magnet across its chaos of elements, picking up those that are significant and, in a welding flash, precipitating the ordered concept. This is "that amazing discrepancy between the stuff of poetry and poetry itself"; in practical terms, between the pictures in Coleridge's head from the dozen huge tomes of his travel reading and the formed beauty of the "Ancient Mariner" or of "Kubla Khan." Coleridge's own explanation, while he was still under the influence of Hartley's association theory, was that shuttles of association weave a patterned woof into the "fabric of visual imagery." "Seeing a mackerel," he said, "it may happen that I immediately think of gooseberries, because I at the same time ate mackerel with gooseberries as the sauce." Lowes thinks "something like that . . . was the case with the strange congeries of shining simulacra which had streamed together and modified each other, and set up a sort of subconscious communal existence of their own."[34] But the aimless flow of association which Coleridge called "reverie-ish and streaming" left things far too much to chance, or at best to simple propinquity.

At one point we are on sure ground. There can be no doubt that the requisite materials and the magnetizing, welding force are continuously present in the transliminal state. Some kind of illuminating spark does blaze up every time we get a new imagined conception. But what amalgam of forces unite in the sparking process? That, in my logic as well as in Lowes', in Poincaré's, and in all the others, is still the challenge.

EDITOR'S NOTE. This rather complex chapter is important in advancing the author's argument. Part of its complexity stems from its use of evidence from fields of study not usually brought into juxtaposition. Findings from psychiatry, parapsychology, physiology, endocrinology, and literary criticism are pressed into the author's service. His purpose is to show that "transliminal mind" has behavioral referents and to indicate that the ways of functioning to which it refers make it a likely candidate as the principal "center" of creative imagination in the human organism. The importance of the "theorem of the transliminal mind" in the author's argument is easy enough to see. It provides a link between the inner autistic processes of the organism and the processes of the external environment which, to some large extent, control conscious, "reality oriented" perception. "Transliminally," the organism functions in a condition of relative "freedom" to create novel forms of image and conception. These forms are not dominated within by the demands of the deep unconscious nor by the demands of external reality. Yet in its transliminal functioning the organism has access to both "internal" and "external" resources.

The variety of the documentation, already noted, actually lends additional illumination to the author's orientation and purpose. In his view, the traditional dichotomy between "body" and "mind" must be undercut if any valid and defensible theory of the imagination is to be formulated. His transliminal mind is not "mental" as opposed to "bodily." Physiological or endocrinological findings are as appropriate to an understanding of his "magical threshold" as are findings from psychiatry or literary scholarship. It is important to note that "inner" processes of the organism are seen by the author to be quite as accessible to study through the scientific methods of the physiologist or endocrinologist as through direct experience as in the poet's vision or in trance states. The author is not here arguing his conviction that the body-mind dichotomy is a mischievous block to fuller understanding of creative human functioning. He is rather, in his attempt to fuse documentation from studies of "body" and studies of "mind," demonstrating how the block may be overcome.

4

The Stuff of Creative Mind

THE ingredients of creative mind accumulate continuously in the nervous and motor systems in a fusion of perceptual tracings and motor adjustments. Reconstructed below the threshold of awareness, these appear in the transliminal mind as a kaleidoscope of fantasy imagery. New concepts, realistic or autistic, are formed from these four-fold materials—percepts, motor adjustments, images, and old concepts. These constitute the stuff of mind.

Of the four ingredients, the fusion I shall call "motor imagery" appears to be the initiating and indispensable requisite of the flash of meaning. The term is used advisedly to center attention on two of the four constituents; incipient movements and images. The other two are percepts, which are continuously being traced on the nervous system, and concepts, which are only intermittently formed. These four items constitute the over-all content of mind. In itemizing them separately, for purposes of definition and analysis, I do not suggest that any one is independent of the others. On the contrary, each act of the normal mind is a complicated tangle of them all and occurs against an ever-moving panorama of autistic fantasy.

MOTOR DETERMINANTS OF MEANING

The continuous streaming of perceptual experience constitutes one important part of the stuff of the transliminal mind. Since perception is a link between the outer scene and inner world of a man, I will deal with it more fully in the next chapter. But much more goes on in the organism than nervous imprinting and storage of percepts. There is also the imprinting of uncountable motor adjustments and their integration into manifold attitudes or sets of expectancy. In physiological terms this activity is both the continuous firing of cells, and overt and incipient movements in nerves, tissues, and muscles. Sherrington's electro-encephalographic picture of the millions of flashing shuttles of the enchanted cerebral loom can be generalized for other parts of the nervous and endothalamic systems.

The entire organism is a mass of tensile pushes and pulls. This is the second aspect of the organism's reservoir of potentially creative materials. Perceptual experience and physiological forms of movement, taken together, comprise what I call the motor determinants of meaning. I suggest that these constitute the primary raw materials of the transliminal mind, from which images and concepts are formed.

This brings to the fore a motor theory of consciousness and meaning as well as of attention and relaxation. It now needs to be demonstrated that we respond to ideas as well as to people, things, situations, by making appropriate incipient or overt muscular adjustments; that shifts in emotion always imply predictable changes in postural set, and that skeletal muscle patterns fit specific emotional patterns; that the new-born baby's first meanings and the aged man's last ones are motor responses to physiological tensions or needs; that electro-encephalographic and myographic measurements verify the hypothesis that motor attitude is the matrix in which perception occurs. Each new increment of perception is built into an organism that is in ceaseless, dynamic movement. It is not only an organism with a history, but one that never pauses, from conception to death, except for the purpose of conscious appraisal and redirection.

It is a truism of contemporary psychology that we respond to objects *with* meaning, and that we are aware of them only as we make appropriate movements with respect to them. To the sound of the word "thin" I react with meaning by incipient contraction; to "broad" by the impulse to move expansively. Try the experiment on yourself of thinking and feeling "thin" and, simultaneously, making expansive movements of the muscles of the torso, shoulders, and arms which are normally appropriate for the meaning "broad." To take another example, how do you judge resistances? You do it by resisting vicariously with the muscular system. Consider the sensitive poise of the fingers as a person responds to the phrase, "fragile as an eggshell." How does one move at night in a dark room, shut off from touch, sound, sight, taste, and smell? By making incipient, groping, sensitive body-responses of his feeling of spatial relations. It is interesting to observe how invariantly the appropriate body gestures accompany the emotion of anger—the clenched fist, the flushed face, the raised voice, the tightening muscular systems of the speech mechanism, the pounding heart.

One responds to concepts by the indicated physical reactions—rigidity of the body's motor-set in responding to the concept "hardness," resilience in its response to "softness." Note the appropriateness with which the sound and tone of the voice are adjusted to the meaning to be conveyed by such words as "giant," "elves," "fairies," "witches."

Our meanings are operational in character; weight means tendency to fall, volume to expand, a ceiling presses down, a floor up, a line seems to have direction, attraction means pulling, repulsion pushing. Rhythm suggests recurrence, antipathy recoiling. The concept of love means going out to; hate, turning away from. Each of these meanings is expressed in action terms, as verb not noun, and the basic gathering together of the total organism is always motor. These inner tensions in the shoulders and other parts of the body are felt abstractions, felt expressions. Through these muscle senses we distinguish weights, dimensions, resistances. Through this capacity to feel movement we recognize shapes, forces, distances. Thus the inner movements of the body constitute an important instrument by which we respond with meaning to the outside world.

The obvious form in which these hidden incipient bodily movements appear is motor attitude or anticipatory set. It is a generally accepted principle today that in each act of response the organism adopts the physical attitude that is appropriate to the meaning with which it is responding. One does not go too far, in fact, in saying that the incipient moving, gathering-together process *is* the meaningful response. Moreover, the consensus taken from diverse schools of thought states that a man's characteristic attitudes determine how he behaves and, still more basically, what he feels and thinks.

Attitude is the total gesture of the organism. It serves the function of framing, projecting the meaning with which we respond to situations. The organism knows by getting appropriately set. We strike appropriate physical attitudes, and corresponding psychological attitudes, or meanings, are inextricably fused with them. Consider, for example, the bodily recoil of fear and the tendency to flight, the outstretched arms of love and sympathy, the clenched fist of anger. Attitudes are the gesture of the organism; taken all together they are the set in which it anticipates its response. We speak, therefore, of attitudes of expectancy or anticipation.

Moreover, the instantaneous flash—the primal awareness of the organism when the man says "I know"—is this tonal gathering-together of the self. The act of knowing is the total gesture of hands, face, torso, autonomic and central nervous systems. In it words play a minor, often negligible part. Indeed, so futile is the struggle of the speech mechanism to find the appropriate words that the clearest meanings the organism achieves are the flashlike fusions of unpremeditated expressions of the whole being. This is what we shall mean by "gesture"; what Isadora Duncan meant when she said, "All my life I've struggled to make one authentic gesture"; what Martha Graham meant by "one primary or true movement"—one movement that would state her view of life. This is what the painter paints, the poet writes, the musician composes, what every scientist endures in the ordeal of framing an hypothesis—the making of the authentic gesture.

Nina Bull's studies, carried out over a period of some twenty years, represent the most extensive attempt to establish experimentally the prior role of motor attitude in emotion. Her basic proposition was (a) "that feeling [she does not distinguish between feeling and emotion] is dependent upon preparatory motor attitude"; (b) "that the particular kind of action prepared for by the motor attitude determines the particular kind of feeling." Her experiments sought to establish whether "consistent patterns of bodily response can be induced which correspond to the familiar affective states known as *disgust, fear, anger, depression, triumph,* and *joy.*" Following a series of preliminary studies in 1938–1939, her principal experiment was carried on in the New York Psychiatric Clinic in 1947–1948 and in 1949–1950. A group of college students were presented, while under hypnosis, with six single stimulus words—disgust, fear, anger, depression, triumph, and joy. Observations were recorded of their behavior and a record was taken of their own retrospections. Hypnosis was employed because of its "well-known freedom from self-consciousness and the general narrowing of consciousness."[1]

There were sixty sessions in the experimental series with the six specific emotions, the subjects responding either by a bodily reaction, by hallucinating, or merely by remembering an appropriate situation for the emotion. Almost all the responses observed were clearly attitudinal, that is postural or preparatory, not consummatory reactions. In anger, for example, the subjects "would clench their hands in readiness to strike, but they never actually struck at anything."[2] Two principal kinds of feeling were experienced—the feeling of the emotion itself—for example, anger, and the various organic sensations—tensions, pressures, movements. These were all spoken of as "feelings" and were hard to distinguish. Nevertheless, the subjects always seemed aware that a difference existed between them, and even described transitions from one feeling to the other.

Mrs. Bull's general conclusions were that "without somatic changes of some kind no new affect of any kind was obtained, neither the contrasting one suggested by the hypnotist, nor any other. The primary affect in every case was either maintained or definitely augmented. It was demonstrated that deeply hypnotized subjects could not obey the suggestion prohibiting any change in posture or organic sensation, if they obeyed the suggestion of feeling a new emotion." Here we find confirmation that a shift in emotion always implies bodily changes, "those in the realm of postural set being particularly marked."[3]

There are important general inferences from the Bull experiments. Cannon always insisted that there was no clear parallelism between endocrine content and emotional reactions. One cannot distinguish anger from joy or depression from elation, for example, by the hormonal or sugar content of the blood. For many years, this was regarded as sufficient evidence that there was no correspondence between patterns of behavior and specific emotions. Yet the more recent physiological evidence, such as I have quoted, and our everyday observation show that the normal man clearly distinguishes between specific emotions and behaves in terms of these distinctions. The Bull experiments and evidence point definitely to the role of the skeletal muscles, of the entire muscular system in these distinctions. In fact, they show that the individual seems to strike the physical attitude before the meaning flashes up. The question of objectivity of measurement, however, should be kept in mind. Mrs. Bull had no measurements of elapsed time and the problem of sequence is still controversial. While my own interpretation confirms her conclusions, it is to be regretted that an objective body of measurements of temporal sequence is still not available.

As a result of her many years of experienced work, Nina Bull developed an attitude theory which divides the production of the affective states into two serial parts: *first,* the motor attitude, or posture of the body (this is preparation, what I call incipient movement or set of expectancy); *second,* the "consummatory movement" or action.

It is not generally appreciated that all action predicates attitude, since *every* kind of bodily movement requires some preliminary postural preparation. Some portion of the organism must always be stabilized to form a fulcrum from which the movement can take place—as when the shoulder joint is relatively fixed in order to permit a measured movement of the forearm. . . . Similarly, the chest of an angry person must be fixed to form a base of operation from which the arms can strike effectively . . . slow motion pictures show this postural preparation and its follow-up movement as one continuous flow, with no dividing line between the two.[4]

All action predicates postural preparation in which feelings of "being moved" arise. Thus Mrs. Bull makes an important revision of James's famous principle of emotion—"we cry and are sorry," that is, we strike the motor attitude of crying and the feeling of being sorry arises. For she says that as we actually cry, that is, as incipient movement (set) gives way to overt movement, the feeling of being sorry subsides. It is the preparatory tendency or impulse to move, the attitudinal incipient behavior, not overt movement, that gives rise to feeling. Mrs. Bull's studies show that the particular way we move determines the kind of emotion—whether of anger, sorrow, fear, disgust, rage, triumph, joy, or depression. Three stages of attitude, or readiness, are postulated: neural readiness or latent attitude which precedes the sequence of actual emotional behavior; activated readiness or motor attitude which starts the emotional sequence going; and conscious readiness or mental attitude of orientation and intention which is the essential part of the feeling in the emotional sequence. I conclude that the "mental" aspect of attitude cannot precede the "motor" part. It "cannot in fact appear at all without an antecedent motor attitude to fire the afferent pathways from the muscles and viscera to the brain."[5] In a personal statement to me she has said that she still lacks conclusive experimental evidence for the generalization that the motor part *precedes* the mental. I accept it, however, as implicit in all that we know of the nature of the act of response as I have interpreted the consensus of physiological-psychological knowledge in the preceding chapters.

According to the Bull theory, motor attitude is labeled "feeling" and mental attitude "thinking." Her second stage of attitude-formation, activated readiness or motor attitude, when taken together with the first, latent attitude, is my stage of incipient movement or set-of-expectancy. There is much reason for thinking that it is the point of actuation, or firing, of the flash of insight. I, too, call its accompaniment (that is, the mood created by it) feeling. But I am convinced that the motor phase can not be distinguished from the mental in the attitude or set. The act is a unit, a fusion of the physiological and the psychological, and we still lack conclusive measured evidence that any one phase precedes the other.

A RHAPSODY OF IMAGES

We know that the perceptual ingredients of the imagined conception are stored in the unconscious, even though the process by which they are traced in the nervous system is largely unknown. They appear to us, however, in the creative threshold mind as images.

We have noted how our conscious-nonconscious continuum projects a corresponding dichotomy in imagery—the reality imagery of conscious perceptual experiences contrasted with autistic imagery based on earlier perceptual experience which has been reconstructed in the unconscious. This distinction between autistic and reality imagery underlies the dichotomy between creative and logical thought discussed in Chapter 2. Among the reality images we should distinguish the memory image from the imagination image. Memory images are vague holdovers from previous perceptual experience. I look at my valley and its mountains, close my eyes and have a memory image. I read the descriptive account of a similar mountain view or try to imagine what Angkor Wat looks like, and I have an imagination image. These types are both called reality imagery, because they are the product of, or are verifiable by, direct personal experience.

By far the most important form of autistic imagery involved in creative work is the dream-image. Time after time it has proved to be the liaison with stored unconscious materials. Second to the dream as a rich resource for creative work we must recognize the hypnoidal (hypnagogic and hypnopompic) imagery which includes hallucinations, eidetic images, crystal images and such images of distortion as synesthesia, diagram forms and body schema. While it is difficult to distinguish image from percept, I regard the image as the liaison between conscious percept and unconsciously projected symbol in the act of response. In fact, symbol or concept is what I shall call, following the early students of philology, "metaphor-image."

We have seen that the hypnoidal mind is a kaleidoscope of fragments in perpetual flux. Each new perceptual increment "dropped . . . into the deep well of unconscious cerebration,"[6] as Henry James described it, touches and fuses with the stored concourse of interpenetrating traces. The incessant activity of amalgamation fashions and refashions memory images and from time to time imagination images. We get a picture of hypnoidal flashes of association like that called up by the picture of Epicurus' atoms, unhooked from the wall and darting in all directions. Blended in vivid incoherence in our dreams and our reveries they become a dissolving panorama of moving pictures. Thus the subliminal blendings and fusings accumulate in the unconscious depository. Network upon network of linked images, fantastic medleys, Coleridge's pet "ocular spectra," tenant the layers just below consciousness.

This is the hypnoidal flux that bursts through into the normal as well as abnormal autistic vestibule as a "saturnalia of the mind." McKellar calls it *"knight's-move thinking."* "You get a picture," one of his patients said, "then another picture, but you can't get the two joined." To a patient of Bleuler's, autistic thinking is "idea joined upon idea in the most bizarre series of associations."[7] Stekel gives a similar description. "We never have single thoughts but always many, an entire polyphony. . . . I picture thinking as a stream of which only the surface [reality] is visible; orchestral music of which only the melody is audible."[8] The reality-mind is like the tiny visible part of the iceberg, autism the huge sub-surface foundation. Quoting a patient who described herself as "so busy chasing hares off the pathway through the woods that I lost the main path,"[9] Stekel made a useful suggestion, calling it "polyphony and not one voice." "What we are after," he said, "lies in the middle voices or even in the counterpoint."[10] Clang associations (caused by terms similar in sound but different in meaning) are frequent; one of McKellar's patients when asked to explain the statement: "Those who live in glass houses shouldn't throw stones," thought first about a castle, then connected the moat of the castle with the mote of the parable of the mote and the beam. "I realized that the 'moat-mote' connection was logically unsound and was puzzled to find that the idea it led to none the less appeared to be relevant."[11]

There is no question that nineteenth-century students of psychology paid close attention to the indispensable role of the image. During the first half of the twentieth century, however, under the mechanistic influence of Pavlov and Thorndike and the parallel positivistic climate in philosophy, the concern about imagery and other constituents of the imagination sharply declined.

Actually, we live our lives, waking and sleeping, against a kaleidoscopic background of imagery. Many of us may not know it, we may even disbelieve it when reminded of it. This Sir Francis Galton discovered eighty years ago when he made a study of the *"Illumination, Definition and Colouring of Mental Images."* To his astonishment he found "that the great majority of the men of science . . . protested that mental imagery was unknown to them, and they looked on me as fanciful and fantastic in supposing that the words 'mental imagery' really expressed what I believed everybody supposed them to mean." But he found "that in general society many men and yet a larger number of women, and many boys and girls, declared that they habitually saw mental imagery, and that it was perfectly distinct to them and full of colour."[12]

Cole interpreted the data on imagery in 1933.

Other investigators have described auditory, motor (kinesthetic), tactile, olfactory types of imagery, although all agree that the visual is the most common. . . . In all probability intensive study of the individuals who seem limited to one modality would reveal the presence of other forms. We have no choice, however, but to accept the subject's word for it, and upon this basis most of us are of the predominantly visual type; a few seem confined mainly to auditory images; and some report only kinesthetic images. The verbal type, common to those who work with abstract, verbal material, may, in turn, be divided into those who "hear," "see," or "feel" the words, and in the last group are those who report incipient speech movements in recall.[13]

Careful students of mental life recognize that their waking hours are lived against an almost unbroken background of imagery.

For creative production the more profitable type of imagery seems to be what Urbanschitsch and Jaensch named "eidetic" imagery. Apparently it is especially prominent in childhood. Introduced first by Urbanschitsch in 1907, the concept was developed by Jaensch at the University of Marburg.[14] The word comes from the Greek noun of the verb "to see." Jaensch speaks of the "out-there-ness," the almost three-dimensional stereoscopic aspect of the eidetic image. Galton (1880) found that one-tenth of his schoolboy subjects could "project their images." One of his most spectacular prodigies was an eidetic imager who could calculate from an imagined slide rule. Jaensch's findings contrasted children with adults. Sixty per cent of the children but only 7 per cent of the adults possessed this faculty in a highly developed state. Why the difference? Certainly there are two factors: the freer, more imaginative tendencies of children; and the predominance of verbalism in the life of the grown-up and its lesser degree in childhood. Gordon Allport reported that 50 per cent of a group of eleven-year-olds had eidetic images with the vividness and substantiality of a visual afterimage, and like the latter they may move with the eye. They are far more persistent than the afterimage, however, and may be revived voluntarily, hours, days, and even months after a few seconds' exposure. On occasion they may be obsessive in character, recurring spontaneously and—as in the case of childhood fears—approach hallucinations. . . .

The images appeared as though "projected" upon a gray background placed at normal reading distance, and they possessed a richness in detail greater than either visual afterimage or memory image commonly shows. The subjects seemed to be able to "read" the items from the image, frequently adding to and occasionally correcting what had previously been reported from memory. . . . Details such as the following were reported: . . . letters composing a word in a "foreign language on a poster in the background," the length and direction of the lines of shading in a stretch of roadway, the number of whiskers on a cat's lip, the correct spelling of the word *Gartenwirtschaft* which appeared in the pictures in small letters over the door.[15]

Murphy confirms this.

Thus a child is shown a picture of a garden scene for ten seconds, and some hours later is able to *see* the scene, reading off from his memory panorama more and more details which he never noticed in the original during the period of exposure. Such images may be poured forth in a volume that is immense in comparison with what can be produced by the ordinary methods of remembering and verbalizing. They also obey optical laws too complex for the child to understand, indicating an orderly perceptual process which is continued in full force long after the removal of the outer stimulus.[16]

So much for the general prevalence of imagery. Although we lack adequate statistical studies, general testimony and the psychological consensus based on the voluminous literature of the last two generations show that the waking as well as the sleeping mind of most people is marked by a kaleidoscope of imagery. The fact of its constant availability seems to be established.

But what, more exactly, is it? What do we mean by image and, more important, by motor image? Can we today, in the light of the accumulation of recent bio-psychological studies, define it more precisely than was formerly possible? We can, indeed, building on the knowledge acquired in recent years from the exploration of the conscious-unconscious continuum.

We must be prepared, however, to make a right-about-face in dealing with the data of the creative flash of insight. Conventional education has predisposed us to rely altogether on the data of reality-oriented thinking. Actually we must learn to deal also with the imagery material of autistic thought.

CONCEPTS AND THOUGHT-MODELS

Percepts, motor adjustments, and images are indispensable constituents of the autistic mind. But they are simply bits and pieces, merely the raw materials. There is no clear suggestion that they contain within themselves the autonomous forming power of which the dynamic preconscious is capable. While the ingredients of the hypnoidal mind are kaleidoscopic, it is a fact that from them are precipitated both the rigorously ordered conceptions of science and the radiantly ordered beauty of art. Some integrating, organizing force must therefore be postulated; some power which, as McKellar says, working like a giant magnet, selectively picking up iron from a heterogeneous scrap heap, gathers together only the mutually attractive fragments. I suggest that there is, in the nature of the act, a tendency of response that turns this miscellany into order.

The primary tendency of the ever-moving organism is to generalize the cumulating accretion of percepts, motor tendencies, and images. Such generalizing is called "conceptualizing." Concepts, generalized from past experience in the inherently necessary motor attitudes, "fire" the flash of meaning. In the act of firing, the concepts become the ordering part of the stored ingredients.

I turn next, therefore, to a preliminary examination of what is known descriptively about concepts.* I say "descriptively" because in the concept we come to grips with the basic form of the flash of insight.

---

* To make this completely clear requires a thorough analysis of the process of conceptualizing, but that can be more effectively accomplished in relation to symbol formation. I shall do little more, therefore, in bringing this chapter to a close, than to indicate the nature of the role of concepts as part of the stored ingredients of the creative imagination, and to show how they make possible the reduction of the confusion of the world to meaningful order.

Consider the case of the neonate learning to talk by naming things in his environment, and by so doing mastering the conceptual meanings. He hears a special moving object being called "dog." He becomes interested in it and in his own peculiar jargon calls it "dog." Later he sees another somewhat different-looking moving object also called "dog"; and this too he learns to call "dog." As time passes, other similar but never identical objects appear, each called "dog" and to each of these he responds with the percept and the name "dog." While this is going on, many other names of things, people, situations, actions are being acquired by the same process.

Slowly the concrete dog percepts take on a more generalized nature, a kind of "dog" configuration. The child notices, at first without much conscious recognition, that different "dogs" are similar to each other in general size and shape of body, in hair, bark, and way of moving. At some point in the learning process, the concrete reaction in terms of what the object is or does or has, gives way to broader generalizing, to abstracting of characteristics. As this happens the dog percepts give way more and more to the dog concept. This is seen in comparing the typical age-level responses on the Binet-Simon intelligence test. Recall the contrast in definitions of "orange" given by the hypnotized man who has been regressed to early childhood. On the four-year level he defined an orange as "something to eat, looks like a ball"; on the twenty-year level, as "a sweet citrus fruit grown in very warm climates."

It is in this way that the young child establishes the concrete beginnings of his thought-models for the external world. As he reaches school age, he has built up meanings for the animals of the locality, the physical things of the community, the people of the family, the neighborhood, the town, the means of transportation and communication, and the obvious tools of production. So far as these are concepts, they are largely *definitional* in character: a dog runs . . . a policeman helps . . . an airplane flies. . . .

Entering the school and mastering the tools of reading, number, and language, the process is vastly broadened and deepened. Generalizations are extended to include *relational* ones of increasing complexity. Now the child is systematically inducted via concepts into every phase of the civilization and culture: man making-and-doing, producing food, shelter and clothing, transporting and communicating, buying and selling, moving about and governing; man meditating, creating, and appreciating with esthetic materials; man's institutions and languages, his uses of science and art, his ideas, beliefs, values, what he wants most and fears most. The perceptual and conceptual environment ranges over the entire earth and its peoples, past and present. To understand more than a few of these by first-hand experience is impossible. To study them at long range in schools and colleges requires thousands of episodes which vary in scope and abstruseness from the learning of the primary school to studies in the higher schools.

To deal with this staggering range of ways of living, ideas, beliefs, and traditions, the cue to selection and organization is the "key concept." Sane and orderly life would be impossible were it not for the conceptualizing capacity which enables man to select and respond to a few key stimuli from the overwhelming fusillade to which he is subjected. It is this capacity that builds thought models of economy and order. Ordering is generalizing. Most acts of response are generalizations; our waking hours are marked by an uninterrupted flow of generalization. From the moment of rising, through the hours of work and relaxation in leisure time, we generalize about the weather, our means of going about our tasks of the day, our relations with other people, things, institutions, and problems.

Each of these statements is a concept which generalizes many specific meanings. Manifold responses to specific occupations, to the data of political, economic, and religious groupings are steadily formed into a manageable hierarchy of concepts. For example, the key concept, "industrial society," generalizes a dozen less comprehensive ones, such as mass production of goods, specialization of labor, standardization of manufacture, corporate capital, precarious interdependence, high standard of living, etc. At the top of the hierarchy and on the most complex level such an ideological concept as "automation" generalizes all the meanings of an industrial society and, in addition, many others—acceleration of atomics and electronics; expansion in the size of producing unit; speed of processes; problems of wages, prices, living standards, and costs of living; the consequent transformation of the democratic structure of power; dehumanization of the individual; concern with things; or-

ganizational conformity; the development of anti-intellectualism. . . .
Thus the thought models of the intelligent man are comprised of
key concepts which embrace the entire culture: the primary characteristics of its over-all structure, the hierarchy of modern revolu-
tions, changing civilizations and great trends of thought, theories of
social change, challenging philosophies, the primary concepts and
unresolved conflicts of the American way of life, and manifold
others.

What then is a concept? How we define it will depend on how
we look at the problem of knowing. If we regard the flashing up of
insight as discovery, as I do in this study, we shall define the act
of knowing from the inside, as intuitive identification. If we are
engaged, however, in the verification of a discovery, we shall look
at the problem logically from the outside and in terms of categories.
A concept is, according to this view, a general idea that stands for
a group of similar objects, persons, ideas, situations, actions. Or
it is "any word or idea that stands for any one of a group of
things." We succeed in conceptualizing to the extent that we can
identify and classify similar characteristics of heterogeneous things
or people. This makes categorizing the essence of conceptualizing,
and reflects the outside-looking-in point of view in knowing. This
is correct for the process of verification. It is what happens in the
use of concept, or in what Bruner calls "concept attainment."[17]
This is what practically all the psychological studies have, mistak-
enly as I believe, called concept-formation. It is not concept-formation. This is our basic problem, for we are seeking the factors that
bring about the flash of illumination, that is, of conceptualizing.

One final word on the descriptive aspects of the conceptual materials of mind. In spite of voluminous data accumulated in fifty years
of experimental and many more of speculative study, the nature of
perception and its unconscious products is far from clear. There are
hundreds of pertinent laboratory investigations and a dozen plausible and well-documented theories.[18] Nevertheless, we still have
large blind spots. One problem is that of distinguishing perception
from sensation on the one hand and from conception on the other.
Another is to show the relation of these to the creative materials of
imagery. A third is to relate them to signal, sign, and symbol. If,
for example, we distribute these materials along a scale, sensory

stimulus and sensation stand at one end, imagined conception at the other. Between them are arranged various stages of symbolic transformation, depending on the extensiveness with which interpretation is involved. Electrochemical signaling is the nonconscious connection between external stimulus and percept. It is equivalent to, or immediately gives rise to, sensation. Sensation becomes percept, which is, in the first instance, a snapshot imprint of a fusion of elements from the external and the intraorganic worlds. Percepts are traced on the nervous system, appear as various forms of imagery and motor adjustments, some of which are recovered as remembered images or ideas. These heterogeneous imprints, stored in the unconscious, are transformed into meanings as the organism generalizes from past experience and organizes new integrations. The image, I suggest, is the liaison between conscious percept and preconsciously projected concept. Perception, in its transformations, forms the bulk of the conscious, reality-oriented mind.

This four-fold flux of percept, motor adjustments, images, and concepts is the stuff of the creative mind. These are not separated and inert bits. They are a glowing, rippling flow of electrical and chemical movement and motor imagery. One fact we can count upon: In meeting each new situation, the body-mind organism is neither inert nor quiescent; it does not have to be "started" to produce a new flash of meaning. On the contrary, it is in continuous wave motion, ever ready to have its electrochemistry and its motor tendencies tuned in and thereby to produce the flash of meaning.

These, then, are the ingredients of the threshold mind. In that powerful alembic they are transformed and purified and emerge as the great conceptions of man's arts and sciences, of his way of life. So the scientist assembles his materials from every conceptual frontier. And the poet knows, as Coleridge said, that "all other men's worlds are the poet's chaos."[19] These are the ingredients of the creative mind. But what gives form to the flash?

5

Outer Scene and Inner Need: The Censors

Tʜᴇ primordial stuff of mind is perceptual, registered continuously in the nervous system. Each act of perception is a conscious, integrated, bi-polar response to stimuli from the outer scene and the inner tension system. Each response is formed by what the total, two-fold situation demands. This is the true field of integration of outer and inner stimuli. Hence positive creativeness and negative censorship exist potentially in the perceptual foundation of every act of thought and overt response.

MAN IN TWO WORLDS

Man must live in two worlds—the external physical world of other men and events and his inner psycho-physiological world of sensations, images, and ideas, moods and fantasies, wishes and needs. From birth to death the primary raw material of his inner life is the dynamic deposit in his nervous system of his percepts of that outer world. Barred off from it by the enclosing somatic covering, like the dazed prisoner in Plato's Cave, his only known access to the world outside is a dozen sensory channels: sight, hearing, touch, taste, smell, pressure, equilibrium, position or spatial orientation, temporal orientation, temperature, pain, and rhythm. Through

78

these channels, sensory percepts of astonishing richness and variety are "imprinted" on his nervous system. Through these visual, auditory, kinesthetic-motor, and other perceptions, he feels, sees, and hears his world. The feeling is done focally through proprioceptive, kinesthetic motor adjustment. By all who see and hear it is done primarily through the visual and auditory senses. It is difficult to know which is more important, the seeing and hearing or the feeling of the world.

Nothing is more important than the generalization that man must live in two worlds. Every act of man is anchored in the integration of stimuli from the outer scene with the inner stresses of the body. As Kubie phrased it: "Every symbol must have roots simultaneously in the internal perceptual experiences of the body and in the external perceptual experiences of the outer world."[1] Ross Mooney, generalizing the essential conditions for the living of man, says that he must be able to operate with respect to a reaching-out and a receiving-in process. The two together constitute, out-and-in-and-out-and-in-again-and-again, man's ordering of his universe, "his continual coming-to-be through give-and-take . . . indicating man's continual fitting of specific in-comings and out-goings."

The act of response, therefore, consists in a bi-polar action of outer situation and inner stress system. The integration is not merely psychological, it is bio-social-psychological, and the integration includes cultural factors as well. This was forecast a century ago by Claude Bernard's discovery that all experience is lived in two environments—the outer, external world of things, living creatures and human beings, and the inner organismic environment. Cannon's researches confirmed Bernard's pioneering. Each act of response is marked by interaction between the outer culturally shaped stimulations of the external environment and the inner, body-mind drives of the organism. It is basic to my theory of imagination that all the contents of the mind—perception, imagery, memory, thinking, feeling, and imagination—are powered by a fusion of outer-inner drives: stimuli from the "real-world" culture of moving people and things, integrated with stimuli from the inner flux of remembered imagery, motor tendencies, and unconsciously produced metaphor-images, symbols, and concepts.

This reaching-out and receiving-in process is the basis of percept-formation, and percepts constitute the primordial material of the flash of insight. In the unconsciously worked-over form of fantasy, imagery, and concept, they comprise, if we include the dominating motor adjustments of the body, the basic materials of the autistic mind. It is in this inclusive sense that perceptual experience is the basically imprinted stuff out of which the act of knowing and of creative imagination forms itself. This is not to say that the flashes of meaning from the unconscious are mere duplicates of the originally stored percepts. Some of the more graphically and traumatically imprinted ones may, as Penfield has shown, be traced and preserved fairly intact over many years. But most of them constitute the kaleidoscope of fantastic imagery of which we become aware in our hypnoidal experiences, a few as background imagery in fully conscious states.

The accepted psychological definition of perception is "awareness ensuing directly from sensory processes," the awareness emerging either from external or from intraorganic stimulus. It is a many-sided, complex process arising from the concurrent action of all or many of the dozen known senses impinging on the unconscious storage. For example, what seems to be the painter's simple visual perception of the objects of his scene has actually been colored by his spatial and temporal orientation to them, his unconscious, kinesthetic responses to the pressures of the air and sky, or the floor, ceiling, and walls of his studio, and to the many-sided play of forces in imbalance and balance. All these perceptions and more are added to the commonplace phenomena of sound, touch, smell, pain, and temperature continually bearing in upon him. Still other factors mold each new bit of perception as it is integrated into an organism with a complex history. The single perceptive response condenses all that the perceiver's intraorganic needs demand and what he knows of an object or a scene as well. And what he knows is, in turn, the product of what he has learned from the culture in which he grew up.

Thus, the perceptual field is the union of the radiating forces of all the sensory channels through which the perceiver can reach to the outside world, and all the unconsciously stored experiences that bear upon it. Whether it should be extended to include "extra-sensory" perception is very much a matter of controversy.

The perceptions experienced in our daily lives fit no single pattern. They vary from simple sensation to subtle, personal interpretations. The simplest are the sensational aspects illustrated by the sights we see, the tones we hear, the odors, tastes, pains, pressures, feelings of warmth and cold in everyday experience. Also fairly simple and direct are specific meanings, perceptions that give "concrete-object" character to the thing or event perceived. This is the simplest form of the flash; we call it "meaning."

Somewhat more complex are the form aspects of perception. These are phenomena in which our perceptions are centered primarily on such properties as contour, outline, shape, bulk, height, and so forth. In all these the well-known figure-ground phenomenon is present. Here the emphasis is upon wholes, patterns, configuration, Gestalts; the key is interrelationship—both between parts and parts, and between parts and wholes. Paralleling these are the percepts that are characterized by a dimensional frame of reference. These are revealed in all experiences where interpretation is involved, with or without a quantitative standard, such as appraisals of such qualities as brightness, loudness, lightness. Moreover, in some acts of perception the interpretation is thoroughly personal and individualistic, depending as it does on the prevailing mental-motor set or attitude.

Finally, on the scale of complexity, there is the phenomenon known as "perceptual constancy": seeing a square as a square, irrespective of position or size, nearness or remoteness; perceiving a melody as a particular melody, irrespective of key. If, indeed, we can explain the "constancy problem," we shall be well on the way toward solving the unsolved problem of meaning and resolving the body-mind controversy.

THE CULTURE-MOLDING OF PERCEPTION

We look, then, for the factors involved in percept-formation in both of the perceiver's worlds—in his inner system of stress and in the external culture. Each individual sees and feels the world in his own way, because each has built a unique body of traces in his organism by having lived his life and interpreted objective events in his own individualistic way throughout infancy, childhood and youth. This amounts to saying that percepts which are traced in the unconscious electrochemistry of the cerebral cortex have been molded by the individual's response to the culture in which he grew up, by that cumulative temperamental and physical development of body and mind which we call life style, and by the dominant wants, purposes, needs which his individual life history has evolved. *Thus perception is much more than imprinting. It is a creative process in itself. The perceiver creates the field from which his percepts, signs, and symbols emerge.*

I begin with the evidence on the role of the outer scene—the way in which the culture molds our perceptions. The evidence is to be found in a voluminously documented literature of social, anthropological studies of primitive life and of the contemporary community.

An Example of the Culture-Molding Process

I shall use one example to show the deep and pervasive influence on our perceptions of membership in particular national cultures— the American and the Egyptian. The account which I wrote during a year's residence in Egypt (1951–1952) as Fulbright Lecturer in Education, asks you to imagine that identical twins are separated at birth and through childhood and youth.[2] One grows up in the United States, the other in Egypt. What have they become at, let us say, thirty years of age?

The American twin has become a vigorous young farmer, living with his equally educated wife (both completed secondary school) and three children in his six-room frame house, which is painted, heated, screened, electrically lighted, and has pure water electrically pumped and piped into his house from his artesian well. Neat barns and sheds house his animals and implements. He plows, cultivates his land, and harvests his crops with a small tractor and other modern machines. He takes his produce to market in his motor truck; he drives his car to town for shopping, visiting, attending church on Sundays, and lodge meetings and movies once or twice a week. With his farm and county newspapers, radio and television, he is in touch with news, not only from his own county, but from the entire earth.

He is an individualist in most matters, although he fulfills his obligations to the community and the country. He pays a school tax and a property tax without question, contributes to his church and lodge and the farmers' cooperative, votes regularly, either Republican or Democratic, and with some understanding, prejudiced though it may be. He attends public meetings in the village community and argues with his neighbors about changes proposed in the local school and other community problems. Although deep down he knows that he and they differ from one another, he believes in a kind of equality of personality. While he teaches his children to fight for a better life through competition, he also constantly reminds them, "You must cooperate with your neighbors and work for your community."

His twin brother, born of the same mother and father, but brought up from infancy in an Egyptian village, has become at thirty years of age a typical fellah. He laboriously cultivates his acre of Nile-watered soil—either as a paid laborer getting three or four piastres (10–12) cents a day, or as an "owner" of a few feddans of land, heavily in debt, with an income of perhaps thirty-five or forty dollars a year. He works with much the same tools and animals as were used by his ancient ancestors: the plow, the shaduf, the saquia, the winnowing-fork, the sickle, and the straw basket. He tattoos his body, circumcises his son, plucks his hair, and colors his skin with kohl and henna, and indulges in many of the old marriage and funeral customs.

Unlike his American twin, although he, too, is self-centered, he has never known what a real "community" is. He was born into a "crowd" and has lived in one all his life; he is gregarious in birth, in love, in daily work, in family and village life. In his two-room, earthen house, dark, unventilated, lacking even primitive sanitation, he crowds with his wife and three children (he was married at seventeen, already has had seven children though only three are living), a grandfather, and two grandmothers, two other relatives, and all their animals (for protection against thieves at night). There, in a crowd, these people are born, become sick, convalesce, cook, eat, sleep, carry on much of their lives, and die. The fellah has no privacy either in his home, village, or fields; people touch him at every point.

Neither physical nor human climate stimulates him. The chronic diseases of his people—bilharziasis, tetanus, malaria, or tuberculosis—have sapped the energy and vigorous mentality of his youthful days. He is almost totally unaware of the world beyond his village. Even though his father was compelled by the law to send him to school, he actually had no more than a total of two years of crude reading and writing and memorizing of the Koran and long ago lost these little beginnings of literacy. The Omda (mayor) of the village has a radio, but the fellah seldom is interested in listening to it and has little that comes over it paraphrased for him. At rare intervals, he is asked to vote. This he does by making a mark on a ballot that the Omda has prepared for him; but he has little awareness of what men, parties, or measures he has approved.

Three Levels of Cultural Influence

Social anthropologists tell us that, while these twins will at thirty have in common many physical characteristics, they will be fundamentally different personalities in mental, social, and spiritual qualities, ways of living, worshiping, marrying, and bringing up their children, burying their dead, in speech and ideas, basic beliefs and loyalties. One will be thoroughly "Egyptian," the other "American." This illustrates what is meant by group-membership and by the culture-molding process.

The basic theory is set by the product of the past fifty years of anthropological studies of the respective roles of the biological individual and the culture in personal development. As a consequence I shall use the concept, "the culture," in terms of current anthropological consensus, to include the total life of a people—what they do, make, contrive; what they think, believe, fear, desire.

First, on the surface, there is the material culture—the ways and means by which a people produces and distributes its physical goods, buys and sells, communicates, and the like—in general, its total economic system.

Second, the social institutions of the people operate beneath the obvious physical culture. These appear as the family life, government, industry and business, social organizations, the press, radio, and other agencies of communication, the ritual of churches, lodges, schools and colleges, the work of forums and other parliamentary and elective procedures, the ritual of courtesy in social life, codified food habits, ways of dress, speech, recreation, and the like. The social institutions include also the language of the people, their way of measuring, recording, and expressing facts, their use of science and art—all of these used as instruments of thinking and feeling.

Third, there is the all-encompassing psychological climate, of much importance in percept-formation. The subtle and hidden "psychology" of a people is even more directing and formulating than their external material culture, and their social institutions. Social patterns are created primarily by drives, attitudes, ideas, feelings, against a background of beliefs and values. What the people have in their heads, what they want most and fear most, determine above all else what they do and what they become. Their desires—for personal security, for a better living, for social approval—dominate their social psychology. But the social psychology of a people also includes the all-pervasive "climate of opinion" of the wider society, molded by such directive concepts and attitudes as freedom, equality of opportunity, justice, patriotism, and so forth. This is what Bateson and the anthropologists, Murphy and the social psychologists, call the "ethos" or "feeling tone" of the culture.

Within this framework, the individual creates his perceptions, whether in primitive tribes or in urban and rural communities of twentieth-century America. The key to the connection between the individual's behavior and the mass behavior of social institutions is what, since Ruth Benedict's work, we have called the psychological "culture-pattern." As she put it: "A culture . . . is a more or less consistent pattern of thought and action." And Herskovitz said that the culture-pattern is "the most important concept . . . from the institutional point of view. . . . It is the multiplicity of patterns which together make up the culture as a whole; it is the particular patterns that impinge on the life of an individual member of society that will shape his behavior."[3]

An Interdependent System of Mores and Role-Taking

Two additional anthropological concepts help to make clear the extent to which percept-formation is molded by the culture. The first is the "mores," now generally defined as the specially sanctioned customs or rules of a living society. Following the pioneering of Sumner and Keller and the more contemporary findings and interpretations of Benedict, Bateson, and Mead, the culture is visualized as a vast interdependent system of mores, or rules of conduct which are suffused with feelings of rightness. Children grow up surrounded by the enfolding climate of opinion—feeling, even hearing constantly that "this is the way things are done, this is the way you are to do them."

Every act of perception, therefore, is shaped in part by four types of activities: (1) the self-maintenance mores which are primarily economic, keeping the society alive, providing for its sustenance; (2) the self-perpetuation mores—marriage, family life, sex relations in general; (3) the self-gratification mores, the activities of expression and appreciation, the leisure aspects of life conceived in broadest scope; and (4) the self-regulation mores, embracing the regulative, controlling, protective activities of the society. The self-maintenance mores, basically the economic institutions and the getting-a-living activities, appear to play a major role. This was illustrated in the example given of the Egyptian and American twins, and is confirmed by the dominant role of economic institutions in the current accelerating industrialization and transformation of the world.

The second concept contributed by the social-psychological anthropologists to the perception-molding process is "role-taking." This was built up in a generation of bio-social-psychological research, partly to correct the extreme interpretations given to the idea that the act of response was completely in the formative grip of the culture. As Murphy phrased it, we think now of acts of response "as enactments of specific *roles* assigned the individual by virtue of age, sex, race, occupational status, religion, or any other category which society emphasizes."[4] His interest was in the manner in which role-playing molds personality; mine is in its influence on percept-formation, but the implications are much the same in both cases.

The evidence has piled up from both the studies of primitive life and those of twentieth-century American community life. Witness the work of Mead and Bateson on the primitives of New Guinea, Mead's on the Manus, and Bateson's on the Iatmul.[5] The Manus are a head-hunting people whose entire lives seem to be devoted to waging war and in which the lives of men and women are determined by the social roles played by each sex. Similar evidence distinguishing the role of male from that of female has accumulated in many other such studies; for example, Bateson's work on the Marquesans and also on the Zuni.

Common sense evidence abounds from a study of the effect of American culture upon growing boys and girls. An obvious example is the tendency of village and small-town children to follow the occupational patterns of their elders, or to respond to the regional or national feeling-tone of what is the profitable thing to do. In 1900 in my own youth it was the "romance of engineering"—building dams and digging the tunnels of the world—that drew youth into the institutes of technology. Today with satellites and sputniks in space, it is the study of science that largely determines college registration. It is not primarily the arts of life, certainly not teaching, that is now the attractive social-occupational role.

PERCEPTION AND INTRAORGANIC NEED

Integrated with the impact of the external world upon perception is the pressure of intraorganic needs. A person sees in part what he wants to see or needs to see in any situation; this holds true in respect to the other senses as well. What he sees and feels is the product of the life style and temperamental outlook developed by his unique life history. Sinclair Lewis, in one of his early novels, describes the diametrically opposed outlooks of twin brothers, reared in the same culture. One was unhappy, insecure, a pessimist who saw nothing good in life; the other was a confident, buoyant chronic optimist who could perceive nothing bad.

Maslow and Mittelmann, in their *Principles of Abnormal Psychology,* published two similarly opposed autobiographical comments from college students. According to one, "Life is a hard thing." He maintained he did not "trust anybody in the world, not even my mother. After all, people are all selfish deep down and are out only to get, not to give." Even your best friends, he said, "will take advantage of you . . . envy you . . . step on you and make fun of you." He never felt "relaxed and happy with other people" because he was "always suspicious of their motives." To the other student life was good, cooperative, comfortable. He liked people, he said, "therefore they like me. . . . I've always assumed that a person was nice until he had proved himself to be otherwise." He reported that one of his friends once told him that he had "such a nice view of the world because I bring out the best side of everybody I know." Some of the same people that he liked behaved very differently to other people because, he said, "they realize that I have no desire to threaten them or to hurt them, that I really like them."[6]

Similarly, perception may be a very different affair in two different periods of the same person's life. Cole documents from *The Letters of William James* how differently James's theory of emotional consciousness would have been interpreted from that given in *Principles of Psychology,* written in his optimistic years, had it been written in his youthful years of deep depression and black pessimism. James describes how, in the earlier years, he "awoke morning after morning with a horrible dread at the pit of my stomach, and with a sense of the insecurity of life that I never knew before." Some years later, however, he was a changed man, convinced that he was master of his own destiny; "this characteristic attitude in me," he said, "always involves an element of active tension, of holding my own, as it were, and trusting outward things to perform their part so as to make it a full harmony, but without any *guaranty* that they will."[7]

From primitive biochemical levels throughout foetal life, childhood, youth and adulthood, the organism is a selector and organizer. The very social pressures that mold the outlook and meanings of the perceiver have to be reconciled with his unique personal need-systems. In every phase of life, the fact of self-selection of diet is established, whether it be a diet of physical food or ideas, thought, and philosophy. We pick our scientific theories, our plays, poetry, and novels, our philosophy, religion and church at least partly in the light of our personal orientations, points of view, our often unphrased theories of life.

We not only live in two environments—the "reality" world of the external environment and the "autistic" world of the inner environment—but our perceptions are inevitably distorted by the molding demands of both.

A study of the need-tension system as the key to creative energy shows that the basis of drive dynamics is a fusion of physiological and psychic tensions. These brain-mind tensions operate as a coordinated system of regional tensions: visceral system, action system of overt and inner movements, brain dynamics, and endothalamic and autonomic systems. The living body may be interpreted as an interrelated system of need-tensions of body and mind, that is, bio-psychological. With our new addition of the role of the culture, they become bio-cultural-psychological. Thus the act of response is "need for acting," but in social terms and as the situation of the moment demands. Thus, our need-system makes over the reality situation, and its crucial characteristics remade are signalled to our brain by our nervous system. Signals are transformed into signs and symbols in the subcortical, or 'tween-brain, and the cerebral cortex as our needs prescribe. Needs and wants "bend the framework" within which we interpret what we see, hear, feel, and remember. Thus there is an ever-recurring tension between new perceptual experience of the real world and the stored experience of the autistic world.

THE CENSORS IN CULTURE AND SELF

The way has now been cleared for a critical sub-theorem about the operation of the transliminal mind. Much of the registered stuff of mind is censored. The culture-molding process censors the basic perceptual record. The Self, constantly on guard, censors what comes in and what goes out.

The idea of the censors is indispensable to understanding one major thesis of my study: *The transliminal mind is the creative center of the continuum because it alone is uniquely free to create.* Neither of the extremes of the continuum—the conscious or the nonconscious—is free; both are marked by warping, inhibiting forces. Censorship is therefore a far-reaching concept, operating at both poles of the outer-inner process; it affects perception as well as imagined conception.

The Censoring Culture

Most Americans grow up in a community which is a hierarchy

of face-to-face interest groups, and in which they are bombarded by partisan ideas, slogans and pressures of national sounding-boards—of press, radio and TV, movies, church, rostrum, education, the vast machinery of publicity. Vigorous, self-conscious pressure groups (chambers of commerce, labor unions, political parties, "good government leagues," church groups, health and educational groups), organized for offense and defense, strive to mold the individual's beliefs and allegiances. It is through constant interaction with these agencies that the process of being inducted into the culture takes place.

Growing up is an unceasing, interactive, culture-molding process. Assailed at once by too many things, labels, pressures, the child picks out a few cue meanings and responds to these. This is "perceiving." The social world is always whispering the Ten Commandments and the Moral Law in his ear, constantly admonishing him to compete hard with his neighbor, but to "serve" him too, directing him to conspicuous aspects of desirable character, pointing out the commendable features of situations and personalities and the acceptable characteristics of institutions. Thus, he learns by a multitude of experiences how he can get along with, or in some degree control, his social world. Back and forth the process goes—action and reaction, egocentric individual adapting to and defending himself against the culture and thereby contributing his bit to its remaking. So the modern man comes to know his fellows, and is known by them, by the characteristics that are associated in the public mind with the groups with which he works and plays, worships and votes, philosophizes and moralizes. Expressed in general terms, we are known, not for the infinitely complex beings that we are, but by the labels that are popularly put on the company we keep.

Psychologists since Walter Lippmann[8] have had a name for this cultural coloring of percept-formation—the stereotype. "We tend to perceive," he said, "that which we have picked out in the form stereotyped for us by the culture." Each of us lives in the psychological world of his own stereotypes. He creates it by his responses, the cues which he has learned from the culture-individual interactive process. But this is a personally created, perceptual world and, in part at least, a pseudo-world.

The law of the stereotype applies to the world of people as well as things. If the purposes and actions of other people bear on ours, we pay attention to those which past experience and present association have taught us will be important to us. Many investigations in the social sciences have shown that our reactions to other people are determined by the special significance which, in developing our habits of attention and awareness, we have attached to their assumed characteristics.

Thus growth is largely governed by learning to adjust to outside censors that deflect our perceptions the moment they invade dangerous territory. We learn that there are some things one just does not do, some things one does not say; there are dangerous thoughts to fight shy of: "This is thin ice, watch your step!" Thus the child grows up ensheathed in the matrix of the "national" way of life, assailed by the diverse patterns of culture of the competing groups of the society.

Following Lippmann, we have learned to say that there are barriers between the public and the event. There are economic, property barriers due to the monopoly of the facts by those who own the agencies of national communication: the great chains of the press, radio, TV, movies, advertising. He who controls the agencies of communication drastically influences the public mind, both by withholding the facts (which is censorship) and by distorting the facts (which is propaganda). Partly as a consequence of the economic barriers, there are political barriers. Young people grow up today in a culture divided against itself by a dozen dichotomies —center-to-right against center-to-left. Even if much of the current propaganda and censorship could be eliminated and there were established a free flow of facts and ideas to the people, there would still be psychological barriers. The scope and intricacy of the meanings that confront the person who tries to understand our current civilization stagger even the well-informed student. The buzzing, booming confusion must be simplified and reduced to some degree of meaningful order if the current conditions and problems are to be grasped, even by the intelligent minority of the population. This is little more than a hint of the generalization that most human events are episodes in censorship.

The Censoring Self

What is the product of the impact of this culture-molding process on the individual in our highly competitive, individualistic society? Is it a normal, healthy, creative self? The kind Walt Whitman sang about in "One's Self I Sing"?

> One's Self I sing, a simple separate person,
> Yet utter the word Democratic, the word En-Masse.[9]

A man for Whitman was a unique personality to be loved and lived with for himself, every part worthy of respect and admiration—but it was the total self that was the important thing. Nothing is greater to one than one's Self, he said. Is this total self-acceptance the normal product of growing up in human society today? Yes, for a few—ideally for all. But the ideal is achieved only in a tiny minority.

And for most of us? The normal, healthy, unified self appears as a greatly divided self-system—a house divided against itself. To understand the conception of the "censoring self," we need a norm with which to conceive of the healthy self.

The Normal, Healthy Self

I assume with Maslow, Cole, and other students of behavior, that pervading each human being there is an intrinsic and unchanging inner nature. This I shall call "the self." The self is the very focus of being, the unifying, motivating, directing, and inhibiting agent which pulls together the ingredients of the act of response. The self is good, not evil. At the least it is neutral. Although it is ineffable, in the sense that it must be experienced to be known, yet it can be studied and its nature discovered. Thanks to Maslow's recent studies [10] from which I quote extensively, we have some objective foundation for a new conception of psychological health. As he says, the healthy self is "delicate and subtle and easily overcome by habit, cultural pressure and wrong attitudes toward it," but it never really disappears in the normal person.

I have used Maslow's statements of the outstanding characteristics of healthy, "self-actualizing" people as a tentative norm in my study of censorship and the self. They perceive the real world frankly, have "an unusual ability to detect the spurious, the fake, and the dishonest in personality." They accept themselves and others and show a marked "lack of defensiveness, cant, guile . . . playing a game, trying to impress in conventional ways."

They are spontaneous in behavior, and are in general strongly focused on problems outside themselves, "as contrasted with the ordinary introspectiveness that one finds in insecure people." They "customarily have some mission in life, some task to fulfill . . . which enlists much of their energies." There is a quality of detachment about them, a need for privacy. They depend largely for their continued growth upon their own potentialities and resources, not on other people or extrinsic satisfactions.

They have a "wonderful capacity to appreciate . . . freshly and naïvely, the basic goods of life—with awe, pleasure, wonder, and even ecstasy." The mystic experience is fairly common among them, if this is divorced from any theological or supernatural meaning. It can be located on a quantitative continuum from strong to mild: "the mild mystic experience occurs in many, perhaps even most, individuals, and . . . in the favored individual it occurs dozens of times a day." They have a deep feeling of identification and sympathy for human beings, *Gemeinschaftsgefühl*, Alfred Adler called it, to describe "the 'flavor' of the feelings for mankind" expressed by such persons. Self-actualizing people have "deeper and more profound interpersonal relations" than most adults, are capable of "more fusion, greater love, more perfect identification . . . than other people would consider possible." Yet their circle of close friends is small, partly "for the reason that being very close to someone in this self-actualizing style seems to require a good deal of time. Devotion is not a matter of a moment." They are democratic in the deepest possible sense; they learn from anybody who has something to teach them, yet there is in them a discriminative, "hard-to-get-at tendency," an unwillingness to give respect to *any* human being just because he is a human individual.

Their sense of humor is also out of the ordinary. It is not hostile (making people laugh by hurting someone). It consists, on the contrary, "in poking fun at human beings in general when they are foolish, or forget their place in the universe, or try to be big when they are actually small." And this can take the form of poking fun at themselves.

They are rarely unsure about the difference between right and wrong, avoiding most of the confusion, inconsistency, and conflict so common in most people. They are strongly ethical, do right and do not do wrong. "Needless to say, their notions of right and wrong are often not the conventional ones."

Finally, mature persons, Maslow's self-actualizing people, are creative. Everyone has "a special kind of creativeness or original-ity," rather like that of unspoiled children. The creativeness of healthy personality seems to affect everything the person does.

This is not to paint a picture of perfection for these normal, healthy personalities. They are human and have the failings of hu-manity. They make foolish mistakes and have "silly, wasteful, or thoughtless habits. They can be boring, stubborn, irritating. They are by no means free from a rather superficial vanity, pride, parti-ality to their own production, family, friends, and children." In intense concentration they "become absent-minded or humorless, and forget their ordinary social politeness." They are even capable of an extraordinary ruthlessness.

Summing it all up, Maslow concludes that the ability of the healthy personality to accept "the nature of his self, of human nature, of much of social life, and of nature and physical reality" accounts for most of his value-judgments—what he approves of, disapproves of, is loyal to, opposes or proposes, what pleases him or displeases him. In fact, the typical human value dichotomies tend to disappear or are resolved. Fundamentally "self-actualization is actualization of a self, and no two selves are altogether alike. There is only one Renoir, one Brahms, one Spinoza." Maslow thinks his subjects "are more completely 'individual' than any group that has ever been described and yet are also more completely socialized, more identified with humanity than any other group yet described."

This, then, is the norm, set by the few who rise above the pressures of society and the culture. But for most of us the never-ending conflict between I and They builds feelings of inferiority and self-defense.

EDITOR'S NOTE. This chapter is basically incomplete. Its place within the design of the book, as the author conceived it, is nevertheless clear. There is, he seems to be saying with Maslow, an inherent potential and drive in all selves to trust, mature, and actualize their auto-symbolizing, creative process. Censorship, from within and from without, undercuts the self-trust, thwarts the actualization, smothers the creativity.

In the transliminal mind there is freedom from censorship and hence freedom to create. If men and women can learn to recognize and use the power and products of this transliminal mind, they can and will become creative and self-actualizing, whole rather than divided, selves. This hope led to the author's tremendous drive to understand and il-luminate the character and operation of this transliminal mind. In knowing it and learning to discipline its power lies, as he saw it, man's best hope to restore wholeness, spontaneity, creativity and progress to a world of men and cultures which has lost confident and balanced command of its truly human powers and resources.

6

Form in Body-mind Functioning

Up to this point, some headway has been made in identifying the central questions that must be answered in reaching any adequate understanding of the creative act in man. One part of the task has been critical in character—to clear away misconceptions that impede contemporary men in asking the central questions meaningfully.

It has been necessary to distinguish clearly between logical verification and creative discovery. The tradition among academic students of thought has been marked by preoccupation with processes of logical verification. Attention has been diverted from processes of discovery in which concepts are imagined and formed out of the tensions between present stimulation and the storage of past experiences in the organism. Yet it is in processes of discovery that the creative dimension of thought is to be found if at all. Thus discovery has been established as the special concern of this book.

Another crippling disjunction is the traditional separation of "body" and "mind" in the study of meaningful human response. This disjunction has tended to keep apart, in the study, knowledges about man which must be seen together if adequate understanding of human behavior, in both its inner and outer aspects, is to be attained. In my treatment, some of these knowledges have been brought together and seen together—knowledge from the arts and from the sciences, from physiology and psychology, from the study

96

of cultures and the study of personalities. The possibility of under-cutting the dichotomy between "body" and "mind" seems prom-ising. But much more needs to be done along the same line.

Another part of the task is constructive in character—to articu-late new ways of looking at human behavior, particularly in its creative aspects. And this part of the task has been advanced along with the critical part. The vital characteristics of the creative act have been described and its typical phases delineated. The notion of a conscious-nonconscious continuum in which life is lived has been broached and evidence marshaled to defend the notion. The "locus" of creative imagination has been identified as an intuitive creative state at the threshold of the nonconscious mind—the trans-liminal state, as I have called it. The materials to be formed novelly in imagination have been reviewed and these have been found to be both "physiological" and "psychological" in character. The relative freedom of transliminal mind from external and internal censorship has been established.

This background permits the articulation of the central questions in more intelligible forms. What is the nature of the process through which the flash of insight occurs? How are electrochemical signal-ings from without and from within the organism formed into mean-ingful response? How are signals transformed into signs and symbols? How do imagined conceptions take form in the translimi-nal mind, when we let it work without imposing the willful tyranny of external or internal demand upon it? All of these questions imply some autonomous forming process at the threshold of conscious-ness. It is to a delineation of this process that we now turn.

THE CREATIVE FLASH AS BODY-MIND ACT

My theory postulates that every creative human response is the act of a whole person. Such a person is one who has so developed from inherited beginnings that factors of growth have been inextricably interrelated. Each act is a two-phased integration of body and mind, these tending always to act as a unit. Nerves do not think, the whole man thinks; the brain does not create, the whole man creates. Fifty years of research in the human sciences have laid the foundation for this theory. It is supported today by the physicists' concept of the field as an organization of forces in tension, the biologists' concept of integration, the Cannon concept of homeostasis, the Gestaltists' concepts of configuration and closure, the personality psychologists' concept of organization, and the expressive artists' basic concept of form.

In this organic framework of the person in action we ask: What are the respective roles of "body" and "mind" in the act of response? Nothing is more basic than the role of the body. We not only move with it, we think with it, feel with it, imagine with it. The history of psychology was marked for a long time by a tendency to forget this. Psychologists spoke as though psychic behavior were all mind and no body. But in recent years that tendency has been corrected. Following the consensus initiated by John B. Watson, we say today: "We think with the whole body." When an individual reacts to an object or a situation, "his whole body reacts . . . manual organization, language organization . . . and visceral organization all function together."

Twenty years after Watson's early work, George Hartmann confirmed this point of view. "The body breathes, runs, and digests, but it also loves, dreams and writes history." He was clear about the unitary character of body and mind, saying: "What is called 'mental life' is just that aspect of life which appears distinctively in our more subtle adaptations as memorizing, painting, debating, etc. Essentially, however, it is the living body . . . and not anything separate and distinct from it which solves algebraic equations, composes sonnets, and predicts eclipses."[1]

The layman understands all this. By his frequent assertion, "I know in my bones," he means that he knows in his muscles, his frame, nerve tissues, his entire organism—he knows "all over." To teachers interested in the child as a person, it makes more sense to say: "He perceives with his body, even with his skeletal muscles," than to say: "He perceives with his mind." There is, in fact, nothing we can do except through the whole body, whether we walk or dance, express ourselves through an art form, understand what another human being is doing or saying, know the meaning of any object, sense its shape, texture or dimension or appreciate the expression of another person.

And yet we know that no single act of human response is of the body alone. Into each act enters something called "mind," something called "purpose" and something called "will." As E. D. Adrian of Cambridge says: "We cannot keep the mind out of it for long," no matter what kind of a human situation we examine. To illustrate this he gives the example of what happens, physically and mentally, on being lost on a clear night, and finding one's way home by studying that familiar pattern of the stars known as the Plow or Dipper.

Adrian contrasts the homing behavior of a man with that of an automatically piloted airplane, saying that the plane "would not, of course, contain more than a trivial fraction of the innumerable mechanisms which our brains would need to make us behave as we do, and it would not adapt itself to new problems as we can." Then he explains carefully that "it is the addition of the mental events which makes the fundamental difference and seems to rule out anything like a purely physical description of all that happens."[2] The contrasts between the homing airplane and the man trying to find his way home are clear. The man is conscious and the plane is not; the man is an organism, the plane is a mechanism; the man can adapt himself to novel situations, the plane cannot unless a code has been built into its mechanism which anticipates the very changes which are necessary. This points to the essential difference between mechanism and organism; namely, the creative powers of the human organism, the imagination which can invent needed responses to unexpected and novel situations.

The Body Beginnings of the Flash of Insight

Perhaps the most convincing evidence that physical movement plays a determining role in the flash of meaning is found in genetic studies. We can now draw upon thirty years of investigation of human growth from a score of child development institutes in Europe and the United States. The outstanding achievements are those of Jean Piaget of Geneva and Arnold Gesell of Yale.[3]

Consider the newly born child's responses to the stimuli of the outside world. They are purely physical movements, demonstrating only what Piaget calls "sensori-motor intelligence." The infant is a squirming, reaching, kicking body in constant movement. Observation of his first perceptual reactions centers attention on these nebulous movements; his attempts to fixate his eyes, to get his fingers around objects, to orient himself in space. Behavior consists of postural adjustments, physical attempts to follow moving objects, kinesthetic adjustments to objects. As Cole says, "There is always an *inter-reflex* readjustment when a steady-state of posture is upset." But even with the newly born child the act is a patterned response. "When he turns his head to his right side as he lies on his back his left arm comes up, crooked at the elbow. . . . Move a bright light across his field of vision and his eyes will follow. . . . The gross ordering of the responses is there at the start. . . . Even the inexperienced organism, confronted with the massive stimulation of a complex field, gives a grossly ordered pattern of reaction."[4]

These first physical movements, themselves, are the sources of the first flashes of meaning, for there is no "mind" except in the reactions of the body. These first motor responses *are* the first meanings, hence the beginnings of mind. For example, the baby acquires a meaning known later as "milk" by making manifold sequences of responses—reachings, eye movements, responses to hearing, manual fumblings, sucking movements. These visual, manual, tactual, tasting movements and reflexes, when shot together in one total reaction, constitute the meaning. Thus we respond with the meaning, we do not get it by some mysterious process. Intellect, motor habit, and emotion are only three names for phases of the act of response. Moreover, what the psychologist calls perception is also the product of a succession of acts of response. Each act builds a new increment of meaning. Each increment is traced upon the nervous system in some as yet unknown way, adding its bit to the storage of modified images, of incipient movements which become motor attitudes and are continuously formed and re-formed. These are the products of experience. Thus we say that the newly born child comes into the social world without "mind," at least with no more of mind than has been produced by nine months of intra-uterine life.

As growth and development continue, the processes called perception, thinking, and imagining all advance together as the cumulative product of manifold responses which, in varying degrees, are flashes of meaning. Following Piaget, these responses are, first, basically physical movements: By six months the child has some control over reaching and grasping; by a year to eighteen months he can walk. These movements are traced as they are made, one by one, on the motor areas of the cerebral cortex (altering thereby manifold other parts of the nervous system). These and the products of other stimuli are traced on the respective sensory association and projection areas of the cortex. In some unknown way they appear to the child in succeeding responses as visual, auditory or other images, pictures centered about incipient and overt movements, and more definitely formed motor habits.

With the advent of language in the second year, sensori-motor intelligence emerges into what can be called "ego-centric thought" because the "child conceives of things only in relation to his own actions." In this period responses are still primarily a flux of motor tendencies. Spatial coordination also advances as the egocentrism of infancy and the early years gives way to increasingly "objective" appraisal. The third stage, Piaget's "rational thought," begins for most children approximately at the seven-year level and reaches maturity during the beginnings of adolescence, with the eleventh or twelfth year.

It is from a study of the earliest development of the sensory-motor responses, that light is shed on what psychologists call the unsolved problem of meaning. Here, in body movement, is one of the keys that will unlock the doors of imagined conception.

The Flash As Body-Mind Transformation

The addition of one more set of facts about the act of response will locate exactly the point of the creative imagination's greatest mystery. These are physiological and psychological facts concerning that process by which stimuli arouse signals in the nervous system which are then transformed into signs or symbols of meaning. To bring these together will take us directly to the crux of the body-mind dichotomy in the unsolved problem of meaning.

Drawing on the world's students of the physiology of the forming process—Sherrington, Adrian, Lashley, Penfield, Gerard, Papez, Fulton, Gellhorn, Cobb, Monnier, and others, I break the act of response into three stages: (1) signal, (2) sign and/or symbol, (3) movement. They appear to occur simultaneously and to be integrated, but actually are in sequence. The first and third steps are primarily physiological, the second is both physiological and psychological. It is in the second stage, I suggest, that the intuitive flash of imagination occurs.

In the first signaling stage, a stimulus upon the sense organs is sent as a pattern of electrochemical impulses or signals via afferent nerves, mainly along the spinal cord, to the subcortical brain— sometimes referred to as the old, mid, or 'tween brain—and on to the projection or receiving areas of the cerebral cortex. In this stage, the waves of electrical impulses are mere signals, registering as a patterned series of digits in the electrically active, cerebral cortex. As Gerard says, "the nerve cell has to make only one decision—a choice between yes and no." Adrian agrees:

There is only one kind of change which can be conducted down a nerve-fibre . . . [Investigations of this problem, including the am-plification of the tiny impulses, establish without question that all these impulses are of the same] relatively simple character. The signalling between one group of nerve cells and another . . . which must play an essential part in our thought and our intelligent activity, is based on the transmission of repeated waves of activity or impulses in the nerve-fibres. . . . We can make records to show us what signals are passing from moment to moment along the fibres . . .

[And then]

impulses travelling to the brain in the fibres of the auditory nerve make us hear sounds and impulses of the same kind arranged in much the same way as the optic nerve makes us see sights. The mental result must differ because a different part of the brain receives the message and not because the message has a different form.[5]

Expressing this first phase in language of cybernetics as "input," it consists of signaling to the brain data needed for perception and understanding in coping with the external world. As a result, coded abstract patterns are electrically imprinted on the cerebral cortex. These have a definite correspondence to the patterns received by the sense organs.

In addition to this new input two other elements come into play. The first of these consists of earlier traced experiences which have been stored in the unconscious and in that tiny and now easily recoverable part of it called "memory." The second element is the never-ceasing electrochemical activity of the cerebral cortex. The three elements, taken together, constitute the "input" part of the transformation that makes up the flash of meaning.

Thus far, the account is straightforward. But we now confront the heart of the mystery. This input of signaled messages is not psychologically usable. The coded patterns that have been imprinted on the cortex, corresponding point for point to the patterns received by the sense organs, do not form an intelligible picture. It is not a portrait of either the outside or the inside world. It is still only a constellation of physical signs. As Adrian says: "When a sense organ is stimulated, impulses are sent up to the brain in appropriate numbers and frequency to form some kind of picture of events in the receiving areas of the cerebral cortex."[6] This much we know; but it has no "meaning." We cannot act upon it.

Second, physiological signals are transformed into psychological meanings. Somewhere in the organism something turns these signals, these signs, into meaning and we act. Insight flashes up, we imagine or speak or move. Thus "mind" intervenes again in the on-going body process, transforming the signals or signs into symbols. This is the key process called "symbolic transformation."

Can its physiology be described? Its psychology? Yes, to a certain extent. Since Hans Berger's discovery of the electro-encephalographic activity of the brain in 1928, many critical gaps in our knowledge have been filled in, and certain of the psychological gaps as well. Some of the confusion can now be cleared up; and where there are gaps, there are intriguing theories. In succeeding chapters I deal with the theories as well as with our reasonably certain knowledge.

The third stage is output in action. In this third stage, the sign or symbol is transmitted to the muscular system as a command, producing speech and/or other meaningful motor responses. Thus physiological signals have given way to psychological processes— perceptual recognition, memory, appraisal, inference, decision, satisfaction. And then the product, some unknown integration of these, produces more electrochemical signaling to the muscular system; this results in movement—and, with much more sign-following, as Adrian says, we "find our way home."

SOME EVIDENCE CONCERNING STORAGE AND
RETRIEVAL OF EXPERIENCE IN THE BRAIN
AND MIND

During the last twenty years many fascinating break-throughs have
occurred in the study of brain functioning. Thousands of brain-dam-
age, mind-damage studies have produced direct evidence of body-
mind unity. Such studies have been made possible by military and
civilian closed-head injuries, by electrical and psychological studies
of epilepsy, and by more than 100,000 frontal lobotomies and other
types of neuro-psychosurgery. No less than six techniques are now
available for studying the relation between "mind" and brain injury: electrical stimulation, ablation, observation of epileptic
patterns, the use of electro-encephalographic records, statistical
correlation of psychological measurements and the testimony of
conscious patients. Many questions remain unanswered. But there
has been a steady advance in theorizing as well as an impressive
massing of evidence. I can only sample this theorizing and evidence
in this study of the imagination. I trust that the sampling will indicate the richness of this field for eventual understanding of meaning
and response in human beings.

The Storage of Experiences in the Brain

The physiological search for the nervous center in which experience is registered has centered attention on the brain. The mind
is "in the head," and particularly in the roof-brain or cerebral
cortex. McCulloch reminds us of the reason for this over-simple
localization.

There and only there are hosts of possible connections to be formed
as time and circumstance demand. Each new connection serves to set
the stage for others yet to come and better fitted to adapt us to the
world, for through the cortex pass the greatest inverse feedbacks whose
function is the purposive life of the human intellect.[7]

The "hosts of possible connections" are possibilities because of the
incredibly interlaced structure and functioning of 13 billion neurons.
But this number alone cannot possibly account for the tracing and

retention of the thousand-billion-billion elements of accumulating adult experience. While some semipermanent modification of nerve cells must be postulated, there must, in addition, be vast supplementary "storage" facilities.

The brain is the great center in which vital body information is gathered and organized. "It knows" about the sugar content and balance of the body; for example, that there should be 1/60 of an ounce for each pint of blood, when to order any excess burned up, and when to order the liver to secrete more. "It knows" the regulating facts about breathing and how to maintain an average of 17 to 20 respirations a minute. It controls heart beats at 70 per minute on the average and regulates body temperature at 98.6 degrees Fahrenheit. As a communication center it is a network of 13 billion cells serving as the organizing clearinghouse for all the organs of the body. It is an active, electrochemical enterprise, its cells firing all the time, whether we are asleep or awake. These nerve cells are self-activating storage batteries. I quote the current consensus from W. Grey Walter's summary of evidence:

Every living cell maintains an electrical potential difference between its inside and the outside world. In [nerve] cells specialised for conduction . . . activity is associated with a dramatic reduction in this potential difference and in the brain the vast congregation of nerve cells generates an enormously complex and continually varying pattern of electrical discharge. These electrical changes are so diminutive that elaborate equipment must be used to detect them from the surface of the head and even more intricate devices are necessary for exact measurement. A record of the electrical changes in the brain is called an electroencephalogram or EEG. In normal adult humans, the most prominent features of the EEG are usually rhythmic oscillations at about ten per second—these are called *alpha* rhythms. Now the size and regularity of the alpha rhythms vary greatly in different individuals and there is evidence that persons with mainly visual habits of thought exhibit smaller and less persistent alpha activity, while those who think in terms of sounds and movements rather than visual images have large, regular alpha rhythms. Furthermore, in nearly all people who show this alpha activity, the rhythms are augmented when the eyes are shut and the mind is tranquil—they are attenuated by opening the eyes or by mental effort.[8]

We know, furthermore, that the whole brain, the cerebral cortex particularly, is in ceaseless electrochemical activity.

It is now practically certain that all the cells of the cerebrospinal axis are being continually bombarded by nerve impulses from various sources and are firing regularly, probably even during sleep. . . . It is probably not far from the truth to say that every nerve cell of the cerebral cortex is involved in thousands of different reactions. The cortex must be regarded as a great network of reverberatory circuits, constantly active. A new stimulus, reaching such a system, does not excite an isolated reflex path but must produce widespread changes in the pattern of excitation throughout a whole system of already interacting neurons.[9]

Retrieval—Memory

Granted that important keys to memory "are in the head," more specifically in the cerebral cortex, just "where" is the nonconscious mind? Does the brain work as a whole in modeling the external world for us? Or do separate parts of it—cerebral cortex and its distinctive regions, for example—do specific and indispensable things? In technical language, are memory and the control of behavior "localized" in specific regions of the cortex? Or have all parts of it "modeling potential?" Since the data upon which we must rely are physiological and highly technical, a graphic case will be used to introduce the problem. I take a famous one, the case of a young Canadian girl, J. V., from Dr. Wilder Penfield's quarter-century of reports of surgical exploration of the cerebral cortex.

At the age of seven J. V. had had a frightening, traumatic experience. Her earlier medical history revealed a major illness in infancy following an anesthetic, which had been marked by convulsions, coma, and transient paralysis. During the seven years between ages seven and fourteen she had suffered epileptic seizures, frightening dreams, and hallucinations. The traumatic experience was described by Penfield in terms of the scene that she remembered to have occurred when she was seven years old.

[She] was walking through a field where the grass was high. It was a lovely day, and her brothers were walking ahead of her. A man came up behind her and said: "How would you like to get into this bag with the snakes?" She was very frightened and screamed to her brothers, and they all ran home, where she told her mother about the event. The mother remembers the fright and the story, and the brothers still recall the occasion and remember seeing the man.

After that, she occasionally had nightmares during her sleep and in the dream the scene was re-enacted. Three or four years later, at the age of 11, it was recognized that she had attacks by day in which she habitually complained that she saw the scene of her fright. There was a little girl, whom she identified with herself, in the now familiar surroundings. During the attack she was conscious of her actual environment and called those present by name; yet she also saw herself as a little girl with such distinctness that she was filled with terror lest she should be struck or smothered from behind. She seemed to be thinking with two minds.[10]

Dr. Penfield exposed the posterior half of the right hemisphere of the cerebral cortex, and with the subject under local anesthesia, probed the entire region with an electrode. Centering attention on the posterior regions of the temporal lobe and certain areas of the auditory and visual centers, he stumbled upon a new "cerebral continent." This was the area covering "most of the superior surfaces of the temporal lobes; as well as the lateral and probably the interior surfaces," and spread over both hemispheres. Repeated stimulations under carefully controlled conditions brought confirmed recall of the childhood traumatic experience, spoken responses of fright, recall of the recurring dreams of her childhood. Stimulation of the auditory centers brought such comments as: "They are yelling at me . . . everybody is yelling . . . I imagine I hear a lot of people shouting at me . . . something dreadful is going to happen."[11]

Penfield says, "This seems to be a perfect experiment, but there is more to it." The girl's condition worsened, the epileptic hallucinations continued, sometimes becoming major seizures leading to unconsciousness in a generalized convulsion. Dr. Penfield removed a large part of the right temporal cortex. "She no longer had the hallucinations," but she could remember her seven-year-old experience of the "meadow, the man, and her fright."

Why the disappearance of the hallucinations but the retention of memory of the earlier experience? Penfield concludes that "another identical neurone pattern" which, when stimulated either by "memory" or by the electrode—"was located in the other temporal cortex," although that "is purely hypothetical."

The conclusion is unavoidable that when complex hallucinations are induced by stimulation of the temporal cortex the music a patient hears and the appearance before him of his mother or friend are *like memories*. It seems evident that in some way the stimulating electrode is activating acquired patterns of neuronal connection which are involved in the mechanism of memory. The patient is conscious of, and thinks over, these hallucinations as he would a memory which he had himself summoned.[12]

Hallucinations and the Temporal Cortex

Penfield cites other cases from his surgical file in which long forgotten experiences were retrieved when certain areas of the temporal lobe were touched with the electrode. One patient reported:

It was not as though I were imagining the tune to myself. I actually heard it. It is not one of my favorite songs, so I don't know why I heard that song.

Many a patient has told me . . . that the experience brought back by the electrode is much more real than remembering. And yet he is still aware of the present situation. There is a doubling of consciousness and yet he knows which is the present. A patient may cry out in astonishment that he is hearing and seeing friends he knows are far away.

Curiously enough . . . two experiences or strips of time are never activated concurrently. Consequently there is no confusion. There seems to be an all-or-nothing organization which inhibits other records from being activated.[13]

There is now definite confirmation of Penfield's earlier hypothesis "that hallucination, dream and memory depend on the neuronal mechanism in the temporal cortex." Before the 1957 annual meeting of the National Academy of Sciences, he reported the major findings of his quarter century of work. In the new "cerebral continent," he said,

. . . there is hidden away a record of the stream of consciousness. It seems to hold the detail of that stream as laid down during each man's waking conscious hours. Contained in this record are all those things of which the individual was once aware; such detail as a man might hope to remember for a few seconds or minutes afterward, but which are largely lost to voluntary recall after that time.[14]

This is regarded by some as confirmation of James's "stream of consciousness" hypothesis. Its record, says Penfield, "might better be compared to a wire recorder or to a continuous film strip with sound track." When specific spots in the exposed temporal cortex were touched by the electrode, each patient relived long-forgotten episodes of his childhood, as did the girl, J. V. Each new stimulation always revived the same episode, as if it were again being lived in the present moment; yet "the patient knew it was something out of the past."

This is perhaps as close as man has ever come to locating the very touching point of body and mind. Penfield's conclusion is that two types of response occur under electrical stimulation of the temporal cortex. They are psychical, of the mind, as well as of the body. One type is a "flash-back of past experience," a part of feedback. "The other is a signalling of interpretation of present experience," involved vitally in symbolic transformation. Together they "would seem to form parts of one *subconscious* process, the process of comparing the present experience with past similar experience." This seems to support my hypothesis that the flash comes in the threshold state between the conscious and the unconscious.

He shows that either epileptic discharge or experimental stimulation in the temporal cortex produces illusions of perception. This carries us into the field of judgment, for an illusion is a flash perception. The alteration in behavior is not in seeing or hearing, it is in "perceiving"—that is, the interpretation of the sights and sounds. He illustrates common perceptual illusions: visual perception, things momentarily seen as larger or nearer, smaller or farther away; auditory illusion of memory—a feeling of *déjà vu*, of familiarity; an illusion of remoteness—feeling of unreality "as though" he were far away and yet perceiving the scene . . . "as though he were a secondary observer." Many mental states were brought about by temporal stimulation which can only be called a kind of scrutiny of the ego, a feeling that it is an epileptic dreamy state, "out of this world." It is not sensory; it consists of changes in one's opinion about himself and his world—an *"illusion of introspection* instead of an illusion of sensory perception."

John Pfeiffer confirms that perceptual illusions are "involved in a kind of false memory or false recognition, a strange feeling *(déjà vu)* that we have been there before." Some students ascribe them to a clairvoyance or intuition, some to "mere coincidence," similarity of stimuli to past experiences. Often "false recognition" follows soon after noticing special odors. Physiologists have recently ascribed it to the old visceral brain. This appears as an extension of the temporal lobe, receiving and sorting nerve impulses from the nose. Moreover, injury to the temporal lobes has been shown to produce these feelings of false recognition. They have been frequently reported in concussion cases, and in other cases of intense emotional strain such as that suffered by soldiers going into battle. In these "everything seems unreal." The reporters are "pepped up, joyous and light-hearted," "lifted out of themselves," like "spectators watching themselves move forward." The situation "seemed to have happened at some previous time"; *déjà vu* again.

Penfield concludes "that these induced mental states are like dreams." The reproduction is "not a picture or a single sound, but a progressive changing psychical phenomenon. If the electrode is held in place, action goes forward as in a dream and the patient may become frightened and cry out."

Penfield suggests that this may cast new light on the physiological mechanism of dreams. "We have stumbled unexpectedly," he says, "upon the location of the neuronal patterns 'which dreams are made of' and have glimpsed other mechanisms within the humming loom of the mind." We know now that the epileptic hallucinations "reproduce a remembered event more or less perfectly and one that may have been dreamed as well." Sometimes the same neuronal pattern is reproduced, at other times the pattern includes alterations and recent memories—probably formed "with each recrudescence of attacks." These recent memory patterns apparently contaminate the long-term memory pattern unless the latter has been strongly conditioned by long habit.

Then come two important conclusions. "In some cases successive stimulation at a point produced the same hallucination time after time." And with respect to a dream that had been frequently repeated during epileptic seizures—"stimulation at different points produced different portions of the hallucination with relative constancy." He emphasizes that such perceptual illusions are produced only by stimulation of the temporal region and the border area of the occipital cortex.

Thus the data strongly suggest that the temporal cortex plays a determining role in memory and in comparisons of past experience with present sensory perceptions. "Here alone electrical stimulation and epileptic discharge activate acquired synaptic patterns . . . it is only in this region that such stimulation produces complex psychical illusions and hallucinations."[15]

What Do Theories of Memory Contribute?

The theories of memory reduce to two types. The first consists of theories which postulate some semipermanent modification in the material of the nervous system. One of these postulates chemical changes in the nerve cell itself, presumably in the protein nucleus, the other at the synapse, in the meshing of the branching nerve fibers. The second type of theory postulates reverberation or resonance among many cells. This includes Lashley's theory which postulates a "multiplicity of interacting circuits"; also McCulloch's theory of closed reverberating circuits.

The theory that the memory trace is an alteration in nerve cells more precisely states that the stimulus causes a "trace" to be imprinted on the cortex. This is the theory of one school of Gestalt psychologists, under the leadership of Köhler. It holds that percept and concept are basically electrochemical fields in continuous wavelike pulsations, a "self-modifying system of tensions." This form of tracing is postulated to be held together in the required form by such internal forces. But, as Cole reminds us, "a *trace* is a scientific construct. No one ever saw a trace. . . . We do not even know where they are located. . . . A trace might be described as that which makes possible the revival of responses made long ago, as that which is preserved when the response to a configuration of stimuli has ceased."[16] Adrian agrees that we must postulate "some semi-permanent modification" in the nervous system itself. Explaining his position, Adrian says that even a "slight outgrowth" in the thickness of the dendrites which have been specially active, or other change in plastic nerve cells, would be enough. He grants that these have never been detected under the microscope, nevertheless, "some kind of material change seems to be needed to account for the persistence of memories over periods when the brain is virtually at rest."[17] I can find no competent dissent to that generalization.

A related theory is that the stimulus imprints traces upon the cell's self-duplicating, protein molecules. Joseph Needham says that "if the keynote of this mode of thought [among biochemists] were to be summarised in a single sentence, it would be that the foundations of morphological form are to be sought in the proteins responsible for cell-structure, and that these are inescapably connected with the normal metabolic processes of the living cell as a going concern."[18]

The quantitative requirements of storage space are met by this theory, for there are probably a thousand-billion-billion protein molecules in the brain. It is known, moreover, that as electrochemical impulses move along the nerve fibers, they do make changes in their protein molecules. Their shortness of life—only about a day—is counteracted by the fact that they, at least, the "giant proteins," "can reproduce like living things . . . they can manufacture images of themselves," and their offspring have the "same markings as their parents."

Pfeiffer elaborates:

In other words, protein molecules representing the memory of something that happened when you were a child have been multiplying or "breeding" ever since. This process may go on for sixty years or more, each generation of new molecules replenishing the old supply and preserving memory traces. . . . Some investigators are convinced that the substances will be definitely identified with memory, and that the evidence may help explain certain familiar observations that baffle us now. For example, alcohol is known to be one of the substances that produces radical and permanent changes in proteins. This process, called denaturing, might account for the hallucinations and loss of memory which are symptoms of certain forms of alcoholism.[19]

Moreover, the genes transmitting hereditary traits and the viruses causing disease also seem to be self-duplicating molecules.

Thus in "snapshot memory," the theory is that billions of passing scenes are photographed through camera-like "shutters" of our eyes at the rate of ten per second; they are "not stored in one place, or in one piece . . . [but] as a pattern of individual traces, producing lasting changes in protein molecules. Each molecule is like one of the silver grains imbedded in the emulsion of a photographic plate, bearing its own fraction of the total picture." The picture in our head is a "mosaic of imprints on up to a thousand protein molecules." The pattern is not located in a particular spot. The theory speculates that its widely scattered bits form a "three-dimensional pattern, a kind of memory constellation in space."[20] Moreover, this could account for memory in spite of extensive cortical damage.

Several arresting facts that question the validity of any "organ" or localized cell-storage theory, were brought out sharply in the Hixon Symposium. As John von Neumann said, most neurologists "seem to be equally convinced that memory is due to some lasting changes somewhere on the body of the nerve cell, somehow connected with alterations of thresholds. Is it not better to say that there probably is a memory organ somewhere, but that we are absolutely ignorant as to where it is—probably as ignorant as the Greeks, who located the whole intelligence in the diaphragm?"[21] He went on to say that there is evidence that much of memory "is static, unerasable, resulting from an irreversible change." He urges that "no memory, once acquired, can be truly forgotten. Once a memory-storage place is occupied, it is occupied forever, the memory capacity that it represents is lost; it will never be possible to store anything else there." Actually this is not really forgetting, "but merely the removal of that particular memory-storage region from . . . easy availability to one of lower availability."[22] The system of files has not been destroyed, merely moved into the cellar, and in response to future situations may be brought up and made available.

Over thirty years ago (1929) Karl Lashley, working on the borderline between brain physiology and psychology, suggested a different answer to the question, "Where is information filed?" Adrian reports Lashley's opinion:

. . . every part of the cortex may be affected when something is learnt, so that the memory traces are everywhere and might be produced from any part, provided that they could be extracted from it. [He asks] By what possible mechanisms might a pattern of stimulation exciting one restricted group of nerve-cells set up a reproduction of itself, reduplicated throughout the whole cerebral area into which those nerve-cells discharge? And he answers in terms of resonance, or interference patterns in the innumerable local circuits made by the cortical cells and their short or long conducting elements.

Memory traces would then be more or less stable resonance patterns which might be reduplicated all over the cortex in small or large collections of cells, and a fresh signal would find the resonating systems ready to be stirred up to increased activity if it fitted more or less into the pattern.[23]

Twenty years later, in the Hixon Symposium, Lashley concluded: "Memory is not stored in a single locus . . . we cannot deal with individual conditioned reflex arcs. . . . [Memory must be stored in] a multiplicity of interacting circuits whose excitatory effects can be transmitted around various types of cortical interruption." His evidence from many physiological-psychological experiments on rats shows that "there must be some sort of multiple representation." He found, he says, "that one-sixtieth of the visual cortex of the rat will mediate visual memories and it may be any sixtieth, provided it includes part of the central projection field."[24] How reconcile this finding on rats with Penfield's findings on human beings? The fact, for example, that a long-forgotten specific episode was revived again and again whenever the electrode touched the same precise spot in the temporal lobe of J.V.'s cortex? May not the answer be that both kinds of memory, specific imprinting on specific cells and cell assemblies, are used on one occasion and some form of resonance or of reverberating regions on other occasions?

In briefest overview, this epitomizes the brain's role in the forming process which we call the flash of insight, or imagined conception. There are, however, parts of the body other than the brain that play critical roles in our behavior. There are indeed many animals capable of complicated and intelligent behavior that have no brain, or at best a very inadequate one. There are multi-celled bodies in our blood stream that behave, more or less, as independent living beings, avoiding what is bad for them and selecting what is good. "Have they any claim to minds?" Adrian asks. "And if so, have their minds any share in the mind of the larger organism in whose blood-vessels they live?" Then he reminds us of the basic biological principle of integration—namely, that since "the organism works as a whole we cannot expect to understand its behavior by studying its parts."[25]

Following that principle we shall relate the mind to what goes on in the whole body, not merely to what takes place in the brain. My theory postulates that the transforming of stimuli into meanings is done in some integration of brain, endothalamic, autonomic, and muscular systems.

The brain is treated as the dynamic center of transformation, control, and communication. There are the physiological controls to sensory perception, imagery, memory, consciousness and unconsciousness, symbolic thought, and imagination. This is the physiological key to the emotional matrix of behavior, to will, purpose and initiative, and to the drive-dynamics of the imagination. The muscular, ideomotor, and incipient movement systems are primary sources of symbolic feeling and gesture.

Thus the transforming organ that brings about the flash of insight is really a complex group of organs, but its mid-brain nucleus, what Papez calls a "harmonizing mechanism," plays the controlling, guiding role in the act.

7

Form in Nature and in Art

A N understanding of the concept of form and the form-ing process becomes indispensable at this point. We know, as a consequence of recent advances in the behavioral sciences, that the forming process is central in all natural phenomena. It is the key to the explanation of growth and development. All higher beings, the embryologists tell us, are endowed with a typical form-pro-ducing mechanism which characterizes both their external features and their internal structures. This is basic, for the "germ . . . pos-sesses in itself the means of creating forms," says Dalcq. It is a certitude that "our very concept of life . . . necessarily implies some definite, always elaborate structure or order; that is, an abstract translation of form."[1] This form-making power is both macroscopic and microscopic. At one end of the scale it binds to-gether the cosmos in an external system; at the other end it brings about crystal forms, for example, which are "a product of the geometry of one unit repeating itself indefinitely."[2] A forming proc-ess holds the molecules of liquids in an equilibrium of tension by a continuous cycle of forces of attraction and repulsion. In plant and animal growth it guarantees a sequence of steps of unfolding. In men the special function of the central nervous system is the perception of form or Gestalt, and when it occurs in the flash of insight it is the forming of the imagined conception. This is the in-tuitive, inside way of knowing through identification with the

116

object. And Lancelot Whyte, projecting the concept into the future, says that "the operations of the intellect . . . require, prior to and beneath their logical rearrangements, a formative process which shapes experience into units which the intellect can employ." Thus "the most comprehensive natural law expresses a formative tendency."[3]

MAN'S RECURRING PREOCCUPATION WITH FORM

In every historical epoch men have dealt with the concept of form. Aristotle recognized the formative principle saying that form "is the qualitative essence of things." Plato, before him, regarded "ideas as pure forms, and the world as forms in the process of being realized." Democritus speculated that the vast multiplicity of forms in things was due to different arrangements of the same atoms. In a sense all study of man and his world has been the study of the forms of things, of people, their institutions, ways of living, problems, and values.

There have been certain luminous moments in the evolution of the concept. In ancient times perhaps the most brilliant was that of Pythagoras (c. 550 B.C.) and his School. Pythagoras, in developing a primitive numerical symbolism, generalized that "all things are numbers . . . including the whole of nature." As one writer phrased it, he and his followers were "drunk with the vision of God in Number." "Every vista in this Pythagorean garden," said Whyte, "is an avenue of perfection, a radiance of number or form revealing the true nature of things."[4] Recurringly throughout modern times, men have come back to this Pythagorean conception. Earlier than the Greek masters, the Egyptians had used the concept of mathematical form in creating decimal systems in the art of mensuration and in calculations involving simple geometrical solids.

By the second century before Christ, men had begun to perceive that the relations between the motions of the planets could be expressed compactly in symbolic form, for example, in mathematics. In the long medieval hiatus, the Mohammedan Arabs preserved and extended the concept of form in algebra, trigonometry, and astronomy and in the arithmetic of India. In the thirteenth century Thomas Aquinas, reconciling Aristotle with medieval theology, saw the world as a "hierarchy of forms," and his followers developed the scholastic theory of matter and form. The Oxford School of logicians sought to "define the conditions which are necessary and sufficient to produce the form of any selected phenomenon." In both the sciences and the arts Leonardo da Vinci recognized form in all fields of life, the esthetic, the scientific and the practical. In other writings of the fourteenth and fifteenth centuries, the concept of form was recognized to be the basis for model, type, pattern and other characteristics of living things.

By 1600 the growing appreciation of form was revealed in the anatomical drawings of Vesalius, the study of planetary ellipses by Kepler, the recognition of dynamic similarity in mechanical phenomena by Galileo, Descartes' invention of analytic geometry and his statement of universal mathematics. And in the seventeenth century, although Newton's dominating mechanistic concepts retarded the growth of organic ideas, Milton was referring to "the form by which a thing is what it is," and Thomas Browne was saying "the formative operator . . . will endeavor the formation of the whole." Francis Bacon summed it all up: "The form of a thing is its very essence."

In the eighteenth and nineteenth centuries from Vico to Buffon, Erasmus Darwin, and Lamarck, the terms "organism" and "organization" came into vogue and the morphological approach was followed in the study of species, natural and human processes, of cultures, and history. Kant (1764) saw form as the fundamental principle that holds the elements of things together and Goethe generalized that the formative process is "the supreme process, indeed the only one, alike in nature and in art." To Hegel (1800) form was the "active determining principle" of the historical process, and to Schelling all nature was characterized by a "single formative energy."

The grip of the concept tightened on the minds of students as its role in the sciences and arts was increasingly recognized. It was apparent in early crystallography, in cytology, in biology, and in the theory of the evolution of organic forms, as well as in the writings of Coleridge and other poets. By 1852, Thomas Huxley was saying that the elements involved in a single life were summed up in "those forms which proceeded from a single egg taken together."

In the 1890s, Von Ehrenfels and the first group of Gestalt psychologists emphasized the role of the "form-qualities" of experience, anticipating the fuller experimental determination of Gestalt after 1910 by Wertheimer, Köhler, and their group.

In the next two generations the great shift in thought from mechanism to organism established the concept of form through the entire intellectual and expressive world. I name only a few examples: D'Arcy Thompson's great mathematical study of organic forms, *Growth and Form* (1917); Einstein's mathematical initiation of study of the morphology of the universe; the morphological approach of Durkheim, Malinowski, and Benedict in the study of cultures; symbolic forms in language, myth, and other aspects of culture as documented by Usener, Cassirer, and Langer; conceptions of patterned organizations in the new physics; Child's pattern concept in animal and human behavior; organic properties recognized as "patterned" rather than "atomic" by Bertalanffy, Woodger, and others; and Berger's discovery of the patterned form of the brain's alpha rhythms.

This selection of high points of the great discoveries does little more than raise the curtain on the dramatic exploration of the basic concept of form.

THE FORMING PROCESS IN ALL NATURAL PHENOMENA

Form-making in nature provides rich illustrative material. As a result of a century's study of form in plants, since Goethe first suggested its name, morphology, it is known today that the final form of a plant arises by a "continual production of appendages within growing points,"[5] called meristems, and persists throughout the life of the plant. Regulating factors exist which maintain equilibrium between cells. While the external factors of water supply, light, temperature and gravity play a part, the basic forming process is now known to be controlled by internal factors. These are the growth hormones called auxins, and B-type vitamins. Although there is uncertainty as to how these control the form of plant growth, it is agreed that the auxins and three B-vitamins (thiamin, nicotinic acid, and pyridoxine) largely explain the reaction of plants to light and gravity and also explain the development of leaves. It seems probable, says Gregory, "that growth regulation is brought about by the mutual control of activators and inhibitors."[6] Recent developments in biochemistry and cytology have found success in extracting growth inhibitors from plants. While knowledge of the electrochemical interplay of inner attraction-repulsion forces is at this point incomplete, the internal anatomy of the plant "can in theory be accounted for by interchange of hormone-like substances between neighboring cells." The crux of the problem of symmetry seems to be "the effective factor determining the position of each localized center of cell division in the meristem."[7]

"Some general character," says Waddington, "pervades the whole realm of organic form."[8] This reveals itself particularly in the control of growth. Development appears to be a continuous unfolding of a sequence of forms. These are self-originated, built up from the inside, "from very many cells, each of which contains and is controlled by a whole host, several hundreds at least, of hereditary factors."[9] One conspicuous characteristic of every item of living material is internal order. Each is a complete, unique whole.

The fullest documentation comes from E. S. Russell. He first illustrates self-directiveness in the healing of wounds. "The stimulus which initiates the process of wound healing is a class or range of substances normally formed as a result of injury to the epidermal cells. . . . The process as a whole moves, or is directive, towards the restoration of the normal functional structure. . . . The restoration of the normal density of cells is achieved by migration, by multiplication of cells, and by the degeneration of unwanted cells, all of which processes are aimed at restoring the norm."[10]

Many other examples of self-directive activity in lower order species are at hand. For example, simple repair and wound healing via "the tactile perception of something missing,"[11] by homeostasis of oxygen supply in the tissue, by regulation of condition of the blood, or by capacity to grow organs from the organ parts.

In the light of such diverse examples, Russell generalizes. "*If in a living animal normal structural and functional relations, ei-*

ther external or internal, are disturbed, activities will usually be set in train that are directive towards restoring structural and functional norms, or establishing new norms which are adapted to the altered circumstances."[12]

Russell not only demonstrates the directiveness of activities throughout the entire range of the animal world. He also insists that they are creative. "I use the word creativeness deliberately, for no other appears adequate to describe the amazing power which living organisms possess."

That human thought, and science itself, are dependent on the directive and creative activities of life becomes very obvious when we consider the development of a human being. . . . The power of conceptual thought, which is the basis of science, is dependent on, and conditioned by, the directive and creative activities of the developing body, which result in the building up of the incredibly complex and orderly organization of the fully functional and normal adult human body. . . . We should remember that intelligence is only a means to life, not life itself. Instead of attempting to explain the "teleological" nature of organic activities in terms of concepts derived from man's knowledge of his own purposive activity, as do the mechanist and the vitalist, we should take precisely the opposite view, and regard human purposive activities (including machine-making) and modes of thought as being a specialised development of the fundamental "purposiveness," or as I prefer to call it, the directiveness and creativeness, of life.[13]

Life and mind are one. At least "psychological activity issuing in purposive behavior is to be regarded as a specialisation of vital activity." Thus we can agree with Russell that directiveness is "an attribute, not of mind but of life"; with Sinnott, that purposive activity "is a specialized and elaborated kind of directive activity, concerned mainly with the mastery of his [man's] material environment"; and with C. S. Myers "that life and mind are at bottom the same."[14]

Our knowledge of embryology sheds added light on the forming process. As a result of the recent advances in the research on micro-organisms, especially with the aid of electronic microscopes, the embryologists and biochemists feel that they can now arrange forms in a hierarchy. Going up the scale, one finds significant forms, "the definite shape of which," says Dalcq, "has an intrinsic importance for the welfare or the future of the organism." These formed structures develop in a constant progression until they attain "a certain equilibrium typical for adult specimens of each species." Thus "morphogenesis displays a continuous activity, apparently striving towards a definite end."[15]

Confirmation of these findings comes also from recent research in biochemistry. Joseph Needham, distinguished British interpreter, following in the tradition of D'Arcy Thompson, F. G. Hopkins, and Whitehead, agrees with the Aristotelian concept, "no matter without form." "Form," he says,

is an essential constituent of the whole realm of organic chemistry . . . nor can it be excluded from "inorganic" chemistry or nuclear physics. Eventually it blends, we might say, into order and organization as such. . . . The only two components required for the understanding of the universe in terms of modern science [are] Organization . . . and Energy.[16]

Forty years ago knowledge of chemistry of molecules was so limited that the structural formulae of organic chemistry were regarded as the products of pure imagination. Then came the pioneer experiments of Langmuir and Harkins with the monomolecular films, enabling the calculation of dimensions of molecules and showing how "they took up positions exactly in accordance with their presumed structures." New methods were developed in addition to those which studied surface phenomena "by which we know that the structural formulae of chemistry correspond to true spatial relations."[17] This is confirmed by studies in X-ray crystallography, in the components of living organisms, and in steroid chemistry. All these have been important in the development of endocrinology and other biological fields.

The pioneering insight on the metabolism of the cell was that of Hopkins, who saw "the protoplasm of the cell as a kind of chemical factory, where a large number of reactions were able to proceed in close contiguity without becoming disorganized." This has been confirmed by modern "techniques of labelling individual atoms by the use of isotopes [which] permitted estimates of the speed of metabolic scrapping and replacement." Biochemists in other countries are developing the method and have gone far in "tracing out of complicated paths and cycles in the flowsheet of the cell's industrial processes."[18]

A new consensus seems to be emerging that the cell's growth, expansion, proliferation, "inspired by some self-propulsive energizer" and controlled by nervous materials, is related to, and organized with, the brain and higher central nervous system. D'Arcy Thompson, using mathematical models, apparently anticipated this, although very crudely, in his studies of induction. Many biologists hold that further advances will be brought about only by the union of biochemistry, embryology and mathematics; and some insist on an even wider multi-disciplinary approach. Needham says, "we need much more knowledge about the responding cell proteins as well as about the substances or surface configurations or whatever they are, which mediate the determination stimulus." Great gains have come recently through the invention of "methods of ultra-micro chemical analysis."[19]

FORM IN THE ARTS

Since the consensus of judgment stated here is confirmed from manifold studies in the other natural sciences, one does not overgeneralize in saying that an autonomous forming process is central to all natural phenomena. And this is true also of man-made objects. The basic esthetic concept of this book is that art is the formed expression of imagined conception. This concept joins form and imagination, for the imagined conception is the product of the forming process. The product of the artist is his statement of what he sees, his way—but *with form*. Forty years ago Clive Bell pointed to form as the "starting-point for all systems of aesthetics. . . . There must be some one quality," he said, "without which a work of art cannot exist; possessing which, in the least degree, no work is altogether worthless." What quality, he asks, "is common to Sta. Sophia and the windows at Chartres, Mexican sculpture, a Persian bowl, Chinese carpets, Giotto's frescoes at Padua, and the masterpieces of Poussin, Piero della Francesca and Cezanne?" There is one, he says, "significant form." "These relations and combinations of lines and colours, these aesthetically

moving forms, I call 'significant form.' "[20] Louis Sullivan, the first
form-seeking architect of America, discovering for himself that
form always "followed function" in natural phenomena, held "organic form" to be basic to the design of a house. Frank Lloyd
Wright, once his assistant, always spoke of architecture as "organic." Isadora Duncan agreed with Sullivan, labeling the gesture
of the dance as "organic form." Robert Frost expressed it: "Let
chaos storm . . . let cloud shapes swarm . . . I wait for form."
Albert Barnes in *The Art in Painting* calls it "plastic form." Sheldon
Cheney prefers "expressive form," saying, "Expressionist advance
[in modern painting] has been made largely by schools that might
reasonably be called *'form-seeking.'* "[21]

PRINCIPLES OF THE FORMING PROCESS

Within the limits of the natural sciences and even beyond them
into the social sciences, as well as in the arts, we can generalize the
principles of the forming process. The history of social, economic,
and political organization and of all forms of creative expression
have produced a definite consensus on three principles of form.

The Principle of Unity

Throughout the development of civilization, man has been,
above all, an orderer. Throughout time and in all places of the earth
he has transformed wild hillsides into gardens of ordered beauty.
Working his will upon the chaotic watershed of the Tennessee, he
organized that huge area into a cultivated valley of farms and
towns, with channels for production and distribution, transportation, communication, and markets. In the recurring episodes of
Western history, creative men have transformed political anarchy
into order, rebuilt disrupted economic systems, and stated the
mood and the mind of the people in poems, songs, plays, paintings,
dances. The creative task is always the same, whether it be in art,
science, or invention: that of reducing a miscellany to order. This
is the first principle of form, variously called "Heaven's first law,"
the "first principle of the universe," "modern science's final explanation," and "the foundation of all art." It is the basis of the sci-

ences and arts of man. Its synonyms are organization, organism, the unity of the whole.

The Principle of Economy or Simplicity

From the study of the behavioral sciences and the arts of man emerges the second basic principle of the ordering process. The significant act always tends to seek the simplest possible solution. This is the historic "principle of parsimony," or economy, "a working rule for treatment of scientific data, according to which the simplest available explanation is to be preferred, i.e., the explanation which involves the fewest or least complexly related concepts that are adequate."[22] The natural scientists and estheticians of Whyte's splendid symposium agreed that "the essence of creative activity [lies] . . . in a simplifying process which automatically involves not only the selection and rearrangement of the available material, but its modification in process of developing a simpler form."[23] Konrad Lorenz reminds us that "What is called a most 'pregnant' form in Gestalt psychology is objectively that of the mathematically simplest regularity."[24] Economy would seem to be implicit in the definition of an organization; the ideally perfect order will be guaranteed only by the simplest possible fusion of elements. The instinctive tendency of the animal body is to act that way. The mathematician, building his beautiful definition, knows it. The expressional artist knows it. The poet seeks the one best word, the briefest possible but most complete phrase to express his feeling. The architect searches for the minimum structural design. Martha Graham (carrying out the Sullivan-Wright principle that form not only follows function, but that the two are one) strove for the "one true movement." To find the irreducible minimum, that is the ordeal of the artist. As Louis Danz put it, *"Form is that kind of organization to which nothing can be added and from which nothing can be taken."*[25]

The Principle of Functionality: Doing What the Situation Demands

This principle is illustrated throughout nature, each living thing tending to do what the situation requires. This is revealed on the most elemental levels of behavior—the tropism or forced movement, as Jacques Loeb called it.[26] The examples occur throughout the plant and animal world. There are *phototropisms,* as in the bending of oat seedlings under the influence of light, or in the forced movement of the gold-tail moth, called "slave of light" because it can move only up the stem of the shrub toward light, to find its indispensable food in the new buds and shoots. *Geotropism* is revealed in the orientation of living things to gravity, *stereotropism* in their orientation to contact pressures, *rheotropism* in their orientation to movement in a visual field, and *chemotropism* in "the circling of fish toward the chemical diffusing of bait."

Analogous to these examples are animal responses to a "biologically relevant situation," as Lorenz puts it. It is as though "the animal 'knows innately' " or " 'recognizes instinctively' " what to do, although the competent ethologist warns against such anthropomorphism. Actually, the animal's response is governed by what Tinbergen and Lorenz have named an "innate releasing mechanism."[27] All species appear to be equipped with electrochemical receptory apparatus which is "selectively tuned" to respond to specific stimuli.

The concept of function gripped thinking men during the past fifty years of social transformation through which the industrializing, democratizing culture of the West has passed. Philosophers, engineers, architects, sociologists, psychologists, all have asked concerning their materials, What function is this thing to carry out? Louis Sullivan, seeking an irreducible principle of form in architecture, asked of every building and every member of every building he designed, What is this thing to do? What is this beam or column to support? Concerning the over-all design he inquired, What kind of life is to be lived in this house? In the current revolution in the arts of expression there are manifold revelations of the functional principle of form. The creative artist asks of every word in a poem, every line of a drawing, every body gesture in the dance, What is its function? What nuance of meaning is this phrase to convey? What mood is this gesture to evoke?

The cultural milieu in which we moderns have grown up is saturated by the functional concept. We have seen it remold our political-economic definitions. Nowadays, property, long defined in law nominalistically, in terms of "thing," is being redefined in terms of social use—What is it for? For whom is it to be developed? For the use of the people has increasingly come to be the answer. Psychology and the other behavioral sciences all have tended to become functional. Certainly the concept of functionality has come to be an accepted first principle in the forming process.

A RHYTHMIC PATTERN-MAKING PROCESS

The very concept, form-making, or forming process, implies that we are concerned not with something static but with a dynamic working model. A sense of rhythmic pattern-making pervades man's inner biological data. Form in all matter is the product of the interaction of internal electrochemical forces. Matter is made up of molecules (groups of atoms) which mutually attract and repel one another. This electrochemical process is ceaseless heat-motion within molecules which in inanimate solids collide and rebound in random vibratory action. Light is thrown on this process by studying the shift from the chaos of movement in gases to the increasing emergence of form in liquids and solids. This process is sometimes referred to as the "taming of heat motion," the lower the temperature the greater the emergence of form. In gases where temperatures are highest, forces cannot hold molecules together and there is no form. In liquids, form is manifested as internal forces more nearly balanced and molecular equilibrium is successfully maintained; with temperatures higher and distances greater, attractive bonds are broken and there is still some random movement but increasing form. Under the low temperatures of solids, heat motion does not exceed vibration across short distances, molecules are held together and there is maximum possibility of form. But the important point seems to be amplitude of electrical vibration. There is an optimal distance from which molecules are in equilibrium because forces are approximately balanced. Thus the internal tensions are balanced against one another in a stable configuration or, rather, nearly balanced. The cautionary phrase "nearly balanced" is very important and I shall return to it in a moment.

The contrast between the inanimate crystal, for example, and an organism will project more clearly the conception of form. "The best manifestation of solid form," says Humphreys-Owen, "is the ideal single crystal, in which one internal pattern is repeated perfectly throughout," and the outer shape is a "consequence of its inner arrangement."[28] Moreover, "the crystal grows towards the shape in which total of the attractive forces emanating from its surface is least."[29] But this is mechanism, the product of a unit which repeats itself endlessly but produces only balance, shape, uniformity. The end result is inert, static, not dynamic. It is death, not life. A crystal is a static array of identical parts.

In sharp contrast to the mechanical shaping of objects is the dynamic form of organisms. In nature's forming processes the linkage between organic molecules is creative. Here we have, not the repetition of molecules as in the crystal, but the addition of new atoms. The attraction-release process is present, producing balance and imbalance, but there is always a surplus tension, which produces imbalance again, and further movement. Thus, while the shaping of the crystal is a one-way affair, the organism is two-way. It is marked by an internal cyclic balance and imbalance, push and pull, down-beat and up-beat, systole and diastole. Enough surplus tension is left over always to keep the pulsation going.

While there is, as yet, no biological or biochemical consensus on the nature of the form-making process, the theory stresses the rhythmic, pulsating attraction-repulsion architechtonics of the single cell. "All the functioning regions of cells and of organisms," says Whyte, "seem to possess a labile but perpetually self-restoring skeleton structure of protein,"[30] pulsating with perpetual cycles of expansion and contraction. Whitehead agreed: "A rhythm involves a pattern. . . . The essence of rhythm is the fusion of sameness and novelty. . . . A mere recurrence kills rhythm as surely as does a mere confusion of differences."[31] This agrees with the Gestalt psychological principle of closure in perception, the tendency of the organism to complete the incompleted act. And this, Lewin speculated and then demonstrated, is one secret of success in memory; it is the incompleted act which is remembered.

There are countless examples of the rhythmic movement of the organs of the living body: the pulsating heart, the synchronized periodicity of breathing, the alpha (or other) rhythms of the brain; there is the characteristic time-beat of walking, the unique personal rhythm in oral speech, the rhythmic responses of the singer, the orator, the actor, musician, acrobat, or the skilled worker in any occupation. Psychologists, similarly, have documented the periodic nature of mental activity. Attention ebbs and flows. Effective performance is grouped rhythmically in a vast range of acts —rate of tapping, estimating numbers, rowing a boat, operating a typewriter, the eye-movements of the best readers, and the finger-hand-wrist movements of the best hand-writers. And personal expression in music, poetry and creative dance, painting and sculpture confirms the role of rhythm.

WHAT BECOMES OF THE BODY-MIND PROBLEM?

Are the traditional controversies over psycho-physical parallelism and over the natures and separate spheres of "body" and "mind" concerned with a phantom problem? Some recent philosophies, like Whitehead's philosophy of organism and Dewey's philosophy of experience, have emphasized the continuity rather than the discontinuity of mental and physical processes and functions. But philosophical systems in which the dichotomy has been bridged are likely to be unconvincing to persons identified with other systems of thought.

To me the conclusions of scientists on the subject are harder to refute. For example, the British psychologist, C. S. Myers, has said, "The notion of any *relation* between mind and body is absurd —because mental activity and living bodily activity are *identical*."[32] Sinnott, American biologist, agrees: "Biological organization . . . and psychical activity . . . *are fundamentally the same thing*."[33] His point of view is that the whole life of man, rich in ideas, in inspirations, in intellectual subtleties, in imagination and emotion is the manifestation of an organized biological system raised to its loftiest levels. Upon this system the outer world impinges as a series of sensations, real or imagined, and out of it come actions, either overt physical responses or more subtle mental ones or the two combined. What takes place between these events is, at bottom, the regulatory activity of the protoplasmic system. In its lowliest expression this appears as regulatory control of growth and function. Such control merges imperceptibly into instinct, and from these simplest of physical phenomena emerge the complex mental activities of the higher animals and finally the enormously rich and varied life of the intelligent and imaginative human being.

From this view, the traditional body-mind problem is a phantom problem. And this is the view which promises progress in understanding and developing the creative forming processes of the human imagination.

Part II

WAYS OF RELEASING

THE IMAGINATION

Editor's Introduction

In Part I, the author was concerned essentially with identifying and describing the creative act in man. In the first instance, he garnered and ordered the evidence provided by recognized innovators in the arts and sciences who had sought to identify and describe their own processes of innovation. This provided a nontechnical framework for his attempts to identify and describe more technically the processes of the creative imagination and the conditions, psychological and physiological, under which these processes manifest themselves. This technical search led him to integrate various evidences concerning the nature of meaningful human response in general. Within the genus of "meaningful human response" he sought the differentia of that species of response with which he was finally concerned—the creative act.

Among the differentia of the creative response, his construct of "transliminal" or "off-conscious" mind-body functioning proved to be central. In off-conscious functioning, the person lets things happen rather than tries to make them happen according to already known and cherished patterns of thought and habit. It is a state of relaxation from the dictates of external censorship or unconscious compulsion. It is a state of relaxation attained through a concentration of attention upon what is to be discovered or known. Yet the process of knowing involved is a coming to know through "inner" identification rather than through "external" categorization of that which is consciously observed—a process of discovery rather than one of logical verification. The process is autistic rather than directly oriented to a consciously perceived reality.

The author found in dreaming, in fantasy, in hypnagogic and hypnopompic imagery "natural" prototypes of the off-conscious creation he sought to describe. But men historically have not been satisfied to depend upon such adventitious natural occurrences in cultivating the resources of the transliminal mind. They have developed arts and artifacts, methods and disciplines, to enter more aimfully into threshold experiences and to garner the fruits of the imagination which flourishes in such experiences.

The author turns in Part II to a study of the ways by which men have thus sought to release their powers of imagination. In a sense, the arts and disciplines which these practices embody constitute technologies for inducing in themselves transliminal states. Here, as elsewhere in human experience, technologies often develop without the benefit of any fully developed "theory" concerning the processes which the technologies are designed to produce and control for human use. Elaborate improvements in fire boxes and drafts took place in producing and controlling fire for man's benefit long before the oxidation theory of fire was articulated or tested. Similarly, men have developed technologies for releasing the human imagination before any adequate theory of the imagination has been formulated. Yet the learnings which have come through the development and use of these technologies can throw additional light upon the conditions and content of an adequate theory. So the author hoped in this study.

The ways of releasing the imagination explored seem various on the surface—trance states induced by hypnotism and drugs, mysticism, the systems of spiritual exercise in the Orient, the disciplines of intuition in the West. Yet they are held together by the author's construct of "transliminal," mind-body functioning as the locus of human imagination. And the practitioners and students of these technologies have relevant lore and knowledge which no theorist of the imagination can sanely ignore.

8

The Opening of Trance Vestibules

M_Y present postulate extends the conception of the transliminal mind, as the creative center of the conscious-nonconscious continuum, to include the light trance of hypnosis but to exclude medium and deep trance. This limitation is justified because, while the deeper trance states have been proved to have access to even the earliest storage of human experience, and while they also have amazing powers of physiological and psychological anesthesia, no evidence has been advanced concerning their creative potentialities. In this respect, the deep hypnotic trance is definitely distinguished from the creative dreaming mind.

HYPNOSIS[1]

The hypnotic trance state is an intriguing phenomenon, but what does it have to do with the creative imagination? While there is no evidence that creative acts take place in either medium or deep trance, the case for light trance is much stronger. Kline concluded that there is a great difference between it and the depth levels; under light trance, he said, "many highly complex and subtle changes in psychological function can be brought about."[2] The evidence shows that, in hypnotic trance, the subject has access to various levels of the nonconscious. It suggests that traits and ca-

135

pacities are revealed which may be directly involved in the creative act, among them suggestion, the concentration of attention, acceptance, and ideomotor action and neuromotor enhancement. It supports the general concept of the conscious-nonconscious continuum. It throws new light on the ability of the organism to suspend both physiological and psychological functions, on amnesia, and on possible connections between the nonconscious and the transliminal mind.

Moreover, it is a fact that all but a negligible few in the general population can draw on these powers. From the estimates of Liebault and Bernheim in the 1870s, to that of Kline in the 1950s, the verdict is approximately the same: 70 to 95 per cent of the people can be hypnotized into a light trance state. Liebault claimed that the correct percentage was 92, Wetterstrand 97, Kline 95. Bernheim said that a hypnotist is no operator if he does not succeed with 80 per cent. It is clear, therefore, that the trance state is a common phenomenon; most people are suggestible. There are, however, great differences in suggestibility. Immature and older people are generally more hypnotizable than the young and tough-minded. But even among the latter, many of advanced intelligence can be subjected to light and medium trance. Kline's final conclusion is, however, that not more than 10 per cent can be brought to "a depth state within which . . . complete amnesia, complete anesthesia, spontaneous amnesia, positive and negative hallucinations, and posthypnotic behavior are capable of being produced easily."[3]

Physiological Functions Suspended—Analgesia

The evidence is conclusive that hypnotic trance anesthetizes the nerve ends that produce sensations of pain. Surgeons' reports in the popular as well as technical press abound in cases which show that in post-surgical therapy where intensely painful tissue damage is involved, hypnosis means relief from torture. In one instance, an arm had been badly burned in a gas heater explosion, dead tissues had been cut away. Exercise was called for, but even with opiates, the pain was so excruciating that the muscles could not be contracted. Under hypnosis, however, the patient felt no pain whatsoever as directions were given to exercise the arm. "Stretch it, stretch it. When you wake up you will continue to move it but this will not be painful." Awakened, the patient moved her arm without pain.

A British workman lost the toes of one foot in an accident. A graft of skin onto the injured foot from another part of his body would save the foot. But to bring this about would require of him an impossibly prolonged and painful task; he would be required to sit up, leaning forward in a rigid position, holding foot and hand together over a period of several weeks. Under hypnosis, however, he "held the wrist-to-ankle position for 28 days without lameness or discomfort." Another hospital patient whose leg had been immobilized with anesthetic was told, under hypnosis, that he could walk—"and he did, as though his leg were normal." Hypnotism is also being used successfully in painless childbirth.

There is a long and successful history of the use of hypnotic anesthesia in surgery. In India, as long ago as the late 1840s, Dr. James Esdaile, using hypnotism, performed thousands of painless operations; three hundred of these were major operations and nineteen were amputations. Many minor operations are being performed painlessly at the present time, and in Germany and Austria the practice has been common for many years.

These are examples of the apparently magical suspension of physiological functions under hypnosis, called analgesia, or insensitivity to pain. The clinical reports are supported by such scientific laboratory studies as those of Robert R. Sears.[4] Using carefully designed apparatus, he measured degrees of painful stimulus by means of precise instruments and techniques, recorded elapsed time, flinch, tracing of facial grimaces, pulse, respiration, leg-withdrawal reflex, galvanic skin reaction, and measured inspirations. Sears' conclusion is that while the subjects show individual differences, hypnotic anesthesia "very nearly or quite abolishes certain reactions and reduces the amount of the reaction to a certain extent in all."[5] Take as a single example exact measurement of galvanic skin reaction to painful stimuli. Sears reported a reduction of pain for voluntary reactions of 95 per cent, for partly voluntary reactions (facial grimace) 92 per cent; for such nonvoluntary oscillations as pulse reduction 77 per cent, but for variability of pulse 50 per cent.

Hull sums up the long history of investigation of anesthesia of the skin, saying that it permitted the operator "to thrust a needle through the skin without eliciting withdrawal reflexes or a grimace of pain from the subject . . . [it] produced a nearly perfect abolition of the ordinary signs of pain in the case of voluntary or semivoluntary processes." Other authorities agree that the anesthesias affect the voluntary system more profoundly than the involuntary or reflex system; although suggestion, for example, produces anesthesia in all voluntary visual activities, "there remains a residue of involuntary reflexes in the pupillary and lens systems." In the nonvoluntary processes the reduction of signs of pain varied from 20 to 75 per cent. It has been suggested that the process is in some way "significantly related to the mechanism of volition." Hull's generalization is that hypnotic anesthesia may result in "the complete abolition of a sense, apparently resulting in a condition such as total blindness, or it may be limited to an apparent blindness to certain specific things or classes of things."[6]

One of the oldest forms of hypnotherapy is the clearing up of symptoms by direct hypnotic suggestion. Brenman and Gill summarized the evidence to 1947 by stating that "almost every syndrome which we might now label 'psychosomatic' has been reported successfully treated by direct suggestion."[7] They then list all varieties of menstrual disturbance, psoriasis and other skin diseases, asthma, muscular rheumatism, migraine, epilepsy, seasickness, and insomnia, mild forms of obsessions and compulsions.

Psychological Functions Controlled By Suggestion

Psychological as well as physiological functions are suspended in the trance state. Evidence concerning the ideational control of psychological functions has come from the experiments on suggested hallucinations. Hull gives an authoritative example of induced hallucination:

I say to him, "You can now open your eyes, though without waking. Mr. X has gone home. Look around and tell me whether you can see him." The subject gazes around sleepily, apparently with some care, and replies that he cannot. I tell him to count the men present aloud, pointing to each with his finger. He does so. When he comes to Mr. X he passes him by without notice, and ends with a sum one less than the number of persons really present. This phenomenon is sometimes called a *negative hallucination*.[8]

The hypnotized subject, says Cole, "accepts [a] paper with a smudge upon it as the passport photo of his wife, taken two years ago," ". . . in the trance state, he not only can recall with unusual vividness, but he seems to be able to see this material as though it were projected upon the page before him." Another subject "struggles to read the page of print which, you have assured him, is a reprint of one of his own compositions written some time ago in English I; and he will do this in spite of the fact that the book in his hands is actually a textbook in organic chemistry."[9]

In such cases of suggested hallucination the subject reacts *to what he accepts as stimuli*. The consensus of judgment is that hypnotized subjects will realistically "act out responses" to suggested pseudo-stimulations. The suggestion that water is vinegar produces the wry face; that it is wine makes them act as though they were tipsy; "the room is very cold" brings about shivering; and, at the converse suggestion, they fan themselves.

A generation ago skeptical psychologists, while granting that these examples are dramatic, insisted that there was a real question as to their validity and that they should be subjected to experimental analysis. Consider, they said, the unstudied problem of pupillary reaction to hallucinations. When a bright light enters the eye, the iris normally contracts. Does it contract when the suggestion is made to a hypnotized subject that he sees such a light and he reports that he does? There are still no direct experimental answers to the question. Since Cason and Hudgins established, independently, that iris response to light can be conditioned to auditory stimuli, it is possible that most people have, in their conscious lives, already been conditioned to iris response via key words of response to brightness.

What about the production of electrical changes in the skin by hallucinated painful stimuli? Hull reports, on measuring the effect of suggestion by the galvanic skin reflex, that ". . . the galvanometer's response following the hallucination of a pin-prick appears

to be substantially like that resulting from a genuine pin-prick";
he adds that the threat of a pin-prick brings the same response in
the waking state.[10]

While Hull's studies were in progress, Heilig and Hoff reported
from Germany the successful induction of cold sores (herpetic blisters) by suggested hallucinations, *but only in connection with an
emotional ordeal*. Mere suggestion that the blisters were beginning
to form on the lips was not sufficient to bring them out.[11] Hull
grants that the recall of the emotional ordeal did reduce the resistance, "that the emotions aroused in the trance were physiologically
genuine . . . and there is consequently strong *a priori* presumption
that if the attempt were made to arouse similar emotional crises in
the normal waking state this also would have been followed by
. . . the appearance of . . . blisters."[12]

Similar studies were reported by Heilig and Hoff on the relation
of the hallucinatory process to changes in secretion and metabolism.
Digestive reactions were evoked by hypnotically induced hallucinations. Chemical analysis of stomach contents revealed "that the
food partially digested under conditions of suggested relish showed
a disinctly greater amount of acid secretion than did a normal control meal." Heilig and Hoff also reported the positive effect of suggestion on the secretion, quality, and quantity of urine. "Pleasant"
suggestions, that they felt fine, made to subjects in trance, were
followed by reduced secretions of water, chlorides, and phosphates;
unpleasant suggestions were followed by excess in secretion and a
parallel loss in body weight.[13]

The Evidence on Post-Hypnotic Phenomena

That the trance state has access to the storage of the unconscious has also been definitely established by three types of data
on post-hypnotic behavior. There is clear evidence of inability to
recall, on waking, events occurring during hypnosis; also of ability
on waking to carry out suggestions given during hypnosis; finally,
of ability to recall under hypnosis, events of earlier experiences.

The fact of inability to recall, when in normal waking states,
the events of trance states, was known to the first investigators of
hypnosis. The Marquis de Puysegur (1784) discovered the phenomenon in his famous patient Victor. A century later (1888)

Binet and Féré quoted a contemporary to the effect that de Puy-segur's hypnotized patients, "as soon as they returned to a normal condition . . . retained no recollection of what had occurred during the three or four hours' crisis."[14] James (1890) reported that a subject "may have been led through the liveliest hallucinations and dramatic performances, and have exhibited the intensest apparent emotion, but on waking he can recall nothing at all."[15] Since the publication of Bernheim's (1886) classic account, post-hypnotic amnesia has been accepted as a symptom of "the most profound degree of hypnosis which it is possible to attain."

The ability to recall, under trance, events occurring in previous trances, has also been known for nearly a century. Binet and Féré reported that while "the hypnotized subject seldom remembers, on awaking, the events which occurred during his hypnotic sleep . . . when he is asleep his memory embraces all the facts of his sleep, his waking state, and of previous hypnotic sleeps."[16] Moll (1913) agreed that "the subjects remember in hypnosis all that had happened in previous hypnoses"; he quoted a case of Wolfert's—a "woman who remembered in the magnetic sleep all that had taken place in a magnetic sleep thirteen years before."[17]

It was in this century-long background that Hull's laboratory studies of learning by conditioning under hypnosis were carried out. Hidden in Hull's material is a distinction of great importance. He agrees with the other investigators that, under trance, amnesia for general symbolic recall is complete. But for specific conditionings learned by practice under hypnosis, it is zero! The latter finding is confirmed by the fact that for certain manual habits, also learned by practice, amnesia is only 50 per cent.

Just what is the distinction? Hull is *comparing the roles of two different phenomena—suggestion and learning by practice.* Where no *suggestions of recall are given* in a trance, events taking place in the neighborhood of the subject "will not be recalled on waking for . . . they will never have been registered." Apparently suggestion and acceptance by the subject are the keys to the registering or tracing and hence to memory. Hull adds the confirmatory comment: ". . . if a definite suggestion has been given that the subject will not be able to recall in a subsequent trance the events of the one in which the suggestion is given, the suggestion will very likely be realized. Indeed, almost any memory phenomenon that is physically possible to the subject will be encountered if specific suggestions to that effect are given."[18] I conclude from these data that suggestion and its acceptance are the critical factors in tracing the idea in the unconscious storage.

Since the work of Bernheim and his contemporaries, voluminous confirmations of post-hypnotic suggestion have accumulated. In one of Erikson's studies he reports an example of post-hypnotic suggestion carried out after a lapse of five years. But more is involved than the registering of the new suggestions and their acceptance by the physical organism. They are traced on a continuously firing electrochemical nervous system which had earlier recorded a multitude of acts and response. These had not only stored specific behaviors; they had also been cumulatively integrated with earlier tracings to form general standards or norms of behavior. Thus, as Cole says, "The censoring system sometimes operates counter to the impulse . . . to do a very foolish thing (to dance upon a table-top, to give the dean a 'Bronx cheer')."[19]

These are the essential facts concerning the powers of the hypnotic trance. It produces anesthesia, either completely or selectively abolishes the functioning of any of the senses, producing blindness, deafness or insensitivity to pain, as the case may be. But of direct significance to our probing of the unconscious, it permits the recovery of lost memories, re-establishes the behavior of earlier childhood years, creates new forms of nonreality-oriented unconscious mind, and controls the flow of experience across the conscious-nonconscious threshold. These facts help us understand what takes place in the act of creative imagination.

GUIDING CONCEPTS OF THE TRANCE STATE

Reduced to simplest terms, the trance state is induced by the successful use of suggestion, concentration of attention and total acceptance of suggestion.

Hypnosis as Suggestibility

The consensus among scientific students confirms that of the earlier speculative evangelists of hypnotism: The first key to the trance state is suggestion. Roughly defined, suggestion is the initiation of a chain of ideas either communicated by another or by oneself. Technically defined, in the carefully chosen words of Weitzenhoffer, *"a suggestion is a group of ideas proposed by one individual . . . to another person . . . such as to cause the subject to react as if the phenomenon for which the ideas stand were actually present."*[20] Weitzenhoffer's definition is general, applies to all forms of suggestion, discriminates between what is and what is not suggestion, and is consistent with the general consensus. If a suggestion is made by another person it is called heterosuggestion, if by oneself, autosuggestion. Autosuggestion plays a constant role in our daily behavior, and is closely related to the imagination.

Psychologists, psychiatrists, and sociologists had been speculating about the concept of suggestion for more than half a century. It was Hull's scientific studies that took the hypnotic trance out of the realm of speculation. Since Hull's work it has been regarded as a state of suggestibility. His generalization is accepted today. "The difference between the hypnotic state and the normal is, therefore, a quantitative rather than a qualitative one. . . . The essence of hypnosis . . . lies in the fact of *change* in suggestibility."[21]

Relaxation Through Concentration of Attention

The cue to bringing about any form of the quiet mind is relaxation. Throughout the history of man's attempts to heighten intuition, every version of knowing through inside identification has utilized techniques to concentrate attention and relax body and mind. Lao-tzu's Taoist direction is "void the mind." The incessant cry of both Zen master artists and Western intuitive philosophers is —"Let thought go; feel, don't think." When we attend closely to music we gather ourselves together to shut off all but the auditory senses; in intense visual attention we exclude all but the sense of sight. In recalling specific events, facts or principles in thinking logically or in imagining new relationships, we draw down all the sensory curtains around our gathered-together selves. Irrespective of the culture or the historical epoch in which there has emerged a technique for bringing about the quiet mind, peoples the world over have developed their own ways of relaxing through concentration of attention.

That both Eastern and Western masters of the quiet mind have developed the same general approach will be seen from the assembly of techniques brought together in the following chapters. I deal here only with those of hypnosis. There are several variations, one of which, by Kraines, fixes attention by reiterated mention of sleep:

I want you to relax. Relax every part of the body. Now when I pick up your hand I want it to fall as a piece of wood without any help from you. (The examiner then picks up the hand and lets it drop to the couch.) . . . Now relax your legs the same way; just let them be limp. Now take a deep breath and let it out slowly. Now concentrate on your toes. A warm sensation starts in the toes and sweeps up your legs, abdomen, chest, into your neck. Now relax your jaws. Relax them more, still more. Now your cheeks; now your eyes. Your eyes are getting heavier and heavier. You can hardly keep them open. Soon they will close. Now smoothe out the wrinkles in your forehead. Good. Now make your mind a blank. Allow no thoughts to enter. Just blank. You see a blackness spreading before you. Now sleep. Sleep. Sleep. Sleep. Your entire body and mind are relaxed—sleep, sleep. (This phrase is repeated several times in a soft and persuasive voice.) Your sleep is becoming deeper, still deeper. You are in a deep, deep sleep.[22]

Termination of the session is brought about by a warning signal— for example: "When I count five you will wake up."

The conviction that sleep and the hypnotic trance are not variants of the same thing led to the development of Wells's technique of "waking hypnosis." This excludes all suggestion of sleep or drowsiness. W. R. Wells makes some preliminary experiments, then asks the patient to fix attention on some object, saying something on this order:

You must exclude all other thoughts and keep your gaze riveted on this point, eyeballs turned up as though you were looking at the middle of your forehead. Watch it steadily, fixedly, thinking of nothing else. Note every detail so that if I ask you to close your eyes you will be able to picture it as though you were still looking at it. You will be able to do this only if you give it your complete attention and literally feel that you are memorizing it. Watch it closely, try not to blink. Don't let your gaze shift to right or left. . . .[23]

From experience with hundreds of subjects Wells insists that by suggestion he can produce the "characteristic phenomena usually associated with deep sleeping hypnosis"; his technique is easier to learn, avoids the taint of being an "occult" method, takes less time and less effort and is more successful than the "sleeping methods."[24]

In some techniques, attention is first concentrated on the relaxing process. Note the reiteration, "relax, relax every part of your body." The parts are named beginning with the toes and ending with the wrinkles in the forehead. Breathing is perceived to be crucial to relaxing. Western students, while recognizing the importance of breathing, have not probed as deeply into its mechanisms or developed it as rigorously as the Eastern masters of Tao, Yoga, and Zen. The monotony of repetition, supplemented by uninterrupted fixation of attention and a conscious willing to exclude all extraneous stimuli are employed to bring about relaxation.

Normal attention span is notoriously short. The endeavor here is to increase it by fixing it *on* something. The devices are manifold. Some center attention on inner points of fixation, others on outer objects. Both Kraines and Wells center attention inwardly. Kraines's technique, using speech, is to fix attention specifically on parts of the body. Relying on the operator's prestige, he gives first general and then specific directions, illustrating each one carefully. He emphasizes regular, deep breathing and uses the monotony of repetition. Wells also fixates attention inwardly in such directions as: "gaze riveted on this point, eyeballs turned up as though . . . looking at the middle of your forehead . . . watch it steadily . . . think of nothing else . . . note every detail . . . try not to blink . . . don't let your gaze shift."

Related to these two techniques is the postural-swaying method. Such directions as these are given: "Stand here . . . heels and toes together . . . body erect, shoulders back . . . breathe comfortably . . . imagine your feet hinged to the floor, your body . . . free to move back and forth. . . . You will become unsteady . . . imagine your body floating in space . . . don't *try* to do anything . . . don't try *not* to do anything . . . let yourself drift . . . don't worry, I'll catch you *when* you fall." The therapist uses rhythm, timing his directions to fit the swaying: "swaying forward, swaying backward, forward, backward," etc.

The foregoing methods are primarily motor fixations, centering attention inwardly and on parts of the body. There are other techniques in which the subject fixates by eye or by ear on some outer object. The eye-fixation techniques generally employ a bright object: a white card, a crystal ball, a mirror, a shiny silver pen or pencil. The object is held close to the eyes and above them to force the subject to look upward. This compels a high degree of convergence, tires the muscles, requires effort, and encourages the closing of eyes. The directions emphasize the use of the imagination in inducing relaxation: "Imagine yourself floating," and suggestions are given through all possible senses—visual, auditory, tactual, kinesthetic; the more senses involved, the more complete and prompt will be the induction of the trance state.

Ear-fixation techniques are also used; for example, the metronome, ticking at such slow rates as 50 beats a minute. The tone is muffled and soothing "to help you go to sleep. . . . Listen carefully . . . and to nothing else . . . imagine each tick saying 'deep-sleep . . . deep-sleep.' . . . How comfortable you feel all over." Another variation is to accompany the metronome's ticking with visual and motor images of slowly stepping down a ladder: ". . . each tick is saying 'step down' . . . step down . . . down . . . down into deeper sleep . . . deep-sleep . . . step down," etc. Or the subject is asked to imagine himself descending a ladder or a stairway, the steps getting darker and darker as he goes down. Counting off the steps with the ticks helps, timing each count to fit the stepping and drawing out the sound of the numbers.

Acceptance of Suggestion

Another step, in addition to suggestion and relaxation through concentration of attention, is necessary to establish the trance state, and is, I think, a cue to understanding the creative, threshold mind. This is acceptance. The subject must *accept* the operator's suggestion, that is, he must react *as if* the suggested phenomenon were actually present. He accepts when he responds to a suggested idea as he would respond to stimuli from "real" situations. All stimuli are not suggestions, although they bring about changes in behavior. A stimulus is turned into a suggestion and made effective by the subject's acceptance of the idea that he should behave in the way suggested. Brenman and Gill, who stated the contemporary view, say that "the hypnotized subject is by no means an automaton . . . a suggestion takes effect only if it is consonant with the balance of forces of the individual's strivings . . . his understanding and elaboration of a suggestion are likewise determined by his own personality structure."[25] Acceptance may consist, therefore, in acting upon a suggestion, or in deciding to act upon it; or it may be merely a conceptual appraisal, the subject finding nothing adverse or menacing in it. But to explain it we must bring together still more materials from physiology and psychology.

Ideomotor Action and Neuromotor Enhancement

Further understanding comes from combining two long known but little applied concepts, ideomotor action and neuromotor enhancement. The principle of ideomotor action states that an idea can produce specific patterns of muscular response. Its supporting concept, neuromotor enhancement, states that the initial responses, minute though they may be, can be vastly built up through accretive and reinforcing processes.

This concept of ideomotor action was grasped and named a century ago by W. B. Carpenter.[26] In practice, however, its close linkage with the imagination antedates Carpenter by hundreds of years. While its early history dealt with its role in thought reading, ways of "divining" and other forms of magic, the concept was so well established in psychology by 1890 that James called it "orthodox." In 1913, Thorndike devoted to this subject his presidential address to the American Psychological Association. It was not until the 1930s, however, under the influence of Hull's work, that the scientific exploration of ideomotor action was seriously undertaken. Since that time a score of investigations, using such objective instruments as the measurement of nervous electrical currents, have gone far, as Eysenck says, "towards re-establishing the ideomotor theory in its previous commanding position."[27]

In brief, the notion is that imagined idea and incipient movement are approximately one and the same thing. Certainly, if there is a distinguishable sequence of steps it is of this order: idea, transmission of signal to muscle, movement. The idea can be implanted by autosuggestion, by suggestion from another, by imagining the movement or by hearing others discussing such movements. "Experimental evidence," Eysenck concludes, "is overwhelmingly in support of the contention that an idea, or image, of a movement tends to produce the precise movement imagined, or a modified form of it."[28]

Suggestion, then, can evoke a thought that will produce a local condition of excitation. But to enhance that excited state to overt movement requires a succession of repetitions of the suggestion. Eventually a critical point is reached at which a wave contraction is produced. For example, if the suggestion were made to move the hand, and if one could stand away from himself and examine his own physiological processes under the microscope, he would see the suggestion producing, after a delay, "slight twitchings, then . . . trembling, and, finally . . . abortive and partial responses."[29] As the suggestion is repeated, over and over again, these partial responses integrate, become stronger and more easily observable, fuse as they move along the line of direction—and then the hand moves. Following Fulton or Houssay, the facts for neuromotor enhancement are established by summating phenomena in which initial contractions in a muscle, caused by a series of stimuli, either increase in amplitude (called treppe) or fuse individual muscular responses (called tetanus). Nerve impulses accumulate in "trains and volleys," steadily augmenting the strength of the muscular response. The total process is given the all-embracing name, tonus or tonicity; it is defined as "a state of normal elastic tension of the tissues, in virtue of which the parts are kept in shape and, as it were, alert and ready to function in response to a suitable stimulus."[30]

The steps of inducing the trance state can now be restated: concentrating attention on the idea, enhancement through tonus, relaxation. Weitzenhoffer says: "The net effect [of the narrowing of attention] is a stronger, steadier stream of nerve impulses to the muscles and the elimination of other patterns of muscular tension which might either oppose or at least mask the desired effect."[31] As muscular contraction actually sets in and is observable, we have enhancement—spreading of ideomotor action from one or more specific nerve channels to other related ones.

There are, however, two additional types of evidence that bear directly upon the unconscious sources of the materials of the creative imagination. One, already emphasized, is an unexpected and positive addition to our powers of recall of previously stored experience. Another finding concerns hypnotic control over the "splitting of the mind." The facts of this last phenomenon must be placed at our disposal.

Dissociation in the Trance State

More than half a century ago Pierre Janet and Morton Prince explored the hypothesis that under hypnosis the splitting of mind, or dissociated personality, is possible. Janet, finding hypnotized patients re-living episodes experienced in earlier normal states, subjected the hypothesis to objective test. To one of his patients, Lucie, he gave the post-hypnotic suggestion that upon awakening from the trance and while otherwise behaving normally, she was to write a letter to a friend. After waking, and while Lucie was carrying on a conversation, her hand automatically wrote the following letter:

MADAM,
I shall not be able to come Sunday as I had intended. I pray you will forgive me. It would give me great pleasure to come to you but I cannot accept for that day.

Your friend,
Lucie

P.S. Best of regards to the children, please.[32]

Later, shown this letter, Lucie disclaimed all knowledge of writing it. In another experiment Janet gave Lucie the post-hypnotic suggestion: "You are going to multiply by writing 739 by 42." When she awoke she recounted the details of her day's work to Janet, but meantime and without interruption of the conversation, her hand did the computation correctly.

Shortly after Janet's study was published, Morton Prince (1909) also published experimental studies of dissociation, a theory of which he had originally been skeptical. Using a more complicated computational experiment than Janet, he concluded that his "experiments to determine co-conscious ideation" established dissociation as a fact.

In 1925, C. T. Burnett published an even more carefully controlled body of experiments on dissociation.[33] The data are so important that they merit a rather full description. Under trance the subject is told that, after waking, he will multiply a pair of numbers automatically, that is, without his knowledge. One number is to be the "number of taps the experimenter makes while the subject is looking at a book," the other is to be the number on the right corner of the page at which the subject is looking when the experimenter asks for the book. On waking, the subject reports amnesia of the trance events, is given a copy of *Aesop's Fables* and ordered to locate a page with three fables. As he turns the pages the experimenter taps three times, takes the book at the moment when the subject is looking at page 41 and directs the latter to recite some well-known verses. As he does so his hand, hidden by a screen, is writing the sum 123 (that is, 3 x 41). Although he insists that he is awake and that the hand is doing nothing, it actually proves to be anesthetic. The subject is re-hypnotized and recalls both his multiplications and automatic writing. Burnett repeated the experiment successfully thirteen times and concluded that his study had produced evidence of a co-conscious activity which he calls "splitting of the mind."

This is the contention of those who accept the concept of dissociation. Hull, the arch-conservative defender of conditioned-response theory, grants that there is "some evidence" for dissociation under trance. Weitzenhoffer, the current outstanding authority, accepts it as fact. So do Cole and Watkins, and the latter has put the principle to work in what is known as the "hand technique." This consists of dissociating the hand from the rest of the person, telling the hypnotized hand that it is not now responsible to any censor, that it can answer questions, that it doesn't need to resist the truth. Watkins presents concrete evidence of writing and drawing done at various ages. He reports that "the hand can be regressed to any desired age level," and will often produce "significant material . . . which cannot be brought out by direct interviewing under trance."[34]

Hull's appraisal of the investigations of Janet, Prince, and Burnett raises two questions. The first is: Can an intellectual process be brought about by hypnosis while the subject remains "in professed ignorance of its existence while it is going on"? His answer is "Yes." "Burnett's work," he says, "is particularly convincing. . . . There seems little room for disagreement . . . that post-hypnotic suggestion rather easily brings about a condition in which a person will perform fairly complex intellectual tasks and yet will deny all knowledge of the process at the very moment that it is taking place."[35]

The second question, he says, is still controversial: "Is the dissociation . . . of such a nature that two distinct intellectual processes may go on quite or nearly independently of each other?"[36] His answer is that "experiments cited above are not nearly so conclusive." With the aid of laboratory assistants, Hull carried out some experiments (although on very few subjects) on the controversial question. He grants some significance to "the clever experimental approach of Barry, Mackinnon, and Murray [which] so far as it goes . . . possibly points in the direction of dissociation as a functional independence."[37]

In Hull's handling of the problem we have the expression of an avowed mechanist of the Pavlovian conditioned-response point of view. Lawrence Cole, from a more organic approach, handling the same data, draws exactly the opposite conclusions. "We are two minds not one. Or perhaps we should try to conceive of a hierarchy of systems, of levels beneath levels, with a top level where full awareness and capacity to verbalize give us an illusion of unity, integrity, and rationality that the study of hypnotic phenomena belies."[38]

DRUGS AND THE CREATIVE MIND

William James comments on the use of drugs in reviewing the ways in which men have sought to achieve the "mystical state." "Drunkenness," he says, "is the great exciter of the *Yes* function in man. . . . The sway of alcohol over mankind is unquestionably due to its power to stimulate the mystical faculties of human nature, usually crushed to earth by the cold facts and dry criticisms of the sober hour. Sobriety diminishes, discriminates, and says no; drunkenness expands, unites, and says yes."[39]

From the earliest writings of man we find this universal interest; in the oldest Vedic rituals, for example, reference is made to the widespread use of the soma juice, a fermented drink from the soma plant. Lin Yutang quotes the early Hindu poet, saying: "The case for intoxication with God is therefore established. And readers may well regard these [few verses of] Hymns as the first cocktail sips of the Hindu religious philosophy":

The heavens and earth themselves have not grown equal to half of me: Have I not drunk of soma-juice?

I in my grandeur have surpassed the heavens and all this spacious earth: Have I not drunk of soma-juice?

. . . .

One of my flanks is in the sky: I let the other trail below: Have I not drunk of soma-juice?[40]

Aldous Huxley, quoting Philippe de Félice, speaks of the universal use of drugs for religious and other purposes "in every region of the earth, among primitives no less than among those who have reached a high pitch of civilization."[41] "The urge to transcend self-conscious selfhood is, as I have said, a principal appetite of the soul."[42] James, who experimented with ether, diluted nitrus oxide, and other drugs concurred: "The drunken consciousness is one bit of the mystic consciousness."[43]

The special "transcending" drug of the American Indian was mescalin, a product of "peyote," a cactus root. Peyote was a favorite "chewing root" of the Indians north and south of the Rio Grande before Cortez's time; one of his company wrote that "they venerate [it] as though it were a deity."[44] The use of it in social and religious ceremonies must have continued among many tribes of North America, for extended records are found of its recent use among the Menomini, the Kiowas, and the Potawatomi in the late 1800s.

In the meantime, Western scientists rediscovered it. Kraepelin, German psychologist, started work in 1883 on connecting the effects of mescalin with schizophrenia. Three years later (1886), Ludwig Lewin, German botanist and pharmacologist, discovered the plant from which it was manufactured—*Anhalonium Lewinii*. By the middle 1890s, Prentiss and Morgan were making systematic studies of the visual hallucinations produced by it, and Jaensch, Havelock Ellis, and Weir Mitchell all were experimenting with its use. Ellis reported in 1897 that its effects on him were "a saturnalia of the specific senses and chiefly an orgy of vision." Mitchell, after taking the drug, saw a succession of what looked like "fragments of stained glass," "delicate floating films of color," "abrupt rush of countless points of white light," landscapes and buildings of Gothic design. "As I gazed, every projecting angle, cornice and even the faces of the stones at their joinings were by degrees covered or hung with clusters of what seemed to be huge precious stones, but uncut stones, some being more like masses of transparent fruit. . . . All seemed to possess an interior light."[45]

In 1952, Dr. J. S. Slotkin of the University of Chicago conducted a careful first-hand study of peyotism among the Menomini Indians, became a member of a "Peyotist Congregation" of the National American Church, and observed their monthly ceremonies. Such rites as the Dancing Rite and the Medicine Dance were initiated by the chewing of the peyote root. The drug was not habit-building. Slotkin's testimony is:

I know many people who have been Peyotists for forty to fifty years. The amount of Peyote they use depends upon the solemnity of the occasion; in general they do not take any more Peyote now than they did years ago. Also, there is sometimes an interval of a month or more between rites, and they go without Peyote during this period without feeling any craving for it. Personally, even after a series of rites occurring on four successive weekends, I neither increased the amount of Peyote consumed nor felt any continued need for it. [He adds that] Peyote has never been legally declared a narcotic, or its use prohibited by the federal government.[46]

The "light-vision" is reported again and again throughout the history of the drugged mind, whether from narcotics, or from "mystic" autosuggestion. Everything is brilliantly illuminated. "The mind's capacity for recognizing fine distinctions of tone and hue is notably heightened."[47]

What is this "visionary world" to which Ellis, Mitchell, Coleridge, and others referred? One of the most recent experimenters with the use of mescalin is Aldous Huxley who (observed by his wife and a friend who is a "scientific sleuth equipped with tape recorder") "one bright May morning (in 1953), swallowed four-tenths of a gram of mescalin . . . and sat down to wait for the results."[48]

The typical mescalin or lysergic-acid experience, [says Huxley], begins with perceptions of colored, moving, living geometrical forms. In time, pure geometry becomes concrete, and the visionary perceives, not patterns, but patterned things, such as carpets, carvings, mosaics. These give place to vast and complicated buildings, in the midst of landscapes, which change continuously, passing from richness to more intensely colored richness, from grandeur to deepening grandeur. Heroic figures, of the kind that Blake called "The Seraphim," may make their appearance, alone or in multitudes. Fabulous animals move across the scene. Everything is novel and amazing. Almost never does the visionary see anything that reminds him of his own past. He is not remembering scenes, persons or objects, and he is not inventing them; he is looking on at a new creation.[49]

Other people might "see" even more; the change in Huxley's world (he is a poor visualizer, he says) was in no sense revolutionary.

Half an hour after swallowing the drug I became aware of a slow dance of golden lights. A little later there were sumptuous red surfaces swelling and expanding from bright nodes of energy that vibrated with a continuously changing, patterned life. At another time the closing of my eyes revealed a complex of gray structures, within which pale bluish spheres kept emerging into intense solidity and, having emerged, would slide noiselessly upwards, out of sight. But at no time were there faces or forms of men or animals. I saw no landscapes, no enormous spaces, no magical growth and metamorphosis of buildings, nothing remotely like a drama or a parable. The other world to which mescalin admitted me was not the world of visions; it existed out there, in what I could see with my eyes open. The great change was in the realm of objective fact. *What had happened to my subjective universe was relatively unimportant.*[50]

What about spatial relationships and time? They had ceased to matter very much. His perceptions were of other things than place and distance and the passage of time. He saw the books on his walls, but what impressed him was "the fact that all of them glowed with living light and that in some the glory was more manifest than in others. In this context position and the three dimensions were beside the point. . . . The mind was primarily concerned, not with measures and locations, but with being and meaning."[51]

It is light and color, their intensity and heightened significance that are of greatest significance in visionary experiences. The sense of intensified significance becomes *"identical with being; for, at the mind's antipodes, objects do not stand for anything but themselves."*[52]

Several of these investigators have commented on the fact that taking mescalin gave them a notion of what it must feel like to be mad; their world seemed like that of the schizophrenic. One man, visiting his mad wife in a hospital to tell her about their children, said: "She listened for a time, then cut him short. How could he bear to waste his time on a couple of absent children, when all that really mattered, here and now, was the unspeakable beauty of the patterns he made, in this brown tweed jacket, every time he moved his arms?"[53]

Renée, in her remarkable *Autobiography of a Schizophrenic Girl,* speaks of the sensations of unreality in the early experiences of approaching madness.

. . . illimitable vastness, brilliant light, and the gloss and smoothness of material things. . . . One day, while I was in the principal's office, suddenly the room became enormous, illuminated by a dreadful electric light that cast false shadows. Everything was exact, smooth, artificial, extremely tense; the chairs and tables seemed models placed here and there. Pupils and teachers were puppets revolving without cause, without objective. I recognized nothing, nobody. It was as though reality, attenuated, had slipped away from all these things and these people. Profound dread over-whelmed me, and as though lost, I looked around desperately for help. I heard people talking but I did not grasp the meaning of the words. The voices were metallic, without warmth or color. From time to time, a word detached itself from the rest. It repeated itself over and over in my head, absurd, as though cut off by a knife. And when one of my schoolmates came toward me, I saw her grow larger and larger, like the haystack.[54]

A COMPARATIVE LOOK AT THE VISIONARY WORLD OF THE MYSTICS

The taking of the drug dredges up from the depths of the nonconscious mind such strange fantasies as these. But it resembles accounts in the *Tibetan Book of the Dead,* the transfigured works of literature and the arts—of Milton's "Darkness Visible," Browning's "Childe Roland," Kafka's *The Trial,* or Blake's, Cezanne's or Van Gogh's paintings. The *Ramayana,* great Hindu book of India's past, describes a land "watered by lakes with golden lotuses. There are rivers by thousands, full of leaves of the color of sapphire and lapis lazuli. . . . The country all around is covered by jewels and precious stones, with gay beds of blue lotus, golden-petalled."[55] And both the Christian and Buddhist Edens are described as having their "Stones of fire." Some primitives, as well as moderns, Europe's Celts, for example, saw worlds of shining glass instead of stones.

Is this ecstatic condition the same ecstasy as that induced by autointoxication, by the rhythmic dance, by the psychics and sensitives of the East? Certainly many mystics perceive preternaturally brilliant colors, and these visions resemble those described by the more reputable "mediums." This visionary world resembles the pictures of the autistic mind described by such seers of the Christian Church as the two Catherines, Meister Eckhart, Jakob Boehme, George Fox, Swedenborg, to name a few of the great modern transcendentalists.

As a transition from drug-produced visions to ecstasy-produced, religious illumination, to be described later, I take a powerful description from a distinguished writer of James's day, J. A. Symonds. James said of it: "With this we make the connection with religious mysticism pure and simple." Symonds had described what James called "a mystical experience with chloroform":

After the choking and stifling had passed away, I seemed at first in a state of utter blankness; then came flashes of intense light, alternating with blackness, and with a keen vision of what was going on in the room around me, but no sensation of touch. I thought that I was near death; when, suddenly, my soul became aware of God, who was manifestly dealing with me, handling me, so to speak, in an intense personal present reality. I felt him streaming in like light upon me. . . . I cannot describe the ecstasy I felt. Then, as I gradually awoke from the influence of the anaesthetics, the old sense of my relation to the world began to return, the new sense of my relation to God began to fade. I suddenly leapt to my ιeet on the chair where I was sitting, and shrieked out, "It is too horrible, it is too horrible, it is too horrible," meaning that I could not bear this disillusionment. . . .

Yet, this question remains, Is it possible that the inner sense of reality which succeeded, when my flesh was dead to impressions from without, to the ordinary sense of physical relations, was not a delusion but an actual experience? Is it possible that I, in that moment, felt what some of the saints have said they always felt, the undemonstrable but irrefragable certainty of God?[56]

SUMMARY

This is the astonishing and enlightening story of the hypnotic trance and of the trance induced by drugs. We have not discovered in these a description of the disciplined creative imagination at work. But it is clear that we have found definite evidence bearing on the nature of the threshold or off-conscious mind—the mind which creative imagination employs—and on some of the ways men have used in releasing its formative powers. Methods of concentrating attention, of relaxing inhibitions against "non-real" images and thoughts, of releasing the powers of autistic mind, all demonstrated in trance states, will find a place in a disciplined use of the creative imagination, whatever additions and differences such a discipline may incorporate.

When the reality principle is relaxed—with its orientation to practical coping with the objects and events of the outer world—forming, shaping motor attitudes, along with the content of stored images and perceptions, remains. The autistic body-mind creates its own imaged situation, a situation shaped to the desires and aversions of the inner world. Hypnosis and drugs relax not alone the reality principle but, in some measure, the propriety principle as well. Images outside the conventionally sanctioned ways of sensing and perceiving are entertained and projected by the poetizing psyche. The power of internal and external censorship over the forming powers of the minded organism is reduced.

Similar processes occur in the operation of creative imagination. Some of the processes are perhaps identical. But we must search further for the complete nature of the ordered creative imagination and for the disciplines by which men have released its ordering powers.

9

The Tao of the East

Void the mind:
Abide in stillness.
Life arises and passes,
Birth, growth and return,
A rhythmic arc from Source to Source.
In the rhythm is quietude,
A tranquil submission . . .
And so, the Great Light!

FRAGMENT FROM AN ANCIENT CHINESE
POEM ASCRIBED TO LAO-TZU, SIXTH
CENTURY B.C.

THREE THOUSAND YEARS AGO Eastern men of wisdom
discovered ways of releasing mind that produce the illuminating
flash. In China this way into the quiet mind was known as Tao, in
India as Yoga, in Japan as Zen. My study shows that these are comparable to the concepts already developed on the unconscious-con-
scious continuum. The threshold mind now appears with Eastern
labels: from the Chinese—the "creative mind of Te," "spontaneous natural functioning"; from the Indian—"the interval of suspense," "creative climax," "poised one-pointed concentration";
from the Japanese—"no-mind," "it shoots." To the cultivated Taoist or Yogin, as to the intuitive artist or philosopher of the West,

158

the clear foveal, active mind of consciousness is distinguished from the peripheral, "no-action" mind of the off-conscious. Instead of concentrating on conscious mind, as do the pragmatic problem-solvers, the men of Tao subordinate it. Their endeavor is to create conditions that will favor *letting* things happen, while ours of the West is to create conditions that will *make* things happen.

The Westerner who has not lived in the East and studied one of the forms of its expression under the direction of a Master Teacher[1] can scarcely grasp the "great meaning" of Tao. It is ineffable; it must be experienced to be known. It is also noetic, for it combines both feeling and thought. Shrouded in impenetrable shadows for two thousand years, *all* attempts to describe it or to translate its native literature into Western languages have resulted in such baffling paradoxes as: the utility of emptiness; knowing by voiding the mind; action through inaction; being purposeless on purpose. For example, in the Tao Teh Ching, Lao-tzu says:

> The Way of Tao is this:
> It strives not, but conquers;
> It speaks not, but all is made clear:
> It summons not, but its house is crowded;
> It contrives not, but the design is perfect.

And in another verse:

> Yield and you need not break:
> Bent you can straighten,
> Emptied you can hold,
> Torn you can mend.
> And as want can reward you,
> So wealth can bewilder you.

The texts of the great Chinese classics seem to the technologically-minded Westerner utterly detached from the space-time world. We shall be well advised to confess, as we undertake to examine them, that we are ill equipped to understand such detachment, or to appreciate the intuitive insight it brings about. But, as C. G. Jung has reminded us, the East can teach us a deeper awareness of life and hence of understanding because their wise men have experienced and taught it. We of the West tend to shun such detachment, Jung says, as "mere shadowy sentiment culled from religious terminology," disposing of it as so-called wisdom and pushing it into the obscurity of faith and superstition. I agree emphatically with his judgment of Tao. "It does not consist of sentimental, exaggeratedly mystical, intuitions bordering on the pathological and emanating from ascetic recluses and cranks; the wisdom of the East is based on practical knowledge coming from the flower of Chinese intelligence, which we have not the slightest justification for undervaluing."[2]

ONE GREAT DOCTRINE THROUGHOUT THE EAST

As the East's books of wisdom[3] were searched for evidence of ways-in to the transliminal state, I found the cue, with mounting excitement, not in several doctrines, but in one all-pervasive way of release. Its universality seems indeed to have been grasped by those Taoists of China who referred to it as the Great Meaning and the Zen masters of Japan who called it the Great Doctrine. The ultimate purposes and goals are somewhat different in the three regions, but irrespective of diversity in schools and sects and labels, the psychological heart of the "way of release" is basically the same throughout the Far East. For reasons which will be clear later, I shall refer to it most often as Tao, and because it seems to me to be congruous with the intuitive way of sensitive Western creative men, I apply it to both East and West.

Independently in widely separated regions and persistently over three thousand years, perceptive men have confirmed one another in the discovery of the intuitive way of knowing. In China it has developed through Taoism, from 1500 B.C. up to the present time; in India through the makers of the Vedas and the Buddhists, from 1500 B.C. until today; in Japan through Zen Buddhism as expressed in the practical arts and crafts, since the twelfth century A.D. In two of these regions, India and China, the ancient massive movements occurred concurrently. While oral beginnings of the teachings and the techniques are unknown, they are believed to have originated in each region earlier than 1000 B.C., and to have been passed down in the form of epic songs from generation to generation. In each of these centers of population, separated by vast distances and enormous mountain systems, several geniuses of intuition emerged at the same moment. I name only the earlier two —in China: Lao-tzu, c. 604–520 B.C.; in India: Buddha, 563–483 B.C.

China and India produced the two longest-lived and most continuous civilizations of mankind. Today their combined populations, still continuous with the earlier ones, total more than a billion human beings; with their cultural affiliations in Ceylon, Burma, Indonesia, and Japan, they constitute over half the world's population. They are the East. It is their wise men who practiced the intuitive way in the largest numbers and over the longest periods of time, and found the path to the very verge of the unconscious and hence to the transliminal antechamber of the mind. The literature of The Great Doctrine of the East stretches, therefore, from the Tao Teh Ching, the I Ching and the Vedic writings to the recent interpretations of modern Taoism and the Zen masters in Japan.

THE NATURAL, CONTEMPLATIVE WAY IN CHINA

As in the case of the Buddhists and their Buddha, so with the Chinese Taoists, one personality, one name, Lao-tzu, is revered and several great books, most important of all the Tao Teh Ching and the I Ching,[4] are treasured by the scholars. Whether there actually was a flesh-and-blood Chinese named Lao-tzu is unknown. The generally accepted belief is that a man of deep wisdom, later referred to as Lao-tzu, did emerge in the sixth century B.C. (c. 604–520 B.C.), but it is thought that the words ascribed to him were the distilled wisdom of generations of contemplative men who observed and speculated upon human life and thought. It seems fairly certain that this wisdom was not written down until two or three hundred years after his death. It is supposed to have been recorded in the second century by Chuang-tzu. In any event, eighty-one remarkable verses have come out of the long process.[5] They constitute the Tao Teh Ching, one of the world's great books.

In the Tao Teh Ching and the I Ching (from which Taoism is believed to have sprung) we have uncovered one of the world's finest sources for the study of the intuitive way. Reading the beautifully measured verses, one misses any note of persuasive fire or burning zeal. One gets from them a feeling of detachment, of profound insight into the ways of men, lessons of humility, quietude, and calm. The "natural way" rings out all through the verses: "leave the people free to flow with nature"; "man's necessity is to conform with the rhythm of life." One reads of the "effortless order of the heavens and the earth." One is told to keep to nature's original simplicity and so attain wisdom.

> How can a man's life keep to its course
> If he will not let it flow:
> Those who flow as life flows, know
> They need no other force . . .
>
> Nature does not have to insist,
> Can blow for only half a morning.
> Rain for only half a day.
> And what are these winds and these rains but natural?
>
> If nature does not have to insist,
> Why should man?

Tao, then, is the "natural way" of human response, not some artificial means conjured up by the politicians to conventionalize and regulate the affairs of men. It is neither a religion nor a code of morals. In our Western sense of the term, Chinese civilization never developed a religion. It did, under the influence of the Confucianists, develop a moral code. But the Tao never was, nor is it today, a "religion" or a code of "ethical behavior," as men of the West interpret these. Tao is, rather, a way of liberating the human mind so that it can act naturally, as it would if it were released from censorship and control.

The Chinese intelligentsia are said, in fact, to have two "philosophical traditions": Confucianism and Taoism. Many stories have been told of imaginary encounters between Lao-tzu and Confucius, the spokesmen of the two traditions. Some of these are said to have been made up by Chuang-tzu as he committed Taoism to written form in the second century B.C. One of these, which I quote from Sheldon Cheney, may have no support in historical fact; it does, however, illustrate the differences we are trying to make clear between the natural and the conventional ways. It is said that Lao-tzu, the Taoist seer, and Confucius, the social reformer, met at a time when Lao-tzu was an old man and Confucius a young one.

The young man, it is said, spoke of "good manners and noble actions . . . etiquette and a just code of law." No one knows exactly what they talked about, but Cheney guesses that Lao-tzu may have talked of his "favourite doctrine of the *Tao* . . . of the natural as against the artificial man, and his necessity to conform with the rhythm of life; of action without assertion, and of non-interference . . . and of the natural honesty and compassion of people not educated to shrewdness and righteousness and morality."[6]

Perhaps Confucius may have said, "They advocate Charity and Righteousness"; to which Lao-tzu is supposed to have replied:

Do Charity and Righteousness constitute the being of man? . . . Take note of the heavens and the earth, how they move in effortless order, of the sun and moon that unfailingly return with their brightness, and of the stars that preserve their courses without exertion. There are, too, the birds and beasts, which need not be told to flock with their kind; and the trees grow naturally upward. Conform to this natural rhythm, follow this Way, and you will attain wisdom. . . . Stop going about as if you were beating a drum. . . .

Lao-tzu went on to caution Confucius about introducing confusion and disorder by his moral meddling. In effect he said (as indeed he shaped the thought for another) : "Take care, my young reformer, not to interfere with the natural goodness of the heart of man. . . . In repose it is profoundly still; it is capable, nevertheless, of every freedom, of every orderly movement. . . . Do not wake men out of their natural purity, avoid excess of arguing, trust to quiet conformance with Order."[7]

THE GREAT DOCTRINE IN JAPAN

During the ancient period, each of the three regions of the East found its own special way into the intuitive mind. In India it was the way developed by sensitive Hindus and Buddhists called "Yoga." From India, Buddhism and the technique of Yoga crossed the Himalayas into China in the second century of our era, when Christianity was still young. There it fused with the best of Taoism as that had developed out of Lao-tzu and other early masters and was written down by Chuang-tzu. A thousand years later it crossed the sea to Japan and appeared as the Great Doctrine called Zen. Although Zen was 1,700 years in developing, the clearest form in which the Great Doctrine can be studied today by Westerners is in the practical arts and crafts of Japan. Its influence finally became so widespread that it affected the entire range of Japanese culture. It created subtle new ceremonies governing family life, such as the tea ceremony and the design of houses and gardens. It molded the educational program of the samurai, the warrior class, and the practical arts of archery and swordsmanship. It created the ritual and techniques in ink painting and the graphic arts and a basic philosophy of the No-theatre, the dance, and the movement arts.

In developing these practical and fine arts, the Japanese practitioners of Zen developed a rigorous educational program of individual instruction that seems in some respects the exact opposite of our modern Western education. Its aphorisms and educational directives all point to the same thing—how to bring about the quiet mind by relaxing the individual. Practical suggestions of method emerge: preparatory ceremonial ritual through which is achieved the physical, mental, and spiritual loosening of the person; never-ending practice for perfect mastery of craft technique; reduction of words and thinking to the barest minimum while emphasizing total feeling through organic body gesture.

I have found greatest help in understanding the method of Zen from the report of the German philosopher, Eugen Herrigel.[8] Herrigel, while serving as professor of philosophy at Tohoku University in Sendai after World War II, studied the Great Doctrine of Zen through a grueling six-year course in archery.

Preparatory Ritual in the Practical Arts

At each lesson, Herrigel says, the preparatory role of ritual is of supreme importance in putting the pupil "simultaneously in the right frame of mind for creating. The meditative repose in which he performs [these rituals] gives him that vital loosening and equability of all his powers, that collectedness and presence of mind, without which no right work can be done."[9] I shall give brief examples of such ceremonial approaches, taking first one from ink painting.

A painter seats himself before his pupils. He examines his brush and slowly makes it ready for use, carefully rubs ink, straightens the long strip of paper that lies before him on the mat, and finally, after lapsing for a while into profound concentration, in which he sits like one inviolable, he produces with rapid, absolute sure strokes a picture which, capable of no further correction and needing none, serves the class as a model.[10]

In flower arrangement the ceremonial technique is the same:

A flower master begins the lesson by cautiously untying the bast which holds together the flowers and sprays of blossom, and laying it to one side, carefully rolled up. Then he inspects the sprays one by one, picks out the best after repeated examination, cautiously bends them into the form which exactly corresponds with the role they are to play, and finally places them together in an exquisite vase. The completed picture looks just as if the Master had guessed what Nature had glimpsed in dark dreams.[11]

Herrigel generalizes from his years of study that these ceremonies

tell the pupil that the right frame of mind for the artist is only reached when the preparing and the creating, the technical and the artistic, the material and the spiritual, the project and the object, flow together without a break. . . . He is now required to exercise perfect control over the various ways of concentration and self-effacement. . . . [After several years he said] Day by day I found myself slipping more easily into the ceremony which sets forth the "Great Doctrine" of archery, carrying it out effortlessly or, to be more precise, feeling myself being carried through it as in a dream.[12]

Mastery of Craftsmanship by Unending Practice

The second great principle in the Zen arts is absolute mastery by drill and more drill. "Practice, repetition, and repetition of the repeated with ever increasing intensity are its distinctive features for long stretches of the way."[13] It substitutes the quiet mind for the active mind. It requires an exact copy of the teacher's model, repeated until the duplicate is perfect. It denies the role of "thinking." It asks the subject to give up all conscious purpose. Its aim is to produce perfect mastery over body and mind, and thus perfect mastery over tools, implements, instruments and methods.

Far from wishing to waken the artist in the pupil prematurely, the teacher considers it his first task to make him a skilled artisan with sovereign control of his craft. The pupil follows out this intention with untiring industry. As though he had no higher aspirations he bows under his burden with a kind of obtuse devotion, only to discover in the course of years that forms which he perfectly masters no longer oppress but liberate. He grows daily more capable of following any inspiration without technical effort, and also of letting inspiration come to him through meticulous observation. The hand that guides the brush has already caught and executed what floated before the mind at the same moment the mind began to form it, and in the end the pupil no longer knows which of the two—mind or hand—was responsible for the work.[14]

Relaxation of the Person: "Don't Think—Feel!"

The ritual of preparation in archery goes on through interminable years of practice in relaxation. There is first a long period devoted to the sheer physical loosening in the handling of the bow, then in the "loosening of the arrow" so that "it shoots itself," and finally "self-detached immersion." "All that I had learned and achieved so far," said Herrigel, "only became intelligible to me from this point of view: relaxed drawing of the bow, relaxed holding at the point of highest tension, relaxed loosing of the shot, relaxed cushioning of the recoil."[15] His account details at great length the meticulous care—through weeks of practice—with which Master Awa taught him the special construction of the bow, its peculiar elasticity, its "noble form" when strung and held back ("the bow encloses the 'All' in itself"), the "nocking" of the arrow on the string, and in watching the Master's demonstration of the process which "looked not only very beautiful, but quite effortless." So Herrigel repeated the act, day after day for months on end; but "despite the most diligent practice [it] refused to become 'spiritual.' "[16] Always the Master watched, almost without spoken directions, letting him struggle with the task, only calling out occasionally, "Relax! Relax!"

Then finally he offered the next teaching suggestion, and it was a direct confirmation of Buddhist Yoga and, as we have seen, of Western hypnotism—correct breathing.

"You cannot do it," explained the Master, "because you do not breathe right. Press your breath down gently after breathing in, so that the abdominal wall is tightly stretched, and hold it there for a while. Then breathe out as slowly and evenly as possible, and, after a short pause, draw a quick breath of air again—out and in continually, in a rhythm that will gradually settle itself. If it is done properly, you will feel the shooting becoming easier every day. For through this breathing you will not only discover the source of all spiritual strength but will also cause this source to flow more abundantly, and to pour more easily through your limbs the more relaxed you are."[17]

When Herrigel protested that he was making an effort to keep relaxed, the Master said:

"That's just the trouble, you make an effort to think about it. Concentrate entirely on your breathing, as if you had nothing else to do!" It took me a considerable time before I succeeded in doing what the Master wanted. But—I succeeded. I learned to lose myself so effortlessly in the breathing that I sometimes had the feeling that I myself was not breathing but—strange as this may sound—being breathed. . . . Now and then . . . I managed to draw the bow and keep it drawn until the moment of release while remaining completely relaxed in body, without my being able to say how it happened . . . at last I understood what was meant by drawing the bow "spiritually."[18]

After a year of ceaseless practice and repeated failure, there came a moment when the Master said to Herrigel that he was "drawing the bow spiritually." But drawing the bow spiritually was, as Master Awa said, "only a preparation for loosing the shot . . . spiritually," and that took several more years of practice! The key to the beauty of the act was the effortless, smooth loosing of the shot.

Finally came the key to mental relaxation—letting oneself feel, not think! Whenever his concentration lagged, he "thought" of what he should do—and failed. Daisetz Suzuki, the chief authority on Zen in America, explains the basic Zen paradox, hence the key to the Great Doctrine: "Man is a thinking reed but his great works are done when he is not calculating and thinking. 'Childlikeness' has to be restored with long years of training in the art of self-forgetfulness. When this is attained, man thinks yet he does not think."[19] "Don't think of what you have to do," said Awa. "The shot will only go smoothly when it takes the archer himself by surprise. It must be as if the bowstring suddenly cut through the thumb that held it. You mustn't open the right hand on purpose."[20] And then it was that the Master told Herrigel that "the right art . . . is purposeless," and the latter finally saw that he "must become purposeless—on purpose!"[21] Thus the process of loosening physically and mentally went on and on, and spiritual posture improved, but the final "spiritual shooting" failed to come. " 'You worry yourself unnecessarily,' the Master comforted me. 'Put the thought of hitting right out of your mind! You can be a Master even if every shot does not hit.' 'How can the shot be loosed if I do not do it?' 'It shoots,' he replied. 'It waits at the highest tension.' "[22] Month after month they sought the moment of "highest tension," when "it" would shoot.

" 'And who or what is this It?' "

" 'Once you have understood that, you will have no further need of me.' "[23]

"One day [much later], after a shot, the Master made a deep bow and stopped the lesson. 'Just then It shot,' he cried, as I stared at him bewildered. . . . Only after a considerable time did more right shots occasionally come off, which the Master signalized by a deep bow. How it happened that they loosed themselves without my doing anything, how it came about that my tightly closed right hand suddenly flew back wide open, I could not explain then and I cannot explain today."[24]

During the many months that followed, Herrigel said he experienced the hardest schooling of his life. It was not always easy for him to accept the disciplined drill, but slowly he saw that it was destroying the "last traces of any preoccupation with myself and the fluctuations of my mood. 'Do you now understand,' the Master asked me one day after a particularly good shot, 'what I mean by *It* shoots, *It* hits?' "[25]

Then, at long last, the Master Teacher was willing to explain the theory of the Great Doctrine. "He dwelt longest," says Herrigel, "on the 'artless art' which must be the goal of archery if it is to reach perfection." When it is mastered, the archer "is Master . . . of the artless art. Indeed, he is the artless art itself and thus Master and No-Master in one. At this point archery, considered as the unmoved movement, the undanced dance, passes over into Zen."[26]

NO-MIND: THE ART OF TAO

The technique of Tao produces a high form of concentration of attention and relaxation; Zen archery illustrates it beautifully. The ceremonial ritual puts the individual in the "frame of mind for creating," says Herrigel, the painter lapses into "profound concentration," becomes vitally loosened and develops optimum "collectedness and presence of mind." After years of its rebuilding, Herrigel found himself carrying out the Great Doctrine effortlessly, feeling himself "being carried through it as in a dream." This is precisely the off-guard composing that I reported earlier.

The secret of the personal rebuilding is subtle. If the ordeal of the preparatory ritual has been endured, the perfect shot or, in our terms, the "flash of illumination" is achieved.[27] How? By letting one's conscious mind alone! That is, by non-action, called *wu-wei* by the Taoists. *Wu* means not or non. *Wei* means action, making, doing, striving, straining, or busyness. *Wu-wei* is non-strivingness, but it is more than that; its resultant is Tao, the way of release.

This helps to clear up the apparent paradox of *wu-hsin,* literally, "no-mind." I depend on Watts here for the clearest interpretation I have found of what Taoism and Chinese thought mean by *hsin.* Apparently the original ideograph pictured the heart or perhaps some other internal organ. But, says Watts, to translate *hsin* as "heart" seems too emotional, while "mind" is too intellectual.

Sometimes it is used for an obstruction to be removed, as in *wu-hsin,* "no-mind." But sometimes it is used in a way that is almost synonymous with the Tao. . . . This apparent contradiction is resolved in the principle that "the true mind is no mind," which is to say that the *hsin* is true, is working properly, when it works as if it were not present. . . .

All in all, it would seem that *hsin* means the totality of our psychic functioning, and, more specifically, the center of that functioning, which is associated with the central point of the upper body.[28]

Watts tells us that "when a man has learned to let his mind alone so that it functions in the integrated and spontaneous way that is natural to it, he begins to show the special kind of 'virtue' or 'power' called *te*." Watts, summing up, defines *te* as: "The unthinkable ingenuity and creative power of man's spontaneous and natural functioning—a power which is blocked when one tries to master it in terms of formal methods and techniques."[29] Lao-tzu spoke of *te* in more of his apparent paradoxes:

> Superior *te* is not *te*,
> and thus has *te*.
> Inferior *te* does not let go of *te*,
> and thus is not *te*.
> Superior *te* is non-active [*Wu-Wei*] and aimless.
> Inferior *te* is active and has an aim.[30]

I cannot escape the conclusion that the Taoist's *te* is creative intuition. It is Galileo's *il lume naturale,* Newton's leap of the imagination, Gauss's sudden lightning flash. This is what I call the autonomous forming process of the unconscious; that is, symbolic transformation. *Wu-hsin,* then, is literally "no-mind," meaning unself-consciousness. It is the true no-mind revealed in the off-conscious, the subconscious, hypnoidal part of the continuum. It is a state of the organism as a whole in which mind flows smoothly, naturally, of itself—as in the hypnagogic state or in the dream. "The Taoist is one who has learned to let the legs walk by themselves."

Being in the Tao, then, is equivalent to the Westerner's being in the quiet mind, relaxed, off-guard. The Tao is the way of releasing the tense, inhibiting conscious mind. The technique developed by Zen master-artisans is centered on such liberation. "Let go, feel, don't think," it says. As Lao-tzu said,

> If nature does not have to insist,
> Why should man?

If a man learns to relax completely, he does not open his hand, it will open of itself at the point of highest tension, and the arrow will be loosed "spiritually." The Taoist's description of the process matches those of other cultures; for example, the great principle of "spontaneity." "It shoots" is the principle of the transliminal mind's "flash of illumination."

"Relax, don't think, feel" is the controlling direction through years of interminable practice. You will never get in the Tao by trying. This is also the admonition of the intuitives of the West. Don't analyze your stroke, they say, feel it, let the movement-centered body do it. Let go, as Poincaré did, and—if the conscious preparation has been masterful—the solution to your problem flashes through. These acts are felt, intuitive, unthought, they are spontaneous *tzu-jan*, "self-so." How are they brought about? By the will? No, they are projected not by conscious design but from the nonconscious mind.

Proper breathing is a key to relaxation, both with the Tao and with the techniques of the West. It is the great goal, the source of "spiritual strength." "Concentrate entirely on your breathing," said Awa. Herrigel reports that eventually he lost himself so effortlessly in the breathing that he was "being breathed." The off-conscious phenomenon again. Then, and then only, he "drew the bow spiritually," that is, "it shot." "It"—the off-conscious organism.

These wise men of the Far East had an elaborate introspective psychology; they generalized constantly about *"ching,"* which means mental power; their classic book is I Ching, their constant phrase is no-mind. By this is meant the peripheral mind on the fringe of the unconscious; "no-mind" is nonconscious mind. Such complete inhibition of conscious mind is brought about that the unconscious can do its work. So "it shoots," the arrow is unloosed, the tennis ball is returned from the most difficult position. The Western examples of physical activities match the commonplace examples of Zen: Pancho Gonzales' perfect cannon-ball serve, Babe Ruth's sixty home runs in a baseball season, the dance artistry of Manolete, master toreador of the world. The perfection of the dance in Martha Graham and José Limon, and Vladimir Horo-witz' piano playing are distinguished as performing arts of the West.

We can hear Lao-tzu saying that this is "the Tao's great principle of spontaneity." Thus, through Taoism is developed the ability to respond to the world spontaneously, as does a child. This natural way is one we know best because we have grown up reacting that way throughout our younger days. As Suzuki put it, childlikeness is restored by years of rigorous training in self-forgetfulness: "When this is attained man thinks, yet he does not think."

Each of the vestibules to the unconscious so far examined provides its own way-in. Tao is no exception. Its way is to release the tensions in the organism and so free the unconscious mind. "Off-conscious mind" is merely a label for an organism that is so loosened that "it" can act. "It" can have a flash of insight, an idea. It can think creatively, can discover. The hallucinatory images of the hypnoidal state can appear to conscious mind as ordered symbols.

The technique of putting oneself "in the Tao" works wonders by developing such masterful control over the bodily processes that attention is directed entirely away from consciousness. The tense conscious mind gets out of the way and the off-conscious organism functions effectively.

To the technique of concentration and relaxation by Japan's master artists is added "sovereign control" over the craft: mastery through practice. The purpose is such perfect control that the total organism is liberated. This is motor-centered education in action. The goal is release through bodily inhibition of all extraneous factors. This is a more perfected form of the Western intuitive way of putting things out of mind, dropping the problem down into unconscious cerebration. Then the act of knowing, the autonomous forming process of the unconscious, can occur—"spiritually," as Zen would put it.

If, even with these explanations, Lao-tzu's paradoxical aphorisms about the art of letting things happen are not clear, be consoled by Chuang-tzu's words: "Were language adequate, it would take but a day fully to set forth Tao. Not being adequate, it takes that time to explain material existences. Tao is something beyond material existences. It cannot be conveyed either by words or by silence."[31] It cannot be explained, it can only be indicated, is the invariable reply to the question: What is the Tao? Hear how Lao-tzu rated men by their reaction to the Tao.

> When the superior man hears of the Tao
> he does his best to practice it.

When the middling man hears of the Tao
he sometimes keeps it and sometimes loses it.

When the inferior man hears of Tao,
he will laugh aloud at it.
If he did not laugh, it would not be the Tao.

Yet the "no-mind" could be no more adequately described in words than in Lao-tzu's political admonitions. In government, he says, true action takes place through a form of inaction.

A leader is best
When people barely know that he exists.
Not so good when people obey and acclaim him.
Worst when they despise him.

Fail to honor people,
They fail to honor you;
But of a good leader, who talks little
When his work is done, his aim is fulfilled,
They will all say, "We did it ourselves."

Lao-tzu sums up the natural way in politics.

You should rule a great country
As you fry small fish—
With the least turning.

"What then did these people do in order to achieve the progress that freed them?" asks Jung. He answers: "They did nothing," and explains: "The key is this: we must be able to let things happen in the psyche."[32] And he, too, points to the confirmation of the manifold paradoxes of the Tao Teh Ching, the I Ching, and the Golden Flower: the utility of emptiness, knowing by voiding the mind, action through inaction, doing by being, "actionless activity," being "purposeless on purpose."

THE WAY OF YOGA

The search for other primordial examples of the Great Doctrine leads one to the way of Dyhana Buddhism called Yoga. Of the several regional records perhaps the most enlightened source to this version of the intuitive way is the large body of Hindu-Buddhistic philosophical and religious writing. One can delve deeply into it through four selections: the Rig-Veda, the Upanishads, the Bhagavad Gita and the Dhamapada of Buddha. In contrast to the Tao Teh Ching and I Ching, these great Vedantic and Hindu writings are basically religious books. Dr. Lin Yutang, one of our best contemporary Chinese students of oriental wisdom, said of the contrast. "Hindu philosophy and the knowledge of God are inseparable as Chinese philosophy and the questions of human conduct are inseparable."[33]

Nevertheless, we are concerned with these because they give us a second view of the Eastern world's conception of both the unconscious and the super-conscious, contemplative mind.

This great literature also gives us access to a historic system for achieving concentration and relaxation and finally the flash of insight. Its name is "Yoga" and those who practice it are "Yogis" or "Yogins." The word means literally, the "yoke"—the yoking of the personal soul or self of the individual to the Brahman, the cosmic force of the universe. The Yogis are concerned with psychology, with mind, as much as with religion and morality. Their goal is to achieve meditative and contemplative states of consciousness; in Yoga, the ancient wise men, molders of the secret teachings, discovered early the intuitive way into the center of creative energy.

Yoga, as we know it today, is the product of more than two thousand years of distilled thought and feeling, but its present form can be traced back to the writings of Patanjali (the Yoga Sutras) in the second century B.C. Little is known about him beyond the fact that he served as the man who recorded the basic ideas and techniques. Dr. Kovoor Behanan,[34] a contemporary Indian student of Western philosophy and psychology, himself trained in Yoga, said: "The cornerstone of the system is a book called Yoga Sutras (*Sutras* means aphorisms) attributed to Patanjali. He did not claim to propound a system of philosophy, but set down valuable instruction to induce certain psychological states."[35] Nevertheless, the Yoga Sutras have become the accepted systematic statement of the discipline of Yoga. This discipline combines a program of physical diet, posture, mastery of the involuntary muscles and breathing, with a program of intellectual concentration, mental and moral discipline. A manual of personal discipline, its aim is to cultivate physical poise, natural insight, and emotional stability.

Sixty years ago William James was one of a considerable group of enlightened Westerners who were greatly intrigued by the psychological conceptions of Yoga. This interest had nothing to do with the hocus-pocus of Westernized forms of occultism, whether theosophy, New Thought, anthroposophy, Hindu rope tricks, illusions of levitation, mediumistic ectoplasms, or table rappings and liftings. Lin and Behanan concur; the theosophists and "such experts in 'psychism,' " says the latter, "insist on treating the fictions of their imagination as realities, mixing philosophy and science, abdicating reason and fact to wishful thinking. Our experience and long conversations with yogins have convinced us that they have a greater appreciation of logic and reason than the mystery-seekers and spirit-chasers."[36]

In sharp contrast to the occultists, said James, the designers of Yoga were trying to create a scientific system.

All the different steps in yoga are intended to bring us scientifically to the superconscious state of Samâdhi. . . . Just as unconscious work is beneath consciousness, so there is another work which is above consciousness, and which, also, is not accompanied with the feeling of egoism. . . . There is no feeling of *I*, and yet the mind works, desireless, free from restlessness, objectless, bodiless. Then the Truth shines in its full effulgence, and we know ourselves—for Samâdhi lies potential in us all—for what we truly are, free, immortal, omnipotent, loosed from the finite, and its contrasts of good and evil altogether, and identical with the Atman or Universal Soul.[37]

PHILOSOPHIC PRINCIPLES UNDERLYING YOGA

Patanjali recognized that it would be necessary to build his program of physical and mental exercise on a theory of matter and mind, and so borrowed from the earlier Hindu philosophic system, *Samkhya*. Behanan interprets this combined doctrine.

Samkhya-yoga offers a naturalistic interpretation of material phenomena, including in this category mind which, in its various modifications or operations, appears as intellect, will and feeling. The concept of evolution, common to all systems of Indian philosophy, enabled samkhya-yoga to regard the world as the result of a gradual process of differentiation. . . . What strikes us in samkhya-yoga as the most characteristic feature of experience is the element of change; that which was is no more, that which is will no more be. Everything is in a process of becoming. . . .

This is equally true of the mental world which can be considered a regular stream of images flowing continuously from moment to moment. . . . In both the physical and mental worlds, samkhya-yoga found this common feature or element of change and called it *rajas* (energy). Without rajas there cannot be any change or motion, and since the universe of experience, both internal and external, is forever in a perpetual state of flux, rajas or energy is its irreducible substratum.[38]

He adds a second element from the world of experience, which is called *sattva* (intelligence or mind-stuff), and a third element, *tamas* (inertia). These are called *gunas,* interpreted variously as quality, self or soul, and are combined in various proportions to constitute the basis of an evolving universe.

Yoga is important to us, in part, because of its belief in new levels to which the evolutionary concept can be applied. *Samkhya* philosophy accepts the concept of the unending evolution of existence and of stages of consciousness. As Coster, the British psychologist, describes it:

. . . to the Darwinian picture of the evolution of the complex from the simple in terms of physical structure there is added the idea of an evolving consciousness, at first vague and instinctual, but gradually becoming more alert, responsive and specialized, and by its own development compelling the evolution of new and subtler physical vehicles for its expression. The potentialities of this expanding life are illimitable: hence the future of the human race is to all intents unpredictable.[39]

Thus the Yogins of the East add psychological levels to our theory of physical and biological evolution. They conceive of varying and successive realms of existence distributed on a continuum, of which that realm which we call earthly life is a single stage preparatory to others. They assume, as I do, the continuity of consciousness in the continuum of mind. Consciousness, variously called direct knowledge or true liberation, is reserved for the very highest levels of development. Thus, in order to understand Yoga or Taoism or Zen we must be prepared, as Watts suggests, to admit the possibility of some view of the world other than our conventional one—the possibility that knowledge does not come merely from our surface consciousness.

Yoga conceives that both the race of man and individual men evolve through several stages of consciousness.* These are referred to by such psychological names as sensory or physical awareness, emotion, concrete thought, abstract or creative thought (insight), and will and intuition. The East's interpretation of the first three stages of growth agrees fairly closely with that of Western psychology. In the lowest stages either of infancy or of primitive life, behavior consists of little more than the bodily responses of direct observation. In the second stage, early childhood and pre-adolescence, whether in the individual or the race, mental life is dominated by dream and feeling states, called "concrete thought" and "emotion" in the East's interpretation. In the third stage, both peoples and individual adolescent youth reach the level called "intelligence." Most of the members of so-called "advanced" civilizations today can be said to live their lives on one or more of the first three of these stages—the sensory, emotional, and the obvious forms of "concrete thinking."

The fourth and fifth stages are of greatest interest to us, being the creative and contemplative levels. The fourth stage is attained by those few sensitive intuitives who are "naturals" and others who survive the ordeal of Patanjali's advanced Yoga program. Descriptions of this stage, portraying a state which seems to be comparable to the threshold mind of this study, borders perhaps on the creative, linguistically-centered mind, in which our Western logical empiricists are now building their programs of verbal symbolism. There is no question that with Yoga, as with Tao and Zen and Western intuition, absorption in language and "thinking" constitutes the important obstacle. The fifth stage of growth is conceived of as a "super-conscious state," the highest spiritual goal of human development, variously called *kaivalya* or *samâdhi,* in our terms, direct knowledge or liberation. This cannot be explained in words, it can only be indicated.

---

* Geraldine Coster outlines these succinctly in her critical study of *Yoga and Western Psychology.* I draw upon the conceptual labels which she has given the respective stages.

THE YOGA TECHNIQUE OF BODY-MIND LIBERATION

The Indian Yogi developed a rigorous method of physical and mental release somewhat comparable to the Zen technique of preparatory ceremonial ritual, mastery of craftsmanship by unending practice, and relaxation of the person. And the purpose seems to be approximately that of releasing the conscious mind so that the unconscious can bring its creative acts to the threshold.

To carry the novitiates through the first three stages, the Patanjali sutras prescribe a five-fold preliminary training series. The first two exercises deal with practical matters of everyday life: the practice of harmlessness; obedience to the moral law; and obedience to the spiritual law. The third builds posture and poise; the fourth develops control over breathing; and the fifth, called "withdrawal" or "abstraction," raises "consciousness from its ordinary state to that of concentration or meditation." These exercises, although covering a considerable period of time, are preliminary. They are designed to carry the student to the verge of creative concentration, which is the point of chief interest in our study of the flash of insight.

The system, guided by religious goals and concepts, recognizes and prepares for specific distractions or obstacles: ignorance, self-esteem, desire, aversion, and the will to live or attachment to life. For example, the obstacle called ignorance is religious in connotation, not equivalent to our psychological concept of ignorance, meaning lack of knowledge. As Coster says:

The eastern idea of ignorance may be compared with the Christian conception of original sin . . . the individual is regarded as being born into ignorance, as existing in a world of illusion built up by ignorance. The goal of evolution [in Yoga] is the dispelling of ignorance, as the goal of a Christian life is the conquest of sin. When ignorance is completely dispelled, the man attains liberation [that is] freedom from the bondage of reincarnation and compulsory experience.[40]

But our use of the term "liberation" is the Taoists' psychological stage—namely, release from the restricting, warping, conscious mind. Yogins hold to that meaning also but in a broader religious background.

As the novitiate enters the third stage there is an elaborate system of posture development, called Hatha-Yoga, through which the student acquires perfect control over movements and positions of the body comparable to the mastery of Zen artists, probably superior to that of acrobats and athletes of the West. Patanjali insists that postural control is indispensable for deep and uninterrupted meditation; the body must be accustomed "to some one position which is easy and poised."[41] This seems to confirm both the elaborate and prolonged ritual of posture-building in Zen and the emphasis in this study on a motor-centered educational program.

For the fourth stage of the preliminary exercises the student is trained through a systematic course of breathing exercises which seem markedly similar to those employed by Zen artists. According to Lin Yutang: "It begins with a unique and unparalleled exploration in the region of the involuntary muscles and bringing them under the control of the mind."[42]

These four exercises are regarded as preliminary in that they constitute the training program for the conscious mind. They take the individual where he is, in a state of confused thought, and through physical as well as mental and "moral" training, bring him to the verge of what the Chinese call "no-mind," or what I call the hypnoidal, threshold mind. In short, they carry him to the verge of the creative action of the unconscious.

CREATIVE CONCENTRATION IN YOGA

We distinguish, therefore, between preliminary Yoga which "has for its object the breaking up of the automatic and unaware habits of thought and feeling which make up the confused picture of life," and the more mature meditative stages. When the preliminary goal has been achieved "the student of yoga sets about the further mastering of the mind by the study of concentration."[43]

The fifth part of the program, as Lin says, "proceeds to the liberation of the mind from its sense impressions, and the deeper residuents and impedimenta that not only clog but form the very fabric of our subconscious life."[44] The fifth exercise, called by Coster "withdrawal and abstraction," accompanies training in breath control "by efforts to withdraw the consciousness from sense contacts, so that it may attain to a state of pure thought."[45] Its method involves practicing to blot out the ticking of a clock, for example, by refusing to hear it. The purpose is to permit the unconscious "to function apart from sensory phenomena." This is the Western psychologists' concentration of attention by inhibiting extraneous stimuli. Thus the Indian practice also confirms the Chinese and Japanese.

There is a step-by-step graded training program, prescribed by the first twelve sutras of Patanjali's Book III. The mastery of the first three produces *samyāma* or "lucid knowledge." I quote them verbatim.

1. *Concentration is holding the attention fixed upon an object.*
2. *Sustained concentration upon one object is deliberation.*
3. *When all consciousness is lost save that of the shape on which the mind is fixed, this state is contemplation.*

The seventh sutra says: "*Samyāma is the first step in true Yoga, the five preliminary exercises merely leading up to this.*" But, says the eighth, "*samyāma is still not the goal.*" The ninth to twelfth sutras direct the way toward the ultimate objective.

9. *When control of mind is achieved in the face of distraction, then the mind takes on a one-pointed form, which is itself a modification or trend in the mind.*
10. *By habitual practice the point of balance at which such one-pointedness dominates can be sustained at will.*
11. *The mind has two inherent tendencies, to consider many things and to become one-pointed. The quality of sustained one-pointedness leads to samâdhi.*
12. *Then, by further achievement of balance between inertia and activity in the mind itself, a point is finally reached where all mental processes are transcended.*[46]

This is *samâdhi*, the highest imagined condition of consciousness.

Two generations ago, William James gave us a parallel description of the stages through which the Yogin passes in reaching "the illumined state." I paraphrase his long account. First, intense concentration of the mind on one entity, a relaxed condition with all emotional concerns dropped off but with mind in the intellectual sense—judgment, reasoning—still functioning. Second, thinking, reasoning, judging mind drops away, leaving a feeling of satisfied wholeness. Third, the satisfaction departs and indifference, memory, and self-consciousness are perfected. Still more advanced stages of contemplation are described where "there exists absolutely nothing"; where "there are neither ideas nor absence of ideas." Finally another region *samâdhi* is reached which is the end of both idea and perception . . . "not yet Nirvâna, but as close an approach to it as this life affords."[47]

In the light of our mid-century psychological and physiological knowledge we can supply supplemental details. In the beginning the student concentrates on an object or idea, and attempts to control the oscillations of attention that mark the conscious life of most people. Yoga provides two alternative ways of dealing with distractions. One is to concentrate by a rigid effort of will on what is called "one-pointedness." The Yogins do this by a "summary dismissal of all intruding images and ideas." The other way is to allow "the oscillations [of attention] gradually to subside,"[48] until the movement is such that it can be fairly easily controlled. In either case the exercise of will is required. Fulton and other neurophysiologists have described this as concentration through inhibition.

As success is achieved in excluding intrusive stimuli the subject reaches a stage called deliberation, but "the process is still one of conscious effort. . . . This is the period of maximum effort and distaste, at which the experiment very commonly breaks down." In a later stage, called contemplation, "there is no longer consciousness of effort, and no longer awareness of the mind as an instrument, but simply awareness of the object of thought."[49]

Up to this point the process seems to be comparable to Western techniques for producing concentration of attention in hypnosis or various forms of autosuggestion. But the Yogin knows the danger to the truly creative process. He warns the student against letting himself fall passively into the hypnotic trance, for that is negative and unproductive. This confirms my conclusion that the trance state per se is uncreative. Instead of the passive "mediumistic trance," he is urged to continue to endure the ordeal of positive concentration. This is a "profound tuning of the mind to the object of study, which results in deep insight and a tapping of a wide range of correlated ideas."[50] This increase in the power of seeing relationships is "the most fruitful and practical aspect of the meditation exercise." This fourth stage in which the mind is profoundly tuned to the object is so positively productive, it can only be described as creative. This supplies further confirmation of the conditions favoring the creative act: the concentration of attention, "the interval of suspense," and then the sudden flash of illumination which the East calls the "creative climax." The stage of "one-pointed" contemplation is described as a "period of suspense and sustained excitement and a creative climax." The program outlined in the sutras strongly suggests that its "creative climax" is my postulated "autonomous forming process of the creative unconscious." My study of the autobiography of the flash of insight has referred to the creative excitement that comes with the liberation of mind as a symbolic transformation takes place and a new conception is grasped.

Moreover, in my interpretations, I shall make much of the flash as determined by anticipatory set, a feeling of imminence—being just "on the verge of," or "about to act." I shall develop it further. The Yogin uses exactly the same terms to describe the same moment. When conscious effort has subsided, and a period of "suspension" sets in, one has a "feeling of poise, of floating, of 'being just about to.' " The period of suspenseful expectancy gives the impression of stillness. It is "accompanied by a sense of boundless power and capacity, a mastery of the subject in hand and is a state of radiant expansion and fulfillment."[51]

In one of his sutras, Patanjali makes the point that the achievement of concentration through habitual practice enables one to "reach and sustain the one-pointed or poised condition at will, and to proceed confidently from it to the creative state." The secret is to achieve a balance between the inertia of the mind on the one hand and its over-activity, its hectic flitting from one thing to another. These prevent creativeness, but so does inertia.[52] Through detachment one gradually achieves poise. The Sankhya psychology constantly emphasizes that "release . . . is attained by achieving a harmonized . . . condition of consciousness"[53] with respect to opposed and distracting opposites.

Behanan appraised Yoga after submitting himself for a year to its total program of physical and mental exercises. Before engaging in Yoga he was in run-down condition. A few months after beginning it his health improved noticeably. He stood up better under physical and mental work. His resistance to illness increased, headaches diminished. His emotional life began to change; it seemed to gain more stability and balance. Trying to analyze "mental, emotional integration," he thinks, "it is that quality of inner feeling which is the subjective counterpart of our reactions to the events of the world, particularly those that immediately affect our own personality." But, he adds, "this discipline has in no way influenced my intellectual outlook." He said it brought emotional as well as physical balance. "Yogic practices perhaps lead to what may be called the homeostasis of emotion. It seems to awaken deeper levels of energy." He thinks the changes in emotional life "may, in all probability, be mediated through transformations in the glandular system. . . . Recent studies have shown the supreme importance of the changes in the secretions of certain endocrine glands for personality development."[54]

Behanan studied several Yogins in their exercises and development for over a year and reports:

I can testify without any reservation that they were the happiest personalities that I have known. Their serenity was contagious and in their presence I felt always that I was dealing with people who held great "power" in reserve. If the saying "radiant personality" means anything, it should be applied to them.[55]

James, after gathering much competent personal testimony, gave a similar evaluation of what he called the Yoga system in Hindustan.

The result claimed, and certainly in many cases accorded by impartial judges, is strength of character, personal power, unshakability of soul . . . a very gifted European friend of mine who, by persistently carrying out for several months . . . its exercises in breathing and thought-concentration, and its fantastic posture-gymnastics, seems to have succeeded in waking up deeper and deeper levels of will and moral and intellectual power in himself, and to have escaped from a decidedly menacing brain-condition of the "circular" type, from which he had suffered for years. . . . A profound modification has unquestionably occurred in the running of his mental machinery. The gearing has changed, and his will is available otherwise than it was.[56]

When a man returns from *samâdhi* to the normal world, James said, he is "enlightened . . . his whole character changed, his life changed, illumined."[57]

Behanan's major conclusion is: "Whatever may be one's opinion of the yogic theory of the mind and its evolution, its success in developing a healthy emotional equilibrium is empirically verifiable."[58] The metaphysical tenets of Yoga

are an audacious and poetic leap in the dark—worthy enough to occupy a spacious hall in the "Mansions of Philosophy" that the human mind has spun in its irresistible desire to explain the warp and woof of the unknown.[59]

This must conclude the story of the Tao of the East. I find in the Great Doctrine of the East impressive validation from widely separated cultures of my notions of the transliminal mind, of the conscious-unconscious continuum, and of the autonomous forming process in the creative unconscious. I find, moreover, mutual corroboration on the technique of developing the intuitive mind of inside identification through concentration of attention and relaxation. I shall postulate that such phrases of the East as "being in the Tao," "no-mind," and "creative climax after the interval of suspense" approximately describe the state which I have called the transliminal mind.

10

The Tao of the West

In the past fifteen hundred years of Western development there have been three clear episodes in the rediscovery of the intuitive mind. Preceding these was a minor and intermittent period in Greek life which has such a limited relation to our search that I will not deal with it here. The first and longest of the major episodes was that of Christian mysticism. One phase of this, the non-theopathic phase, makes an important corroborative contribution to my study, and I deal with it briefly. The second was the modern development of the intuitive way by philosophers and artists of Western Europe and America. The third was the rise of an organic conception of mind among twentieth-century behavioral scientists, a new understanding that was to confirm and greatly illuminate the pre-visions of the artists and philosophers. The combined contributions of these three groups has produced what I tentatively call the Tao of the West. In this chapter, I shall deal particularly with the poets and philosophers; in later chapters with confirmations and extensions coming from men of science.

WESTERN MYSTICISM

In exploring the intuitive characteristics of the mystic way I have been greatly helped by three important appraisals—those by James

(1901), Underhill (1910), and Cheney (1945).[1] Miss Underhill's world-acclaimed study of mysticism embraced the entire sweep of intuitive wisdom from the Vedantic and Buddhist writers of India two thousand years ago, including the medieval seers of the Christian church, and up through the major poets of modern times. One of her conclusions is so pertinent that I quote it: "Mysticism . . . is not an opinion; it is not a philosophy. . . . On the one hand it is not merely the power of contemplating Eternity; on the other, it is not to be identified with any kind of religious queerness." The mystic way, as Underhill defines it, is an "arduous psychological and spiritual process . . . entailing the complete remaking of character." It has "nothing in common with the pursuit of occult knowledge." Underhill sums it all up as "the achievement here and now of the immortal heritage of man."[2]

It is apparent, however, that she is discussing the mystic-*theopathic* way, with clear religious goals and overtones. The mystic-*theopathic* way goes much further and toward a different goal than that which I am calling the intuitive mind of creative imagination. Nevertheless, I have leaned heavily and gratefully on a part of Miss Underhill's masterly analysis; specifically, on the first three of her five stages of the mystic way—the Awakening, the Purgation, and the Illumination of the Self. I suggest that the preparatory stages of the mystic experience are identical with the entrance into the intuitive threshold mind of man's creative imagination. The evidence is clear that with man working as artist as with the man of religion, the self and its abilities must be awakened and disciplined, and, as this is done, *illuminated*. From Buddha to Blake and Coleridge and on to Bergson, the record abounds in instances of those in whom the illumination of the self provided, in an intuitive antechamber of mind, clear accessibility to the illuminating flash of imagination. I am asking, then, to what extent does such an experience open the doors of conception, giving access to successively receding antechambers of the unconscious?

The Illumination of the Self

The records of psychological analysis of mysticism help to open the doors of conception, if the first three of Underhill's stages are separated from the last two:

The Stages of Illumination   *The Theopathic Stages*

1. The Awakening of the Self
2. The Purgation of the Self
3. Illumination of the Self

4. Purification of the Self—the Dark Night of the Soul
5. Union: the Self and the Absolute, God, are One—the true goal of the mystic quest

The last two stages mark the "mystic way" as "theopathic"—completing the purifying withdrawal from the world of human reality and consummating final Union with God. The first three stages, however, are a process of concentration and "emptying the mind," comparable to the corresponding stages in Yoga. I suggest that in these first stages of awakening, purgation, and illumination of the self can be found a confirmation of the East's Great Doctrine, and a model also for the creative experience of Western artists, philosophers, and scientists.

The first stage, the awakening of the self, leads in religion to conversion. But in expression it leads to creative imagination. In it *the self's increasing awareness that its illusory life is not the truest real world* is comparable to the processes of awakening described by Plato for denizens of his "cave of sensory illusion." The records read much like those we have already given from the autobiography of the flash of insight. It is in the third stage, illumination, that the man of mystic persuasion and the creative man concerned with clear-seeing come together. Underhill states the case so definitively that I quote her at some length:

In illumination we come to that state of consciousness which is popularly supposed to be peculiar to the mystic. . . . Those who still go with him a little way—certain prophets, poets, artists, dreamers—do so in virtue of that mystical genius, that instinct for transcendental reality, of which all seers and creators have some trace. The initiates of beauty or of wisdom, as the great mystic is the initiate of love, they share in some degree the experiences of the way of illumination. . . .

Responding to the intimations received in that awakening, ordering itself in their interest, concentrating its scattered energies on this one thing, the self emerges from long and varied acts of purification to find that it is able to apprehend another order of reality.[3]

Underhill says such "a radiant consciousness has been true of all great poets."

. . . all real artists, as well as all pure mystics, are sharers to some degree in the Illuminated Life. They have drunk, with Blake, from that cup of intellectual vision which is the chalice of the Spirit of Life: know something of its divine inebriation whenever Beauty inspires them to create. . . . Amongst those who cannot be called pure mystics we can detect in the works of Plato and Heracleitus, Wordsworth, Tennyson, and Walt Whitman indications that they too were acquainted, beyond most poets and seers, with the phenomena of the illuminated life. In studying it then, we shall be confronted by a mass of apparently irreconcilable material: the results of the relation set up between every degree of lucidity, every kind of character, and the suprasensible world. . . .[4]

Here poet, mystic, and musician are on common ground: for it is only by the oblique methods of the artist, by the use of aesthetic suggestion and musical rhythm, that the wonder of that vision can be expressed. . . . The natural mind is conscious only of succession: the special *differentia* of the mystic is the power of apprehending simultaneity. In the peculiarities of the illuminated consciousness we recognize the effort of the mind to bridge the gap between Simultaneity and Succession: the characters of Creator and Creation. Here the successive is called upon to carry the values of the Eternal.[5]

The Gathering of the Self and the Development of the Quiet Mind

But it is from the mystic's art of introversion and contemplation that the education of the creative man can take its cue. It is to withdraw from the hurly-burly of the external world, cut himself off from all outside influences, and dedicate his mind to "communion with the real." This it is that "conditions the creative activity of musician, painter and poet." Thus the Western seer confirms the wise man of the East. Contemplation is the quiet mind that both releases and magnetizes the antechambers of the unconscious mind. The growth of the creative man, says the Tao of the West, is conditioned by this advancing education in the art of contemplation. This is one of the pedagogical lessons from a millennium of mysticism.

But there are others. There is, for example, the importance of knowledge and disciplined ability. "The painter, however great his natural powers, can hardly dispense with some technical training," says Underhill, and then confirms our earlier generalizations about the indispensable role of rigorous conscious preparation. "It is true that he [artist or mystic] sometimes seems to spring abruptly to the heights, to be caught into ecstasy without previous preparation: as a poet may startle the world by a sudden masterpiece. But unless they be backed by discipline, these sudden and isolated flashes of inspiration will not long avail for the production of great works."[6] Our full powers cannot be developed without this kind of education which "consists largely in a humble willingness to submit to the discipline, and profit by the lessons, of the past. Tradition runs side by side with experience; the past collaborates with the present." And then a perceptive insight into the psychological task:

The condition of all valid seeing and hearing, upon every plane of consciousness, lies not in the sharpening of the senses, but in a peculiar attitude of the whole personality: in a self-forgetting attentiveness, a profound concentration, a self-merging, which operates a real communion between the seer and the seen—in a word, in *Contemplation*.[7]

The method seems, in essentials, to be a replica of the Great Doctrine of the East.

Creative Concentration

Concentration of attention, relaxation, and illumination mark the road to be traveled. Evelyn Underhill's beautiful "sutras" confirm Patanjali, the Zen Master-Artist, and findings of the Western scientific psychologist:

All that is asked is that we shall look for a little time, in a special and undivided manner, at some simple, concrete, and external thing. This object of our contemplation may be almost anything we please: a picture, a statue, a tree, a distant hillside, a growing plant, running water, little living things. We need not, with Kant, go to the starry heavens. "A little thing the quantity of an hazel nut" will do for us, as it did for Lady Julian long ago. Remember, it is a practical experiment on which we are set; not an opportunity of pretty and pantheistic meditation.

Look, then, at this thing which you have chosen. Wilfully yet tranquilly refuse the messages which countless other aspects of the world are sending; and so concentrate your whole attention on this one act of loving sight that all other objects are excluded from the conscious field. Do not think, but as it were pour out your personality towards it: let your soul be your eyes. Almost at once, this new method of perception will reveal unsuspected qualities in the external world. First, you will perceive about you a strange and deepening quietness; a slowing down of our feverish mental time. Next, you will become aware of a heightened significance, an intensified existence in the thing at which you look. As you, with all your consciousness, lean out towards it, an answering current will meet yours. It seems as though the barrier between its life and your own, between subject and object, had melted away. You are merged with it, in an act of true communion: and you *know* the secret of its being, deeply and unforgettably, yet in a way which you can never hope to express. . . .

The price of this experience has been a stilling of that surface-mind, a calling in of all our scattered interests: an entire giving of ourselves to this one activity, without self-consciousness, without reflective thought. To reflect is always to distort: our minds are not good mirrors. The contemplative, on whatever level his faculty may operate, is contented to absorb and be absorbed: and by this humble access he attains to a plane of knowledge which no intellectual process can come near.[8]

Thus introversion and contemplation constitute an art that can be acquired through the discipline of education and put at the command of every man.

But we must not miss the paradox involved. The truly quiet mind is passive, but only in an active sense. Relaxation is not merely "letting go." It is relaxation *with control* that we seek. It is truly dynamic and purposive, marked by an intense condition of peace through designed tension; its "repose is the result of stress." This is Tao, the Great Doctrine, re-emerging in the West. This is letting things happen; action through inaction, purposelessness on purpose. And this is the condition in which the transliminal state permits the flash to occur. When "it shoots" (as Zen Master Awa described it) the flash comes from the unconscious.

OPENING THE DOORS OF IMAGINATION

A new chapter in the Tao of the West—to be gleaned from the autobiography of the human imagination—dates from the beginning of the second intellectual revolution in the first decades of the nineteenth century. In A.D. 1800 the intuitive way was still grasped by only a few sensitive men of the West; in fact, it is only in our own generation that we have learned that William Blake, for example, was really prologue to a new period. He knew the illumination of the self, the intuitive way, internally, in its own terms, but he also saw the function of the imaginative artist in a world of men. Coleridge was also a bridge between transcendent and mundane views. Feeling with him determined thinking. Although they were contemporaries, there seems to have been no contact between the two men. In fact, when, in *Biographia Literaria,* Coleridge recites the honor roll of the great intuitives, mentioning specifically Pythagoras, Plato, Plotinus, various Christian churchmen of the Middle Ages, Jakob Boehme and George Fox, he ignores Blake. Yet we, who can see the nineteenth-century record in perspective, sense that they are the first two in the West to become major actors in the modern drama of human imagination. Both were curious and articulate about the intuitive process. With them the flash *becomes* the imagination, and the illumined self is also concerned with the betterment of the earthly life of men.

So I turn to Blake and Coleridge for light on the opening of the doors of imagined conception. There were many lesser men, for the study of mind was becoming a life occupation for thousands of feeling, thinking persons. But from this little company we can draw the essence of what our great intuitives learned about knowing and imagining, expressing, and communicating.

WILLIAM BLAKE: THE MODERN MAN
OF THE IMAGINATION

Blake was, as I have said, prologue to our modern drama. Of all the poet-artists and philosopher-seers whom I have drawn upon he is the best bridge between East and West, between the Christian mystics and the agnostic rationalists, the "illumined self" and the creative act. He not only utters the word "imagination" more often and more pointedly than any other, he is more than any other the creative imagination personified. And he was the first of the great intuitives to stand on the frontier of the new industrializing democracy and form a vision of what creative man might do toward making a good society of it. From every standpoint Blake is our man.

Man of Intuitive Insight

This is the man who was contemptuously discarded in his own times as a "mystic," a visionary dreamer, even a mad man, and then ignored by the entire Victorian world. Not till the rebellious and improvisational revolution in the expressive arts after 1900 was Blake rediscovered. Blake was not a mystic, but he was a man of rare insight. He was especially the true precipitant of the imagination, the forerunner of Coleridge and Whitman and Bergson. It is true that these men followed the intuitive path in acts of partial withdrawal from the physical world. But instead of continuing on in that path to the point of final union with the absolute, they endured the ordeal of return. They produced, indeed, a fine balance between withdrawal and return. In a sense this constitutes a fusion of the sensory and the intuitive paths.

Cheney agrees that

far from denying the senses, Blake pleaded for richer use of them, though for enjoyment not with them so much as *through* them. They are often the channels to vision, to detection of the divine—"the chief inlet of the soul," he called them. His own contact with, as it might be, angels, or the Spirits of Milton and Shakspere, or with God was sometimes spontaneous and sometimes evoked by the sights and sounds and smells of nature. When he had gone to the seashore to live he wrote: "Heaven opens here on all sides her golden gates." He spoke too of the pleasures of sex as a gateway to vision, a holy gateway opening upon the clearest Eternal seeing of which the soul is capable. He is tolerant of sense enjoyment as he is tolerant of reason when utilized for its own necessary purposes. But as he thundered at reason usurping the place of intuition, imagination, and vision, he thundered at imprisonment to the senses.[9]

D. H. Lawrence exclaimed: "They'll say [of my work] as they said of Blake's: 'It's mysticism,' but they shan't get away with it, not this time: Blake's wasn't mysticism, neither is this." And I add: "Neither is this!" *The way of creative imagination is not mysticism.*

A Vision of Creative Men

When we turn to the productive record of this great creative artist we see the full significance of creative illumination. How it abounds in the vocabulary of "madness" . . . "inebriation" . . . "intellectual vision." Take, for example, Blake's letter to a friend:

. . . excuse my enthusiasm or rather madness, for I am really drunk with intellectual vision whenever I take a pencil or graver into my hand. . . .[10]

The great function of these precipitants of the imagination is, in Blake's words, to "cleanse the doors of perception." He saw his great task as that of "bringing down Imagination and Divinity to man." I quote from *Auguries of Innocence:*

> To see a World in a Grain of Sand
> And a Heaven in a Wild Flower,
> Hold Infinity in the palm of your hand
> And Eternity in an hour.[11]

And the powerful lines: "Let the world of rationalization and of the senses be consumed in the fires of imagination. Free the eternal soul; let it taste again Infinity." And then the most significant lines of all: *"If the doors of percepton were cleansed everything would appear to man as it is, infinite."*

He was a student of the imaginative past, but with a clear vision toward the future. He was vastly more than a rebel, for he saw that modern man, being debauched by Western industrialism and colonialism, had within him enormous creative potential. Holding a man-centered view of the universe, the earth and living creatures upon it, Blake saw what his beloved England, or Albion, might be, what a wonderful life human imagination could produce on earth if men would let their imaginations have full sway. But it could not be done by man's withdrawing from that world to lose himself in God. The return, facing the world of men, was as necessary, and wonderful, as the ecstasy of withdrawal. He summed it all up in that much misunderstood book, *The Marriage of Heaven and Hell,* part prose, part epigrammatic essay, and part verse.

Speaking as the Devil himself—he always identified himself

with the agencies of the energy he was picturing—he searches for the great source of creative energy. It can be brought to earth from Hell as well as from Heaven. "The Eternal Hell revives,"[12] he affirms.

> Death and Hell
> Teem with Life.

Cheney appraised him:

A saint William Blake was, though a saint with a difference, a saint curiously enamoured of the Devil; a loving, forgiving saint in living, but flawed with some very human frailties.[13]

Cleansing the Doors of Perception

Blake's way of "cleansing perception," then, was to rid oneself of the illusion of the primary or the sensory world. It was to lift oneself out of the sham world of hypocrisy and cant, to cut off false, selfish desires, to straighten out values. It was to transform sensory perception with a kind of "extra" sensory perception.

And in Blake we see the new role of the self. The great "saints" of the theopathic way opened the cleansed doors of perception to bring about the selfless life in union with God. Blake led the great poet-artists of modern times in self-affirmation in a world of men. How it rang out in Walt Whitman (born in Blake's old age, 1819) only a generation later: "One's Self I sing . . ."

Here, then, is the suggestion that the act of creative imagination may be a fusing of sensory perception and intuitive vision. Provocative concepts arise from studying Blake—a restatement of the boundaries of the real and the unreal, a widening understanding of what perception is. It is more than sense perception, more like the perception-in-depth we found in Cezanne. We begin to suspect the version of the world we get only through the eyes and ears. We are startled into taking off the blinders that we wear in the act of perceiving through the senses. We speculate concerning the clearer understanding that appears to come via kinesthesis, and we have a premonition of the role of body gesture. And is not perception-in-depth really *conception?* We shall see.

COLERIDGE AND THE IMAGINATION CREATRIX

I had long felt that in Samuel Taylor Coleridge I would find another stimulating cue to the study of the creative act. His total contribution to the modern creative record and its clarification has been immense. Contemporary with Blake, Coleridge was an expressive Man of Imagination—especially in his three world-acclaimed poems, "The Ancient Mariner," "Kubla Khan," and "Christabel." But beyond this, he was the first creative artist to make much conscious effort to understand the psychology of the imagination. Thus he becomes an important resource for my study as both imaginative poet and critic of the poetic imagination. Arthur Symons called him "the high priest" of criticism, saying: "No one has ever gone deeper down into the substance of creation itself, or more nearly reached that unknown point where creation begins."[14] John Livingstone Lowes who, after 1900, spent half an academic life in the literary detection of the way in which Coleridge created his great poems, said of him:

Few human beings, I take it, have ever pondered more deeply than Coleridge the mysterious "goings-on" of their own minds, and few who so pondered ever had, perhaps, such complex workings to explore, or such lynx-like intellect with which to track them.[15]

The record is clear that he pondered more deeply the mysterious goings-on in the mind than most other men of imagination, that he committed himself to "the absolute sanction of intuition." He explored deeply into "the substance of creation itself."

Devotee of Intuitive Identification

The nature of his psychological ideas is important to our study of the creative process. He was early immersed in the significance of the "meaning of an idea." Accepting at first the mechanistic associationism of the philosophers Hobbes, Locke, and Hartley, he was later, in Germany, converted from Hartley to Kant, and somewhat to Jakob Boehme and Christian mysticism. The conversion matured after he had returned to Greta Hall at Keswick in 1800, to find freedom and quiet to meditate. His letters of this period are revealing, especially one to his friend Poole in 1801. I quote a single generalization that marks the completeness of his conversion from mechanism to the organic, intuitive way of knowing "My opinion is this: that deep thinking is attainable only by a man of deep feeling, and that all truth is a species of revelation."

This twentieth-century dichotomy—the inside-outside controversy over knowing—was definitely reflected in Coleridge. He continues in his letter to Poole, "One *word* with *meaning* in it is worth the whole alphabet together."[16] The word can be given meaning only by the Self (Coleridge would have said the Soul) expressing it; the alphabet is merely a concatenation of unrelated elements—twenty-six alphabetized letters. How does the flash of insight come about? Does it not come, he asks, from inside the personality, rather than from the outside observation of things and men? "By meditation rather than by observation? And by the latter in consequence only of the former? As eyes, for which the former has pre-determined their field of vision, and to which, as to *its* organ, it communicates a microscopic power?"[17]

How much Coleridge anticipated of recent psychology can be glimpsed by his references to the self, to feeling, to memory and the unconscious. For example, in 1801 he wrote:

By deep feeling we make our *ideas dim,* and this is what we mean by our life, ourselves. I think of the wall—it is before me a distinct image. Here I necessarily think of the *idea* and the thinking *I* as two distinct and opposite things. Now let me think of myself, of the thinking being. The idea becomes dim, whatever it be—so dim that I know not what it is; but the feeling is deep and steady, and this I call *I*—identifying the percipient and the perceived. . . .

Again, what is a thought? What are its circumscriptions, what the interspaces between it and another? When does it begin? Where end? Far more readily could one apply these questions to an ocean billow, or the drops of water which we may imagine as the component integers of the ocean. As by a billow we mean no more than a particular movement of the sea, so neither by a thought can we mean more than the mind thinking in some direction.[18]

In his speculations concerning the Imagination and the Fancy he was something more than a casual student of what Lowes called "the flowing in of memory upon perception." In the much debated

Chapters XII and XIII of *Biographia Literaria,* he defines Imagination, distinguishing it from what he calls Fancy. The primary phase of Imagination, the living power and prime agent of perception, gives us, Coleridge says, the raw materials with which the secondary phase—the creative, organizing, unifying, forming phase—works. The two together—I interpret them to be but two phases of one continuous organic process—constitute the eternal act of creation, the "Esemplastic Power." This is a premonition, I think, of the concept of the "Forming Process."

To this esemplastic power, "imagination creatrix," he opposes the Fancy, which is "no other than a mode of memory . . . [which must] receive all its materials ready made from the law of association."[19] Much energy and printing has been wasted, it seems to me, in a century of controversial argument over the meanings of his two definitions. Richards points out that Coleridge himself did not think too highly of them as indicated eighteen years later in *Table Talk,* a month before he died.

The metaphysical disquisition at the end of the first volume of *Biographia Literaria* is unformed and immature; it contains fragments of the truth, but it is not fully thought out. It is wonderful to myself to think how infinitely more profound my views now are and yet how much clearer they are withal. The circle is completing; the idea is coming round to, and to be, the reality.[20]

Let us be content with Richards' view that they are "merely a preparatory exercise intended by Coleridge to discount certain current assumptions (they are still current in literary circles) about the modes of operation of the mind."[21]

On Feeling and Form

But in his more mature years he became clearer about the operation of the creative mind. In his appraisal of feeling as opposed to thinking, and in his conception of the role of the self, he anticipates important concepts of our biosocial-psychology of today. For example, on feeling he writes:

I hold that association depends in a much greater degree on the recurrence of states of feeling than on trains of ideas. . . . Believe me, Southey! a metaphysical solution, that does not *tell* you something in the heart is grievously to be suspected as apocryphal. I almost think that ideas *never* recall ideas, as far as they are ideas, any more than leaves in a forest create each other's motion. The breeze it is that runs through them—it is the soul, the state of feeling.[22]

And in the *Anima Poetae*, (1804) there is an anticipation of our growing psychology of feeling and form:

One of the most noticeable and fruitful facts in psychology is the modification of the same feeling by difference of form. The Heaven lifts up my soul, the sight of the ocean seems to widen it. We feel the same force at work, but the difference, whether in mind or body that we should feel in actual travelling horizontally or in direct ascent, *that* we feel in fancy.

For what are our feelings of this kind but a motion imagined (together) with the feelings that would accompany that motion, but less distinguished, more blended, more rapid, more confused, and, thereby, co-adunated?[23]

Thus "feeling" is used by Coleridge as a kind of matrix in which thinking is done "with intense energy." He speaks the language of the intuitive path. Such concepts as "realizing acts of intuition," "acts of contemplation," "concepts of the understanding," are instruments with which to explore the nature of poetry.

Coleridge's anticipatory intuitions can be connected to corresponding concepts of twentieth-century behavioral scientists, working on the farthest frontiers of the body-mind problem. He speaks as one of the earliest "meaning of meaning" men, projecting "motion [meaning] into form."

LOWES' STUDY OF COLERIDGE'S CREATIVE UNCONSCIOUS

It may be that Coleridge's distinguished place in the study of the imagination will owe far more to the work of a literary man who lived a century after him than to his own critical achievements. Lowes' *Road to Xanadu* is the most successful attempt of our times to document and appraise the effects on a poet's conscious work of his unconscious creative imagery. The title implies, says Lowes, "the road of the human spirit." It was an attempt to get at "the workings of the imaginative energy itself," to discover how, out of chaos, the imagination "fashions its elements into lucid and ordered unity."[24] It was his effort to clarify "that nebulous theory [of the imagination] propounded in the twelfth and thirteenth chapters of *Biographia Literaria.*"

By the time *The Road to Xanadu* was finished, Lowes had trailed Coleridge through what he had read and found, sometimes on the last page of a great tome, the phrases which had exploded later into vivid pictures and meanings in the lines of "The Ancient Mariner" and "Kubla Khan." He gives us documentary evidence of the sources which gave Coleridge, who had never traveled outside of Britain and Western Europe, the images of arctic and tropical regions, the flora and fauna of six continents, and the islands of the seven seas. And we must remember that, added to this unconscious storage of voracious reading, there was the accretion which came from thousands of hours of talk by one of the world's greatest masters of the art of conversation. Coleridge was obsessed with language, eternally inventing new words and phrases. In a letter to Sir Humphry Davy (1800) he uses one—"ultra-crepidated"—and adds, "I give myself credit for that word *'ultra-crepidated,'* it started up in my brain like a creation." And in another letter: "I envy dear Southey's power of saying one thing at a time, in short and close sentences, whereas my thoughts bustle along like a Surinam toad, with little toads sprouting out of back, side, and belly, vegitating while it crawls." Lowes comments: ". . . sometimes . . . we are vouchsafed dizzying glimpses into those circles upon circles of association which used to break against the shore of his auditors' patience. . . ."[25]

Peopling the Twilight Realms of Consciousness with Images

The first phrase in my caption is Coleridge's, the second is Lowes'; together they point to the true significance of Lowes' literary detection. *Xanadu* shows how Coleridge peopled his unconscious, and hence the threshold center of creativeness, with images. And Lowes adds that they give us "some inkling of what those subliminal 'atomes crochus' were—those mysterious elements out of whose confluences and coalescences suddenly emerged the poem."[26] But the vital and new idea that takes us forward in our study of the imagination is Coleridge's (and Lowes') conception that the materials from which the poetic line is formed are images precipitated from conscious experience. Coleridge made much of the role of the image in his work. In a letter to Davy he described how, when he was composing a poem, "voluntary ideas were every minute passing, more or less transformed into vivid spectra."[27] Describing the same composition to Southey, he adds: "While I wrote that last sentence I had a vivid recollection, *indeed an ocular spectrum,* of our room in College Street, a curious instance of association." And to Godwin in 1801: "I bent down to pick something from the ground . . . as I bent my head there came a *distinct, vivid spectrum* upon my eyes; it was one little picture—a rock, with birches and ferns on it, a cottage backed by it, and a small stream. Were I a painter I would give an outward existence to this, but it will always live in my memory."[28] Throughout his life Coleridge's letters, notes, and "table talk" abounded in mental pictures.

For when Coleridge's imagination was working at high tension, actual pictures seem to have passed before it with the preternatural vividness of those after-images which the eighteenth century loved to call "ocular spectra"—not spectra as we to-day understand the term, but impressions retained on the retina of the eye with an independent luminousness and precision after the passing of some flash of vision, as a window which has leaped at night into dazzling configuration in a blaze of lightning hangs printed for an instant in sharp definition upon the dark.[29]

Linking intense concentration and the kaleidoscope of imagery touched off by it, Coleridge refers to Ben Jonson who "in those racy conversations with Drummond of Hawthornden, told his host that 'he heth consumed a whole night in lying looking at his great toe, about which he hath seen Tartars and Turks, Romans and Carthaginians feight in his imagination.' "[30] Lowes describes the state of concentration as one in which in the "intense luminousness of Coleridge's brain scraps of remembered fact, or lines on the printed page flashed, as he says, 'into vivid spectra,' and words sprang into pictures as he read or wrote."[31]

That the unconscious is a vast storehouse in which the stuff of imagination is partly worked over, without our conscious help, all reporters on their own processes of creation bear witness.

Does the Unconscious Mind Create?

Lowes asks again and again whether "the chaos of elements or shattered fragments of memory"[32] are organized on the unconscious level, and makes the obvious guesses as to where and how it is done. By association, he says; by propinquity, which "does business merrily in the unconscious world, as well as up in the realms of light, and in both strange couples mate. Dew-drops blended together on the bosom of a new-blown rose, and Mars rising over a gibbet; diamond quarries in some Golconda of faëryland, and Tartarean forests of Upas trees—such conceptions could not coexist in a region charged with secret currents, and remain unmodified." They are modified; that we know, but what is the process? Lowes says, " 'that synthetic and magical power . . . the imagination' (it is Coleridge's own words that I am using) must perforce 'blend and (as it were) *fuse* them, each into each.' Mars willy-nilly must shed a baleful light upon the dew-drop, and the diamonds of faëryland blink dull in the shade of Upas trees. Or else the Tartarean forests must glimmer with faint rays from faëry Golcondas, and Mars be reflected, mild and luminous, in a drop of dew. Or else both processes at once and all together must go on, until, as in 'The Ancient Mariner' and 'Christabel' and 'Kubla Khan,' beauty insensibly takes on something elfin and uncanny, and the fantastic and the sinister an unearthly radiance."[33] By the magical power of the imagination, says Lowes—and Coleridge. Yes—but how?

Lowes himself provides a dramatic example from the workings of his own imagination. A full thirty years after reading O. W. Holmes's *Autocrat of the Breakfast-Table,* he recalled a passage from it. Holmes's printed passage had read:

Put an idea into your intelligence and leave it there an hour, a day, a year, without ever having occasion to refer to it. When, at last, you return to it, you do not find it as it was when acquired. It has domiciliated itself, so to speak,—become at home,—entered into relations with your other thoughts, and integrated itself with the whole fabric of the mind.[34]

But the passage flashed back into Lowes' memory a full generation later, Lowes says, in so striking a configuration that when I looked it up I could barely believe my eyes. . . . What I recalled (or thought I had recalled) had been cast in a vividly figurative form—the figure of something germinating and expanding, dimly and occultly, with white and spreading tentacles, like the plant life which sprouts beneath a stone, or burgeons in the obscure depths of a pool. And that was not on the page before my eyes at all; it was, so to speak, a creature of the well [the Unconscious]. But it was a creature, as I soon discovered on reading farther, which had had associations with the well. For in another passage, elsewhere in the book, in an entirely different context, the Autocrat *had* used the figure of the uncanny life which breeds beneath a stone, and far below the surface of my consciousness the two had undergone amalgamation. And the result was neither the Autocrat's nor mine. It was, despite its utter triviality, a veritable birth of the subliminal deep.[35]

This seems to me to be evidence that "an idea put into your intelligence" is not merely stored intact in the unconscious for thirty years; the changing experiences have indeed integrated it "with the whole fabric of the mind." But it indicates still another theory, one to which I shall return for careful study. The new blend of stored experiences created by the unconscious is recovered in the transliminal mind *in symbolic form*.

Coleridge himself supplies what he thinks is the key to the unconscious process in that perceptive line in *The Notebooks:* ". . . *the streamy nature of association, which thinking curbs and rudders"*;[36] this is the "true birth of the subliminal deep." The unconscious *is* creative, he says, and "association" is the method. But no one, Lowes or Coleridge, Freud or anyone else, has ever observed it at its amazing welding and transmuting work and we still can only guess as to how it is done. Somewhere and somehow in the dark recesses below the threshold of awareness the psychological alchemy takes place. Coleridge and Lowes take a necessary first step by providing names, labels, with which to think about it. In Coleridge's own words, it is "that synthetic and magic power . . . the imagination . . . [that] dissolves, diffuses, dissipates, in order to re-create"; and Lowes later speculated: ". . . there was moving among the reassembling images a conscious power whose operations we have yet to see."[37]

Lowes renames it "a selective exercise of the imagination . . .

that very flux of interweaving phantasms of association." Then the mysterious blending power becomes "Will," and the phantasm of association "when the creative energy imposes its will upon it, becomes the plastic stuff both of life and art. And we are doggedly making our way . . . because it is worth infinite pains to see that the difference between art, in whatever sphere, and the chaotic welter of the stream of consciousness lies not in their constituents, but in the presence or absence of imaginative control."[38] So now Coleridge's "esemplastic power" becomes "imaginative control" and Lowes makes a five-fold synthesis of the elements of the process of creative imagination: "The deep Well, with its chaos of fortuitously blending images; but there is likewise the Vision which sees shining in and through the chaos the potential lines of Form, and with the Vision the controlling Will, which gives to that potential beauty actuality."[39]

This is the final breaking down and naming of the factors which Lowes and Coleridge conclude are involved in the creative process; of these, three stand out: the Well of the unconscious, the flash of Vision, and the shaping of Will. But what special power, what forming process resolves the chaos, forges the exquisitely balanced unity? "The Imagination," says Coleridge, which *"sees all things in one."* And Lowes, building on his idea, says that "when it acts on what it sees, through the long patience of the will, the flux itself is transformed and fixed in the clarity of a realized design."[40] Between them they have given us an inspiring description and raised before us several possible theories of how the unconscious functions.

Several Possible Explanations of the Forming Process

Viewing the conscious-unconscious continuum as a whole, there are four gross possibilities: The forming process can take place in the working of the conscious, in the unconscious, in the transliminal state connecting the two, or in some union of all. Was the resolution of the chaos enhanced by a slow *conscious ordering* of the accretion of images that are dropped, bit by bit, into the unconscious by the artist's reading, conversations, speculations? Was it what the psychologists of 1915 used to call "the higher thought processes"? Was this done by some intrinsic organizing power of the unconscious itself, so hidden that we shall never be able to lay bare its mysterious power? Or are we left with some unconscious power of ordering the chaos, equally mysterious, that takes place in the center of creative energy—our transliminal state? Is it done at the very last moment by the conscious flash of insight, but with no previous accumulating unconscious welding? Is it done by some upward pull from conscious need, some fusion of intensely quiet mind and body-response of meaning? Lawrence Cole, studying the Coleridge-Lowes material, questioned in much the same way: "Is the process of creation an intrinsically regulated affair, or are the 'matings' and 'crossings over' determined by repeated assaults from without? What causes the disintegration and reassemblage of these layers of constellations stored at such widely separated times? And what are the regulating conditions?"[41]

One possibility is flatly denied: "no synthesis," says Lowes, "based on mere mnemonic joiners-work will . . . serve."[42] Whatever else the unknown may be, the thing it is not is the sum of the unconscious fragments. "The unity that has somehow come about is as integral as the union of the seven colours which blend in a beam of white light. You may break up the beam into its spectrum, as we have resolved our shapes of light into their elements. The result in either case is the same: the enhancement of the miracle of their unity."[43] In short, no mechanical additive explanation will account for the miracle of the flash.

There are other possible explanations. One is that it occurs by sheer chance-like operation of the streamy nature of association itself. Referring to Goethe's "dæmon" of the *Conversations,* which is comparable to his own "spirit of the Well," Lowes speaks of the chance-like behavior of the associative processes of the Unconscious. " 'But,' Goethe insists, 'the dæmonic is not the only factor in creation. In such matters it is much as in the game the French call Codille, in which the fall of the dice is to a large degree decisive, but in which it is left to the skill of the player to meet the situation thus created.'[44] That is strangely like Epictetus's answer to the question how one is to deal with the same two elements of chance and volition in *life*. 'If he take example,' says Epictetus, 'of dice players. The numbers are indifferent, the dice are indifferent. How can I tell what may be thrown up? *But carefully and skillfully to make use of what is thrown,* that is where my proper business begins.' "[45]

Lowes himself gives a place to chance in this mystery of the operation of the unconscious: ". . . the subliminal ego doubtless deals the cards, as the throng of sleeping images . . . move toward the light." Then Lowes provides for the mysterious force: "But the fall of the cards accepted, the shaping spirit of imagination conceives and masterfully carries out the strategy of the game. Grant all you will to the involuntary and automatic operations of the Well —its blendings and fusings, each into each, of animalcules, and rainbows, and luminous tracks across the sea, and all the other elements of chaos." Then the creative power is renamed: "There still remains the architectonic imagination, moving, *sua sponte,* among the scattered fragments, and discerning, latent in their confusion, the pattern of the whole."[46]

Weighing the possibilities within the unconscious itself, Lowes quotes Poincaré's famous piece about his own creative processes. "How can we explain the fact," asks Poincaré, "that, of the thousand products of our unconscious activity, some are invited to cross the threshold, while others remain outside? Is it mere chance?" He answers: "Evidently not." But Poincaré's use of the hypothesis of the "hooked atoms" of Epicurus sounds like chance: ". . . *they plough through space in all directions . . . Their mutual collisions may then produce new combinations.*" And then Poincaré, like Coleridge, like Lowes, like many others from whom my consensus has emerged, insists that flashes that do not cross the threshold are "points of departure for [our] calculations." And these *"must be made in the second period of conscious work which follows the inspiration."*[47] This is the generalization that one finds in the record of dozens of the world's creative men.

Lowes still faced the question: "How were the latent images raised up? And with what body did they come? That is the question which I mean to try to answer."[48] But he never succeeded. He tries, through four hundred beautiful pages, but gives us finally little more than brilliant namings, guesses, and descriptions. The end point of it all is that the great poem was "a work of pure imaginative vision." Three factors created it: the unconscious storage of experience and its strange combustion of new weldings, the flash of Vision, and the Will to put it all together. In another place, his three factors have become four: "the thronged yet sleeping subliminal chambers; the summons which unlocks their secret doors; the pouring up of images linked in new conjunctions provocative of unexpected *aperçus;* the conscious seizing and directing to an end of suggestions which the unconscious operations have supplied." The process is not a monopoly of creative poetry, "it is the stuff of which life weaves patterns on its loom." He sums up the entire process: "Intensified and sublimated and controlled though they be, the ways of the creative faculty are the universal ways of that streaming yet consciously directed something which we know (*or* think we know) as life."[49]

So Lowes goes on for several hundred pages of splendidly written passages, trying one descriptive name after another: "inward creatrix" . . . "controlling Will" . . . "imaginative control" . . . "creative energy" . . . "creative genius" . . . "the power of seeing whole" . . . "the leap of imagination" . . . and dozens more. With Goethe, Kipling and others already quoted, Lowes often rests his case on the "dæmonic" element in creative genius.

But even at the end of the twenty years of magnificent literary detection, the creative act itself remained to Lowes a mystery. Again and again Lowes labels the dæmonic power but is unable to explain how it works.

HENRI BERGSON, MODERN PHILOSOPHER
OF THE INTUITIVE WAY

In 1907, Henri Bergson (1859–1941), professor at the Collège de France, published *Creative Evolution.* It was acclaimed widely in the West, in spite of its devotion to the intuitive way of knowing. James, on reading it, wrote to Bergson, saying: "Oh, my Bergson, you are a magician and your book is a marvel, a real wonder . . . unlike the works of genius of the Transcendentalist movement (which are so obscurely and abominably and inaccessibly written), a pure classic in point of form."[50] And Irwin Edman, who wrote the Foreword to its re-publication, said of it: "Here . . . was one . . . who, while a consummate literary artist, could beat precise analysts at their own game, and analyze nuances of feeling, action and thought which seemed to escape through the nets of logic and to be crushed by the tight schemes of matter in motion."[51]

In 1889, at the age of thirty, Bergson had written a paper on "intuition" that later (1903) was published as *Introduction to Metaphysics*. It is in this work that he presented his most systematic view that "knowledge lay in intuition." Wild says of his efforts:

. . . it is to Bergson that we owe the most strenuous philosophical attempt ever made to establish intuition as an independent mental function. Not only did he seek to persuade the world that, would it but use the faculty, intuition is a useful instrument in the search for reality, the most powerful, indeed, in man's possession, but that it is owing to man's neglect of it that he has so long wandered in the maze of contradictory theories and conclusions.[52]

The contrast between Bergson and James is sharp and clear: James the great empiric, the gatherer of documents and evidence, the world's most voluminous quoter, the apostle of the open mind, the pluralist ever loathe to conclude. "What is concluded that we might conclude in regard to it?" James quoted and interpreted the authorities on "the mystic state," on the image and imagination, and yet failed to state a tightly reasoned position. Bergson was the very antithesis. He, too, had been a student of biology and psychology and as a philosopher centered his studies of growth on life, on the process of knowing and remembering, and the concept of time or "duration." He was the greatest philosophic exponent of knowledge via intuition of our times; to him knowledge lay "in intuition, in the self-immolating and absorbed insights of the poet, the artist, the saint, of men at the acme of life, in the creative activity of genius, worship or love."

In the *Introduction to Metaphysics,* Bergson formulated the principles of his theory of intuitive knowing. In the final interpretive paragraph of this famous little book he takes us to the heart of his theory of knowing, expressing, and communicating, and likewise to the essence of the intuitive path:

Every one of us has had occasion to exercise it to a certain extent. Any one of us, for instance, who has attempted literary composition, knows that when the subject has been studied at length, the materials all collected, and the notes all made, something more is needed in order to set about the work of composition itself, and that is an often very painful effort to place ourselves directly at the heart of the subject, and to seek as deeply as possible an impulse, after which we need only let ourselves go. This impulse, once received, starts the mind on a path where it rediscovers all the information it had collected, and a thousand other details besides; it develops and analyses itself into terms which could be enumerated indefinitely. The farther we go, the more terms we discover; we shall never say all that could be said, and yet, if we turn back suddenly upon the impulse that we feel behind us, and try to seize it, it is gone; for it was not a thing, but the direction of a movement. . . .[53]

This is the "prime reality" of his theory—"for it was not a thing, but the direction of a movement." This is magnified by Bergson into an importance coordinate with intuition. It is difficult to illustrate concretely. He tries first the example of the unrolling of a coil, and second that of the myriad-tinted spectrum with its gradation of color from one shade into another. But he prefers the example of an infinitely small elastic body, contracted to a mathematical point, drawn out gradually so that a constantly lengthening line emerges from it. Fixing attention on the action by which the line is traced rather than on the line, considering "only the movement itself, the act of tension or extension; in short pure mobility," or duration, he says, will give us "a more faithful image of ourself." The self is the only reality by "which we shall see from within by intuition." Now the concept of duration (time) is continually "in the making"; hence you cannot represent duration, the inner life, by abstract ideas. Duration is a unitary affair and can be appreciated only by an effort of intuition and this is the essence of simplicity.[54]

Thus Bergson differs sharply with the Lockean School and takes his stand with the Leibnitzians, asserting that the self, the personality, is not an aggregate of mechanisms, not a mosaic of acts. From his organic point of view, we must stress the concept of becoming, not of being—to understand the personality we must know the direction of its values, interests and tendencies. We cannot reconstruct the whole of an object "by setting concept beside concept," the scientific way. This is additive, the mosaic-building method, not the truly integrative way. We cannot, for example, "form a faithful representation of duration by setting in line the concepts of unity, multiplicity, continuity, finite or infinite divisibility." Abstract ideas are "incapable of replacing intuition."[55] In all of this Bergson is saying that the scientific, conceptual way of knowing is an artificial reconstruction via the assembling of parts. One never really gets inside the object that way in order to know it.

All of this is in direct opposition to the scientific, mechanistic, stimulus-response, positivistic, empirical psychologies which have dominated the thought of most laboratories and libraries since the mid-nineteenth century. As Bergson put it, this point of view maintains that "the external and visible is more fundamental than what is not . . . the 'cause' remains external to the organism." It is interesting to note that Bergson was writing his little book on intuition at the very moment that Pavlov was describing behavior in terms of the conditioned reflex. Most of Western psychology and philosophy was to follow Pavlov and deny Bergson during the next fifty years.

Thus Bergson picked from three centuries of physical and natural science the basic concept—motion, movement, change, tendency, things in the making, becoming, *not* being. The first of his nine principles is "mobility." "Not *things* made, but things in the making, not self-maintaining *states,* but only changing states, exist. . . . *All reality, therefore, is tendency, if we agree to mean by tendency an incipient change of direction.*"[56] Here Bergson points straight to the nub of the contrast between science and art as applied to knowing. Science studies the subject at length, collects all the materials, makes all the notes, knows through analysis of elements, of parts. Art knows through the "effort to place ourselves directly at the heart of the subject"; the heart of the method is "intuition." This contrast between intuition and analysis is made clear at the beginning of Bergson's little book:

By intuition is meant the kind of *intellectual sympathy* by which one places oneself within an object in order to coincide with what is unique in it and consequently inexpressible. Analysis, on the contrary, is the operation which reduces the object to elements already known, that is, to elements common both to it and other objects. To analyze, therefore, is to express a thing as a function of something other than itself. All analysis is thus a translation, a development into symbols, a representation taken from successive points of view from which we note as many resemblances as possible between the new object which we are studying and others which we believe we know already. In its eternally unsatisfied desire to embrace the object around which it is compelled to turn, analysis multiplies without end the number of its points of view in order to complete its always incomplete representation, and ceaselessly varies its symbols that it may perfect the always imperfect translation. It goes on, therefore, to infinity. But intuition, if intuition is possible, is a simple act.[57]

Later he adds, "There is one reality, at least, which we all seize from within, by intuition and not by simple analysis. It is our own personality in its flowing through time—our self which endures."[58]

SUMMARY

There has been no clear-cut Tao of the West to match in power the Tao of the East. Yet there has played through our dominantly reality-oriented and intellectualistic Western tradition a minor theme counseling men to cultivate and depend upon the powers and products of inner processes of imagination, contemplation and intuition. Disciplines for releasing these inner powers have not developed into conscious articulation as they have developed in the East.

The disciplines have tended to be at once idiosyncratically individual and tied to some area or another of specific artistic production. They have not become communal or generalized into a way of managing human life. Perhaps, ironically, new developments in the sciences will succeed in building acceptable foundations for a Tao of the West where mystics, poets, and intuitive philosophers have met with a very limited hearing. This is one of the convictions on which this book is based.

11

Off-conscious Freedom to Create

THE major episodes of what Blake called "cleansing the doors of perception" have left us a picture of a twilight realm of mind that is relatively free from both conscious and nonconscious censors. The poets and their esthetic sleuths have demolished the notion that the forming process takes place in the conscious mind, or that chance or mere additive synthesis can bring it about. It occurs nonconsciously and rests upon an overflowing subliminal storehouse of fantasy images. Blake was one of the first to see that the creative impulse must be freed from the noise and cant of defensive conscious mind; "Consume the sensory perceptual illusions," he said, "in the fires of imagination." Putting Blake and Cezanne together, I get the cue to the imagined conception which is perception-in-depth. Moreover, the physiologist's and psychiatrist's scientific knowledge that the channels between inner life and outer scene are enteroceptive as well as exteroceptive has been confirmed by the artist's knowing that they are both intuitively inside and observationally outside. But what turns the stuff of poetry into poetry still remains a mystery, relegated to the dæmonic traits of creative genius.

The dream and the daydream also give clues to the creative act. These are free from the normal restraints of waking behavior, manifest the unrestricted, spontaneous play of free association, have access to many levels of nonconscious tracings of perceptual experiences, and display autonomous powers of picking up and coalescing scattered fragments of fantasy imagery. Two aspects of the dream give support to my thesis about the creativeness of the threshold mind. These are its distortional nature and its powers of condensation. The first (the quasi-hallucinatory, illogical jumps and jerks of dream behavior, its denial of the normal categories of gravity and sensory expectations of location in time and space) can be used to document the autistic nature of the transliminal mind. The second is the dream's proved capacity to condense, to short-circuit the flash of insight and avoid the unsolved and baffling floundering of conscious effort. This latter point may provide a crucial clue to the nature of creative imagination.

While little if any definite evidence has been found that the creative act in any complete sense takes place in trance states, an impressive body of clues for research and interpretation on the problem has been built up by the past generation of scientific study and the preceding century of evangelism. Moreover, the evidence of hypermnesia in the hypnotic trance is conclusive; the organism registers and recovers under the hypnotic trance at least ten times as many perceptual reactions as with conscious effort alone. Thus it is known that trance states do have access to many levels of the nonconscious mind; the recovery of "lost memories" is a fact.

The mystifying ability of the organism in the trance state to shut off sensory stimuli, suspend both physiological and psychological functions, and set up controls that function effectively in later conscious behavior, is now traced to the physiology and psychology of the concentration of attention via suggestion, acceptance, ideomotor action and neuromotor enhancement. While great gaps still exist in our knowledge of the physiology of attention, the consensus on the importance of the motor nature of adjustment is steadily being confirmed. Incidentally, additional evidence in integrated physiological-psychological terms has been supplied concerning the nature of thinking.

But most important is the idea that suggestion, especially autosuggestion is the key to the trance state, and may be a clue to the act of imagination. Related to it is the long-ignored but basic act of "acceptance" which has also confirmed the central role of motor tendencies.

No one of these approaches to the threshold mind has emphasized freedom from the censors of conscious and unconscious mind more importantly than the Tao-Zen-Yoga "Great Doctrine" of the East. Chinese Tao is the natural way of relaxed contemplation. Japanese Zen and Indian Yoga provide similar techniques of body-mind liberation from censorious and frustrating conscious mind. By a discipline of ceremonial posture, breathing and moral-spiritual law, they confirm processes of fixation of attention in Western hypnosis. Moreover, they lead to a stage of concentrated, withdrawn meditation that produces creative abstraction. Finally, the art of Tao builds the creative no-mind (that is, no-conscious mind), as do its Western counterparts, on the principle of spontaneity—the West's principle of free association, one of Freud's great contributions to cleansing the doors of perception.

THE LOCUS OF CREATIVE IMAGINATION:
THE OFF-CONSCIOUS

In continuing our search for the center of creative energy in the transliminal mind, I suggest that we can build firmly on the foundations laid by the analyses of the poet's intuition, the dream's proved creativeness, the West's successes in producing the trance state, and their confirmation by the East's Great Doctrine of body-mind liberation. By implication, this also supports the case against two powerful current points of view toward the nature of creative mind. These are pragmatic psychology and classical psychoanalysis. The key to the creative act lies neither in the conscious mind nor in the deep unconscious. It lies in the threshold antechamber between them. In both the conscious or the unconscious the flash is definitely censored. The creative act, which depends upon freedom, is blocked at both rigid ends of the continuum. In the conscious alert mind it is prevented from breaking through by the incessant demands of sensory stimuli and the lopsided, stereotyped nature of perception. In the deep unconscious levels, about which documented knowledge is all too limited, a generation of analysis suggests another rigidity—that caused by the pervading effects of emotional frustration, and by the inaccessibility of much of the nervous storage for conscious use. But in the transliminal chamber the creative mind is free. I can do no better than quote Kubie's agreement that it is the preconscious state that frees the searching mind from rigidity.

Where *conscious* processes predominate at one end of the spectrum, rigidity is imposed by the fact that conscious symbolic functions are anchored by their precise and literal relationships to specific conceptual and perceptual units. Where unconscious processes predominate at the other end of the spectrum there is an even more rigid anchorage, but in this instance to unreality: that is, to those unacceptable conflicts, objects, aims, and impulses which have been rendered inaccessible both to conscious introspection and to the corrective influence of experience, and which are represented by their own special symbols in impenetrable and fixed disguises. As long as their roots remain unconscious, the symbolic representative will remain unmodifiable. That is what renders them rigid.[1]

Hence the evidence points towards Coleridge's "twilight realm," toward the autistic hypnoidal state, toward my transliminal mind, as the creative zone of the continuum.

I recognize that in my synonyms for the characteristics of the threshold state, I am indulging in "bad" words from the viewpoint of conventional psychology: intuition (which positivists still regard as irrational non-sense); autism; distortion of hypnoidal experiences; fantasy images and hallucinations; processes of condensation. Most of these, the pragmatic mind relegates to psychopathology. Actually, they all are indispensable to any interpretation of the normal mind which draws upon the entire continuum of experience. While this can be made clear only by further documentation, I shall anticipate here a bit of the structure of the argument. Perhaps the best way is to see how these roots of intuition are grown in infancy and early childhood.

The Genetics of Intuition: Felt-thought

Recall the picture of the body-mind beginnings of meaning portrayed in Chapter 5, the processes by which the fusion of the first visual, manual, tactual, tasting movements, reflexes and motor images constitute, when shot together in total response, the meaning. While some say these are learned by repetition, without thinking, I prefer to say they are produced through a kind of thinking which can best be described as *felt-thought*. This conception has, in fact, become a major concept in my theory of the act of response.

All learning in neonate life is learning without words, and much learning in later years takes place without verbalized thinking. Watch any three- or four-year-old trotting about the house or family yard. Note the shortness of attention and interest span, measured in half minutes or less; the constant shifting of goal; the momentary character of learning to adjust to differences and likenesses in the physical world. These experiences involve learning to adapt to differences in size, sound, light, weight, texture, motion, what-not, which are universal and commonplace. More subtle are the self-other experiences involved in building relations with the outer world. "These universals," says Kubie, "are among the child's disturbing, primary encounters with reality, about which our elementary symbolic potential develops. . . . To none of these differences have men ever become fully reconciled, either in the course of individual lives, or through the history of human culture. This fact is one of the great unsolved conundrums of human development."[2] But the important fact is that, once the processes of learning are experienced consciously,

they drop out of the central focus of conscious awareness . . . through the repetition which is essential to the early steps by which we learn anything. Even those simple activities which are vital to life itself, such as breathing, sucking, excreting, moving, and crying, start as random and often explosive acts. The ability to execute them purposefully and economically is acquired (i.e., "learned") through repetition, in the course of which they became economically organized into goal-directed synergetic patterns which include somatosensory, somatomuscular and autonomic components. At first all of these activities are triggered by biochemical warning and prodding devices, which operate at this stage in the absence of any symbolic representation. In each instance, however, the *goals* of even the simplest acts soon acquire symbolic representation; and from that moment on in the human being symbolic processes begin to play continuously on the simple physiological mechanisms.[3]

The fundamental process of condensation, characteristic of the threshold state, is related in some unknown way to the contemplation of the goal of any given act. Doing what the situation demands is a principle of the forming process. Kubie thinks that "Once any . . . act is fully learned, it can be initiated quite independently of inner physical prodding merely by contemplating the goal. . . . It is in this way that our thinking processes acquire the ability to leap over many intervening steps as we perform complex arithmetical processes. Moreover, this is the root of intuitive thinking, whether in science or the arts."[4]

This dropping out of consciousness is the amazing process of condensation, the short-circuiting of meaningful response which is characteristic of the threshold mind.

Creative Discovery via Free Association

The stage is set, therefore, for a cardinal concept: freedom to create. When the mind is freed of inhibitions and blockages, a process known throughout the history of thought as "free association" can and does take place. That the materials of reverie or daydream are startling examples of free association is shown by an experience of Lowes, which began with the receipt of a letter from England:[5]

The panorama was set in motion and unrolled without my will. For the moment I simply allowed the images to stream. Then I deliberately assumed control. For when, an hour later, I came back to write, I saw that here, like manna from heaven, was grist for my mill. The sentence about the world of images at the center of which we live stood already on the page, and the skeleton of a plan was in my head. And with the play of free associations fresh in mind, a new agency was interposed. For I have now consciously selected and rejected among the crowding elements of the phantasmagoria, and the elements accepted have been fitted into my design. The streamy nature of association has been curbed and ruddered—and the result is as innocent of poetry as a paradigm.[6]

His further statements about his "normal and typical proceedings" is very important grist for *my* mill, and I quote the half page, partially quoted before, breaking it up with my own numbering:

[1] The thronged yet sleeping subliminal chambers; [2] the summons which unlocks their secret doors; [3] the pouring up of images linked in new conjunctions provocative of unexpected *apercus;* [4] the conscious seizing and directing to an end of suggestions which the unconscious

operations have supplied—not one stage of the process, nor even the transaction as·a whole, is the monopoly of poetry. It is the stuff of which life weaves patterns on its loom; and poetry, which is life enhanced and glorified, employs it too in fashioning more rarely beautiful designs. Intensified and sublimated and controlled though they be, the ways of the creative faculty are the universal ways of that streaming yet consciously directed something which we know (or think we know) as life.

Creative genius, in plainer terms, works through processes which are common to our kind, but these processes are superlatively enhanced. The subliminal agencies are endowed with an extraordinary potency; the faculty which conceives and executes operates with sovereign power; and the two blend in untrammelled interplay. There is always in genius, I imagine, the element which Goethe, who knew whereof he spoke, was wont to designate as "the Dæmonic." But in genius of the highest order that sudden, incalculable, and puissant energy which pours up from the hidden depths is controlled by a will which serves a vision—the vision which sees in chaos the potentiality of Form.[7]

The very young child learns by free association. Freud learned to help patients recover meanings from the unconscious storage by a method and discipline of free association. The cyberneticists of today have taken it, along with the conditioned reflex, as one of their guiding concepts. So the new consensus, supporting somewhat the early associationists, and building on twentieth-century psychology, documents again the ancient concept. Jacques Hadamard, brought together St. Augustine, fourth-century divine, and Max Müller, nineteenth-century philologist, to arrive at a clearer interpretation of the processes of invention. "Max Müller," he says, "observes that the Latin verb 'cogito,' for 'to think,' etymologically means 'to shake together.' St. Augustine had already noticed that and also observed that 'intelligo' means to 'select among.' "[8] Kubie uses the same building stones for his structure of the preconscious mind: "Cogitation and intelligence: *'Cogito,'* to shake things up, to roll the bones of one's ideas, memories and feelings, to make a great melting-pot of experience; plus the superimposed process of *'intelligo,'* i.e., consciously, self-critically but retrospectively, an after-the-act process of choosing from among unanticipated combinations those patterns which have new significance."[9] Then he clinches the argument for my sharp distinction between discovery and verification in the complete act of thought: ". . . the *'cogito'* component i.e., the assembling of new combinations, is predominantly a *preconscious* process . . . whereas *'intelligo'* is of necessity preponderantly *conscious* (although here too preconscious processes play an essential contributory and economizing role)."[10]

Free association thus provides an important cue to freedom to create. I suggest that the two processes are nearly identical. Moreover, this confirms our findings concerning the necessity of the quiet mind of relaxed concentration, an interlude following conscious preparation in which the worker gives up, pushes the problem back or down out of conscious mind. The psychiatrist interprets this as necessary in order for the worker to come back to it with more objective scrutiny.

The processes of free association, moreover, are founded on the facts of neuro-physiology.[11] They are the "obverse of the conditioned reflex [which] depends upon the fact that within any limited period of time no two experiences can impinge on the nervous system without setting up a connecting link."* It is a process of sampling the content of mind which is pertinent to the immediate situation. These free associations are, as I have named them earlier, *what the situation, inner and outer, demands.* Finally, it must be understood that the term "free" does not imply any exemption from natural causation; there is nothing supernatural about this concept, as there is nothing supernatural about intuition. In fact, the intuitive act is, simply put, the freely associative act.

The Paradox: Freedom and Distortion in the Threshold State

We must realize that in providing for more freedom to create, we confront an inescapable paradox. On the one hand, free association facilitates the scanning, analogic process because, by shutting off the conscious mind through concentration of attention, it has eliminated the rigidities of the censoring conscious mind. It also exposes it, however, to whatever distortions are introduced by the subject's autistic kaleidoscope of hallucinatory and fantasy imagery.

---

* See Chapter 13 for the current cybernetics interpretation of the alpha rhythm of the brain as a possible scanning mechanism.

Classical psychoanalysis interprets these as related to rigidities in the unconscious—suppressed guilt feelings, fears, and hates.

But these freely associating motor tendencies and moving images, spring not only from the nervous storage. Their distortional nature is the very essence of the creative act. The logic of the creative artist's ways of working makes that very clear. The basic postulate is that every creative act abstracts. "Abstract" is opposed to "concrete." It is "withdrawn or separate from matter." Attributes, forces, relations between things are what the expressive artist expresses; they are all synonyms for the one central concept. Every creative act, therefore, if it expresses the attributes of a thing, is an act of abstraction. Cheney reminds us that the insistent effort of expressional artists of our time "to reveal the expressive form quality . . . has led to increased *abstraction*"; that is, there has been "progressive neglect of nature's causal aspects . . . distortion of natural shapes and textures; and in frequent cases, utter abandonment of recognizable objectivity."[12] If every expressive act abstracts, then every expressive act distorts; distortion is the name given technically to the process of producing an abstraction.

The steps in the logic back of the thesis that every esthetic act is an act of abstraction, and hence of distortion, are these. First, the artist-as-self expresses his unique view of life as stimulated by the subject with which he starts—physical thing, imagined conception, whatever it may be. Only by chance could it be, if it is truly expressional, a photographic likeness. Second, the artist can produce a creative and unified work of art only by distorting. As Leo Stein put it, distortion "is of the essence of aesthetic expression."[13] In the paintings of both Matisse and Cezanne, for example, no esthetic whole could be obtained by the painter "by keeping a group of normally seen objects constant to their normal appearances." Matisse said that "he never began a picture without hoping that this time he would be able to carry it through without any distortion that would disturb the ordinary onlooker." But in every case the creative requirements upon him led to pictorial dimensions which "had been pulled entirely out of shape."[14]

THE AUTISTIC NATURE OF THE THRESHOLD STATE

The notion of a "preconscious" state is not in itself novel. But we are now discovering the traits of this condition of mind that make it the unique state in which the creative act takes place. At the turn of the century the studies of such pioneering psychiatrists as Janet, Freud, Silberer, and Bleuler distinguished a preconscious mind whose characteristics set it off definitely from conscious mind. Janet and Prince went further and definitely distinguished two "minds," the conscious and what Prince named the "co-conscious." In 1912, Bleuler gave the state the name that has persisted. This was "autism," meaning the "preponderance of inner life as marked by a turning away from the external world."[15] The evidence of the last three chapters shows that the true meaning of "turning away" is that the process is marked by a shutting off of stimuli of the external world and of corresponding inner states.

Bleuler, and many others since his day, presented evidence that autism is a universal normal phenomenon. It is as characteristic of the feeling processes of Einstein, Poincaré, and other scientific theorists as it is of Western artists, the Taoist-Zen artists and philosophers, or the seers of the Western churches. Bleuler found that while the dreamlike thinking of schizophrenics "has laws of its own . . . the same mechanisms [appear] in dreams, in the daydreams of normals and hysterics, in mythology, in superstition, as well as in other deviations of thought from reality."[16] He noted that ". . . the play of fantasy in itself may be autistic or realistic."[17] There were only quantitative differences, he said, between the play dreams of children and those of "the poet whose poem abreacts his unhappy love or transforms it into a happy one, the twilight state of the hysteric, and the hallucinations of the schizophrenic."[18] The real difference is that while the autism of the schizophrenics is independent of reality, normal people "always . . . [know] how to distinguish it from reality."[19]

Thus Janet and his successors were documenting the philosophic speculations of James, Bergson, and other contemporaries concerning the intuitive nature of the fringe mind. After World War I, James's influence was carried forward in psychology by the "feeling" orientation of the personality students, particularly in this country by Gordon Allport and Gardner Murphy; in psychiatry especially by Lawrence Kubie. Under their impact a new conception of mind has slowly formed. It is one that increasingly draws its materials from the whole conscious-nonconscious continuum. Among these men narrow absorption in rational, reality thinking gives way slowly to include an equal concern for the long-ignored nonconscious. Today, as a consequence, those who stand with this school of thought can theorize about life and knowing with the facts of the nonconscious as well as those of the conscious before them.

Autism in Hypnoidal and Distorted Imagery

The study of the transliminal mind as the creative center of the continuum fixes attention on that daily hypnoidal event of transition in and out of sleep, whether it be hypnagogic (as we drift from wakefulness to sleep) or hypnopompic (from sleep to wakefulness). The studies all point to the off-conscious character of hypnoidal experiences. Kubie calls the daily hypnoidal event a "fundamental and recurring tidal process . . . during [which] these universal experiences are re-experienced in dreamlike symbolic representations, altered, fragmented, reworked, distorted, lost, recaptured, resynthesized, and in some measure digested."[20]

In many attempts in my own work to bring about the hospitable mind of intuitive concentration, hypnoidal imagery has provided the most favorable materials for the creative act. I find that there are, for me, two specially favored hypnoidal periods in the twenty-four hour day. One, almost daily in my experience, is during the period of slow awakening from an early afternoon sleep. The other, less frequent, but of critical importance when it happens, is a period of awakening from a deep sleep in the middle of the night. In such cases, I have taken a current problem to bed with me, and, just before drowsiness sets in, have consciously centered my attention on the confused and baffling factors of the problem on which I am working.

The hypnopompic state is especially favored. Then, as at no other time, all environmental pressures are off; not only is the body in repose, the mind is relaxed, too. The quiet mind is achieved to a degree never attained at my desk while I am engaged in conscious effortful thought. Many days when I am on the edge of awakening and auditory imagery is dominant, I "hear" a discussion of the problem with which I went to sleep. I seem to be a witness to a dialogue of analysis which strongly suggests the no-mind state of Tao. Sleep seems to have taken the hectic, fuzzy, conscious mind out of the picture, made way for the nonconscious to do its work and rise to the hypnoidal threshold. The content of the imagery is succinctly conceptual, has crystal clarity, is marked by sharpness and brevity. Ideas flow in, one after another, and I hear each in succession. All uncertainty and confusion have disappeared.

As the threshold mind is autistic, so, too, it moves with hallucinatory, fantastic imagery. We have seen that the images are stored in infancy and early childhood and continue throughout adult life in incessant and continuous fluctuations in the states of consciousness which occur during the waking state, during sleep, and in all transitions between the two. Kubie says that because "of its relevance to creativity I would re-emphasize . . . the fact that these shifts occur during . . . hypnagogic and fully hypnoidal processes and states, in abstracted states and states of maximally focused attention, under the influence of alcohol and of other drugs which affect cortical and/or emotional processes, and in toxic-delirious processes."[21]

While this technique, designed to bring on hypnoidal imagery relating directly to a specific problem, is not always successful, it does yield results far more often than the chancelike occurrences of everyday life. Even in the latter, however, studies such as McKellar's show that "hypnagogic imagining is, like dreaming, a 'normal' rather than 'abnormal' psychological occurrence."[22] He reported the prevalence of a considerable amount of hypnoidal imagery in the general population. Sixty-three per cent of his group experienced some kind of hypnagogic imagery, and of that, the auditory type was by far the most common; 43 per cent was auditory, compared with 37 per cent visual.

Twenty years after Bleuler, Gardner Murphy and his colleagues attacked the problem of the autistic mind experimentally. A dozen studies were made of the influence of autism on perception, memory, and thought by Sanford, Sherif, Bartlett, Murray, Schafer, Clark, Levine, Allport, Kramer, Postman, and others.[23] From the evidence piled up in these studies Murphy built a theory of the forces playing on the whole range of the reality-autistic continuum. In developing my theory of the feeling-thinking continuum, I have drawn heavily on this work. My point of view implies that in every situation what a man needs most will largely determine how he feels and thinks, what his felt-thoughts are. Behavior is drive-motivated; perception, memory, thought are all influenced by needs, drives, satisfactions, and frustrations. "The molding of perception," says Murphy, "or thought or memory in the drive-satisfying direction follows directly from the satisfying or frustrating quality of past perception. . . . All cognitive processes are apparently continually shaped in greater or lesser degree by the pressure of wants."[24]

The accumulating weight of general testimony, therefore, shifts attention from the reality image of logical thought to the autistic, felt imagery of creative discovery. There is no question that in acts of discovery autistic imagery plays a basic role. It is of great importance, therefore, that a solid foundation be laid for understanding the nature of autistic materials from which the flash of insight composes itself.

Reality Imagery and Autistic Imagery

Gardner Murphy, finding an adequate explanation of both imagination and thought only in a bipolar interpretation of reality and autistic experience, distinguishes several classes of images in normal persons:

(1) the most obvious, images of the dream;

(2) the "tied" images of familiar percepts, as instanced in the sixth finger of the conjurer;

(3) the images developing from a neutral matrix, like voices sometimes heard in the conch shell;

(4) the images, ordinarily called hypnagogic, which realize themselves as one is about to fall asleep . . .

(5) the hypnopompic . . . which are similar to the hypnagogic but appear as one wakens;

(6) full-fledged hallucinations, usually in the form of a visual presentation of a person or his voice—at least one normal person in ten experiences such hallucinations occasionally;

(7) the eidetic images, which are so vivid and so "external" that they are often confused with percepts; they are most common in young children.[25]

I know no better biopsychological description of the reality image than this. Condensed and paraphrased, it recognizes four steps in the imaging process: *first,* the sensory stimulation of receptor and cortical cells; *second,* an interval of time during which the stimulus ceases and bodily tissues respond; *third,* perseveration of receptor and cortical cells; *fourth,* in some unknown way, the "reinstatement" of the stimulating object. If the reinstated appearance approximates the original, we call it "image."

This distinction between autistic and reality image still further clarifies the dichotomy between creative thought and logical thought set up in Chapter 2, contrasting the threshold autistic imagery of discovery with the reality imagery of verification. This checks with Galton's findings that mathematicians and other students of logical fields are weak in autistic imagery. This is accentuated by their almost constant emphasis on abstraction. Compare the logician with the graphic artist. The latter cultivates visual, kinesthetic, and motor imagery as his stock-in-trade, while the scientific analyst allows it to atrophy. "Something like this," Murphy says, "apparently happens also in cortical cells" since we know, for example, that those tissues that are surgically deprived of innervation tend to atrophy. He adds that it would be reasonable to conclude that the "cultivation of imagery is in part the physiological cultivation of certain cortical functions."[26] After trying to explain such cases in which two sets of ideas, autistic-associative and logical-reasoning, occur either simultaneously or in rapid alternation, Stekel is convinced that the "notion of thinking in a single direction is no longer tenable." Stekel's testimony agrees with that of many others, that "the thought-process shows a remarkable condensation."[27] Autistic thinking tends to be concrete and discontinuous; reality-thinking to be more abstract. Moreover, abstract in contrast to concrete thought seems to involve some form of censorship. Thurstone in 1924 pointed out that abstraction "is an inhibitory process." Highly intelligent persons inhibit, delay the response, "holding the data in mind" long enough to appraise them, the less intelligent respond more impulsively with concrete images. Galton pointed out two generations ago that the more abstract-minded people inhibit imagery. It is clear that some form of censor is at work.

There is another contrast. In normal reality-thinking we are able to distinguish a situation in which "it is so" from one in which it is "as if it were so." But in autistic thinking we constantly lose our grip on the difference. McKellar himself was experimented on with nitrous oxide. On regaining consciousness, he reported that "enemies had been putting thoughts into his mind and preventing him from saying what he wanted to say." His experience was not an example of "as though," it was like a schizophrenic's "it is so"; "with loss of insight into the difference between analogy and the literally meant, the responses assumed psychotic-like forms."[28] One subject's response was very much like that of Aldous Huxley in his mescalin experiments already described. It revealed extreme empathy for material objects; for example, knowing exactly what it felt like to "be a table." McKellar adds that these descriptions of empathy are like those of people with great esthetic sensitivity. Hoffer, Osmond, and Smythies, using adrenochrome on Osmond, approximated forms of exaggerated psychotic empathy. Osmond says: " 'I felt I was at the bottom of the sea or in an aquarium among a shoal of brilliant fishes.' "[29] Happily, however, the moment in which he concluded he was a sea anemone in the pool was short indeed.

Hallucinations and Fantasies

Autistic imagery entirely beyond conscious control takes on many forms of distortion. The most common one is called hallucination, a term defined technically as an "abnormal interpretation of ideational experiences as perceptions." It can be either positive or negative. In positive hallucinations we perceive objects when the sense receptor is actually receiving no stimulation; in negative hallucination, we fail to perceive facts present to a sense. Thus it is either a supplying of a percept when none is present, or an ignoring of present percepts. Hallucination, therefore, is to be distinguished from illusion, which is false perception, and from delusion, which is false judgment.

Hallucination and other forms of distortion have been studied psychologically for over a century. The hallucinations of schizophrenics, of alcoholics in delirium tremens, and of normal individuals under the sedative influence of drugs, are *paralleled in the normal mind* by quasi-hallucinations or other forms of distorted imagery. Quasi-hallucinations are, in fact, difficult to distinguish from perceptual images. Visual hypnagogic imaging is close to hallucinatory experience. In reports of childhood experiences, there are frequent references to "faces in the dark"—"terrifying faces, one replacing the other. This happened quite often when I was younger. . . . They seemed too vivid and extraordinarily evil not to belong to something real, somewhere."[30] McKellar's sound-recordings include that of one subject who had a vision of an alligator, that lasted two and a half minutes; another had a vision of a field of wheat that remained for fifty seconds. Many cases of "broad daylight" hallucinations among normal adults can be found in the literature. For example, one person while living in the desert "heard peals of girlish laughter outside," but on dashing out found that "there wasn't even a camel to be seen." Another described what might have been a negative hallucination. "I can play pieces of music and not hear a note," perhaps accounted for by intense concentration on other matters.[31]

These autistic images take on a great variety of forms. The most common ones are *déjà vu,* which has already been mentioned, synesthesia and body schema.

Synesthesia, according to the psychological dictionary, is an experience "in which certain sensations belonging to one sense or mode attach to certain sensations of another group and appear regularly whenever a stimulus of the latter type occurs."[32] It appears to be at its height in early childhood and declines steadily toward adulthood. Twenty-one per cent of McKellar's Aberdeen University subjects reported it. He suggested hyphenated names for special forms—"visual-auditory," "tactile-auditory," and "visual-temperature"; one of his colleagues reported a kinesthetic-olfactory example.

Synesthesia seems to be especially common in music. One reporter said: " 'I tend to visualize images of patterns and shapes when I hear music, particularly that of Bach.' " Sometimes tactile imagery is related to auditory; for example, " 'a trumpet sound is the feel of some sort of . . . plastic cloth!' "[33] Gombrich reports a case of a musician who found that there was " 'only one position in the bed which is in *F sharp major,* and that is the only one which makes sleep possible.' "[34]

Body schema is the name given to autistic images related to the body as an object in space. Lewis Carroll drew on this phenomenon in creating Alice's amazing changes in size during her Wonderland experiences. McKellar comments that "Lewis Carroll may . . . well have had imagination experiences not unlike those which Alice underwent." It is known that, "as Lippmann . . . and Bexton . . . have pointed out, body schema experiences occur in migraine, from which Dodgson is known to have suffered."[35]

Thirteen of Lancaster's psychiatric patients reported body schema; five of the instances were related to hypnagogic imagery. One of McKellar's subjects said, "All my body size was swelling like a balloon and I was being held together by thin bands of string in place of bones." Another reported, "When overtired I occasionally feel as if some part of my face, e.g., nose or ears, has become much larger than normal."[36] McKellar and his colleagues reported successful experiments with sound recordings of subjects experiencing vivid body schema images; for example, "It looks like a large face. . . . Oh, it's horrible! It's like a large turnip. The eyes are a purple color." The images appeared to "come out of a pin point of light, and sort of grow, magnify and become clearer."[37]

The empathic experience of feeling one's way inside an object, of vicariously living the function of the object, as Theodor Lipps taught us to understand it, is of importance in creative work. But it is also revealed in the distorted imagery of everyday life. McKellar reports a case in which the patient said that "when anyone describes a pain, toothache, etc., I experience the pain of toothache for a few minutes."[38] I regard empathy as a most important form of kinesthetic-motor imagery and hence of incipient body movement in the creative process.

Galton reported various "other unnamed experiences" as "imagery associations"; for example, the subject who "when hearing the interrogation 'What?' invariably experienced a visual image of a fat man cracking a long whip." Galton reported that some people associate character traits with numbers.[39] Conditions of fatigue "may produce *exaggerated perseveration* and blockages of thought." Such phenomena perhaps can be accounted for on the grounds of the blurring of images, feelings, or thoughts under conditions of fatigue, narcosis, and so forth.

In my accumulated data from investigations since Galton, I find convincing evidence that the imagery of the normal hypnoidal states not only supplies rich sources for creative imaginations, but that the characteristics of the autistic mind facilitate the passage of unconscious materials across the threshold. We know, for instance, that the bulk of the pictures in our heads are autonomous. They are outside our waking control, rising to consciousness without our so willing. One of Galton's subjects, for example, said, "When the process is in full activity I feel as if I were a mere spectator at a diorama of a very eccentric kind."[40] We have confirmatory evidence from Gordon's studies which distinguish autonomous and controlled images, and go far toward establishing the predominance of autonomous imaging in our everyday lives.

The autistic mind is very clearly set off from the reality-oriented mind by the lack of conscious control. While autistic images are spontaneous, conscious-reality mind works with the imagery of perceptual experience in full awareness and control. This confirms the thesis that the conscious-reality mind is rarely successful in producing the flash of discovery. The latter occurs in the quiet mind, when one is off-guard, relaxed. Yet we must not lose sight of the fact that both are on the conscious-unconscious continuum, as are the autistic-thinking of both the normal and the psychotic. This is revealed in dreams, nightmares, and hypnagogic experiences. Hallucinations occur and are autonomous in the normal person, the neurotic, and the true psychotic. But while the normal man adjusts to and explains away his hallucinations, the psychotic is unable to do so; witness the sudden unexpected and apparently uncontrollable upsurges of emotion in psychotic behavior. Skinner says it is as though these emotions were "emitted by the organism." Thus autistic thinking and normal reality-thinking seem to be distinguished by the "ability to select relevantly and to inhibit the irrelevant." But in all autistic-thinking, whether normal or psychotic, loss of conscious control is evident.

The distinction between autistic and reality-oriented mind stands out clearly in comparing early childhood with mature adulthood. As studies of eidetic imagery have shown, autism predominates in the early childhood mind. Body movement is almost continuous during waking hours; perceptual experience—seeing, hearing, touching, smelling, tasting, and becoming oriented in space and time—are central to the growth process. Feeling is at a maximum, thinking at a minimum. Although linguistic vocabulary increases, verbalizing is limited and concept-forming takes place slowly. In adulthood, however, if home and school have been "successful," the feeling-autistic mind has dropped into the background, the reality-mind has taken over. Body movement has been greatly reduced, but incipient movement continues to play its constant role in all meaningful acts of response. Perceptual experience continues its major functions, but clear distinctions between it and conceptual experience have not yet been made. Verbalization is at a maximum as is to be expected in our world of words.

THE HEALTHY MIND DEPRIVED OF CUSTOMARY STIMULI

A totally independent literature from studies of human isolation[41] produced in the last decade throws new and confirming light on the conception of the normal mind as a state of delicate balance and as a potential center of creative activity. I have drawn on the recent writings of today's outstanding student of this problem, Dr. John Lilly, and have studied the best autobiographies of lonely travelers.

The clue to understanding the relevance of human isolation to the problem of the threshold mind lies in its deprivation of stimuli from the outside environment. Because of this deprivation of stimuli it is necessary to distinguish precisely the experimental isolation data from the reports of effects of limited environmental stimuli in autobiographies of lonely travelers. Certainly experiences of all the lonely reporters were normal in one respect—they were never deprived of a wide range of physical stimuli. No one of their dozen sensory channels was shut off. They saw, heard, touched, smelt, tasted, responded to objects in space and time. In those physical senses they were not isolated. Psychologically, however, they were "isolated," especially those who were alone. I shall state the chief conclusions from the latter cases first.

Psychological isolation itself "acts on most persons," says Lilly, with "effects . . . similar to those of any extreme stress." Mental symptoms are caused "to appear rapidly and intensely." But he adds that, "as is well known, stresses other than isolation can cause the same symptoms to appear in individuals in an isolated group." Gibson, in *The Boat,* reports the case in which only four persons (out of an initial thirty-five) survived in a lifeboat in the Indian Ocean in World War II. Lilly sums up the symptoms, reported by Gibson, resulting from the loss of hope, dehydration, thirst, sunburn, and physical combat.

Most of the group hallucinated rescue planes and drank salt water thinking it fresh; many despaired and committed suicide; others were murdered; and some were eaten by others. The whole structure of egos was shaken and recast in desperate efforts at survival. (It is interesting to note that many of those who committed suicide tried to sink the boat by removing the drain plugs before jumping overboard, i.e., sink the boat [and other persons] as well as the self; this dual destruction may be used by some of the non-surviving solitary sailors.) [42]

Among factors reported by Gibson which were oriented to survival under extreme isolation were these: having previously acquired the ability to become completely physically and mentally passive; being able to maintain the conviction that one would come through the experience; and "having a woman . . . beside him, who shared his passivity and convictions." In all cases, either surviving at sea or from isolation in the polar night, "it was the first exposure which caused the greatest fears and hence the greatest danger of giving way to symptoms; previous experience is a powerful aid." Bombard, for example, was emphatic that "if the terror of the first week can be overcome, one can survive. Apparently, many do not survive this first period."

Slocum's hallucination of the "savior" type involving the pilot of Columbus' ship, the *Pinta,* was one of the most graphic examples:

Slocum had a severe gastro-intestinal upset just before a gale hit his boat; he had reefed his sails, but should have taken them down. Under the circumstances, he was unable to move from the cabin. At this point he saw a man take over the tiller. At first he thought it was a pirate, but the man reassured him and said that he was the pilot of the *Pinta* and that he would take his boat safely through the storm. Slocum asked him to take down the sail, but the man said, no, they must catch the *Pinta* ahead. The next morning Slocum recovered, and found his boat had covered 93 miles on true course, sailing itself. (His boat was quite capable of such a performance; he arranged it that way for long trips without his hand at the helm.) In a dream that night the pilot appeared and said he would come whenever Slocum needed him. During the next three years the helmsman appeared to Slocum several times, during gales.[43]

Christiane Ritter, isolated "for periods up to 16 days at a time," hallucinated a dreadful monster and saw past experiences "as if in bright sunshine." She said she "became 'at one' with the moon, and developed a monomania to go out over the snow." Lilly comments that "she was saved by an experienced Norwegian who put her to bed and fed her lavishly." But she developed such an intense love for polar isolation that she found it very hard to leave the North.

There have been many examples of hallucinatory symptoms involving superstition. Bombard, for example, "thought the number of matches necessary to light a damp cigarette represented the number of days until the end of the voyage. He was wrong several times." Bombard had two-way conversations with a doll mascot. Slocum passed a dangerous reef named M reef which he regarded as "lucky because M is the thirteenth letter of the alphabet." Other cases of superstition were reported such as refusal to eat fish because of "intense love of any living things."

During such complete psychological isolation the person lives so intense an inner life that it takes considerable time to live again in the company of other people and "to reestablish one's inner criteria of sanity." After eighteen months of solitary confinement in World War II, "Christopher Burney was afraid to speak for fear that he would show himself to be insane." Only after listening to other people for several days did he finally feel that he had recovered the usual criteria of sanity, and was able to engage in conversation. Others reported deep feelings that when one lands one "had best be careful to listen before speaking to avoid being considered insane." "Bernicot refused an invitation to dinner on another yacht after crossing the Atlantic alone until he could recapture the proper things to talk about."

What are the chief factors in survival? The quiet mind again, the mood of relaxation and confidence. Only through either physical or mental "passivity" did the survivors build the firm confidence that "he or she will survive" or when there were "definite reassurances from others that each will be rescued." Lilly points out that "in those cases of a man and a woman together, or even the probability of such a union within a few days, there is apparently not only a real assurance of survival, but a love of the situation can appear." Of course, such couples do not represent psychological isolation; "many symptoms can be avoided by healthy persons with such an arrangement."

After interviewing two polar solitaries and studying the literature of the lonely travelers, Lilly concludes that the healthy ego is "dependent . . . in some degree, on exchanges with the surroundings to maintain its structure." He grants that the autobiographies are incomplete because of "social taboos, discretion to one's self, suppression and repression of painful or uncomfortable material, secondary elaboration, and rationalization." Nevertheless, it is clear that "persons in isolation experience many, if not all, of the symptoms of the mentally ill." In some of the survivors these symptoms were found to be reversible—namely, that the experience of the isolation-produced symptoms, on return to normal social life, actually serve to build up symptoms of an even more normal inner security and integration. "Most survivors report, after several weeks exposure to isolation, a new inner security and a new integration of themselves on a deep and basic level."

The "underlying mechanisms are obscure." But Lilly is convinced that

some of the mind's activity which is usually reality-bound now becomes free to turn to phantasy and ultimately to hallucination and delusion. It is as if the laws of thought are projected into the realm of the laws of inanimate matter and of the universe. The primary process tends to absorb more and more of the time and energy usually taken by the secondary process. Such experiences either lead to improved mental functioning or to destruction. Why one person takes the healthy path and another person the sick one is not yet clear.[44]

In the light of the limited physical isolation revealed by the autobiographical accounts, Lilly set up an experimental attempt at the National Institute of Mental Health to investigate the major question. What happens to a brain and its contained mind in the relative absence of physical stimulation? There are really two separate problems. One is neuro-physiological and the other psychiatric. The former he states in this form. "Freed of normal efferent and afferent activities, does the activity of the brain soon become that of coma or sleep, or is there some inherent mechanism which keeps it going, a pacemaker of the 'awake' type of activity?" The statement of the psychiatric problem—"If we expose a healthy whole person to certain stresses, such as physical isolation from patterned stimuli, can it be demonstrated that mental symptoms develop?" I quote his description of his own experiment:

. . . the subject is suspended with the body and all but the top of the head immersed in a tank containing slowly flowing water at 34.5° C. (94.5° F.), wears a blacked-out mask (enclosing the whole head) for breathing, and wears nothing else. The water temperature is such that the subject feels neither hot nor cold. The experience is such that one tactually feels the supports and the mask, but not much else; a large fraction of the usual pressures on the body caused by gravity are lacking. The sound level is low; one hears only one's own breathing and some faint water sounds from the piping; the water-air interface does not transmit air-borne sounds very efficiently. It is one of the most even and monotonous environments I have experienced. After the initial training period, no observer is present. Immediately after exposure, the subject writes personal notes on his experience.[45]

Lilly had only two subjects including himself. The longest exposure was three hours. Lilly found that an "initial set of training exposures overcomes the fears of the situation itself." The subject always had a full night's rest before entering the tank and was advised to inhibit all movements as far as possible.

I summarize Lilly's conclusions about the stages of the tank experience. The first three-quarters of an hour are marked by general awareness of surroundings and other normal experience; the "day's residues are predominant" and recent problems are surveyed. It is a period of gradual relaxation and a good deal of enjoyment. There is a feeling of being isolated in space and having nothing to do is restful and relaxing.

In the second hour tension develops. There is a "stimulus-action hunger." The subject stimulates himself by hidden movements— "twitching muscles, slow swimming movements . . . stroking one finger with another." If these are inhibited over a considerable period of time they can later produce intense satisfaction. But, if prolonged inhibition wins, "tension may ultimately develop to the point of forcing the subject to leave the tank." As this goes on, the subject concentrates on the mask, the suspension, on any "residual stimuli" and each one becomes "the whole content of consciousness to an almost unbearable degree." If this stage is passed without leaving the tank, reality-thinking has given way to ". . . reveries and fantasies of a highly personal and emotionally charged nature. These are too personal to relate publicly, and probably vary greatly from subject to subject. The individual reactions to such fantasy material also probably varies considerably, from complete suppression to relaxing and enjoying them."

Lilly describes the hallucinatory limit of the exploration which he has once experienced: ". . . after a two and one-half hour period, the black curtain in front of the eyes (such as one 'sees' in a dark room with eyes closed) gradually opens out into a three-dimensional, dark, empty space in front of the body. This phenomenon captures one's interest immediately, and one waits to find out what comes next. Gradually forms of the type sometimes seen in hypnagogic states appear. In this case, they were small, strangely shaped objects with self-luminous borders. A tunnel whose inside 'space' seemed to be emitting a blue light then appeared straight ahead." A kind of training effect develops; one learns "to be more tolerant of many internal activities. Fear lessens with experience, and personal integration can be speeded up. . . . The opposite effects may also be accelerated in certain cases. Fantasies about the experience (such as the illusion of 'return to the womb,' which is quite common) are dispelled; one realizes that at birth we start breathing air and hence cannot 'return to the womb.' One's breathing in the tank is extremely important; as a comforting, constant safeguard and a source of rhythmic stimulation."

Hebb's experiments at McGill, although they did not approximate the physical isolation of Lilly's, did supply confirming data.

A subject is placed on a bed in an air-conditioned box with arms and hands restrained with cardboard sleeves, and eyes covered completely with translucent ski goggles. The subjects are college students motivated by payment of $20 per day for as long as they will stay in the box. An observer is present, watching through a window, and tests the subject in various ways verbally through a communication set.[46]

Hebb confirms Lilly in several ways. Greatly increased need for stimuli and action developed, illustrated by "periods of thrashing around in the box. . . ." "The borderline between sleep and awakedness became diffuse and confused." The subjects found it "difficult to carry on organized, directed thinking for any sustained period. Suggestibility was very much increased." At times varying from one to three days the subjects "couldn't stand it any longer and left. Hallucinations and delusions of various sorts developed, mostly in those who could stay longer than two days."

The after-effects in both Lilly's and Hebb's experiment are similar to those reported by solitaries of polar living and sailing. If one is alone long enough with stimulation low enough

. . . the mind turns inward and projects outward its own contents and processes; the brain not only stays active despite the lowered levels of input and output, but accumulates surplus energy to extreme degrees. In terms of libido theory, the total *amount* of libido increases with time of deprivation; body-libido reaches new high levels. If body-libido is not discharged somatically, discharge starts through fantasy; but apparently this is neither an adequate mode nor can it achieve an adequate rate of discharge in the presence of the rapidly rising level. At some point a new threshold appears for more definite phenomena of regression: hallucinations, delusions, oceanic bliss, etc. At this stage, given any opportunities for action or stimulation by external reality, the healthy ego seizes them and re-establishes more secondary process.[47]

In both the Lilly and Hebb experiments, the subjects had difficulty in reorientation of perceptual mechanisms under normal conditions. Illusions persisted for several hours. Lilly felt then that the day started all over again, "as if he had just arisen from bed afresh; this effect persists, and the subject finds he is out of step with the clock for the rest of that day. He also has to re-adjust to social intercourse in subtle ways. The night of the day of the exposure he finds that his bed exerts great pressure against his body. No bed is as comfortable as floating in water."

There may be an important by-product in these studies for understanding the nature of imagination. Isolation-produced hallucinations appear to be about the same as those accompanying mescalin intoxication. At their maximum vividness, the visual hallucinations were three-dimensional, and "could be scanned by eye and head movements . . . [their] contents surprising to the ego." The material of the hallucinations seemed very like that of dreams, with story-bits of past memories mixed with some recent real events. The subject's reactions to these phenomena were generally "amusement and a sense of relief from the pressing boredom. They could describe them vocally without abolishing the sequences [of imagery]. A small number of subjects experienced doubling of their body images. A few developed transient paranoid delusions."

Isolation of men from the bombardment of sensory stimuli does induce autistic activity in their off-conscious minds. The states induced are "abnormal" and studies of them were undertaken to illuminate pathology and its conditions. But the results may also be read as indicative of the inner processes by which new forms of perception and conception are created. Creative imagination must always go beyond the normal and conventional in providing new orientations, new imagined conceptions, new hypotheses. Perhaps overcoming the fear of the "abnormal" and "pathological" in ourselves and others is one important pre-condition of effectively freeing the powers of the off-conscious mind.

Part III

TOWARD A THEORY

OF THE

CREATIVE IMAGINATION

12

Conditions of an Adequate Theory

For this book, the data-gathering stage of the search for understanding is over. We may have missed some minor bits, but, I believe, nothing of great importance. The stuff of creative mind, screened from the sciences and arts of man and the tested wisdom of the ages, is now available to our own insights. And more than conceptual findings, a considerable body of theory has appeared to fill in the gaps. These primordial materials contain within themselves whatever answer can now be given to the query: What is the nature of the act of thought when, in one brilliant moment, there is a sudden veering of attention, a consequent grasp of new dimensions, and a new idea is born? We know that some autonomous forming process characteristic in some degree of the behavior of all living organisms, sweeps like a magnet across the chaotic elements of the threshold state, picking up the significant segments and, in a welding flash, precipitates the meaningful response. This has been the principal clue to answering the question: What, in the creative act, gives form to the bits and pieces of the stuff of mind?

From various sources not usually brought together and interrelated, I have sought and found a factual and conceptual consensus of answers to specific parts of this large question. When we run out of factual and conceptual consensus, we turn to theory. Just what do I mean by theory? It is the best imagined model we can conceive of a given situation. It is our imagined conception of how a given thing or act or situation might work or be explained. Many definitions of theory have been given. One example is "a body of credible hypotheses to guide experimentation." A more rigorous one is "hypotheses having their sources in validated conceptual knowledge on the frontiers of science."

In practical life, before we can build anything with assurance that it will work, we must conceive of it in imagination. We call this imagined conception a model or a design. Both artists and engineers speak of it as design. For any truly creative person, the criteria for theory are rigorous. As the foregoing definition has emphasized, the imagined design, to be valid, must be based on all the known pertinent conceptual knowledge. It must fit the facts and spring from a plausible conceptual orientation. It must be functional; that is, it must account for what human situations demand of the act. It must have generality, that is, it must be capable of generalizing all comparable cases. It must meet the conditions of parsimony and economy. In other words, it must provide an organization to which nothing can be added and from which nothing can be taken away. Its structure must have logical consistency and its design or model must be susceptible to both logical and experimental testing and demonstration. Finally, the theory and its design or model must have clear and sufficient explanatory value.

These criteria are general, applying to a theory of anything. More specifically, a theory of the creative imagination must meet the following specific requirements.

1. It must be a theory of the whole mind, not the half mind of conventional psychology. It must visualize life as lived and behavior as governed by the entire vast conscious-nonconscious continuum, not just by the tiny, censorious conscious part.

2. It must postulate that there is really no body-mind problem; that those who say, with Sherrington, that the gap between physiology and psychology will never be bridged, are wrong; that those who say that there is either a parallelism or an interaction or relatedness between them are equally wrong. Actually, each act of human response is a total, integrated, organic response. Some phases (such as the signalling of messages from receptors to midbrain and cortex and their integration with the endo-thalamic and autonomic systems) are obviously physiological; others, such as

perception and fantasy, imaging and recognition of symbolic meanings, are psychological. But all are fused functions of a total act, made up of a flux of imagery, bodily (muscular) movements and incipient tendencies to act, which are really attitudes of anticipation and seem to play a determining role in the nature of the meaning conveyed by the response.

3. Seeking primarily the body-mind conditions of freedom to create (the abolition of all censors), the theory must concentrate attention on the freely associative autistic mind of the threshold state, rather than on the reality conscious mind. It is concerned, therefore, with the pre-logical and preconscious rather than the logical, the analytical, and the conscious. This is the first key to its explanation:—that the creative flash of insight takes place in the transliminal, across-the-threshold border between the unconscious and the conscious states. This is the "off-conscious, quiet mind" that, by freeing the organism of its censors, *lets things happen.*

4. It must distinguish the creative act of discovery from the problem-solving, reasoning act of logical verification. In the light of the present neglect of the creative act, it must center attention upon it.

5. The theory must postulate that there are two ways of knowing: an intuitive, inside way of identification with the object, or person, and an outside, scientific, observational and measuring approach. Both are postulated as necessary to fully adequate knowledge. The widespread acceptance of this theory will go far toward welding the great perennial dichotomy that has divided men of thought and men of feeling throughout human history.

6. Since the present concern is with the *creative act,* the theory must take its cues primarily from the inside identification point of view, organically from the center outward, not mechanistically from the outside looking in. Thus, the organism is viewed as active and self-directive, not as a re-active automaton, controlled by stimuli from the outside.

7. The inside, intuitive identification must be considered as an autonomous forming process which characterizes the human being, as well as every other organism, from cell to whole animal. A sufficient physiological body of knowledge is available on the continuously pulsating multi-trillion-celled organism. The correspond-

ing psychological stuff of mind is available in the flux of fantasy imaging and motor tendencies.

8. The theory must postulate that absolute concentration of attention (involving the shutting out of all extraneous outer or inner stimuli) is a prerequisite for the creative act. This condition inheres particularly in the quiet, hypnoidal, transliminal state.

9. Creative thought (in contra-distinction to logical thought) must be conceived as felt-thought. It is expressed primarily through *gesture* rather than through words. The present theory of the creative act, therefore, builds chiefly on the nonverbal, gestural expression of feeling. It postulates that logical verification is done primarily through verbalized thinking. *This makes felt-thought, rather than verbally-reasoned thought, the crux of a theory of the creative act.*

10. The underlying theory of the complete act of thought must provide for two symbolisms: a nonverbal gestural symbolism for the imagined conception; a verbal, symbolic logic for its validation.

11. The theory must postulate that the motor-imaging stuff of mind is in ceaseless, pulsating action of electrochemical cellular movement in the central nervous system and throughout the nervous organization of the organism. Thus the nonconscious storage of experience is always available in the sense that the organism never stops or starts, never has to be "turned on." Hence it can be "tuned in to" with the proper fusion of electronic, physiological and psychological stimuli which we call the *determining tendency* to act.

12. The anchorages of the tuning-in process of every meaningful response must be seen as bipolar. It is a fusion of stimuli from the outer-scene and the inner-stress system—a merging of the stereotypes of the external civilization and the unconsciously worked-over personality traits and dominant beliefs and conceptions of the individual.

13. Because of the infinite complexity of the ceaselessly moving human organism, its every movement of life must be seen as precariously unstable. Life is possible only through the basic continuity of the tension-release-tension cycle, each phase passing from imbalance to balance, but always with enough surplus energy to carry the organism over dead center to imbalance. The theory must

account for the on-going, never-ceasing, accumulating structure-building. Its very foundation is a conception of rhythmic pulsation as the basis of the autonomous forming process. Being intermittently a bit off-balance is the key to the continuity of the life process. This is the basic notion of the incompleted act, and this supplies an important key to the nature of the act of meaningful response. It is, therefore, basic to any adequate theory of the creative act.

EDITOR'S NOTE. This chapter shows that the author was well aware of the requirements of the theory he was seeking to formulate. The next two chapters represent separate attempts to push toward the articulation of a theory which met these requirements. Each attempt follows a major trend in contemporary studies of mental functioning. The first builds upon the analogical relations between brain functioning and the processing of data by electronic computers. The second focuses upon studies of symbolic operation and symbolic transformation seen as central to "mental" functioning.

Neither chapter was completed by the author at the time of his death. Yet each as it stands, is of intrinsic importance to students of creative imagination for two reasons. First, each assembles and presents contemporary materials which any serious theory of creative response must take into account. Second, the author makes the assembled material his own and uses it to advance his own developing theory.

As the chapters now stand, the interrelations between the two approaches to a theory of the imagination are not developed. However, in the final chapter, the author attempts to interrelate the two sets of ideas. Readers may prefer to study the final chapter first and then return to Chapters 13 and 14 for the more detailed treatment which they provide.

13

An Approach through Brain-mind Modeling

W E need a basic over-all theory of the act of response upon which can be developed contributory theories of the creative act and its basis in perceiving, conceiving and recalling. In the last twenty years no less than a dozen such theories have been advanced from an encyclopedic range of physiological, psychological, psychiatric, mathematical, and philosophical data. In this present study some of these, especially the earlier ones which are outmoded and others which have not been substantiated, have been discarded. Several are founded on the organic orientation which has been developed in this book. Others of sharply differing and even atomistic orientation have attracted the attention and survived the critical appraisal of distinguished minds in the behavioral sciences, philosophy, and the arts of expression.

Not the least among recent gains is a large body of provocative theory offered in answer to the question: How does the brain-mind model reality? I have brought together a critical selection of those theories that have been produced on the frontiers between the physiological, psychological, psychiatric, and philosophical disciplines. Some of these represent primarily the limited point of view of brain neurologists, although physiologists concerned with emotions have also been involved in the building of the theories, and I

244

have drawn upon them. Others have been produced by psychologists and psychiatrists with physiological experience. These men have also considered carefully the findings of pioneers in the development of a new philosophy and psychology of the act.

CRAIK'S PIONEER HYPOTHESIS

So far as I have been able to determine, Kenneth Craik offered the pioneer suggestion as to how the brain-mind may model the real world.[1] He was a pre-cyberneticist who advanced the hypothesis that the human being carries in his head a mapping "contrivance" that can model, or parallel, the events of the external world and its events. He was one of the first to visualize the possible analogy between the then hypothetical "communication machine" and the human nervous system, and the importance of physical models or "mock-ups" such as abounded in the designing rooms and laboratories of great industrial plants and of the military commands in World War II. His suggestions apparently preceded the original discovery of radar by the allied engineers and mathematicians who put the new electronics to work in the communication control of machines. And he went even beyond this. From his multi-discipline interests in philosophy and psychology, he advanced the theory that "the whole of thought may . . . consist of a process of symbolism."[2]

In Craik's own language the twofold hypothesis is:

that thought models, or parallels, reality—that its essential feature is not "the mind," "the self," "sense-data," nor propositions but symbolism, and that this symbolism is largely of the same kind as that which is familiar to us in mechanical devices which aid thought and calculation.[3]

He found three stages in the thought process: first, the perception of events as translated into words or other symbols; second, the manipulation of these ideas as words or other symbols until another idea or symbol appears; third, retranslation of the ideas or symbols into the predicted design of the process or event in the real world. It is in this way that the brain-mind modeling power enables us "to design bridges with a sufficient factor of safety instead of building them haphazard and waiting to see whether they collapse."[4]

Craik was reaching for an explanation of the basis of "concepts or sensations of objects in the nervous system." He restated his thesis provocatively: *"In a neural calculating machine there may well be patterns of excitation in the cortex,* temporal and spatial groupings of impulses, and so forth which, to a physiologist sufficiently skilled, would 'represent' concepts or sensations of objects."[5]

Has the human nervous system the capacity for doing these things? Yes, there is, on the one hand, abundant evidence of its "great mechanical possibilities" and, on the other, of the power of the nervous system to transform the recorded experience of the past into symbolic form. As for the former, the three processes of translation, inference and re-translation "become the translation of external events into some kind of neural patterns by stimulation of the sense-organs, the interaction and stimulation of other neural patterns, as in 'association'; and the excitation by these of effectors or motor organs."[6] As for the connection of the nervous system with the symbol, these three processes are carried on with words, numbers, and other coded symbols. Thus a working model stresses the similarity of its relation-structure and that of external events. He suggests that the key to the relation of the symbol to the pattern in the nervous system lies "in causal chains and physical or chemical combinations." In modeling physical processes the nervous system *"has only to produce combinations of excited arcs,* not physical objects; its 'answer' need only be a combination of *consistent patterns of excitation*—not a new object that is physically and chemically stable."[7]

Craik advances several other provocative suggestions, especially intriguing is one which deals with the problem of recognition of absolute and relative qualities and quantities. I shall return to these, however, after stating some basic general concepts.

THE CYBERNETICS THEORY OF BRAIN-MIND
MODELING

The most sustained and, I think, far-reaching theoretical efforts, in this area have been those of the multi-discipline group of physiologists, psychologists, psychiatrists, mathematicians, and electronics engineers known as cyberneticians.[8] I turn to them with a caution concerning the limitations in their sources and techniques which are created by their frankly mechanistic point of view. Their hypotheses have been developed with little or no concern for feeling factors and other physiological foundations of emotional life, nor for interdependent psychological functions.

It was this multi-discipline group who, from their work in World War II in the discovery and practical application of radar to communication control in the machine, provided, in the decade after the last war, the most provocative body of logical extensions of Craik's theory. This began in Britain in 1940 with the work of W. Ross Ashby, and was continued in the United States immediately after the war by the group formed under the leadership of Norbert Wiener and the Josiah Macy Foundation. The total body of theory was given the name "cybernetics" by Wiener, from a Greek word meaning "steersman."

Although Ashby's pronouncements in Britain antedated those of the American cybernetics group by several years, I turn first to the material of Wiener, McCulloch and Pitts, and Walter, because Ashby's theory is completely mechanistic and on the whole does not seem to throw clear light on my over-all problem. Craik's work is far from Ashby's, employing both physiological and psychological vocabularies, giving a place to feeling as well as thinking, and to creative and esthetic experience. While both McCulloch and Walter are pretty thoroughly mechanistic, Wiener has always seemed to me rather begrudgingly to leave a place open for the "emotional" qualities in characteristics which distinguish the animal from the machine. With these qualifications in mind, I turn to their first major point, the fact of parallelism between men and machines.

Wiener's statement of his basic thesis uses the vocabulary of parallelism:

It is my thesis that the operation of the living individual and the operation of some of the newer communication machines are precisely parallel. Both of them have sensory receptors as one stage in their cycle of operation; that is, in both of them there exists a special apparatus for collecting information from the outer world at low energy levels, and for making it available in the operation of the individual or of the machine. In both cases these external messages are not taken *neat*, but through the internal transforming powers of the apparatus, whether it be alive or dead. The information is then turned into a new form available for the further stages of performance. In both the animal and the machine this performance is made to be effective on the outer world. In both of them, their *performed* action on the outer world, and not merely their *intended* action, is reported back to the central regulatory apparatus. This complex of behavior is ignored by the average man, and in particular does not play the role that it should in our habitual analysis of society.[9]

F. H. Allport, in a monumental appraisal of sixty years of theorizing about perception,[10] cites many such parallelisms and agrees that "the organism and the computing machine have much in common." Both have inputs and outputs. Both have "switching apparatus"; the electrical machine's relays are paralleled by the human nervous system's switching function of the brain's ten billion neurons. "Both have receptors into which 'information' is fed"; in the computer these are photo-electric cells, microphones, radar systems, etc.; in the organism they are the sense organs. Both are systems of communicating messages and manipulating information. Both have "effectors"—man's muscles and glands, the machine's motors. Both can store and recollect "experience," that is, there is a form of "memory" and "recall" in both. Both can produce the "input-output synthesis" of "messages" coming from the outside world with others that come from the inside. The input-output synthesis is achieved in both by "negative feedback"; this will be fully detailed in a moment. They both operate on a very small amount of energy. The structure of both consists primarily of "circular arrangements rather than straight-line operations."

Summing up the analogies between brain and machine another way, both man and machine *solve* problems and *answer* questions, but *only man can state a problem or ask a question*. The machine can solve only those problems, the data for which have been coded and built into the machine by a man. This points to a fundamental distinction between man and machine. Both man and machine solve problems by feeding information through coded electrical impulses; the codes represent atomistic signals—numbers, words, etc. Both can classify and manipulate and compare information. In the human being examples of these operations abound. Coming out into a brightly lighted place, just as one example, the pupils of the eye contract, the brain measuring intensity of light by counting the number of electrical impulses it receives through the optic nerve. Thus the brain "knows" how much contraction of pupils is needed and "directs the act."

Both the brain and the machine "compute" or otherwise work with electrical circuits. For example, the nerve cells act as relays, as in vacuum tubes, switching, opening and closing and so passing or blocking a current. They operate on the binary principle—off or on, yes or no, 0 or 1. Both can work as digital mechanisms, *but in man only part of the time*. They both operate, in man at least part of the time, in an all-or-none manner, the neuron firing or not firing as is also true of the vacuum tube and the electromagnetic relay. In both, the firing is determined by the state immediately preceding the receipt of excitation; in man "by the number of branched axone terminations of preceding neurons that feed into that state." Hence in man neuron relays appear to work in ways similar to those of the machine. "The situation . . . is well adapted to the transmission of information by the two-digit categories, 0 and 1, of the binary number code." "Just as grid biases modify the tube's timing, so the after-potentials of neurons are important in regulating the passing on of impulses through modification of synaptic excitability." Hoagland said in 1949, there is in the organism, as well as in the machine, a master internal timing device. Summation of impulses at the synapse in the organism has been compared with the use of amplifiers in the machine, and inhibitory impulses, in part, with mechanisms for damping oscillations.

Thus the nervous system codes sensations and sends messages to the brain where more subtle transformations take place. Moreover, both the brain and the machine can check their own accuracies. For example, the computer known as Vinac contains two sub-assemblies of 700 tubes in parallel. Both assemblies work the steps of the problem simultaneously. The machine stops whenever answers differ. There is little chance of both sub-assemblies making the same error. In the brain also, information from sense organs pours into parallel nerve paths and is checked for consistency.

The parallelisms seem impressive. We have, in both man and machine, what seem to be (1) relays, (2) information units, (3) physical decisions, (4) networks, (5) reverberating circuits, (6) storage devices, (7) oscillations, (8) transformation-groups, (9) scanning circuits, and (10)—*both have provisions for feedback.* This last feature is especially important. For this concept has been accepted and incorporated into the consensus of the behavioral as well as the physical sciences. But before it can be dealt with satisfactorily, a basic fact about the cybernetics point of view must be made clear.

In their theory of behavior, the cyberneticians are conformists, concerned primarily with the adaptability of the organism to the world in which it lives, not with the creative reconstruction and improvement of that world. They are builders of *logical* machines and regard the human organism as a logical machine. They have no concern for the *creative* act.

Hence their chief psychological conception is homeostasis, the self-regulation, the self-balancing of behavior. They seek the static condition of balance, not the on-going, dynamic conditions of imbalance. Ashby, for example, is gripped completely by the concerns with changes that produce stability. The goal of all his work is to provide for bringing the organism into a state of equilibrium. The more comprehensive problem of equilibrium and change, balance and the surplus energy to produce imbalance, is not considered. The theory of adaptation, moreover, recognizes only two types of behavior—reflex and learned. Since we can do nothing about the reflexes, the cyberneticians center on learning and how it achieves equilibrium.

The cyberneticians base their entire case on the assumption that the nervous system of the animal, particularly that of the human animal, is a machine. There are no important distinctions, they assert, between the quick and the dead. "The living organism," says Ashby, "in its nature and processes is not essentially different from other matter," and adds "the truth of the assumption will not be discussed."[11] The aim of both theory and model-building is to specify the animal's behavior by variables which can be measured and recorded on dial readings. Adjustive action is the desideratum.

A second major cybernetics conception is that we shall know the nature of the various forms of human behavior only when we can successfully build a model that will work in those ways. Studying man and the machine, Ashby's aim is to deduce "what sort of a mechanism it must be that behaves so differently from any machine made so far." From Craik and Ashby to Walter, Wiener, and Mc-Culloch, the cyberneticians have all been physical model builders. Ashby asks "What properties the nervous system must have if it is to behave at once mechanistically and adaptively." He assumes that the nervous system behaves adaptively, that "it is essentially mechanistic" and that "these two *data* are not irreconcilable."[12] Thus the cyberneticians state their problem as communication control in the animal through successful model-building of communication control in the machine.

FEEDBACK AND ADAPTATION TO THE NORMAL
WORLD

Granted that in the animal as well as in the machine self-regulated homeostasis is a fact, though in man not the whole fact, how then can it be brought about? It is brought about by "feedback," a century-old concept in mathematics and engine-building, now being spectacularly applied to human behavior through the efforts of the cyberneticians. It is a fact that electronic machines "work in a manner reminiscent in some striking way of animal and human behavior," says Sluckin, and such machines employ some form of automatic control. As a result of the past fifteen years of work, the mathematical engineers have come to call these controls, "servomechanisms." They control the machine, says Wiener, "on the basis of its *actual* performance rather than its *expected* performance."[13] Using the jargon of communication control, "the feedback mechanism receives information from the working parts of the machine and transmits this information back to the working parts in the form of orders." This is what is meant by "feedback." Most often, in order to maintain equilibrium, it must oppose the system's chronic tendency to go too far; hence we call this "negative" feedback. When the system needs more push, acceleration, energy, to do more of just what it is doing, the feedback is "positive." Since our bio-psychological concerns for restoring balance from imbalance are primarily with negative feedback, I shall generally refer to examples of it simply as "feedback."

The operation of the centrifugal "governor" of the recent descendants of the Watt steam engine is a good example of feedback. I recall, from my youth in a New England textile mill at the turn of the century, watching the movement of the governor of the Corliss engine which supplied the power for our machines. From each side of the engine two balls attached to pendulum rods swung on opposite sides of a rotating shaft. The speed of the shaft regulated their angular rise and fall by increasing the distance between the weights, cutting down the velocity of the flow of steam and thereby the speed of the engine. The changing speed actuated a collar on the rotating shaft, opened or closed valves of the engine cylinder; they opened when the engine slowed down and the balls fell; they closed when the engine speeded up and the balls rose. This is the self-regulating governor. The equations describing its action James Clerk Maxwell derived as early as 1865. The feedback mechanism is, therefore, a control of the relation between input and output, part of the energy of output being fed back as input of a regulatory nature. Thus a steady or balanced state is maintained.

Examples abound in modern living; for instance, in the thermostatic control of fuel flow in the heating of houses, in anti-aircraft guns, in automatic elevators, in the switching apparatus of the telephone exchange, in high-speed computing machines, and in some automatic factory operations. To cite a single example from Wiener's work, electronic control by feedback was used successfully in World War II as an element built into anti-aircraft guns. The engineers discovered a new principle of far-reaching application in social life as well as in the psychology of individual behavior. They learned that the gun must be aimed not where the plane is at a given moment, but at a future point on the trajectory of the airplane where the gun's missile and the plane will meet. Under ideal conditions, including warm weather, when the gun swings in response to command, the mathematics of this self-pointing process is complex enough. But under abnormal conditions, when the gun's grease "is frozen or mixed with sand, and the gun is slow to answer the orders given to it," it is still more complicated. A feedback element is built into the gun which "reads the lag of the gun behind the position it should have according to the orders given it, and which uses this difference to give the gun an extra push."[14] If this is too hard and the gun swings too far, the feedback in the machine will pull it back, perhaps too far the other way and a series of oscillations will follow. In the automatic elevator the feedback mechanism causes it to come to rest exactly at floor-level, at which point and moment both doors open. The mechanism, controlled by "input of stored data" as well as by new messages, must be synchronized with "the output behavior" of the elevator and the doors. Wiener sums up other well-known cases of feedback control. There are, he says,

examples of negative feed-backs to stabilize temperature and negative feed-backs to stabilize velocity. There are also negative feed-backs to stabilize position, as in the case of the steering engines of a ship, which are actuated by the angular difference between the position of the wheel and the position of the rudder, and always act so as to bring the position of the rudder into accord with that of the wheel.[15]

So much for feedback in the machine. Something very similar occurs in human behavior. Take as an example the behavior of a man in winter steering a car on an icy road. Moment by moment, information is fed into the nervous system concerning the slipperiness of road surface. As intimations are given through our kinesthetic sense of spatial and temporal coordination, we adjust the steering wheel accordingly, moving it quickly in sensitive back and forth movements. We *feel* the situation; thinking, reasoning as such, is at low ebb.

The cyberneticians speak of these feedback sub-systems as "teleological" or purposeful mechanisms. When we pick up a glass of water, for example, the feedback mechanism of the effectors adjusts our grasping behavior; this is regarded as "goal-directed purpose" in action. F. H. Allport makes the point that mechanism can be regarded as teleological if it is equipped with negative feedback and Northrop has suggested that this may be the way to reconcile the "purposive idealists and the positivistic behaviorists."

As in the case of the self-regulating anti-aircraft gun, so the homeostatic duck hunter regulates the error between the position of his gun and the anticipated location of the duck. The amount of information that is fed back into the nervous system is the amount that the actual condition departs from the desired condition; it is analogous to the shift in the direction of the anti-aircraft gun to move it into the needed position, or the amount of oil that the heater should be burning to bring the temperature back to the indicated point on the scale.

Involved in the physiological operation of feedback mechanisms is the established Cannon principle of homeostasis. I quote Wiener.

The conditions under which life, especially healthy life, can continue in the higher animals, are quite narrow. A variation of one half degree centigrade in the body temperature is generally a sign of illness, and a permanent variation of five degrees is scarcely consistent with life. The osmotic pressure of the blood and its hydrogen-ion concentration must be held within strict limits. The waste products of the body must be excreted before they rise to toxic concentrations. Besides all these, our leucocytes and our chemical defenses against infection must be kept at adequate levels; our heart rate and blood pressure must neither be too high nor too low; our sex cycle must conform to the racial needs of reproduction; our calcium metabolism must be such as neither to soften our bones nor to calcify our tissues; and so on. In short, *our inner economy must contain an assembly of thermostats, automatic hydrogen-ion concentration controls, governors, and the like, which would be adequate for a great chemical plant. These are what we know collectively as our homeostatic mechanism.*[16]

High up in the roster of feedback controls are the hypothalamic nuclei. According to Cobb,

The hypothalamus is at present generally accepted as the center for the integration and externalization of the motor impulses that cause emotional expression. It is, moreover, the head-ganglion of the autonomic nervous system which mediates so many of man's emotional manifestations: blushing, sweating, erection of hairs, palpitation of the heart, raised blood pressure, urination and defecation, to mention the most obvious.[17]

The hypothalamic nuclei control many vital functions. They are not arranged in centers for one special function or another, but probably work in a more general way, receiving many stimuli and coordinating them before sending out appropriate motor messages. These go downward to midbrain connections for expression in striated muscles, to bulbar and spinal autonomic connections and to the neurohypophysis. They go upward to give their contribution toward keeping the rest of the brain alert and conscious.[18]

While we are not yet clear about the relation of the hypothalamus to the pituitary gland, especially the anterior pituitary, the relation of the cerebral cortex to the hypothalamus and of the latter to the other parts of the midbrain, still many self-regulating functions of the hypothalamic nuclei have been established. They play a major part, for example, in water secretion, temperature control, fat metabolism, carbohydrate metabolism, and an important role in sexual functions, the operation of the cardiovascular system and the gastrointestinal system. Moreover, the hypothalamus is to be regarded as a wakefulness center, the activity of which tends to keep the cortex alert. "Finally there is much new evidence from the study of electroencephalograms that the hypothalamus has an influence upon the electrical activity of the cerebral cortex."[19] In short, the nuclei of the midbrain are shown to go far toward accounting for the concept of feedback in human behavior.

Apparently, it is impossible to operate any complex system in a completely steady state; there is always some oscillation of the gun, the elevator, the movement of the car wheels, the hand controlling the tool, and so forth. Too great oscillations in human beings mean a pathological condition, as in spastic cases, palsy tremor, Parkinson's disease. This is partly because the "negative feedback mechanism is subject to self-excitation," basically because intertia will carry the gun, car, or tool, beyond the desired point unless it is self-corrected. Hence the designing engineers, or the human being, alter the output, speed it up to match the input. We know that there is a delay in transmission from input to output, and that this will cause output to lag behind. The greater the frequency of variation in the input, the greater the lag in the output. Hence we build into the mechanism a device to match output more closely with input. Some oscillations are self-maintaining, as in those instances in which they are sent completely around the "feedback loop until they affect the original quantity."

In illuminating the effect of oscillations, the physiologist, Rosenblueth, and Wiener studied the frequency of clonus contractions under stretch stimulation in the leg muscle of the cat; they attained results in harmony with their prediction based on this principle. Oscillations support the inference that feedback is occurring since, as accompaniments of the behavioral mechanism, they become marked in its degenerative changes. Some evidence of this sort has been accumulated in such pathological conditions as "purpose tremor" neuroses, with their reiterative character of obsessions and compulsions. These have been attributed to defective feedback or to feedback that has become positive, producing oscillating excesses that may sweep other braincells into their orbit and dominate the behavior of the patient in an inescapable vicious circle.

The notion involved in feedback of input-from-storage, integrated with incoming impressions and producing a modified output is implicit in the past century of theorizing about the act of human response by psychologists and educationists. This is evidenced by the cumulative doctrines of experience (the central theme of the new education) stated by Dewey and many others. I regard the concept as now definitely established and have incorporated it in my own theory of behavior. The feedback element, built into the stored data of organized human experience (memory) becomes an enormously intricate fusion of cortical-cell-assembly, of tensile dynamics in the musculature, of release of endocrine secretions in the circulating blood stream, and of overt as well as incipient movements in the eyes, head, arms, hands, torso. The nub of the complex process is the organism's attempt to perceive (partly visual, partly muscular response in the torso, I think) the relations of parts that will produce the felt (imagined) organization.

In problem-solving this adjusting process does indeed seem to act in the manner of feedback, reflected in cut-and-try oscillations before the correct adjustment is hit upon. Some phases of it can be seen also in the first stages of the creative process of the painter, writer, dancer, or musician: the improvising of a first statement . . . its comparison (a total body-response) with the imagined conception . . . the putting down of the new bit of color or shifting of line, mass, or texture . . . its bodily appraisal, again with a new imagined conception as the norm, . . . oscillations of adjustments (sets or attitudes of anticipation), all tending to come to a more stable rest along a line of direction. This line of direction appears clearly in expressive work—in all creative acts, as well as in problem-solving thought.

It makes a good deal of sense to carry over Wiener's language concerning the feedback behavior of the self-directed mechanical system to the act of logical thought and perhaps to creative acts as well in human beings. "Behavior is scanned for its result and success or failure of this result modifies the future behavior. . . . Feedback is the control of a system by reinserting into a system the result of its performance."

Finally, a note on the basic role of feedback in my own experience. Turning around on my own creative processes as quickly as possible (trying to study them at the moment of doing them) I find a good deal of feedback in my own acts of writing. I put down a new idea, write notes, make tentative sentence statements. Each becomes a part of stored experience, changing the previous storage of concepts. Its juxtaposition with a new imagined conception produces another statement, which acts in turn to push in one direction or another. This is a total process, the union of the specific cell-assembly and the general broadcasting phases. This is the feeling-for-relationship, the tensile sense expressed in the incipient movements of the body. This is prehensile awareness, the first "I know." This is the true form of cut-and-try-and-appraise.

THE GENERAL THEORY OF ORGANISMS AS COMPUTERS

During the nineteen-forties, widely separated behavioral scientists, other than the cyberneticians, on both sides of the Atlantic independently reiterated an hypothesis closely resembling Craik's that the flashing-up of either a new perception or conception is due to some unknown power of averaging the organism's learned assumptions. Year by year, these various independent workers confirmed Craik's primary suggestion that the organism "carries a small-scale model of external reality and of its own possible actions around in its head; [with this] it is able to try out various alternatives, conclude which is the best of them, react to future situations before they arise, utilize the knowledge of past events in dealing with the present and the future."

Humphreys-Owen, crystallographer of the University of London, suggested that organisms have within themselves mechanisms which can integrate with incoming stimuli "similar related experiences of the past," in a sort of "weighted average." Discussing physical principles underlying inorganic form, he says that "spontaneous forms of nature . . . which are sensorily perceived," can be described by "regarding the atoms merely as centres for forces exerted on each other, so that these centres tended to arrange themselves regularly in space." Such a description would be done "by a piece of intellectual imagination, drawing a surface through the average positions of those centers on the boundary of bulk matter." The perception of such form, he says, "is an act of averaging, for the light reflected from each atom is not individually detected by the sensitive surface of the retina. What is detected is the merged emission from very many atoms, and this produces the smooth sensation of form."[20]

The experiments on the perception of motion carried on at Hanover, New Hampshire, by Ames and Ittelson, extend this "averaging" notion to the role of the assumptions that the perceiver has built into his ways of perceiving such events as motion from past experience. According to Cantril, they show "that people actually change the focus of their eyes when looking at a stationary object which is so arranged that it changes size and therefore is experienced as being at different distances.[21] Ittelson reported that "of two objects similar in size and moving at the same speed, the one which we assume to be larger, and hence farther away, will always appear to be moving faster. But even more important is the experimental evidence suggesting that we have assumptions of characteristic speeds for different objects." Cantril goes on to say:

Experiments of Ames and Kilpatrick have demonstrated, for example, that when different objects are seen in a paradoxical context created by having a trapezoidal window revolve about its vertical axis, a rod will appear to *bend,* a bird will appear to *fly,* a carton of cigarettes will remain unchanged, etc., even though each object is in reality simply slowly revolving with the window.[22]

This amounts to saying that in order to make the percept a reasonable approximation of the "real" situation, "we must have built up fairly reliable assumptions concerning its nature." Guiding us in making the perception will be immediately preceding stimuli, established habits of response, customary ways of conceiving. Hebb, from many experiments in perception, concludes that the "apparent simplicity" of perceptions "is only the end result of a long learning process."[23]

The key to understanding the psychologists' interpretation of these laboratory studies is the role of the assumptions which the individual learns to make in reading meaning into sense impressions. Cantril, apparently depending on the Hanover experiments, concludes that the human organism has within itself a mechanism which, when confronted with sensory stimuli, has the capacity to integrate with them similar, related experiences of the past "into a sort of weighted average. It is this weighted average derived from related experiences that is used as the standard in determining the significance of the environment in the next experience." Such mechanisms are not mere arithmetical sums of experience, for one intensely dramatic episode, with its massive mulling over, can outweight a multitude of commonplace ones which are forgotten. "These assumptions are *probabilities* only but if they have proved highly reliable in past action, we begin to think of them as certainties and we act accordingly."[24]

The Hanover group were not especially concerned with quantitative dimensionality. Perception studies, in fact, since the psychophysics of Weber and Fechner, have tended to ignore it. Helson,[25] in a series of experimental studies, provided for it in a theory called "adaptation level as frame of reference." Human organisms tend to *order* their perceptual interpretation of the world in judging distances, sizes, weights, beauty of organization, etc., by unconscious "averaging" or "pooling" of the range of their experiences of judgment. Each individual establishes, from the accumulation of his experiences in judging weights and other dimensions, a standard of reference, a kind of middle zero point against which objects are heavier or lighter, darker or brighter. This medium standard is the individual's "adaptation-level" for the particular function, in a particular situation and time. The pooling process is physiological-psychological and occurs below the threshold of awareness. Being quantitative, Helson's theory is mathematically developed and leads to a specific formula; the average used is not arithmetical but is the weighted logarithmic harmonic mean of all stimuli involved. The theory has been tested experimentally and predicted adaptation levels agreed well with observations. As to how the averaging process takes place (physiologically and psychologically) Helson advances no independent theory of his own.

F. H. Allport,[26] interpreting Helson, has referred to his theory as a quantitative, frame of reference theory, and points out that many other such theories, for example, those of Sherif and Cantril, have developed as a foundation for social psychology. Many experiments in group reactions to situations have shown that the individual's judgments, beliefs and behavior are swayed toward the "social norm" of the group. But again no theoretical explanation is provided of *how* either the frame of reference or the "social norm" is brought about. About all that can be said for the frame of reference speculations is that they are further evidence of growing concern with the nature of the forming process as it operates in perception.

While students of perception have been working from diverse orientations—some from the mechanistic conditioned reflex, others from Gestalt or more organic psychologies, still others studying animal behavior in the new science of ethology—all come to approximately the same conclusion. An unconsciously working "calculator," they say, averages, in some unknown way, stimuli and previously recorded experiences. Organisms not only reveal autonomous forming processes; they are also endowed with systems of "constancy calculus"; for example, human responses to sizes, shapes and melodies are due to the averaging of assumptions that we have learned to make concerning them.

"We perceive the colour of any given object as the 'same,' " says Konrad Lorenz, pioneer in ethology, "whether we see it in the blueish morning light, in the more reddish light of the evening, or in the yellowish light of an electric lamp." In these three cases the object actually reflects very different wave-lengths, and Lorenz suggests that an unconsciously working "calculator" within either the central nervous system or the motor mechanism of response, "averages" in some unknown way the colors of the light reflected from the various objects, deducing the prevailing wave-length through some constant relation between the color of illumination and the color reflected by the object. "Thus," he says, "what we perceive as the colour of the object is nothing else than its inherent property of reflecting wave-lengths in preference to others, . . . so that the mixture of wave-lengths reflected by them adds up to what we perceive as 'white' light." Lorenz postulates that perception is "nothing else than the function of another constancy computer which enables us to perceive the shape of an object as one of its permanent properties."

This theory suggests that the organism is endowed with a constancy calculus, not only for the perception of color, but also for many other types of response. The constancy in our responses to differences in size, shape, melody, and so forth, is due to assumptions we have learned to make in the accumulation of many experiences. This was the conclusion that Cantril drew from the Ames-Ittelson experiments. Lorenz refers to the startling achievement of his own body-mind computer in producing perceptions of constancy of the shape of his pipe as he turns it in his hands. As the ever-changing contours of the moving pipe are shown on the retina, unconsciously to us, he says, the "interpreted movements . . . must involve computations fully equivalent to complicated operations of projective geometry." He cites E. von Holst's similar interpretation of size constancy, saying that "the motor impulses which are sent out to the muscles performing the accommodation or focussing of the eyes, are partly re-conducted to a computer which relates them to the absolute size of the retinal image. From this relation between two variables the constant size of objects is computed."[27]

But Lorenz generalizes beyond the phenomenon of perception, and carries his hypothesis to the very core of my study of the intuitive flash of insight. His statement may serve as a summary to this chapter. Gestalt perception, he holds, is

identical with that mysterious function which is generally called "Intuition"; and which indubitably is one of the most important cognitive faculties of Man. . . . the scientist, confronted with a multitude of irregular and apparently irreconcilable facts, suddenly "sees" the general regularity ruling them all; the explanation of the hitherto inexplicable all at once "jumps out" at him with the suddenness of a revelation.

Without intuition, the world would present to us nothing but an impenetrable and chaotic tangle of unconnected facts. It would be quite impossible to us to find the laws and regularities prevailing in this apparent chaos, if the mathematical and statistical operations of our conscious mind were all that we had at our disposal. It is here that the unconsciously working computer of our Gestalt perception is distinctly superior to all consciously performed computations.

This superiority is due to the fact that intuition, like other highly differentiated types of Gestalt perception, is able to draw into simultaneous consideration *a far greater number of premises* than any of our conscious conclusions. It is the practically unlimited capacity for taking in relevant details and leaving out the irrelevant ones which makes the computer of this highest form of Gestalt perception so immensely sensitive an organ.

The most important advantage of intuition is that it is "seeing" in the deepest sense of the word. Like other kinds of Gestalt perception and unlike inductive research, it does not only find what is expected, but the totally unexpected as well. Thus intuition is forever guiding inductive research. Though he may be quite unconscious of it, even the most exact and "inartistic" of research workers is invariably guided by intuition in the choice of his object, in the choice of the direction in which to look for important results.

Intuition is generally regarded as the prerogative of artists and poets. I would assert that it plays an indispensable rôle in all human recognition, even in the most disciplined forms of inductive research. Though in the latter the important part taken by intuition is very frequently overlooked, no important scientific fact has ever been "proved" that had not previously been simply and immediately seen by intuitive Gestalt perception.[28]

14

Felt-thought through Gestural Symbol

Oᴜʀ conceptual synthesis next focuses on another, and I should think one of the most revealing, clues to the nature of the autonomous forming process. This is the capacity of the autistic mind to turn its fantasy stuff into meaningful concepts and symbols.

Hence, in examining the flash of insight as symbol, as we shall do in this chapter, we once more reorient our study in new dimensions. The flash of meaning as a brain-mind, input-output synthesis explored in Chapter 13, will now be dealt with as a transformation of motor-imagery into symbol. While symbolization is one promising key to the locked doors of imagined conception, there are actually two means interdependent with it. The first is gesture which is the organ of feeling; the second is the verbalizing, naming process, the essence of thinking. I postulate a synthesis of the two means— *gesture as felt-thought*—as one inadequately explored key to the flash of imagined conception.

THE AUTO-SYMBOLIZING PROCESS: A HUMAN NECESSITY

The flash of insight emerges from the unconscious as a full-blown conceptual symbol because the organism can behave in no other way. It is an inner necessity. Herbert Silberer, the German psychiatrist, described it as an "auto-symbolizing" process. Silberer was among the first (1909) to recognize the tendency of masses of hypnoidal imagery to take the form of meaningful symbol. His graphic description of the experience merits extended quotation.

One afternoon (after lunch) I was lying on my couch. Though extremely sleepy, I forced myself to think through a problem of philosophy, which was to compare the views of Kant and Schopenhauer concerning time. In my drowsiness I was unable to sustain their ideas side by side. After several unsuccessful attempts, I once more fixed Kant's argument in my mind as firmly as I could and turned my attention to Schopenhauer's. But when I tried to reach back to Kant, his argument was gone again, and beyond recovery. The futile effort to find the Kant record which was somehow misplaced in my mind *suddenly represented itself to me*—as I was lying there with my eyes closed, as in a dream—*as a perceptual symbol:* I am asking a morose secretary for some information; he is leaning over his desk and disregards me entirely; he straightens up for a moment to give me an unfriendly and rejecting look.

The vividness of the unexpected phenomenon surprised, indeed almost frightened me. I was impressed by the appropriateness of this *unconsciously selected symbol.* I sensed what might be the conditions for the occurrence of such phenomena, and decided to be on the lookout for them and even to attempt to elicit them. In the beginning I hoped that this would yield a key to "natural symbolism." From its relation to art-symbolism I expected and still expect the clarification of many psychological, characterological and aesthetic issues.[1]

Immediately after his first auto-symbolic experience, Silberer systematically set about gathering similar data from his patients and organized experiments to elicit such hallucination phenomena. His reports throw light on the contents of the off-conscious mind and their relation to preceding conscious experiences.

His basic conclusion is that imagery and other unconscious materials are turned into symbols suddenly and without conscious control, *by the conflict between two "antagonistic elements":* first, the hypnagogic state; second, the conscious effort to think reflectively and comparatively. Silberer speaks of the auto-symbolizing phenomenon as an "hallucinatory experience which puts forth 'automatically' . . . an adequate symbol for what is thought."[2] Rapaport calls the exploration of natural symbolism "the search for the laws determining the images that may be coordinated with given ideas as their symbols."[3] Thus some formative process selects just the pertinent images, movements, and other storage materials that in past experience have projected a given idea or symbol across the threshold. The form which the projecting flash of meaning takes, whether sign or symbol, is determined by the material with which the unconscious has to work. Hence the nature of the unconscious constituents becomes of crucial importance.

What Silberer calls auto-symbolizing is, then, a key to understanding the hypnoidal imagery of the transliminal, preconscious mind and the more inaccessible chambers of the nonconscious. His technique makes it possible to observe directly and with a good deal of precision what can be studied only indirectly and vaguely (because of the passage of time) in the case of dreams. He himself says that symbol-formation "effects an understanding of that which is as yet not understandable. Thus . . . symbol-formation serves as a substitute mechanism, which enables ideas and complexes to manifest themselves in spite of the disturbed condition of apperception."[4]

His development of this point is worth further quotation.

The hallucination phenomena . . . present the picturing-process which produces symbols in its purest form and in strictest isolation from side issues. In these . . . thought contents, prevailing psychological-functional states, and to a lesser degree somatic states, are translated into images. These images carry not only unmistakable earmarks of their origin, but give one the indescribable conviction that they are only a translation into a pictorial symbol of the thought, feeling, and so on.[5]

Auto-symbolizing is, then, still another name for the flashing-up of conceptual meaning. Langer, quoting Ritchie, corroborates this. "The essential act of thought is symbolization."[6] There is critical support for the conception that "symbolism is the recognized key to that mental life which is characteristically human and above the level of sheer animality. Symbol and meaning make man's world, far more than sensation."[7]

CONCEPTUALIZING: A BASIC PRINCIPLE OF MIND

We now bring together several basic ideas: that the primary "need" of the organism is to respond as the situation demands; that the organism's response *with meaning* is itself the very process of conceiving, of idea-forming. Conceiving is always accomplished in the matrix of a general conception or orienting attitude or motor set. All of these notions taken together constitute what I call mind-in-action. I find in Lashley, Washburn, Langer, Murphy, the mythologists, the students of metaphor—in all of them, a recurring emphasis on the exploding, detonating, determining role of the total orienting set of the organism. No new flash appears to come *except in a new orienting conception*. In a discussion group one participant says, "My conception of the matter is somewhat different from yours." Or, he may say, "No, I see it from another point of view." We behave first via our conceptions, second, through our concepts. The former is primarily feeling, the latter, thinking.

In Einstein's search, acts of discovery came about through a felt re-centering of imagined conception; for example, his sudden recognition of time as a new dimension. This reset the total problem and turned him onto a new and successful path. But the flash came only through a long, preparatory, conscious struggle to locate and define the problem, a groping stage marked by mixed feelings of uncertainty about concept, but by certitude about his general conception. He knew he was moving in the right direction. A series of intuitive, tentative, exploratory episodes occurred over the years of work, but each emerged only as new dimensions of the whole structure were felt by the whole organism. Each of these re-orienting flashes epitomized his conception at the moment. If analyzed, the conception would be shown to fuse a hierarchy of specific concepts. With Cezanne, creative artist, discovery in the complete act of expression developed similarly—a long period of deep feeling, of looking and absorbing, a preparatory gathering together of self and task. It was a period of recurring flashes of perception-in-depth. These, too, were episodes in conceptualizing. These were his imagined conceptions. It was these that he tried to paint, his realistic conceptions of the nature-thing before him in the real world.

The key seems to lie in the generalizing nature of the act, which we have variously described as feeling-tone, orienting motor attitude, set, or mood of understanding. I shall, therefore, employ the term "conceptualizing" to stand as general label for any and all of these. It is, moreover, of the greatest importance to distinguish conception from concept, that is, the general shotgun, nonverbal response of conceptualizing from the specific rifle-shot use of the verbal label or concept. It will also be necessary to discriminate clearly between concepts and symbols, between signs and symbols (that is, pointers and conceivers), and between fantasy-images and metaphor-images.

The discussion of signs and symbols therefore will be set in a matrix of conception and conceptualizing. I shall show the role of the concept in the forming of conceptions. The term "conception" has a more organismic, all-embracing, mood-like quality; "concept" a sharper, more linguistically determined significance. If we analyze the constituents of mood or conception linguistically in building conceptions of people, things, actions, situations, institutions, we come out with a set of concepts. For example, my conception of our current automated society is *a feeling* of a social order caught between near-abundance and near-catastrophe. It can be defined and clarified only as I build an advancing hierarchy of concepts into my changing conceptions; for example—engine, atom, reactor, fuel, factory, corporation, interdependence, concentration of control, market, cartel, automation. Each of these concepts serves as a linguistic term to epitomize bodies of concrete meanings arranged in deepening, expanding feelings of scope and interrelationship. The definitional key to the two sets of terms—the conception or conceptualizing way of looking at things, on the one hand, and specific concepts on the other—is language. In the broader terms of the learned disciplines our task of intellectual synthesis here is to embrace psychology, physiology, and the other human sciences in close relation to philology—the study of language.

GESTURE AS FELT-THOUGHT

First, the way must be prepared by a clarification of feeling and its organ—gesture. It is at this point that one of the keys to the stuff of mind becomes indispensable. This is gesture as felt-thought.

The basic data are already at hand in the imagery and motor sources of the imagination. Of the four constituents of the creative act, the two which I fuse as motor-imagery are the cue to the activity of the creative threshold. The kaleidoscope of imagery and motor adjustments is more than a reproduction of the traced impression; it is *projected,* either from and by the nonconscious or solely by the offconscious organism. I have come to regard it as *the basic raw material* of orderly thought and design with which the offconscious welding process works. Its roster includes the obvious images of the dream, those called hypnagogic and hypnopompic, eidetic images and full-fledged, three-dimensional hallucinations. Langer uses the term "fantasy-imagery," calling it the stock-in-trade of the perceptual process. She goes so far as to say, "Every process we perceive, if it is to be retained in memory, must record itself as a fantasy, an envisagement, by virtue of which it can be called up in imagination or recognized when it occurs again."

This is the way in which we know a recurring event that comes in somewhat related situations. "We assimilate it from the fantasy abstracted in the previous instance." But we must take care not to give a distorted psychopathic meaning to the terms fantasy or hallucination. We are referring to the stuff of normal mind. Its universal presence in creative production has been shown in the work of poets, painters and other artists; in the prevalence of a background of auditory and visual imagery in the general population, especially prominent in hypnoidal states; and in the role of eidetic imagery in the creative process, particularly in children. The accumulating weight of experiential and experimental testimony shifts attention, therefore, from the reality image of logical thought to the autistic, felt imagery of creative discovery; hence the postulate that in acts of discovery *the felt motor-image plays a basic role.*

Since felt-thought is to play such a foundational role in the proposed theory and program, it is important to make clear the concept of feeling. We are dealing with more than is conveyed by its common-sense connotation. There are several senses in which we all use "feeling" as "sensation" or as "emotion." Using feeling to mean sensation one says: "This room feels hot," or "the radiator feels stone cold"; one speaks of feelings of texture, colors, sounds, odors. The carpenter enjoys the feel of his wood as the sculptor does his stone, the tailor the texture of his cloth. As emotion, one speaks of feelings of rage or anger, delight or depression, pleasure or pain. The everyday experience of feeling can be either sensuous or emotional and the two are often fused together, unified.

Let it be said at once that the concept "feeling" is used here in neither of these casual senses. To me, feeling is the very foundation of the act of response. It sets the meaning of the act. It is the matrix in which all coming to know takes place. Since it is *primarily the nonverbal* part of the act, it is not easy to find words to describe it, but I shall try. I shall begin by distinguishing between "feeling" and "thinking."

Let us first grant the generalizing nature of every act of response and grant, too, that there is, in both scientific and esthetic situations, an intuitive generalizing stage of discovery and a logical analyzing stage of verification. Let us further grant that there are two ways of knowing: the intuitive inside way of identification and the scientific, outside way of observation. In this framework two types of experience can be distinguished: *first,* those in which feeling is uppermost, in which meaning is felt and expressed without words, by the total gesture of the body; *second,* those in which thinking is central and is clarified and expressed primarily by means of words. Each of the two ways of knowing, and of the two types of response, has its respective symbolism.

My theory asserts that every act—be it problem-solving, appreciation, or creation—has two clearly marked-out phases. Whether they are concurrent or in temporal sequence is unclear. There is, first, a primal awareness taking place in the organism-as-a-whole. This is a general over-all phase which I shall call "feeling." This seems to play the leading part in discovery or creative imagination. There is, second, a more precise verbal and logical documentary phase. This is the specific and analytical one, and it is this that most contemporary psychologists call "thinking." It plays the leading part in logical verification.

Since both phases are involved in the complete act of thought, I shall give the name *"felt-thought"* to the first part which we have already shown to be *discovery*. It is largely based on feeling, although it also employs some of the processes commonly called thinking. The second part of the act, verification, employs logical thought. It consists essentially of systematic logical thinking and the establishment of clear verbalized or mathematically formulated relationships. Breaking down the total process called thinking into its steps will show how it is colored throughout by feeling. First, there is a tendency to delay response, a withholding, a gathering-together of self, which is primarily a feeling of motor set; second, a grasping of relationships, fundamentally a feeling process; third, sensing and holding a continuing, directed line of thought, also a feeling process; fourth, imaginative use of symbols, probably basically a feeling process; fifth, skill in drawing diagrams and building other forms of "thought models"; sixth, generalizing, using concepts. While this total process is universally called "thinking," it is shot through and through with feeling. Hence my agreement with Coleridge's dictum that "deep thinking is attainable only by a man of deep feeling."[8] The consensus on the physiology of the imagination also seems to confirm Coleridge; there is no deep thinking without deep feeling. Feeling is the matrix of thought.

One of the most discriminating discussions of feeling and thinking that I have encountered is that of Collingwood.[9] Noting the baffling complexity of the two acts, he points out several familiar differences between them. Perhaps the most obvious is his "bipolarity of thought . . . the distinction between right and wrong, good and bad, true and false." In thinking there is an all-or-nothingness, a thinking correctly or incorrectly, measured by whether or not it succeeds. Not so with feeling; it is not a question of feeling right or wrong; it is a question of *how* you feel. Another contrast is that feelings are personal and private to the individual, whereas thinking is necessarily public. As Collingwood says, a hundred people in the street may all feel cold, but each person's feeling is private to himself. Hence "thoughts can corroborate or contradict each other, but feelings cannot." Still another contrast is that feelings are momentary, they exist here and now, whereas "in thinking we are concerned with something that lasts, even if it does not last forever." Finally—and here they are similar—both concepts, thought and feeling, are double-barreled. They refer to the activity of thinking and to what we think; to the activity of feeling and to what we feel.

Such differences between thinking and feeling, therefore, identify feeling as a foundational aspect of the act of human response, something independent of thinking and prior to it in action. This is the view of an increasing body of such careful students as Collingwood, Creighton, Reid, and Langer. Collingwood's conclusion is:

feeling appears to rise in us independently of all thinking, in a part of our nature which exists and functions below the level of thought and is unaffected by it . . . it seems that our sensuous-emotional nature, as feeling creatures, is independent of our thinking nature, as rational creatures. . . . When thought comes into existence . . . it brings with it . . . emotions that can arise only in a thinker, and only because he thinks in certain ways.[10]

Gardner Murphy discusses the basic "feel" of thought, what Santayana called "the odor of the individual thinker's mind." This concept has appeared in the psychological literature ever since the Greek "psycho-gnostics." The feeling quality emerges, for example, in the individuality of a creative work, in the possibility of recognizing authorship by a study of the product. Moreover, we have experimental proof that "we can recognize . . . authorship of musical compositions or scraps of handwriting." This means "that sensory elements and their interrelations play a predominating role in such individuality."[11] The way the concepts are felt, "in terms of the organic and kinesthetic sensations, the inarticulate feels and stresses of each moment," all illustrate both the individuality of imagination and its initiation in biological needs. It also stresses the unconscious emphasis in thought: "All thinking . . . is in its core unconscious; it is only its shadow which is conscious, and this is true of free as of directed thought." Murphy insists that both the unconscious and the conscious processes are "perfectly goal-directed; both are perfectly 'physiological' in their movement toward this goal."[12]

In order to show the role of imagination and thought in personality, our recourse is to that vast "half-conscious storehouse of

material on motivation, canalization, conditioning, perceptual structure, dissociation, and organization." Murphy's conclusion is "that
thought and imagination are merely the more complex organized
expressions of all the tendencies which we see in humankind, even
when off guard, in undirected and 'thoughtless' form." And he confirms my thesis that there is experimental evidence on practically all
the aspects of behavior "from the delayed reaction to a lifelong
quest for a scientific answer." Moreover, there is no reason for
questioning that this behavior lies on a "continuum of responses, a
hierarchical progression." The actual substance of imagination and
thought "thus comprises both the quest for reality and the effort to
escape it, both curiosity about the world and the need to improve
upon the world."[13]

DISTINGUISHING FEELING FROM EMOTION

Emotion is primarily the product of the endocrines in the blood
stream; the red face of anger and the stimulation of the heartbeat
are due to the increase of adrenalin in the blood stream and the
release of glycogen stored in the liver. It is the inhibition of salivary
gland action that induces the emotional "dry mouth" of fright of
the novice in public speaking. But neither creating nor appreciating
an esthetic object is a function of emotional excitement, although
the creative artist producing it and the sensitive observer experiencing it may be emotionally stirred. As Leo Stein says, ". . . a person with a strongly felt emotion may write a poem or heave a brick.
. . . Neither the heaving of bricks nor the writing of poems is essentially an emotional act."[14] Hearing a loud explosion, falling suddenly from a height, the recall of a tragic personal experience, an
unexpected scent of a special kind may, probably will, produce
emotional excitement. Emotion, then, is a name given to body
excitement, and, while it is an accompaniment, it is not a determin-
ative factor in the esthetic act.

Feeling, on the contrary, is indispensable to the esthetic act—
either creative or appreciative, and to the complete act of thought
in scientific inquiry. As Stein put it, "Emotion is just emotion, while
feelings are as numerous as appropriate adjustments."[15] The evidence is clear for the distinction between feeling and emotion; physi-

ological and psychological evidence confirms the astute observation of the esthetician.

Cobb, summing up the controversial evidence on the question: "Can emotions be distinguished physiologically?" goes along with Cannon in saying that even the strong emotions of rage, fear, and hate are expressed physiologically in much the same way. At the Wittenberg Symposium (1928), Cannon said that although rage and anger distinguish two different experiences and two different sources of behavior, "yet, so far as the changes in the viscera are concerned, they are very much alike. It is hard to see how you can differentiate such emotions, such different emotions as these, on the basis of phenomena that are so alike as the visceral changes in the two." He had found in the laboratory that the viscera have the same changes "when the animal is exposed to cold, when the animal is given an injection of dead bacteria and has fever; also when it is given insulin and the blood sugar drops down to about half of its amount."

Then he makes a most significant comment concerning feeling and motor adjustments. "We have going on, in the lower part of the brain, processes of a pattern character. . . . When a person weeps he is displaying a very different skeletal muscle pattern from that which he displays when he is angry or when he is glad and laughs. The external pattern [muscular] is indicative of an internal pattern."[16]

Cobb definitely bases feelings on "impulses to act," that is, *on incipient body movement.* From the days of earliest infancy we look into our mother's eyes and face, read the expression of her moods and emotions, and label them. We continue this process throughout the cumulative experience of our lives and feel that we become very accurate in our intuitive interpretations. In each type of emotion there is a common body-movement factor—namely, the impulse to act, the impulse to move, to attack, to flee, to draw near, to shout, to laugh, to dance. This is not overt, but incipient movement; the attitudinal, preparatory stage, the *tendency to move,* is the important thing.

I find corroboration of the physiologist's conclusion by an equally competent esthetician. Leo Stein, after spending most of his life studying creative production and appreciation, finds the cue to feeling in the skeletal muscles. Stein stands with the biologist Cannon in the "one emotion" school of thought. Emotions cannot be discriminated. "I doubt very much that there is more than one, which is just emotion. . . . What seems like multiplicity of emotions, is the colouring of the emotion by factors that blend with the emotion, but are not of it." After years of analysis in esthetics, experimenting on himself to locate the relation between situation and emotion, he distinguishes clearly between emotion and feeling.

There is nothing in any way peculiar to the relation of emotion to art, though there are cases when that which is peculiar to art and that which is peculiar to emotion come together. [Moreover, we must remember that] one who looks at a picture will often have stronger emotions than the man who painted it; the spectators at a game will be more emotionally stirred than the players; the audience at the theatre than the actors . . . most painters when they try to make a picture are perfectly cool . . . [although] this is not always true.[17]

Then he puts his finger on the same key to the differentiation of emotion from feeling as did Cannon, Cobb, and the physiologists— namely, the muscular system.

I have found in studying conflicts, repressions and so on, that it is quite possible to have an intense emotional disturbance which has no definable character other than that of being emotion, on condition that the skeletal muscles remained at rest, or continued undisturbed their indifferent movements, such as walking. . . . On the other hand, an adjustment of skeletal muscles, even those of the larynx and throat, in the appropriate attitudes, would at once give to the emotion a similar colouring. It is obvious enough why it should be generally thought that the emotions have in their essence this diversity. Usually a situation leads to a responsive attitude in which the emotion arises. When I first began to do this sort of thing, my emotions were of different kinds, because I responded to the thought with more definite muscular reactions. It was only when I maintained the bodily poise practically unaltered, that I began to obtain these indeterminate emotions.[18]

FEELING AND MOVEMENT IN THE
EXPRESSIONAL ARTS

Creative workers in the expressional revolution of our time also rediscovered the key role of movement. Modern art, says Cheney, is marked by the expressive concept because of its mastery of movement. In his greatest book, *Expressionism in Art,* he said: ". . . the primary element which pleases the observer in painting can best be described as 'movement in the canvas.' "[19] And with respect to modern painting: "In creative painting, control of movement, of interrelated plastic means, is the first secret of formal design. From the opening of a picture with a partitioning of the field, through a main thrust into deep space, back to a stabilization or equipoise, with innumerable minor thrusts, tensions, recessions and returns along the way, the artist must foresee how the movement skeleton will be coiled within the picture enclosure."[20] Cheney says Cezanne would stand "for a quarter-hour" before the canvas, "feeling through to the movement relationship of that color plane to main plastic rhythm and contrapuntal effect."[21]

In every human culture and epoch the creative artist knew these facts. Long ago, in China, I rediscovered for myself the movement effects that T. S. Eliot, Laurence Binyon, and others saw in ancient Chinese painting. Eliot said, for example, that a Chinese vase "moves perpetually in its stillness." The great Renaissance artists were equally aware of the dynamics of expression. Leonardo da Vinci said that any painting of a living creature that lacks this movement quality is "doubly dead, since it is dead because it is a figment, and dead again when it shows neither movement of the mind nor of the body." El Greco was a master of the plastic concept, as Rudolph Arnheim illustrates convincingly.[22] In El Greco's *St. Jerome,* he says, movement is produced by the counterpoint of the right movement of the beard and the left movement of the hands below. Cover the lower part of the picture, then remove the covering and the movement is sharp and clear. The great painters, from the classic past to Cezanne and the modern plastic artists, succeeded in painting so that the observer moves. They produced a "skeleton of movement" in the canvas. A "path of main movement" was organized from the opening of the picture to the final successful organization of the movement forces within the frames. Order is produced in the canvas by a "structure of thrusts and counter-thrusts." To see a painting, that is to feel it, the eye must be moved in and by the picture plane. Thus, dynamic feeling, expressed by the artist is correspondingly felt by the observer, by means of "back and forth, thrust and return." Feeling-as-body-tension is basic. Kandinsky said that by putting some yellow on blue he got "movement without motion," or "directed tensions."

Eisenstein, motion picture genius of the Russian Revolution, in a powerful analysis of the creative process,[23] cites many examples of movement in the work of the great European creative artists. Dürer produced it by alternation of mathematically precise formulae through the proportions of his figures, Michelangelo by "the undulating and swelling muscles" of figures, Rembrandt by "shifting densities of his chiaroscuro," Delacroix by the "path followed by the spectator's eye in moving from form to form," Van Gogh by "thick running splashes of color." Thus "the line," the path of movement, is, in every artist, seeking "continuance of the movement of the music with the movement of the visual contour." In a masterly study of compositional and structural elements, Eisenstein shows that music and motion picture are related by their "fundamental movements," their "structural laws" of process and rhythm. Visual and auditory elements in music are fused by the movement of hands and feet. The poet also produces rhythms and meter through images of movement; Eisenstein tells of Pushkin's translating into verse the crashing movement of a great wave.[24]

John Marin takes us to the heart of the whole expressional movement in his description of what he was trying to state. To those who exclaim protestingly over the chaotic nonobjective appearance of his water colors, Marin replies he is not trying to reproduce the city. On the contrary, he is trying to express the moving effect which the life of the great city has upon him: ". . . great forces at work; great movements; the large buildings and the small buildings; the warring of the great and the small; influences of one mass on another greater or smaller mass . . . these warring, pushing, pulling forces."[25] "Feelings are aroused which give me the desire to express the reaction of these 'pull forces,' those influences which play with one another; great masses pulling smaller masses, each subject in some degree to the other's power. . . . And so I try to express graphically."[26]

We can now build on the foundation laid in Chapter 4 concerning the motor determinants of the act of thought and motor theories of the act. There it was shown that the primary raw materials of the transliminal mind are the fusion of imprinted percepts, images and concepts with motor adjustments. Playing a formative role in the projection of fantasy-images of the autistic mind are the countless imprinted integrations of motor adjustments as attitudes or sets of expectancy. This has been the result of the never-ceasing firing of cells, revealed by the electronic camera (magnifying the unseen a hundred-thousand-fold) as a seething cauldron of activity in nerves, tissues and muscles. Perceptual experience of mind and physiological forms of movement comprise the motor determinants of meaning. The transformation of motor-image into symbol will be interpreted in the light of a theory of consciousness and meaning that includes the following elements. Meanings are operational in character. We are aware of ideas as well as people, things and situations by making appropriate incipient and overt muscular movements with respect to them. Shifts in emotion imply predictable changes in postural set. Skeletal muscle patterns fit specific emotional patterns. The new-born baby's first meanings and the octogenarian's last ones are motor responses to physiological tensions or needs. Electro-encephalographic and myographic measurements verify the hypothesis that attitude is the matrix in which perception occurs; that a man's attitude—the total gesture of the organism—determines how he behaves, what he feels and thinks. The act of knowing is indeed the total gesture of hands, limbs, face, torso, autonomic and central nervous systems.

MOTOR ADJUSTMENTS AS FEELINGS OF

RELATIONSHIP

This recognition of the pervasive feeling nature of the act of response helps to account for the basic motor determinants of meaning. For more than half a century the avant-garde of Western psychology has kept one eye fixed upon the motor foundations of the act of response. A few leaders went further and saw that there was a connection between movement and feeling. One at least, William James, saw that *grasp of relationship* which is certainly central to thought, functioned through feelings of movement. In his *Psychology,* James established the new orientation with a tremendous emphasis upon the felt experience of the moving body.

Discussing the psychology of the feeling of relationship as the focus of the actual stuff of experience, James said, "If there be such things as feelings at all, *then so surely as relations between objects exist . . . so surely . . . do feelings exist to which these relations are known.* There is not a conjunction or a preposition, and hardly an adverbial phrase, syntactic form, or inflection of voice, in human speech, that does not express some shading or other of relation which we at some moment actually feel to exist between the larger objects of our thought." Then he gives examples showing how language forms—prepositions and other relational words— carry the felt meaning. "We ought to say a feeling of *and,* a feeling of *if,* a feeling of *but,* and a feeling of *by,* quite as readily as we say a feeling of *blue* or a feeling of *cold.* Yet we do not: so inveterate has our habit become of recognizing the existence of the substantive parts alone, that language almost refuses to lend itself to any other use."[27]

Twenty years later John B. Watson continued the motor emphasis, making movement the key to response. To Watson the "higher thought processes" as well as habits are examples of body response. He identified thinking with tiny incipient movements of the vocal chords. "My theory does hold that the muscular habits learned in overt speech are responsible for implicit or internal speech (thought)."[28] We "think" then primarily with the body and especially through the utterance of words. *"Whenever the individual is thinking, the whole of his bodily organization is at work (implicitly)*—even though the final solution shall be a spoken, written or subvocally expressed verbal formulation."[29]

Jacobson demonstrated what Watson and others guessed; namely, the presence of implicit movements in thinking (actually Jacobson meant imagining): ". . . action potentials arise in muscles simultaneously with the meaning processes with which the activity of the muscle, if overtly carried out, would correspond. For example, if one thinks of a tall object, the effect is shown in the action-current of the muscles that would be involved in looking up."[30] Jacobson did not differentiate movements involved in conceptual thinking from other types of implicit response.

AN ORGANIC DETERMINING TENDENCY TO ACT

For seventy years one basic conception has gripped theorists of the act of response. This is that prior to and literally "making" the response there is what many have independently called a "determining tendency to act," the "idea of" or "intention to" act. Külpe of the Wurzburg School in Germany, used all three descriptive terms. James in one of scores of documentations of the motor, attitudinal bases of response, discussed "relations as feelings of tendency." He speaks specifically of "the feeling of an absence," the meanings conveyed in such phrases as "naught but" . . . "although it is, nevertheless."[31] The perception of space he interprets in terms of feelings of motion . . . "the feeling of crude extensity . . . *the line is the relation;* feel it and you feel the relation, the feelings of movement in joints."[32] His recurring conclusion is "that every possible feeling produces a movement and that the movement is a movement of the entire organism, and of each in all its parts."

Thirty years ago, Margaret Washburn, in the most extended study of movement of that day,[33] developed a theory that the *unifying influence* in the act of response was what she called a "problem idea." The most essential thing "is the *persistence of its influence*"; to explain this persistence "we need to invoke something over and above ordinary associative dispositions." Then she, too, uses James's and Külpe's term, saying "an associative tendency becomes a determining tendency through the operation of some factor that is not itself an ordinary associative tendency." Such a "determining tendency proceeds from the idea of an end, and is responsible for the fact that the same stimulus may suggest different ideas under the influence of different problems."[34]

The "distinguishing characteristic of a problem idea, which differentiates it from other kinds of ideas, is the *persistence of its influence.*"[35] In reverie we flit from one idea to another but a problem-idea exerts its influence for a very long time. She suggests "that a problem idea becomes the starting-point of effective and directed thought towards its solution only when the incipient motor innervation which the problem involves connects itself, not simply with general restlessness and uneasiness, but with the steady innervations of the activity attitude. Through their inherent and characteristic persistence, as members of a static movement system, the problem of innervation is kept from lapsing and may continue to exert an influence upon associated motor innervations and to arouse imagery which bears on its solution."[36] Thus, in order to transform an idea into a problem idea, incipient motor excitation must be linked with some excitation relatively static and enduring in its nature. And a determining tendency is an associative disposition one of whose exciting influences is the activity attitude.

The most elaborate attempt to study the process using verbal materials is Lashley's (1951) report on "The Problem of Serial Order in Behavior."[37] He takes as his material the study of serial order in spoken and written language. He shows by experimental examples that "associative chain theories cannot adequately explain the phenomenon, [because] the order of words has little relation to the order of meaning." He illustrates the complex nature of the forces, the conflicting impulses which may distort the order of details of structure while leaving the meaning entirely unchanged: such mistakes in the order of writing and speaking as the Spoonerism, " ' our queer old dean' for 'our dear old queen' " or the manifold examples in Freud's *Psychopathology of Everyday Life* which were interpreted as examples of repressed wish. "Behind the overtly expressed sequences," he says, one can infer only a "multiplicity of integrative processes."[38]

If the associations of successive words in reading matter do not explain the order of words, what does? A word can take its position, says Lashley, only when a particular one of its many possible meanings becomes dominant. This dominance is inherent in the essential structure of speech that determines some fusion of serial and temporal order. At this point Lashley, too, turns to the perennial concept of "determining tendency to act," that is, the idea of, or intention to act. (This, it seems to me, is a key to understanding the flash of meaning, with the nature of which this whole study is involved.) There appears to exist, says Lashley, "generalized schemata of action which determine the sequence of specific acts . . . a syntax of the act which can be described as an habitual order or mode of relating the expressive elements; a generalized pattern or schema of integration which may be imposed upon a wide range and a wide variety of specific acts."[39]

All of this requires a theory of central control, not of sequential sensory control—"some central nervous mechanism which fires with predetermined intensity and duration or activates different muscles in predetermined order."[40]

What about the role of set or idea in the preliminary facilitation of movements by the meaning of the words in the sentence? There is certainly "partial activation or priming of aggregates of words before the sentence is actually formulated from them." This is confirmed by the reaction-time studies of preparatory set. Lashley agrees: ". . . the facts of behavior assure that it is a genuine phenomenon and plays a decisive role in determining the character of the response."[41]

POSTULATING GESTURE AS THE ORGAN OF FEELING

To place both the general and the specific phase of the act in my theory and make them coordinate in importance, each must be dealt with in terms of its organ. No behavior without a mediating organ! There is a hypothesis that the fusion of cerebral cortex, old brain and sub-cortical center serves as the primary organ of the thinking-focus. But this should be accompanied by a conception of a hypothetical organ that can account for the explosive general matrix—intuition, motor imagery, set, attitude, the grasping of the problem, poised attention, expectancy, anticipation-of-what-follows-what. It is necessary, therefore, to postulate a dynamic movement sense which is general throughout the organism and which will stand for the total tensing adjustment of the body.

Somewhere in that tension there is the firing contact that sets off the act. I use tension in the dynamic sense of attraction-repulsion, putting to work concepts developed in the physical and natural sciences: motion, irritability, stimulus-response. Movement, the plastic concept, is basic to every kind of human situation. In our study of the act we have seen it in the set of expectancy, in anticipation of what follows what. Notice the labels we have used to convey the sense of potential energy: the tensed condition of the organism, the preparatory organizing attitude. We "strike an attitude" we say; the emphasis is on action; verbs are used rather than adjectives. Over many years of trying one lead after another, I have always come back to this over-all concept of the tensile sense of the body. It is, I am convinced, an important key to the creative act. It may prove to be the crucial step in the act of thought. But it must have a name—a conceptual label, as clear and direct as "thinking." Its name is "feeling."

Gesture as felt-thought, therefore, is the label I give to the total motor adjustment of the skeletal frame, muscles, tissues, organs, nervous system, circulatory and reverberatory systems, of the endothalamic and the autonomic systems. All of these reverberate as the self, through the agency of the many senses. The essence of the point of view is that gesture is feeling in tensed body movement. The view has historical support from the students of the sciences and arts, it generalizes studies of the psychology of meaning and defines more sharply our interpretation of the role of anticipatory body-adjustments in the perceptual field. Thus in my theory of the flash of insight and of knowing, communicating, and imagining, the tensed body acts as a sounding board responding to the world in the form of feeling.

THE "DETERMINING TENDENCY" OF THE SYMBOL

This extended treatment of felt-thought as gesture enables us to take a critical step. This is to see *felt-thought as gestural symbol.* The connecting idea is the familiar "determining tendency" as it is revealed in the basic nature of the symbol.

One definition of symbol stresses that it is something that stands for, represents or denotes something else—not by exact resemblance but by *vague suggestion.* To emphasize the psychology of the symbolic act and to capitalize on the known role of suggestibility, I shall use "suggest" rather than "represent." As a material object, a symbol can be a mark, letter, word, figure, or other written character to suggest something immaterial or abstract—as an idea, a quality, or a condition. It may be an algebraic or chemical symbol. In religious practices, a symbol is something sacred; for example, the elements in the Eucharist suggesting the body and blood of Christ. In the art of political persuasion, the log cabin birthplace of Lincoln becomes a symbol suggesting grass-roots Americanism. Gestures as well as objects or words serve as dramatic symbols, as in the symbol of genuflection, the kneeling man suggesting the attitude of prayerful reverence; the baseball umpire's downward gesture of the arms as symbolizing "You're out"; the circled thumb and forefinger symbolizing "Perfect"; Churchill's famous "V" for victory, and many others.

It is important to distinguish the symbol from the sign. A sign is an indicator; such as "Follow the green light," or "Follow the arrow." Signs announce objects or conditions: the patter of rain on the trees announces the arrival of the storm; the ringing doorbell, a visitor; the town alarm, a fire. Thus the sign indicates the existence of something or the need to do something. These are the elemental stimuli which set off behavior in either animals or men.

But the symbol seems to be the unique and subtle possession of man. An animal can respond only to signs; a man can *do* something *with* objects which serve as signs and, in addition, can respond to them as symbols. He uses symbols to *think about* or to *conceive of* things, actions or conditions. A sign so used by man becomes a symbol. For example, our country's flag above a town structure may be a sign indicating the presence of a public building, such as a court house or school. But to the deep-feeling citizen the flag is also a symbol suggesting "our America," a deeply embedded constellation of emotionalized concepts—democracy, freedom, equality, brotherhood—which we call the American way of life. Hence "flag" as percept can be either a sign or a symbol, but as symbol it is *conceptual*. It incites and provides a vehicle for feeling and thought.

At this point an example will be helpful. I know no simple one more revealing than that in which Helen Keller described the very dawn of language upon her mind. Blind, deaf, and mute, she had been under the tutelage of a remarkable teacher, Anne Sullivan, from whom she had learned the rudiments of a manual sign-language. But she had never sensed that a "particular act of her fingers constituted a word"; nor that things had names "and each name gave birth to a new thought." There came a wonderful day on which she made the leap from sensation to symbol. She describes how

some one was drawing water and my teacher placed my hand under the spout. As the cool stream gushed over my hand, she spelled into the other the word *water,* first slowly, then rapidly. I stood still, my whole attention fixed upon the motions of her fingers. Suddenly I felt a misty consciousness as of something forgotten—a thrill of returning thought; and somehow the mystery of language was revealed to me. I knew then that "w-a-t-e-r" meant the wonderful cool something that was flowing over my hand. That living word awakened my soul, gave it light, hope, joy, set it free! There were barriers still, it is true, but barriers that could in time be swept away.

I left the well-house eager to learn. Everything had a name, and each name gave birth to a new thought. As we returned to the house every object which I touched seemed to quiver with life. That was because I saw everything with the strange, new sight that had come to me.[42]

Here, then, is the key not only to the distinction between sign and symbol, but to the critical stage in the symbolizing process—the naming. In the qualification which Miss Keller made of the mental reorientation that produced her first understanding of the *use of a word as a name,* she spoke of "this thought, *if a wordless sensation may be called a thought.*" Langer, referring to this episode, adds: "Real thinking is possible only in the light of genuine language . . . in her case, it became possible with the discovery that 'w-a-t-e-r' was not necessarily a sign that water was wanted or expected, but was the *name* of its substance, by which it could be mentioned, conceived, remembered."[43]

Here, then, is the simplest symbolic form—*a word which, as name, points not to a thing, not to a concept, but to a conception.* Langer calls it a "conceptual sign, an artificial sign which announces the presence of a certain idea." Note carefully, "w-a-t-e-r" points not to the thing "water," but to the idea of water. For the first time in her life Helen Keller connected the symbol (written by her teacher's hand in hers) with the idea, and the explosive connecting device was the simultaneous splashing of the water and the registering of the symbol "w-a-t-e-r." That is, the word served as a conceptual sign. It called attention to a conception, not to a thing. At this point Miss Keller began to "think" verbally. In the morning of that wonderful day, she had no words; before night she had learned fifty.

Not the idea, the concept, but the *idea of* the thing—this is the critical distinction. A gesture used as symbol directs attention to an idea or a conception of a thing, not to the thing itself. So does a word or another instrument used as symbol. This is the point that rings out in our whole discussion of symbolism in intellectual as well as expressive activities. The key phrases are: *ideas about, conceptions of, thinking about, feelings with respect to.* Bearing this in mind, one senses that some psychological experimenters on concept-formation (Reed, for example) had a vague sense of the truth when, in their attempts to explain how concepts burst through, they reiterated "it is as though he was *about to have an idea* . . . one senses in the responses that 'something lurked behind' the statement of the subject."

Finally, we connect conceptualizing and symbolizing. The connective tissue is metaphor. Since the explanation of the flashing-up of meaning as symbolic transformation depends on the concept of metaphor, it is important to have its use defined in close relation to the symbol.

A symbol, we said, operates by *suggesting* another meaning. But that is exactly comparable to a metaphor. Metaphor is, according to the Oxford Dictionary, "the figure of speech in which a name . . . is transferred to some object different from, but analogous to, that to which it is properly applicable." As Cassirer put it, "one is semantically made to stand proxy for the other"; and he concludes, "betwixt them . . . the conceptual process takes place."[44]

When Silberer's three-dimensional symbol appeared before him, warning him of his behavior, it was suggesting a hidden meaning, it was metaphorical. Metaphors are figures of speech which help to account for symbolic transformation. Wegener gives us the cue when he says a symbol is "used metaphorically to describe whatever its meaning can symbolize." That is, "literal meaning is slowly defined by cumulative figurative meanings." As Langer states it, "In a genuine metaphor, an image of the literal meaning is our symbol for the figurative meaning, the thing that has no name of its own."[45] Silberer also spoke of the metaphorical nature of the auto-symbolizing process; and Langer referred to the materials, the images, from which symbols are projected as "madly metaphorical fantasies, that often make no literal sense whatever."[46]

I rely upon metaphor at this point, not only for its figurative characteristics, but because it appears to be a basic principle of symbolic transformation. It was Cassirer, again in *Language and Myth,* who gave us this cue to the nature of symbolic transformation. The symbol, he said, is the transformation of sense-image into metaphor-image. Putting the idea to work in this study, we say that the raw materials traced on the unconscious and appearing fantastically as a kaleidoscope of sense-images, motor images, pictures, and word substitutes for story material, are projected in the transliminal creative state as metaphor-image or concept-symbol. My theory makes use of the basic idea that conceptualizing takes place through metaphor, that conceiving is metaphorical thinking.

An unresolved issue of great difficulty will continue to confront us and it may help to state it here. Both Cassirer and Langer seem to postulate that all images, fantasy and otherwise, are symbolic. Langer says, "Their tendency is to become metaphorical . . . they also have an inalienable tendency to 'mean' things that have only a logical analogy to their primary meanings. The image of a rose symbolizes feminine beauty so readily that it is actually harder to associate roses with vegetables than with girls."[47]

But do all images tend to become metaphors? The vast body of them seem to be bizarre arrangements of "object" images, of the paraphernalia of our environment—animals, physical things, persons, actions, situations. Some, perhaps many, are unquestionably metaphorical but not all. In any event, we can agree that the image is one of "our readiest instruments for abstracting concept from the tumbling stream of actual impressions. They make our primitive abstractions for us, they are our spontaneous embodiments of general ideas." Image-symbolism, Langer says, "grows from the momentary, single, static image presenting a simple concept, to greater and greater units of successive images having reference to each other; changing scenes, even visions of things in motion, by which we conceive the passage of events. That is to say, the first thing we *do* with images is to envisage a story; just as the first thing we do with words is to tell something, to make a statement."[48] So, lacking words, we use images and build up, as Lippmann in *Public Opinion* called them many years ago, "pictures in our heads."

EDITOR'S NOTE. The author outlined a next step in his theorizing which he did not live to complete. His plan for this further development will help to place the work of this chapter in clearer perspective.

"We see today that twentieth-century philosophy and education must have a foundation broad enough to include two symbolisms: *first*, a nonverbal symbolism for the situations in which human response is primarily through the gesture of the body, and not dependent basically on language; *second*, a linguistic symbolism with which to deal with the problems of logical verification via scientific and practical thinking.

"Such a twofold symbolism must provide for both phases of the inside-outside process of knowing. It must account for the intuitive 'feeling' way of inside identification, of knowing a man or an object internally, in his or its own terms, which is the creative act of discovery via the detached mind. It must also provide for the analytic way of scientific observation from the outside, utilizing man's best instruments of observation, measurement, and interpretation in the act of verification by logical problem-solving. Moreover, such a comprehensive symbolism must lay a solid theoretical foundation for interrelating the two phases of the act of thought—the intuitive, feeling phase of discovery and the logical, analytic phase of verification."

15

The Creative Imagination: Imperatives for Educational Theory*

W HAT is the nature of the act of creative thought when, after prolonged confusion, in one brilliant moment there is a sudden veering of attention, a consequent grasp of new dimensions, and a new idea is born? We know that some autonomous forming process sweeps like a magnet across the chaotic elements of mind, picks up the significant segments and, in a welding flash, precipitates the creative response. But we do not yet know the nature of that forming process. Although we have lived a hundred years into the second intellectual revolution, we still continue to ask: What was the complete act of feeling and thought that created the Taj Mahal? That lighted the first atomic fire? Each of such acts, whether of art or of science, is an act of creative imagination but, in spite of our astonishing gains in knowledge, we still continue to ask: What is the magical force that forms the bits and pieces from the stuff of mind? Until we know the answer to that question we shall continue to

---

* This chapter is a revised version of a paper read by the author before the Philosophy of Education Society shortly before his death. The paper was printed in the Proceedings of the Philosophy of Education Society, 1960. It provides a comprehensive summary of his theory in the form of a series of theorems.

work without an adequate theory of teaching.

Where can one find out what men now know in answer to this question? Years of intensive study confirmed me in my conviction that there are two great sources of knowledge. One is the creative tradition of man; the tested wisdom of the ages which accumulated first in the East and more recently in the West. The other is the newer conceptual consensus and the more valid theories of what today we are calling the behavioral sciences. The conceptual essence of both sources has to be brought together.

On my retirement in 1952, I continued my study of the autobiography of the creative act. This produced the first theorem.

The Theorem of the Three Stages of Creative Work

This preliminary work transformed into consensus what had long been guessed concerning the stages through which creative work is done. There is first a long, *conscious* preparatory period of baffled struggle; second, an interlude in which the scientist or artist apparently gives up, pushes the problem back or down or "out of mind," leaving it for the nonconscious to work upon. Then, third, comes the blinding and unexpected "flash of insight," and it comes with such certitude that a logical statement of it can be immediately prepared. These stages are present whether in art, science, technology, or philosophy.

Because it was depressingly revealed in my own experiences, I was especially consoled by the unanimity with which the autobiographers point to the presence in their work of long preparatory periods of baffled confusion. It was not until the end of two years of uncertainty that I became clear that the key to the nature of the creative act lay in *giving up* long-held presuppositions concerning the *conscious problem-solving* nature of the act of thought and in beginning again with a new orientation. It is fifty years since Dewey first set us on the track of problem-solving. Since his first edition of *How We Think,* most educational philosophy has followed his emphasis on problem-*solving* and has neglected the prior phase— *discovery* of the problem. This reorientation led to the second theorem.

The Theorem of the Two-fold Act of Thought

The great scientists and artists and their biographers (Einstein-Wertheimer, Kepler-Koestler, Cezanne-Gasquet, Coleridge-Lowes, to cite only four) saw the problem in new dimensions, centering attention on the nature of discovery. The examination of scores of such reports, buttressed by thirty years of handling the experimental data from the biosocial-psychology of thinking, brought to light a reorienting new dimension in the study of the act of thought. While there is only one basic human act of response, *it is governed by two different orientations:* the *feeling mood* of discovering and the logical *thinking mood* of verifying. The first emphasis of my study is, therefore, the sharp distinction between discovery and verification. Both are indispensable to productive thought, hence to the work of the school, but the act of discovery is our special concern and the creative imagination is its instrument.

An impressive body of evidence suggests that an all-pervasive motor-feeling factor is one important key that unlocks the door to the off-conscious forming process. This theorem runs so counter to the practice today of making feeling and emotion synonymous, that it has been necessary to distinguish them precisely. Emotion is a name given to the power-factor revealed in body excitement, primarily the fusion of endocrine action in the blood stream with mid-brain-mind controls. Feeling—the name I have just given to the motor qualities of the act, those which I call body-mind gesture—is indispensable to the imagined conception, whether in science or in art. The evidence from both physiology and esthetics is conclusive.

But the theorem also runs counter to the current absorption in what is called "thinking," to the total neglect of the factors which I call "feeling." The historic Einstein discovery of the relativity principle shows that his six-year struggle to locate and define the problem was primarily a groping, feeling stage. His dazed uncertainty was marked by recurring feelings of being right; of moving in the *right* direction. This was the creative, imaginative stage in which occurred a succession of intuitive flashes of insight; some minor, others major and rare. These followed exploratory episodes of feeling and emerged only as new dimensions of the whole structure were felt via feedback transformations. Verbal, logical analysis was never resorted to until after the flash of illumination, and then *only for verification, never for discovery.* As Einstein said, in the six-year, baffling search for the new conception, his verbal statements of hypothetical propositions "did not grow out of any manipulation of axioms." More specifically, "The way the two triple sets of axioms are contrasted in the Einstein-Infeld book," he said, "is not at all the way things happened in the process of actual thinking." Speaking of his ways of working at the problem, Einstein added: "These thoughts did not come in any verbal formulation. I very rarely think in words at all." Then he adds what seems to me to be most significant: "A thought comes, and I may try to express it in words afterward."[1]

Since both phases are involved in the complete act of thought, I shall give the name *"felt-thought"* to the first part—*discovery.* It is largely based on feeling, although it also employs some of the processes conventionally called thinking. The second part of the act—verification—is called *"logical thought";* it consists essentially of systematic logical thinking and the establishment of clear, verbalized relationships.

The Theorem of the Two-fold Way of Knowing

This theorem confronts us with a perennial controversy, one which I have studied since my graduate days at Illinois. There are two approaches to knowing: an inside identification *with* the object, and an outside measured observation of it. The position seems to me to be inescapable that, although there is only one basic act of response, it is governed by two very different orientations. Both are postulated as necessary to adequate knowledge. Identification, whether it be that of Cezanne as artist or that of a hypothesizing brother of science and philosophy such as Einstein or Poincaré, is the East's "Great Doctrine"—the doctrine of *release of conscious mind*—the no-mind of Tao or of Zen. It is confirmed by the identifying way of Western artists and philosophers of organism; both are forms of knowing a man or an object, internally, in its own terms. The theory of the creative act takes its cue primarily from the inside-identification point of view; that is, organically from the center outward, not mechanistically from the outside looking in.

Thus, the organism is viewed as active and self-directed, not as a reactive automaton controlled by stimuli from the outside.

Each region—East and West—holds a key to the doors of conception and there has been a tendency for each to use only its special key. During three visits to the Far East, I observed and questioned in my search for understanding. For many years I have studied its classics, the great books which uncovered the East's approach to the release of mind. I found that today Western philosophers of organism and creative artists have confirmed the reports of Eastern men of wisdom that there is a basic, inside, identifying approach to knowing.

I must pass over the provocative light thrown on it by our modern artists of the West—the confirmation by Lipps and James, Bergson's emphasis on intuition, Whitehead's concurrence that all knowledge is derived from, and verified by, direct intuitive observation. Lorenz, founder of scientific ethology, agrees that Gestalt perception is "identical with that mysterious function which is generally called 'Intuition,' and which indubitably is one of the most important cognitive faculties of Man."[2]

But these first three theorems are merely preliminary, and I come now to the crux. Its most far-reaching new dimension and reorienting conception is the fourth theorem.

The Theorem of the Transliminal Mind

The illuminating flash occurs at a critical threshold of the conscious-nonconscious continuum on which all of life is lived. This conception emerged only when I stopped working in the narrow dimensions of conscious problem-solving and took in the wider ones of the whole conscious-nonconscious continuum. My study turned the theorem into a postulate that all human experience is lived not on a dual conscious-nonconscious continuum, but that three regions are now distinguishable upon it—two end sections, the conscious and the unconscious, connected by a dynamic, transliminal antechamber in which the creative flash occurs.

Competent testimony had suggested for more than two generations that there exists a fertile border state between the alert, conscious problem-solving mind and the receding depths of the unconscious. Galton, James, Schelling, Freud, Varendonck, and others were aware of it, but did little more than name it. During the last twenty-five years, Kubie alone has accumulated scientific psychiatric studies of it. My study suggests that the phenomenon is identical with the Taoist's state of "no-mind," the state of "letting things happen." This is the state wherein we know before we know we know. It is the quiet mind of concentration of attention. I call it the transliminal mind—the mind across the threshold between the conscious and the nonconscious. Most of my past four years have been devoted to the study of its nature.

A convincing number of requisites of the flash are present in the threshold state. While it is a conscious state, it has antechamber access to the traced storage of experience called the unconscious. *Most significant, it is the only part of the continuum that is clearly free from censorship.* It is off-guard, relaxed, receptive to messages, but it is also magnetic, with a dynamic forming power. I think of it as "off-conscious," not unconscious, for the organism is awake, alert, and very much in control. It is hypnoidal, resembling the light trance of autohypnosis. It satisfies the criteria of the intuitively identifying mind of intense concentration, characteristic of the work of an Einstein, a Cezanne, a Lao-tzu, a true Indian Yogin, or a Zen master-artist.

The conceptual consensus which I developed from the physiological-psychological sciences showed that the threshold state satisfies four requisites. First, it has uninterrupted access to a continuous flow of perceptual experience which is traced and preserved electrochemically in the nervous system, most of its continuous action below the threshold of awareness. Second, a continuing flux of imagery pervades the entire conscious-nonconscious continuum. (Although visual and auditory imagery seem to be most prevalent, actually all of the dozen or more senses are involved.) Third, equally *ceaseless ideomotor action* is traced in the form of motor adjustments, incipient movements, and anticipatory sets or attitudes. The latter two, together, produce what now appears to be the initiating and *indispensable* requisite for every act of response, that is, *imagery*. Fourth, the ordered, conceptual content of the mind, which becomes synonymous with symbol and with metaphor image, involves Gestalts of figure-ground relationships, and is the key to thinking and judging, this also being traced and preserved in the unconscious storage.

These four potential ingredients—which are sufficient to account for the flash—are alive, pulsing with movement, not only permissive but magnetically attractive. From conception to death each of the 250 trillion cells of the human organism is in rhythmic pulsation, "firing" steadily in electrochemical action. Only yesterday our guesses were turned into eye-witness observations by the 100,000-fold magnification of the electron-camera. It is known that this system autonomously renews itself through a never-finished, tension-release-tension cycle. At every pulsation, as long as life endures, a difference in electrical potential always remains left over, an imbalance of surplus tension which keeps the organism alive.

The significance of uninterrupted movement of the motor-imaging materials, largely below awareness, is that from birth to death they and the electrochemical current are always on. There is nothing to be started or stopped, nothing to be turned on or off. My theory is that in each momentary situation the organism strives to tune into the continuously available nonconscious materials, *in terms of what the current situation demands.*

All perceptual acts of response consist of the bipolar action of outer situation and inner stress-systems. The integration is not merely physiological-psychological. It always includes cultural factors. This was forecast a century ago by Claude Bernard's discovery that all experience is lived in two environments—the outer, external world of things, living creatures, and human beings, and the inner organismic environment. Cannon's researches confirmed Bernard's pioneering. It is basic to my theory of the imagination that all the contents of the mind—perception, imagery, memory, thinking, feeling, and imagination—all are powered by a fusion of outer-inner drives; stimuli from the real world culture of moving people and things, integrated with stimuli from the inner flux of remembered imagery, motor tendencies, and unconsciously produced metaphor-images, symbols, and concepts.

But are these "unconscious" activities themselves creative? That is a much studied and debated question, contributed to by two generations of research in five major fields, all of which had impinged in some way on the nonconscious: historic studies of the poet's access to it, such as Lowes' *Road to Xanadu;* studies of the dreaming mind; the hypnotic trance; the mind of drug-narcosis; classical psychoanalysis; and neo-Janet research psychiatry. Here I point to two sets of facts. The dreaming mind reveals two requisites for the creative act: a state of relaxed readiness to establish contact and of magnetizing power to fire the cells of storage. Several hundred studies of hypnosis, published since Hull's first laboratory experiments (1925), show that the hypnotic trance gives access to the storage of the unconscious, eliminates the censoring inhibitions of normal conscious life, suspends both sensory and psychological functions and the rational-logical aspects of the self, provides provocative neurophysiological and psychosomatic ideas about the nature of the act of response, and opens many hitherto closed doors on the flash of insight. Although I can find no evidence that these states in themselves have creative potentiality, I am convinced that their further study will greatly illuminate the nature of autistic states in general.

In 1912, Bleuler gave such hypnoidal states a name that has persisted. This was "autism," meaning the "preponderance of inner life as marked by a turning away from the external world." To me, the true meaning of "turning away" is that the process is "off-conscious," marked by utter concentration of attention which, in some as yet unknown way, shuts off all stimuli from the external world and from corresponding inner states. The autistic nature of the threshold mind has been established by a library of studies. These show that in acts of discovery autistic imagery plays the basic role. In the last fifty years, a new conception of mind has slowly formed, one that draws its materials from the whole conscious-nonconscious continuum and points inescapably to the autistic and creative character of hypnoidal and distorted imagery-experience.

But the *true significance* of the fifty-year documentation of autism is that in the transliminal mind there is freedom to create. All censors have disappeared. In no other section of the continuum is this true. The story of the discovery of the creative process in education is really *the story of two freedoms* and the corresponding abolition of censorship. The first freedom is freedom to move about and to speak, freedom from the external censorship of home and school, of family and teachers, and of a repressive, regimented climate of opinion in the community. This freedom was found and clarified by artist-teachers in the first half of our century, and is so well known that it is unnecessary to discuss it here. But my study steadily laid bare a subtle and little-known inner freedom, which is one of the controlling factors in the creative flash of insight. While this *second freedom* was for 2,500 years known intuitively by the wise, contemplative men of the East, only in the last century has it been rediscovered by sensitive artists and students of the West.

Thus, the stage was set for the guiding concept—freedom to create, that is, to associate freely. When the mind is freed from blockages and inhibitions, a process known throughout the history of thought as "free association" can and does take place. The very young child learns by free association, the psychoanalyst regresses his patient to hidden childhood experiences by free association, and the cyberneticists of today have taken it, along with feedback, as a key concept. Free association fits not only the known facts of neurophysiology, but also those of psychology. In sampling the contents of mind which are pertinent to the immediate situation, free associations reveal those that the situation demands.

This laborious documentation of the autistic freedom of the threshold state is, after all, merely preliminary to coming directly to grips with the great unknown. What is the shaping spirit that "saw and seized upon a hint of Form," in Coleridge's twilight of the imagination, and "through the miracle of conscious art . . . moulded a radiant and ordered whole"?

Three general concepts—one long sensed by men of thought and feeling, the second the product of my study, and the third the contribution of the cyberneticians put me—I am now convinced—on the right track.

The Theorem of the Forming Process

Every creative act is an autonomous forming, patterned process below the threshold of awareness. We now know, and I have documented the generalization from the gamut of the behavioral sciences, that this forming process is central to all natural phenomena. In every historical epoch, from Aristotle and Plato to the crystallographers, biochemists, embryologists, biologists, ethologists, and plastic artists today, man has been recurringly preoccupied with form. The corollary of the forming principle is that the act of response is indivisible into body and mind. It is a two-phased transformation of nervous message into organic, meaningful response. This takes place through an integration of nervous cellular action in brain, endothalamic, autonomic, and muscular systems. Whatever theory of the creative imagination emerges must postulate a totally fused physiology, a biosocial-psychology, and psychiatry of the act. The boundaries between the natural sciences are being obliterated. I can no longer speak of "mind," only of body-mind, sometimes of brain-mind. Under the weight of an overwhelming body of evidence, the dichotomy between brain and mind is disappearing and the so-called body-mind problem has become a phantom one.

The forming process is autonomous and self-directive and has three clearly established principles. The first is "Heaven's first law," the principle of unity, order, organization. The bipolar action of outer scene and inner need means not only that form follows function; the parts are formed thereby into ordered unity. The second principle is the historic concept of parsimony, variously expressed as economy or simplicity. The organism always seeks the simplest possible act in response to what the situation demands. The most pregnant form, says Gestalt, is the simplest. The master of literary style and the master artist, the mathematician, the poet, the tennis champion and the master golfer, the modern dancer and the creative architect—all seek the natural, irreducible minimum. The third principle is that of functionality. This means doing what the situation demands. It is the basic cue to the welding force that pulls all the chaotic pieces of the stuff of the creative act together and gives it form. On the simplest level, it is confirmed by the biological law of tropism or forced movement.

The theory postulates, therefore, that the brain alone does not create. The brain computes, regulates, guides, searches for fit, but it does this in the matrix set by more general bodily factors. All, taken together, seek to complete the incompleted act. This is the consensus validated by the physicists' field concept, the biologists' homeostasis and integration, the Gestalt psychologists' configuration and closure, the personality psychologists' organization, and the artists' concept of significant form. And the forming process is documented without exception in every natural science and every art of expression.

The second general concept which my study brings to the forefront is that of *transformation*. The consensus is clear that the flash of insight is not only a self-forming process, it is also a trans-forming process. The stuff of mind is transformed into meaningful response. Physiological message is transformed into psychological meanings; input is synthesized into output. Fantasy motor-images are transformed into metaphor-images.

The key seems to lie in the generalizing nature of the act. An impressive consensus appears among students of the creative process that both creative art products and scientific hypotheses are the formed statements of imagined conceptions. Thus, the imagined conception is the key to all creative acts.

I draw the conclusion, from studies by Lashley, Washburn, Langer, Murphy, the organic psychologists, the linguists, the mythologists, and the students of metaphor, that no new flash appears except in a new orienting conception. We behave first on the basis of our felt conceptions, only after that through verbalized concepts. I distinguish conceptions, which are shot through and through by feeling, from verbalized concepts, which are dominant in what we conventionally call "thinking." In Einstein's search, explosive acts of discovery came about through a *felt* re-centering of imagined conceptions. This reset the total problem and turned him onto a new and successful path.

The Theorem of the Off-conscious Mind of Relaxed Concentration

There is emphatic agreement among Western students that the flash comes when the person is in a state of relaxed tension. Being off guard seems to be a central condition. But this new Western insight is merely a rediscovery of the Great Doctrine of Tao-Zen-Yoga of the ancient East. Three millennia of contemplative wisdom developed the art of the quiet mind, of relaxed concentration of attention. Juxtaposing it with related concepts from a century of Western behavioral science not only confirms it, but supplies the steps in a plausible theory which implements it as well.

First, then, this theorum restates the East's ancient principle of "one-pointedness," that is, of concentration of attention to a point. Following Fulton and other neuro-physiologists, this is concentration through inhibition. But, of the nature of the relevant neuro-physiology, almost nothing is known. The process seems comparable to Western techniques for producing concentration of attention leading to hypnosis or to other forms of autosuggestion. But both Eastern and Western students know the possible danger to the truly creative process. They warn the student against letting himself fall passively into the hypnotic trance, confirming our conclusion that the trance state is itself not creative. Instead of the passive "mediumistic trance," he is urged to continue to endure the ordeal of positive concentration on the goal. This results in deep insight and a tapping of a wide range of correlated ideas. This stage in which the mind is profoundly tuned to the goal is so positively productive that it can only be described as creative. It supplies further confirmation of the conditions favoring the creative act: the concentration of attention, the interval of suspense, and then the sudden flash of illumination which the East calls the "creative climax."

The program outlined in Patanjali's sutras strongly suggests that its "creative climax" is my postulated "autonomous forming process of the creative unconscious." Our study of the autobiography of the flash of insight constantly refers to the creative excitement that comes with the liberation of mind as symbolic transformation takes place and a new conception is grasped.

Turning from the East's intuitive wisdom to the best of Western psychology's facts and theories of the conceptualizing process, I state its essence as the sub-theorem of the brain-mind as a modeling computer, averaging the organism's learned assumptions.

During the decade of the ninteen-forties, behavioral scientists on both sides of the Atlantic independently generalized that the flashing-up of either a new perception or a conception is due to some power of averaging the organism's learned assumptions. Humphreys-Owen of the University of London, suggested that the perception of form in crystallography "is an act of averaging, for the light reflected from each atom is not individually detected by the sensitive surface of the retina."[3] The experiments on the perception of motion carried on by Ames and Ittleson confirm the averaging process. Helson, in a series of experimental studies, established that human organisms tend to order their perceptual interpretation of the world in judging distances, sizes, weights, beauty of organization, etc., by unconscious "averaging" or "pooling" their experiences of judgment. Lorenz, studying animal behavior, came to approximately the same conclusion. The calculator in the central-nervous apparatus automatically "assumes" that all objects within the visual field reflect on the average any wave-lengths reflected by them; this adds up to what we perceive as white light.

Thus, a steadily accumulating behavioral consensus has developed in the last twenty years that the brain-mind models the external world as a computer, averaging in feed-back manner new perceptual experience with old recorded experience.

But once more we ask the central question: What force picks up the essentials of the fantasia of imagery and movement and forms it into orderly meaning?

The most sustained and, I think, far-reaching theoretical efforts have been those of the multi-discipline group of physiologists, psychologists, psychiatrists, mathematicians, and electronic engineers, generally known on both sides of the Atlantic as cyberneticians. The leaders are Walter and Ashby in England, and Wiener and McCulloch in America. I use the findings of these workers with a caution concerning the limitations in their sources and techniques —limitations created by their frankly mechanistic point of view and their neglect of feeling and other physiological foundations of emotional life.

The cyberneticians have shown an impressive body of behavior parallelisms between man and the computing machine. Both have relays and information units and make physical decisions; both have networks, reverberating circuits, storage devices, oscillations, transformation groups, scanning circuits, and provisions for feedback. The last is especially important, for the concept has been accepted and incorporated into the consensus of the behavioral sciences as well as the physical sciences.

Although the parallelisms are suggestive, far more stimulating to theory and research are the cyberneticians' two hypotheses of "scanning" and "meaning." The first is the most plausible theoretical explanation of the brain's computational guidance of an organism's act of response.

The alpha rhythm is a scanning mechanism, and I add, *searching for completion*. It picks out, from the bombardment of relevant and chance stimuli of the real world, just those stimuli that are "worth paying attention to." Walter—British physiologist, pioneer electro-encephalographer, and leading exponent of Pavlovian, conditioned-response psychology—discovered that four brain-rhythms group themselves in recurring patterns and that through them it is possible to detect behavior patterns. Also by the use of "flicker" stimuli, "illusions" or "hallucinations" become a function of brain electro-chemical activity. The rhythmical electrical evidence obtained from the use of flicker is impressive that the ceaseless brain-mind background activity is communicated to and sets up rhythmic response over *the entire brain,* including the so-called "silent" frontal lobes which Penfield, Halstead, *et al,* regard as the area of thought and of creative imagination. Walter concludes, from brilliant analysis of the effects of flicker and plausible use of simultaneous equations, that the alpha rhythm is a process of searching or "scanning" for form or pattern as in television. To cite typical examples of his facts and logic: (1) The alpha rhythm always stops when pattern is found; (2) the average frequency of the alpha rhythm matches "the period of visual persistence in reading"; (3) the scanning-interval accounts for the optical illusion of the apparent movement from one of two lights to the other, as one light is turned off.

About the same time as Walter's work in England, McCulloch and Pitts in America by another intellectual route arrived at the same "scanning hypothesis." Asking what is the factor that, throughout the signaling and transforming process, preserves the pattern irrespective of spatial and temporal changes, they have developed a theory of transformation of electrochemical message information into patterned response (meaning) based on a new mathematics of transformation-groups. By a group they mean "a set of displacements *bringing an object into identity with itself,* like rotations about an axis of symmetry."

But much is left out by this brilliant brain-guiding theory. Much more is involved in the "searching for completion" than the mid-and-cortical brain. The totalizing factors below the brain, the ener-gizing emotional factors of drive (probably endocrine and hormonal and central-analogical rather than digital), and the over-all body-mind, motor-adjustment system—all of these are involved.

The attitude of imminence suggests a total body-mind searching for the fit that will complete the act. The continued fixation of attention in the threshold state frees a cumulative, "suggesting," "determining tendency to act." This is a factor in the release of the flash of insight.

No less than six lines of research have independently contributed to the validation of this theorem. For two generations, expert testimony among organic psychologists has increasingly agreed that prior to the response, and literally making it, is a motor "determining tendency to act," a "set" or "intention" to act. James in many documentations discussed "relations as feelings of tendency." Külpe laid great stress upon what he called "determining tendency," "being *about* to have an idea . . . a *Bewusstseinlage.*" The Gestaltists, shortly afterwards, used the language of closure. Washburn, in the most extended study of movement, developed the theory that the *unifying influence* in the act of response was what she called a "problem idea." The concept of determining tendency is close to, if not identical with, Goldstein's conception of the abstracting attitude. Reed and others, in conducting psychological studies of concept formation, recognized this same determining tendency of the organism, of its being "on the verge of getting an idea." The most elaborate attempt to study the process using verbal materials is Lashley's (1951) report on "The Problem of Serial Order in Behavior." He, too, turns to the perennial concept of "determining tendency to act," that is, the idea of acting, or intention to act. There appears to exist, he says, "generalized schemata of action . . . which determine the sequence of specific acts."[4]

We find confirmation for the doctrine of imminence in the evidence of the incompleted act in the studies of temporary memory made under the direction of Kurt Lewin. Other things being equal, we remember the incompleted act. An extensive body of laboratory research has confirmed Lewin. Whyte sums up the confirming evidence from the physical sciences.

For the mere abstract idea of an incomplete pattern becomes alive of its own accord; it has a hole which must be filled and this sets going the whole machinery of process, the valences of chemistry, and the attractions and repulsions of life.

This is one great secret of pattern philosophy: incomplete patterns possess their own inherent *élan*. The mathematical symbolism of patterns displays a tendency and movement of its own: toward completion.[5]

A generation of research has established the further fact that no situation is ever perceived except within an orienting, preparatory attitude. This is the matrix of the imagined conception. The most conclusive body of evidence is in several hundred psychological studies of motor attitude and sets of expectancy or anticipation. There is an extensive confirming body of expert testimony and laboratory evidence from Darwin to Landis and Hunt on the startle-reaction. Finally, Bull's experimental studies, carried on for more than twenty years, establish conclusively the prior role of motor attitude in emotional responses. It is a generally accepted principle, therefore, that in each act of response the organism adopts the physical attitude that is appropriate to the meaning with which it is responding.

The scientific study of hypnosis as suggestibility provides further confidence in the notion of imminence. "Suggestion" is technically defined as a group of ideas proposed to an individual "such as to cause him to react *as if* the phenomenon for which the ideas stand were actually present." But the suggestion will be effective only under two conditions: first, relaxation through concentration of attention upon the goal; second, acceptance of the suggestion. Acceptance is a subtle concept, but can be explained most clearly by the fact of the subject's acting as if the phenomenon suggested were actually present—as he would react to stimuli from similar normal situations.

The concept of suggestion is still further illuminated by two other established concepts of hypnosis-research. These are (1) ideomotor action, namely, that an idea can produce a specific pattern of muscular response; and (2) its supporting concept, neuromotor enhancement, which states that the initial responses, minute though they may be, can be vastly built up through accretive and reinforcing processes. Jacobson's various studies established that imagined arm movements were accompanied by actual movements, and "microvoltage during recollection is about equal to that during . . . various acts of imagination." This was confirmed in the analysis of the physiology of thought and speech: "Experimental evidence," Eysenck concludes, "is overwhelming . . . that an idea, or image, of a movement tends to produce the precise movement imagined, or a modified form of it."[6]

This evidence for the organism's basic tendency to complete the act leads to several basic theorems of the symbol. The discovery of the capacity of the body-mind's autistic state to turn its fantasy-stuff into meaningful concepts and symbols was a step of prime significance.

The Theorem of the Two-fold Symbolic Act

The human being knows, feels, thinks, expresses, communicates, by means of two types of symbolic act: (a) felt-thought through the gesture-symbol, (b) verbalized-thought through the name-symbol.

The clearest evidence for the theorem is from the data of genetic bio-psychology from such men as Piaget and Gesell. How does the wordless infant cope with or *know* his world? From conception to the second year of life—that is, before language—we know only by the gesture of movement, and with each movement both motor-adjustments and images are being traced on the nervous system. From the second year to death, most recorded acts have verbal concomitants and in the growth of intelligence they are of supreme importance. But, until death, each act is still motor-centered in the nonverbal gesture of the body. The motor-feeling factor is, there-fore, one important key that unlocks the door to the off-conscious forming process. The human organism is both motor-focused and word-focused. Through its entire life history the organism is tense with incipient movements and expectant attitudes. Its meaningful acts are basically motor responses, interjected into a continuously reconstructing storage of motor attitudes in the musculature and the nervous system. Their integration we call motor attitude which precedes imagery and concept formation. It constitutes the prior determining factor in perception and so in the flashing of meaning.

Since, if we are to analyze and discuss the whole motor complex, we must have a distinctive label, I name it "gesture." From two generations of studies of primitives, higher apes, and language-less young children, we know that all of these have the capacity to turn fantasy-images into motor-centered, gestural symbols. The distinction between the higher ape and man is that the latter can turn fantasy-images into verbal symbols; hence Cassirer's name for man, *animale symbolicum*.

From the second year of life, language via the naming process increasingly becomes an instrument by which the child knows, and copes with, his world. Consider the infant learning to talk by naming things in his environment, and by so doing mastering abstract conceptual meanings of it. A young child establishes the concrete beginnings of his thought-models for the external world, not by learning symbol-names only, but by responding with the gestural symbol. By school age he has built up meanings—that is, responses to objects by means of their names—for the entire environment. Entering school and mastering the tools of reading, number, and language, the process of naming and symbolizing is vastly broadened and deepened. Concrete definitional generalizations are extended to include relational ones of increasing complexity. Now the child is systematically inducted via concepts—that is, conceptual symbols—into various phases of civilization and culture.

To deal with the staggering range of human ways of living, of man's ideas, beliefs, and traditions, the cue to selection and organization is the "key concept." Sane and orderly life would be impossible were it not for the conceptualizing capacity which enables man to select and respond to a few key-stimuli from the overwhelming fusillade to which he is subjected. It is this capacity that builds thought-models of economy and order. Manifold responses to specific occupations, to the data of political, economic, and religious groupings are steadily formed into a manageable hierarchy of concepts.

The forming process is controlled by what the bipolar situation (outer scene and inner need) demands. In most stimulus-situations it is a flash of "meaning"—either a directive "sign" to act (a pointer) or an interpretive symbol of imagined conceiving. The latter is either definitional or relational. Under special conditions the forming process is an auto-symbolizing process, occurring through the transformation of fantasy images into metaphor images. This voluminous illustrating of "concepts" can now be generalized. Each of these concepts is a conceptual symbol. A symbol is something that stands for, represents, or denotes something else—not by exact resemblance but by vague suggestion. To emphasize the psychology of the symbolic act and to capitalize on the known role of imminence or suggestibility, I shall use "suggest" rather than "represent."

The key, not only to the distinction between sign and symbol but also to the critical stage in the symbolizing process, is the naming. This is the simplest symbolic form—a word which, as name, completes the conceptualizing process. In the famous case of Helen Keller's first awareness of the concept *water,* "w-a-t-e-r" pointed not to the thing "water," but to the *idea* of water.

Finally, the language and myth studies, from Usener, Donovan, Wegener, and Silberer to Cassirer and Langer, connected symbol to metaphor in the conceptualizing process. As a symbol operates by *suggesting* a set of meanings, so also does a metaphor. When, in the well-known case reported by Silberer, a frightening, three-dimensional symbol appeared before him warning him of his behavior, it was metaphorically suggesting a hidden meaning. Metaphors are figures of speech which help to account for symbolic transformation. Wegener gives us the cue when he says a symbol is "used metaphorically to describe whatever it can symbolize." As Langer states it: "In a genuine metaphor, an image of the literal meaning is our symbol for the figurative meaning, the thing that has no name of its own."[7]

There is critical corroboration of these findings concerning the naming process, from both genetic psychology and the philosophical studies of myth and language from Usener to Cassirer and Langer. Evidently one does not exaggerate in saying that noticing-naming was one of the giant steps in man's mental development. Usener proposed the hypothesis which, I suggest, has since been confirmed independently by pioneers in several of the behavioral sciences. This is the hypothesis of "noticing" and "naming." The noticing-naming synthesis is brought about by a process of "running-through-a-realm-of-experience" which Cassirer calls "discursive thinking." Gerard, physiologist, seems to be commenting on the same phenomenon of "running-through-a-realm-of-experience" when he asks what ". . . occurred in Goethe's brain when news of his friend's suicide 'crystallized' the plan of 'Werther' as, 'the whole shot together from all directions and became a solid mass.' "[8] Cassirer says that this is noticing and naming, the alerting action of the organism which focuses attention on a point, enabling the spark "to jump across." This sounds much like Wertheimer's "re-centering of the problem," Silberer's autonomous action of unconscious imaging which he called the "auto-symbolizing act," the cyberneticians' picking out relevant stimuli from "noise," Whitehead's "prehension," Wild's "primal awareness," Coleridge's "imagination creatrix." This is close to, if indeed it is not precisely, the "actionless action" of the Tao. For our Western study this is rediscovery of the symbol. Usener and Cassirer were not alone in centering attention on "noticing" and the "naming process," as the crux of conceptualizing and symbolizing. While in Usener's day Donovan was making the same point in England, in Cassirer's generation of the 1920s, an American student of language, Edward Sapir, and Ludwig Wittgenstein, member of the Vienna Circle of "symbolic logic" fame—each, I think, unknown to the other—were converging on a similar theory.

After World War I, physiologists, psychiatrists, and other students of psychopathology and the relation of brain damage to conceptual thought corroborated the stress on the speech factor and specifically on the naming process. One of the most impressive documentations is Goldstein's thirty years of work on language, naming, conceptualizing, and the abstract attitude, confirmed by Halstead's twelve-year study on conceptualizing and the frontal lobes. The evidence is conclusive that conceptual-symbolizing is abstracting. Among Goldstein's amnesic-aphasia patients were many who were "totally or partially unable to find names for concrete things." Their spontaneous language "is conspicuously lacking in nouns and verbs. When shown such an object as a cup or a pen or an umbrella, they adopt a concrete attitude." For example, a patient, asked to give some "girl names," gave the names of several girls in one specific family; he had visualized actual concrete persons. The abstraction, "girl names," was beyond his generalizing abilities.

Goldstein, asking why the patient can not use words as names or symbols to stand for the object, answers: because "the patients have the same concrete attitude toward the words that they have toward objects they are asked to sort." They lack the capacity to create any sort of abstraction.

We seem to have narrowed the source of the power or its deficiency to certain areas of the brain or to such areas in collaboration with maturation and environmental development; the special areas being the frontal and pre-frontal lobes and their connections with the mid-brain. Moreover, Goldstein's interpretation supports the thesis of the transliminal mind. Concrete behavior is universally active, but abstract behavior is "passive," a "surrendering," letting-one's-self-go. The focus is on the inner life, the autistic mind; in concrete behavior the focus is on the stimulus from the outer world.

One final bit of integrating of hitherto separated concepts. The naming-abstracting-symbolizing process appears to be identical with the process of condensation which is characteristic of the dreaming mind, and also of the autistic, off-conscious, threshold, creative mind.

We can see it at work in the genetics of intuition by studying the behavior of young children learning to adjust to differences and likenesses in the physical world (differences in size, sound, light, weight, texture, motion, what-not) which are universal and commonplace. Once the processes of learning are experienced consciously, they "drop out of the central focus of conscious awareness . . . through the repetition which is essential to the early steps by which we learn anything."[9] This dropping out of consciousness is the amazing process of abstracting, of naming, of symbolizing, of intuitive identification.

The foundations of a theory for the two-fold symbolic act that is both gesture and language are broad enough to embrace all the situations of life—the nonverbal as well as the linguistic ones. They provide for both phases of the inside-outside problem of knowing, and account for the "feeling" way of inside identification, of knowing a man or an object internally in his or its own terms, which is the creative act of discovery of the free completion-seeking mind. But they also provide for scientific observation from the outside, utilizing man's best instruments of measurement and interpretation in the act of verification by logical problem-solving.

The chief gap in the present digest of my study is on the biochemistry of mind. The new electro-encephalographic knowledge helps, but it alone is insufficient. Here is one of the next two or three greatest frontiers in behavioral studies. Much better answers will be given shortly to the baffling problem of the creative act when we know much more of the chemical functioning of that motor-feeling complex I have called the "gesture-symbol," "determining tendency to complete the act," the act of acceptance, acting imaginatively "as if" the suggested phenomena were real. We need insight into the chemistry of the act in the moment when the searching movement of the organism turns up the needed pattern.

Evidence juxtaposed from several independent sources suggests that the key to the flashing-up of insight is *the incompleted act.* My study lays bare the following factors which are present in the off-conscious state and which, I now believe, contain within themselves the explanation of the secret of the creative flash: first, utter concentration of attention on the goal, to the exclusion of outer and inner stimuli; second, continuous scanning or *searching movement of the total organism,* uninterruptedly *seeking completion;* third, completion (that is, "flash of meaning") achieved when the adjustment of the organism to the demands of the situation has reached "the canonical position," to use McCulloch's term, that is, when the group of space-time coordinates "brings the object into identity with itself like rotations about an axis of symmetry," as Walter phrased it. The complete absorption in contemplation of the goal seems to pull together the needed elements into perfect fit.

How is the adjusting, searching process carried on? A series of mutually corroborative hypotheses supplies the most plausible theory: first, that the brain-mind works continually as a modeling computer, averaging through feedback the organism's learned (stored) assumptions; second, that the brain-mind's alpha rhythm is the mechanism that scans for best fit; third, that the mid-brain continually computes the changing space-time coordinates; fourth, that the complete freedom of the transliminal state, in which the computing is done, permits a cumulative, organic, motor-feeling factor, a suggesting, determining tendency to complete the act, a motor-adjustment of imminence; fifth, that the total act is carried on in a bipolar fusion of perception of outer-scene and drive of inner stress-system.

New light is thrown on the mystery by juxtaposing the foregoing with the theory of knowing via a two-fold symbolic act: felt-thought through gesture-symbol, and verbalized thought through name-symbol. Every meaningful act, imagined as well as overt, is gestural-symbolic (even if only incipiently so); it is an act of completion, the act of acceptance—acting "as if" the imagined phenomenon were real. This is the only way a human being can conceive—only by suggestion through metaphor.

IMPERATIVES FOR EDUCATION

What, then, from my study are the imperatives for educational theory?

1. A re-examination of behavior theory is called for, a systematic, even encyclopedic one; one that will be founded on the key sources of knowledge, including the latest critical findings of the behavioral sciences. Building upon the brilliant recent past, we are now forced to restudy the foundations of a new theory of curriculum, teaching and administration.

This will require nothing less than a revolution in the education of teachers. For a generation we have given lip service to "the whole man" and the "complete act of thought," but few of us have put the full scope of the available and essential concepts to work. We teach the teachers *semi-psychology*—a psychology of conscious, verbal problem-solving. We proclaim that the proper study of mankind is man, but we deal with less than half of man. We have had science of a sort but almost no art. We have ignored or scoffed at what profoundly wise men for three millennia have called intuitive identification with man and the world. We have had thinking, thinking, thinking of a hyperanalytical kind, but no understanding of the crucial role of the feeling which molds it into felt-thought and thereby brings about creative discovery. We have a magnificent verbal-symbolic logic, but no logic of the gesture, and that is half of life. We have had millions of hours devoted to training in solving problems by reasoning, but almost none devoted to cultivation of the imagination. First, then, the study suggests new dimensions in which to re-examine the act of thought and plot new directions, based on a consensus of the behavioral sciences and the tested wisdom of man.

2. A similar re-examination is needed of our established doctrine of experience; in terms of current behavioral science, this is "information theory." One of the requisites of the creative act of discovery as of the logical act of verifying thought is copious and ordered information; a well-filled storehouse of imagery to guarantee richness and freedom of association, and of ordered key concepts to guarantee organization of thought. A critical weakness of the past era of education has been our lack of mastery; neither the teachers of teachers nor the teachers they taught knew enough. They were not really students, and the effects become evident in the superficiality of the entire educational product. Since no educational theory will be worth making that is not founded on a sound behavioral theory, I suggest that a first step in reconstruction is that we become master students of the conceptual foundations of the behavioral sciences.

3. We must build the foundations for the school of Freedom. While keeping the dynamic power of the theory of the active school, we face the incredibly difficult task of finding the way to match it—in theory and in practice—with the quiet school of intense concentration and intuitive identification. The cue to the quiet mind is the creation of conditions which favor the ancient commonplace of concentration of attention. To create it in our go-getting, activity-for-activity's-sake civilization, and our hyperactive school will require what seems to be superhuman sensitivity, openness of mind, and persistence. Under Parker, Dewey, and the artist-teachers we built the School of the First Freedom—freedom from external restrictions. Now we must build the School of the Second Freedom—that of the inner freedom of the relaxed, threshold-mind of intuitive discovery. The concept of discovery will revitalize our established conception of freedom to investigate.

4. While keeping all the gains on the side of logical thought and continuing to develop mastery of written and spoken language, we are called to parallel our current verbal programs with truly coordinate nonverbal ones. A word-education is only half an education. To provide a whole education, our theory must contain a nonverbal symbolism as sound as the symbolic logic of the logical empiricists.

In practical terms this can be implemented only in a school program that is as motor-focused as it is word-focused. This is the key to the building of a complete school of living. Beginning with the education of teachers, our theory and practice must *provide a program of designed movement.* The felt-thought of discovery can be produced only by a program that provides for the development of the gestural symbol through a complete movement-program in the school, as well as for logical thought through a program of reasoned verbal-processes. The study calls for a motor-and-verbal theory, for a motor-and-verbal program of education. To produce such a program will force our own felt-thought to profound new depths of theory.

5. For the past quarter-century, there has been a world-wide recrudescence of the ancient dichotomy between mechanical and organic explanations of behavior. The current spurt in the natural sciences and the renewal of the label "behavioral" has also given new life to the mechanistic concept, and the generation's organic discoveries again seem to be called in question or at least to be minimized. The great dichotomy persists in the expressive arts and in the foundations of education. Scientific scholars, artists, and philosophers are still split in a great cleavage between particles and patterns; some center attention on the physical particles, others on the field-forces or relations that hold the particles together. Lancelot Whyte has described the split in the physical sciences. "The old regime spoke mainly of particles, forces, reversible motions and conservation laws; the new must learn to speak of complex arrangements of different kinds, their symmetry and asymmetry, one-way changes and rhythmic pulsations." This cleavage in attitude toward life is still the greatest single obstacle to the widespread adoption of a theory of behavior that will build on the conception of the forming-process and on a two-fold approach; intuitive-identification and scientific observation.

Actually, we do not have to choose between particles and patterns. The evidence strongly suggests that our theory will be focused on two poles rather than on a single center. The examples of points and patterns from the new physics are paralleled in neurophysiology by fusion of the digital findings of the cyberneticians, on the one hand, with the analogical discoveries of the endothalamic and motor-systems school on the other. The bipolar emphasis has dominated the studies of the philosophers of nonverbal and verbal symbols since Cassirer; the human being knows through two types of symbolic act. In the two-fold act of felt-thought, both feeling and thinking play coordinate roles. Perhaps the most obvious example lies in the two ways of knowing—outside observation unified with inner identification. Our theory can, in fact, build on the bipolar foundation of stimuli from the outer scene of the culture and the inner stress-system of the organism. In short, the great dichotomy of mechanism *vs.* organism can be obliterated if we start with the premise that the conception of a fundamental particle itself is meaningless. "Ultimate structure must exist," as Whyte says, "there must be last indivisible particles, final units, which act as the markers of the root patterns of this universe." But my study is emphatic that a biosocial-psychological vocabulary which will unify understanding will speak only of "patterns of particles."

6. No new idea appears except in a new recentering, dynamizing conception. This confronts us with our irreducible task: to state in gripping terms a clear, over-arching philosophy that will motivate our youth today. The longer I live and work, the more important to the individual seems to be his overarching *concern*. Granted a modicum of brains, a man's guiding concern determines the nature and limits of his contribution. Correspondingly, the heart of our current philosophic problem is the over-arching framework of the people's thought and feeling.

This theoretical principle has special pertinence today. It is a truism that our mid-century years constitute a critical point in world industrialization, in which the two halves of mankind—half slave and half free—are now caught in a frightening struggle for the minds as well as the bodies of men. I have returned this week from a first hand look at schools and teacher-education in that small sector of the earth, from India to Japan, where half of humanity lives today, where the leaders of nearly a billion illiterate, poverty-stricken, crowded, religion-and-caste-ridden men are trying to set up quickly a new society that will have some prospects of being democratic. I can count on the fingers of two hands the schools of truly democratic living that I found, schools which give promise of making work this thing we call "the democratic way." Moreover, even if we could build 50,000 such schools in East Asia, in the Near East, and in Africa, we could make no appreciable change in the culture in less than fifty years. Adult education is our only recourse, but in adult education our total effort is puny; nowhere on earth is it making more than a dent on the mammoth problem. Nevertheless, we can do nothing less than assume that we have the needed fifty years to modernize and democratize the undeveloped and uncommitted regions of the earth—and build our new theory and practice of a true school of living.

But educational theory, to be appropriate to a revolutionary culture, must be revolutionarily new. We are living in one of those recurring cycles in the history of thought when many old conceptions are outmoded, have served their tentative usefulness; some have actually been disproved. New horizons of theory loom before us, comparable to those faced by Kepler, Galileo, and Newton, and we listen now to new physical theorists, new behavioral theorists, and new expressional artists.

At this point, my study is, admittedly, still unfinished, not least because of vast blind spots in our behavioral knowledge. Notably, we know little about the release of that energy and enthusiasm which fire creative common action and move human beings along a line of valid direction. I have uncovered previously fragmented knowledge about the role of the image as a factor in the individual creative act. And I have sought to join these fragments creatively. But we know little of the processes of mind that create within us an energizing "image of man" to propel, unite, and guide a people and their leaders. Yet that seems to be the crux of our social-psychological problem: first of all, to create a sense of mission in forty millions of American young people freely to lead the uncommitted, potentially free world—now. The heart of their over-arching concern will be "live and help live"; no longer can it be "live and let live." In this task, understanding and unlocking the powers of creative imagination in all men acquire stupendous importance.

NOTES

Notes

1. The single best source in this field is in selected issues of *Industrial Design*. See especially January 1957, "The Question of Creativity," a major report on the MIT seminar on creative techniques for engineers, designers, and executives. See also October 1954; June 1955; August 1955; April and June 1957; January, March, May, August, and September 1958.
2. See William J. J. Gordon, *Synectics: The Development of Creative Capacity* (New York: Harper & Brothers, 1961).

1. AUTOBIOGRAPHY OF THE CREATIVE ACT

1. The record is impressive: two score of plastic artists and composers and critics of the arts, a dozen mathematicians, as many physical and natural scientists, ten philosophers, several sociologists and anthropologists, half a dozen dancers, and a score of masters of physical and mental skills, including fifteen lightning calculators. Typical of those whose introspections have been reviewed in this study are:

Men of science: Galileo, Newton, Darwin, Einstein

Mathematicians: Gauss, Poincaré, Russell, Hadamard

Painters, sculptors: Cezanne, Van Gogh, Gauguin, Kuniyoshi, Moore, Shahn, Ernst

Writers: Blake, Coleridge, Goethe, Dryden, Wordsworth, Chekhov, Tennyson, Kipling, Henry James, John Cowper Powys, Wolfe, Housman, Cocteau, Valéry, Spender, Shapiro, Auden, Tate

Dancers: Duncan, Wigman, Graham

Philosophers: James, Bergson, Russell, Whitehead
Estheticians: Croce, Koestler, Gertrude and Leo Stein, Arnheim, Stauffer, Marin
Psychiatrists: Janet, Prince, Freud, Jung, Fromm, Rank, Kubie

2. Henri Poincaré in Jacques Hadamard, *Psychology of Invention in the Mathematical Field* (Princeton, N.J.: Princeton University Press, 1949), pp. 13, 14.

3. A. E. Housman, *The Name and Nature of Poetry*, The Leslie Stephen Lecture delivered at Cambridge, May 9, 1933 (New York: Macmillan, 1933), pp. 48, 49, 50.

4. *Ibid.*, pp. 49, 50.

5. Henri Poincaré, *Science and Method* (New York: Dover, 1952), p. 61.

6. Eugène Delacroix, "L'Invention et le Génie," and Hadamard in Hadamard, *op cit.*, p. 44.

7. Anton Chekhov in Brewster Ghiselin, *The Creative Process* (Berkeley and Los Angeles, Calif.: University of California Press, 1952), p. 6.

8. *Ibid.*, p. 5.

9. Alfred North Whitehead in Ghiselin, *ibid.*, pp. 4, 5.

10. Isadora Duncan in Ghiselin, *ibid.*, p. 5.

11. Stephen Spender, "The Making of a Poem," in Ghiselin, *ibid.*, p. 119.

12. *Ibid.*, pp. 15, 16.

13. John Livingston Lowes, *The Road to Xanadu, A Study in the Ways of the Imagination* (Boston: Houghton Mifflin, 1927), p. 433.

14. Sir Isaac Newton, in Lowes, *ibid.*, p. 433.

15. Jean Cocteau, "The Process of Inspiration," in Ghiselin, *op. cit.*, p. 80.

16. Paul Valéry in Hadamard, *op. cit.*, p. 17.

17. Hadamard, *ibid.*, pp. 8, 15, 16.

18. Karl Friedrich Gauss in Hadamard, *ibid*, p. 15.

19. Katharine Camp Mayhew and Anna Camp Edwards, *The Dewey School* (New York: Appleton-Century, 1936), p. 423.

20. Wolfgang Amadeus Mozart, in Hadamard, *op. cit.*, p. 16.

21. Claude Bernard, in Hadamard, *ibid.*, p. 48.

22. Amy Lowell, *Poetry and Poets* (Boston: Houghton Mifflin, 1930), p. 29; also in Ghiselin, *op. cit.*, p. 112.

23. Lawrence E. Cole and William F. Bruce, *Educational Psychology* (Yonkers, N.Y.: World Book, 1950), p. 469.

24. Edouard Claparède, in Hadamard, *op. cit.*, p. 50.

25. Hadamard, *ibid.*, p. 50.

26. David O. Woodbury, *Let ERMA Do It* (New York: Harcourt, Brace, 1956), pp. 268, 269.

27. *Ibid.*, pp. 267, 268.

28. Peter McKellar, *Imagination and Thinking, A Psychological Analysis* (London: Cohen and West, 1957), p. 124.
29. *Ibid.*, p. 127.
30. Edwin B. Holt, *Animal Drive and the Learning Process* (New York: Henry Holt, 1931), I, 224.
31. McKellar, *op. cit.*, p. 125.
32. Malcolm Cowley, "Remembering Hart Crane," in Ghiselin, *op. cit.*, p. 148-149.
33. John Dryden, dedicatory letter to "The Rival Ladies," in Ghiselin, *op. cit.*, p. 78.
34. Lowes, *op. cit.*, p. 31.
35. *Ibid.*, p. 103.
36. *Ibid.*, p. 74.
37. Roger Sessions, in Augusto Centano, *The Intent of the Artist* (Princeton, N.J.: Princeton University Press, 1941), pp. 123, 126, 127.
38. Jean Cocteau, "The Process of Inspiration" in Ghiselin, *op. cit.*, p. 79.
39. Julian Levi, in part quoting Georges Rouault in "Before Paris and After" in Ghiselin, *ibid.*, pp. 56, 57.
40. Plato, quoted by A. E. Housman, in Ghiselin, *ibid.*, p. 85.
41. C. G. Jung, "Psychology and Literature," in Ghiselin, *ibid.*, p. 230.
42. Vincent van Gogh, in Ghiselin, *ibid.*, pp. 3, 4.

2. CREATIVE DISCOVERY AND LOGICAL VERIFICATION

1. John Dewey, *How We Think* (Boston: D. C. Heath, 1910).
2. Albert Einstein, in Max Wertheimer, *Productive Thinking* (New York: Harper & Brothers, 1945), pp. 183, 184.
3. Wertheimer, *ibid.*, p. 182.
4. *Ibid.*, pp. 182, 183.
5. *Ibid.*, pp. 168-188. See also Paul Arthur Schilpp (ed.), *Albert Einstein: Philosopher Scientist* (New York: Tudor, 1951). In this volume see especially the essays by Wolfgang Pauli of Zürich, Max Born of Edinburgh, Louis de Broglie of the Institute of France, Walter Heitler of Dublin, Niels Bohr of Denmark, Henry Margenau of Yale, Philipp Frank of Harvard, and Hans Reichenbach of the University of California at Los Angeles. And see A. Einstein and others, *The Principle of Relativity, Original Papers*, trans. from the 1907 papers (New York: Dover); A. Einstein, *Relativity, the Special and General Theory* (New York: Crown, 1920).
6. Wertheimer, *op. cit.*, pp. 176-177.
7. Arthur Koestler, *The Sleepwalkers* (New York: Macmillan, 1959), pp. 518, 519.

8. To cite a few of the best: Vincent van Gogh, *Dear Theo, the Autobiography of Vincent van Gogh,* ed. by Irving Stone (New York: Doubleday, 1946); Eugène Delacroix, *Journal,* trans. by Walter Pach (New York: Crown); Leonardo Da Vinci, *Notebooks,* Edward McCurdy, ed. (New York: Tudor); Benvenuto Cellini, *Autobiography,* trans. by John Addington Symonds (New York: Hermitage), also in Everyman's Library, no. 51 (New York: Dutton); Joachim Gasquet, *Cézanne* (Berlin: Bruno Cassirer, 1930); Paul Gauguin, *Intimate Journals.* trans. by Van Wyck Brooks (London: Heinemann, 1952); John Marin, *Selected Writings,* ed. with an introduction by Dorothy Norman (New York: Pellegrini and Cudahy, 1949).

Among the few systematic books of importance written by artists are the following: Constantin Stanislavski, *Building a Character,* trans. by Elizabeth Reynolds Hapgood (New York: Theatre Arts Book, 1949); Adolf Hildebrand, *The Problem of Form* (New York: G. E. Stechert, 1945); Robert Henri, *The Art Spirit* (New York: Lippincott, 1923); Wassily Kandinsky, *The Art of Spiritual Harmony,* trans. by M.T.H. Sadler (Boston: Houghton Mifflin, 1914); Robert Goldwater and Marco Treves (eds.), *Artists on Art* (New York: Pantheon, 1947). This volume, based on 150 sources, gives the essence of the statements of painters and sculptors from the fourteenth to the twentieth century.

9. Paul Cezanne, in Gasquet, *op. cit.,* pp. 105, 106.

10. William Blake, *Poems and Prophecies,* Everyman's Library, no. 792 (New York: Dutton), "Jerusalem," chap. I [5] lines 16-20, p. 165.

11. E. M. Benson, *John Marin* (Washington: The American Federation of Arts, 1935), p. 107.

12. Paul Cezanne, in Gasquet, *op. cit.,* pp. 105, 106.

3. The Magic Threshold

1. Edward Carpenter, "The Art of Creation," in Sheldon Cheney, *Men Who Have Walked With God* (New York: Knopf, 1948), p. 379.

2. Francis Galton, in Jacques Hadamard, *The Psychology of Invention in the Mathematical Field* (Princeton, N.J.: Princeton University Press, 1949), p. 25.

3. H. A. Taine, "On Intelligence," in Hadamard, *ibid.,* p. 27.

4. Graham Wallas, *The Art of Thought* (New York: Harcourt Brace, 1926), p. 52.

5. Erich Fromm, *The Forgotten Language* (New York: Rinehart, 1951), p. 29.

6. Morton Prince, in Margaret Brenman and Merton M. Gill, *Hypno-*

therapy, A Survey of the Literature, The Menninger Foundation Monograph, series no. 5 (New York: International Universities Press, 1947), pp. 11, 12.

7. William James, *The Varieties of Religious Experience: A Study in Human Nature,* Gifford Lectures on Natural Religion delivered at Edinburgh, 1901–1902 (New York: The Modern Library).

8. In this and the preceding paragraph. *Ibid.,* p. 371.

9. Amy Lowell, *Poetry and Poets* (Boston: Houghton Mifflin, 1930), pp. 25, 26.

10. Rudyard Kipling, *Something of Myself* (New York: Doubleday, Doran, 1937), pp. 226, 227.

11. Johann Peter Eckermann, *Conversations With Goethe,* trans. by John Oxenford, Everyman's Library, no. 851 (New York: Dutton), p. 398.

12. *Ibid.,* p. 394.

13. André M. Weitzenhoffer, *Hypnotism, An Objective Study in Suggestibility* (New York: Wiley, 1953), p. 97.

14. Selected References drawn from sources used by Kubie: Rose H. Alschuler and LaBerta Weiss Hattwick, *Painting and Personality, a Study of Young Children* (Chicago, 1947); Charles Fisher, "Dreams, Images and Perception," *Journal of the American Psychoanalytic Association,* IV, no. 1, January 1956, 5-48; Lawrence S. Kubie and M. H. Erickson, "The Use of Automatic Drawing in the Interpretation and Relief of a State of Acute Obsessional Depression," *Psychoanalytic Quarterly,* VII (1938), 443-466; Lawrence S. Kubie, "The Experimental Induction of Neurotic Reactions in Man," *Yale Journal of Biology and Medicine,* II (1939), 541-545; Lawrence S. Kubie and Sydney G. Margolin, "The Process of Hypnotism and the Nature of the Hypnotic State," *American Journal of Psychiatry,* C (1944), 611-622; Lawrence S. Kubie, "The Relationship of Symbolic Function in Language Formation and in Neurosis," *Transactions of the Seventh Conference on Cybernetics,* pp. 209-235, ed. Heinz von Foerster, Josiah Macy, Jr., Foundation of New York, 1950; Lawrence S. Kubie, "The Distortion of the Symbolic Process in Neurosis and Psychosis," in *Journal of the American Psychoanalytic Association,* I (1953), pp. 59-86; and "On Preconscious Processes," etc., read before American Academy of Neurology, April 1957, in press; Donald Lindley, "Basic Perceptual Processes and the Electroencephalogram," in *Psychiatric Research Reports,* no. 6, American Psychiatric Association (January 1956), 161-171; James T. Marsh and F. G. Worden, "Perceptual Approaches to Personality" in *Psychiatric Research Reports,* no. 6, American Psychiatric Association (January 1956), 171-177.

15. Lawrence S. Kubie, *Neurotic Distortion of the Creative Process,*

Porter Lecture Series 22 (Lawrence, Kan.: University of Kansas Press, 1958), pp. 22, 23.
16. *Ibid.*, p. 137.
17. *Ibid.*, p. 29.
18. *Ibid.*, pp. 24, 25.
19. *Ibid.*, pp. 27, 28.
20. *Ibid.*, p. 30.
21. Sir Charles Sherrington, *Man on His Nature* (Garden City, New York: Doubleday, 1953), pp. 183, 184.
22. Paul I. Yakovlev, "Motility, Behavior and the Brain: Stereodynamic Organization & Neural Coordinates of Behavior," *Journal of Nervous Mental Diseases,* 1948, 107, pp. 313-335.
23. William James, *The Energies of Men* (New York: Dodd, Mead, 1926), p. 21. See all 29 pages of this valuable little book.
24. Charles Darwin, *Expression of the Emotions in Animals and Men* (1872) (New York: Appleton, 1924), pp. 79, 80.
25. Walter B. Cannon, *Bodily Changes in Pain, Hunger, Fear and Rage* (New York: Appleton, 1927), pp. 215, 216.
26. *Ibid.*, p. 221.
27. Stanley Cobb, *Emotions and Clinical Medicine* (New York: Norton, 1950), pp. 90, 91.
28. Gardner Murphy, *Personality: A Biosocial Approach to Origins and Structure* (New York: Harper & Brothers, 1947), p. 88.
29. *Ibid.*, p. 107.
30. *Ibid.*, p. 109.
31. John Livingston Lowes, *The Road to Xanadu, A Study in the Ways of the Imagination* (Boston: Houghton Mifflin, 1927), pp. 426-427.
32. John Dryden, dedicatory letter to "The Rival Ladies," in Brewster Ghiselin, *The Creative Process, A Symposium* (Berkeley and Los Angeles, Calif.: University of California Press, 1952), p. 77.
33. Lowes, *op. cit.*, p. 44.
34. Lowes, in part quoting Coleridge, *ibid.*, p. 91.

4. The Stuff of Creative Mind

1. Nina Bull, *The Attitude Theory of Emotion* (New York: Nervous and Mental Disease Monograph, no. 81, Coolidge Foundation Publishers, 1951), pp. 43, 44.
2. *Ibid.*, p. 47.
3. *Ibid.*, p. 86.
4. *Ibid.*, p. 4.
5. *Ibid.*, p. 19.
6. Henry James, "The American," in John Livingston Lowes, *The*

Road to Xanadu, A Study in the Ways of the Imagination (Boston: Houghton Mifflin, 1927), p. 56.

7. Peter McKellar, *Imagination and Thinking* (London: Cohen and West, 1957), p. 98.

8. Wilhelm Stekel, "The Polyphony of Thought," in David Rapaport, *Organization and Pathology of Thought,* Austen Riggs Foundation, Monograph no. 1 (New York: Columbia University Press, 1951), pp. 313, 314.

9. McKellar, *op. cit.,* pp. 99, 100.

10. Stekel in Rapaport, *op. cit.,* p. 314.

11. McKellar, *op. cit.,* pp. 100, 101.

12. Sir Francis Galton, *Inquiries into Human Faculties* (New York: Dutton, 1928), pp. 58, 59.

13. Lawrence Edwin Cole, *General Psychology* (New York: McGraw-Hill, 1939), p. 506.

14. Erich R. Jaensch, *Eidetic Imagery and Typological Methods of Investigation* (New York: Harcourt, Brace, 1930).

15. Gordon W. Allport, "Eidetic Imagery," *Brit. J. Psych.,* 1924, 15, pp. 99-120 in Cole, *op. cit.,* pp. 507, 508.

16. Gardner Murphy, *Personality: A Biosocial Approach to Origins and Structure* (New York: Harper & Brothers, 1947), p. 393.

17. Jerome S. Bruner, Jacqueline J. Goodnow, George A. Austin, *A Study of Thinking* (New York: Wiley, 1957).

18. Floyd H. Allport, *Theories of Perception and the Concept of Structure* (New York: Wiley, 1955).

19. Lowes, *op. cit.,* p. 426.

5. OUTER SCENE AND INNER NEED: THE CENSORS

1. Lawrence S. Kubie, *Neurotic Distortion of the Creative Process,* Porter Lectures, series 22 (Lawrence, Kan.: University of Kansas Press, 1958), p. 85.

2. Harold Rugg and William Withers, *Social Foundations of Education* (New York: Prentice-Hall, 1955), pp. 27-30.

3. Melville J. Herskovits, "The Processes of Cultural Change" in Ralph Linton, *The Science of Man in the World Crisis* (New York: Columbia University Press, 1945), p. 158.

4. Gardner Murphy, *Personality: A Biosocial Approach to Origins and Structure* (New York: Harper & Brothers, 1947), p. 866.

5. Margaret Mead, *Growing Up in New Guinea* (New York: Morrow, 1930). Gregory Bateson, *Naven* (Stanford, Calif.: Stanford University Press, 1958).

6. A. H. Maslow and Béla Mittelmann, "Principles of Abnormal Psychology" in Lawrence E. Cole and William F. Bruce, *Educational Psychology* (Yonkers, N.Y.: World Book, 1950), pp. 499, 500.

7. William James, in Lawrence E. Cole, *Human Behavior: Psychology as a Bio-Social Science* (Yonkers, N.Y.: World Book, 1953), pp. 392, 393.
8. Walter Lippmann, *Public Opinion* (New York: Harcourt, Brace, 1922). It was Lippmann who first used the concept of the stereotype.
9. Walt Whitman, "One's Self I Sing," from *Leaves of Grass* (New York: Doubleday, Doran, 1940) [first copyright 1855], p. 15.
10. A. H. Maslow, "Self-Actualizing People: A Study of Psychological Health," in Clark E. Moustakas (ed.), *The Self, Explorations in Personal Growth* (New York: Harper & Brothers, 1956), Chapter XIV, pp. 160-192. Several published and unpublished studies are summarized and interpreted in this chapter. Among those published see especially: "Cognition of the Particular and of the Genetic," *Psychological Review*, 55:20-40 (1948); "Higher and Lower Needs," *Journal of Psychology*, 25:433-436 (1948); "Some Theoretical Consequences of Basic Need-Gratification," *Journal of Personality*, 16:402-416, 1948; "Our Maligned Animal Nature," *Journal of Psychology*, 28:273-278, 1949; "The Expressive Component of Behavior," *Psychological Review*, 56:261-272, 1949.

Maslow's study was "not planned as an ordinary research; it was not a social venture but a private one, motivated by my own curiosity and pointed toward the solution of various personal moral, ethical and scientific problems." He found forty-five persons who, by his criteria, were suitable subjects "from among personal acquaintances and friends, and from among public and historical figures" (for example, Whitman, Thoreau). His data consisted "not so much of the usual gathering of specific and discrete facts as in the slow development of a global or holistic impression of the sort that we form of our friends and acquaintances. . . . The holistic analysis of these total impressions yields [the following] as the most important and useful whole-characteristics of self-actualizing people."

The above quotations are from Maslow, in Moustakas, *ibid.*, pp. 160, 161, 164, 165.

6. FORM IN BODY-MIND FUNCTIONING

1. George W. Hartmann, *Educational Psychology* (New York: American Book Company, 1941), pp. 44, 45.
2. E. D. Adrian, *The Physical Background of Perception*, being the Waynflete Lectures delivered in the College of St. Mary Magdalen, Oxford in Hilary Term, 1946 (Oxford, Eng.: Oxford University Press, 1947), pp. 3, 4.
3. I have relied largely on the following writings by Jean Piaget: *The*

Origins of Intelligence in Children (New York: International Universities Press, 1952); "The Biological Problems of Intelligence," trans. and printed in David Rapaport, *Organization and Psychology of Thought* (New York: Columbia University Press, 1951); *The Language and Thought of the Child* (New York: Harcourt, Brace, 1926); "Principle Factors Determining Intellectual Evolution from Childhood to Adult Life," in *Factors Determining Human Behavior*, Harvard Tercentenary Publication (Cambridge: Harvard University Press, 1937); *The Child's Conception of Number* (New York: Humanities Press, 1952); *The Child's Conception of Space* (with Barbel Inhelder) (New York: Humanities Press, 1956).

I have also used Arnold Gesell's *The Embryology of Behavior* (New York: Harper & Brothers, 1945); with Helen Thompson, *Infant Behavior* (New York: McGraw-Hill, 1934).

4. Lawrence E. Cole, *Human Behavior: Psychology as a Bio-Social Science* (Yonkers, N.Y.: World Book, 1953), pp. 469, 470.

5. Adrian, *op. cit.*, pp. 13, 14.

6. *Ibid.*, p. 63.

7. Warren S. McCulloch, "Why the Mind is in the Head," in *Cerebral Mechanisms in Behavior;* The Hixon Symposium, ed. by Lloyd A. Jeffress (New York: Wiley, 1951), pp. 56, 57. For further discussion of feedback see chap. 13 of this book.

8. W. Grey Walter, "Activity Patterns in the Human Brain" in *Aspects of Form, a Symposium on Form in Nature and Art,* ed. by Lancelot Law Whyte (New York: Pellegrini and Cudahy, 1951), p. 182.

9. Karl S. Lashley, "The Problem of Serial Order in Behavior," in *Hixon Symposium, op. cit.*, p. 131.

10. Wilder Penfield, and Theodore Rasmussen, *The Cerebral Cortex of Man, a Clinical Study of Localization of Function* (New York: Macmillan, 1952), p. 164.

11. *Ibid.*, p. 166.

12. *Ibid.*, pp. 180, 181.

13. Penfield, quoted by William A. Lawrence in *The New York Times,* November 24, 1957.

14. Penfield, quoted by Lawrence, *ibid.*

15. The quotations in the preceeding paragraphs are from Penfield and Rasmussen, *op. cit.*, pp. 178, 179.

16. Cole, *op. cit.*, p. 544.

17. Adrian, *op. cit.*, p. 92.

18. Joseph Needham, "Biochemical Aspect of Form and Growth," in Whyte (ed.), *Aspects of Form, op. cit.*, p. 86.

19. John Pfeiffer, *The Human Brain* (New York: Harper & Brothers, 1955), p. 87.

20. *Ibid.*, p. 95.

21. John von Neumann, in discussion reported by The Hixon Symposium, *op. cit.*, p. 58.
22. *Ibid.*, pp. 62, 63.
23. Adrian, in part quoting Karl Lashley, *op. cit.*, p. 91.
24. Lashley, in The Hixon Symposium, *op. cit.*, pp. 71, 72.
25. Adrian, *op. cit.*, p. 4.

7. FORM IN NATURE AND IN ART

1. Albert M. Dalcq, "Form and Modern Embryology," in *Aspects of Form, A Symposium on Form in Nature and Art* ed. by Lancelot Law Whyte (New York: Pellegrini and Cudahy, 1951), pp. 94, 95. For additional brief statements by Waddington, Humphreys-Owen, F. G. Gregory, K. Z. Lorenz, W. Grey Walter, and J. N. Needham, see L. L. Whyte's symposium, *Aspects of Form, op. cit.* Selected sources on structure and the forming process: Sheldon Cheney, *Expressionism in Art* (New York: Liveright, 1934); A. M. Dalcq, *Form and Causality in Early Development* (Cambridge: Harvard University Press, 1938); Sergei Eisenstein, *Film Form* (New York: Harcourt, Brace, 1949), and *The Film Sense* (New York: Harcourt, Brace, 1942); Adolf Hildebrand, *The Problem of Form* (New York: G. E. Stechert, 1945); Susanne K. Langer, *Feeling and Form* (New York: Scribner's, 1953), and *Philosophy in a New Key* (Cambridge: Harvard University Press, 1942); Konrad Lorenz, *King Solomon's Ring* (New York: Crowell, 1952); Erwin Schrödinger, *What is Life?* (New York: Macmillan, 1947); D'Arcy Wentworth Thompson, *On Growth and Form* (Cambridge, Eng.: Cambridge University Press, 1952), 2 vols.; N. Tinbergen, *The Study of Instinct* (Oxford, Eng.: Oxford University Press, 1951); C. H. Waddington, *How Animals Develop*, Torchbook (New York: Harper & Brothers); Hermann Weyl, *Symmetry* (Princeton, N.J.: Princeton University Press, 1952); Lancelot Law Whyte, *Accent on Form* (New York: Harper & Brothers, 1954), and *The Next Development in Man* (New York: Holt, 1948), and *The Unitary Principle in Physics and Biology* (New York: Holt, 1949); Lancelot Law Whyte (ed.), *Aspects of Form, A Symposium on Form in Nature and Art, op. cit.*
2. S.P.F. Humphreys-Owen, "Physical Principles Underlying Inorganic Form," in Whyte (ed.), *Aspects of Form, op. cit.*, p. 19.
3. Whyte, *Accent on Form, op. cit.*, pp. 135, 137.
4. *Ibid.*, pp. 18, 19.
5. F. G. Gregory, "Form in Plants," in Whyte (ed.), *Aspects of Form, op. cit.*, p. 59.
6. *Ibid.*, p. 71.
7. *Ibid.*, p. 75.

8. C. H. Waddington, "The Character of Biological Form," in Whyte, *ibid.,* p. 43.
9. *Ibid.,* p. 45.
10. E. S. Russell, *The Directiveness of Organic Activities* (Cambridge, Eng.: Cambridge University Press, 1946), p. 18.
11. *Ibid.,* p. 21.
12. *Ibid.,* p. 44.
13. *Ibid.,* pp. 174, 175, 176.
14. *Ibid.,* pp. 178, 179.
15. Dalcq, in *Aspects of Form, op. cit.,* p. 95.
16. Joseph Needham, "Biological Aspect of Form and Growth." in Whyte (ed.), *Aspects of Form, op. cit.,* pp. 79, 80.
17. *Ibid.,* p. 80.
18. *Ibid.,* p. 83.
19. *Ibid.,* pp. 84, 85.
20. Clive Bell, *Art* (New York: Stokes [pref. 1913]), pp. 6, 7, 8.
21. Sheldon Cheney, *Expressionism in Art* (New York: Liveright, 1934), p. 99.
22. *Dictionary of Psychology,* ed. by Howard C. Warren (Boston: Houghton Mifflin, 1934). Definition of "economy/principle (or canon) of." It was originally proposed by William of Occam and came to be called "Occam's Razor." According to the Oxford Dictionary, it was "the leading principle of the nominalism of William of Occam that for purposes of explanation things not known to exist should not, unless it is absolutely necessary, be postulated as existing; usually called the Law of Parsimony."

 In animal psychology it was formulated by Lloyd Morgan as a canon for the evaluation of data. It states that "an act of behavior may not be interpreted as due to the operation of a higher mental faculty or function if it can be interpreted as the outcome of one which stands lower in the psychological scale."
23. Whyte, *Accent on Form, op. cit.,* pp. 159, 160.
24. Konrad Z. Lorenz, "The Role of Gestalt Perception in Animal and Human Behavior," in *ibid.,* p. 165.
25. Louis Danz, *The Psychologist Looks at Art* (New York: Longmans, 1937), p. 80.
26. See Jacques Loeb, *Forced Movement, Tropisms and Animal Conduct* (Philadelphia: Lippincott, 1918).
27. Lorenz, *op. cit.,* pp. 160, 161.
28. Humphreys-Owen, *op. cit.,* p. 14.
29. *Ibid.,* p. 17.
30. Whyte, *Accent on Form, op. cit.,* p. 113.
31. Alfred North Whitehead, *An Enquiry Concerning the Principles of Natural Knowledge* (Cambridge, Eng.: Cambridge University Press, 1919), p. 198.

32. Charles S. Myers, *In the Realm of Mind* (Cambridge, Eng.: Cambridge University Press, 1937), p. 189.
33. Edmund W. Sinnott, *Cell and Psyche, The Biology of Purpose* (Chapel Hill, N.C.: University of North Carolina Press, 1950), p. 48.

8. THE OPENING OF TRANCE VESTIBULES

1. Selected sources used on hypnotism and creative imagination:
    I. On the historical background: H. Bernheim, *Suggestive Therapeutics* (New York: Putnam, 1902); J. M. Bramwell, *Hypnotism, Its History, Practice and Theory* (London: Rider, 1913); Clark Hull, *Hypnosis and Suggestibility: An Experimental Approach* (New York: Appleton-Century-Crofts, 1933), chap. I; William James, *The Principles of Psychology* II (New York: Holt, 1890), 593-616; Pierre Janet, *Psychological Healing* I (New York: Macmillan, 1925), 151-207; W. McDougall, "Hypnotism," article in *Encyclopaedia Britannica*, 11th ed.; Morton Prince, *The Unconscious* (New York: Macmillan, 1914); W. H. R. Rivers, *Instinct and the Unconscious* (Cambridge, Eng.: Cambridge University Press, 1922).
    II. On the scientific study of hypnotism since 1925: G. H. Estabrook, *Hypnotism* (New York: Dutton, 1943); Hull, *Hypnosis and Suggestibility, op. cit.;* André Weitzenhoffer, *Hypnotism* (New York: Wiley, 1953).
    III. On hypnotherapy: Margaret Brenman and Merton M. Gill, *Hypnotherapy, A Survey of the Literature,* The Menninger Foundation, Monograph Series no. 5 (New York: International Universities Press, 1947); M. V. Kline et al., "A Scientific Report on 'The Search for Bridey Murphy,' " authoritative appraisal of the book by Morey Bernstein (New York: Julian Press, 1956); John G. Watkins, *Hypnotherapy of War Neuroses* (New York: Ronald, 1949); Lewis R. Wolberg, *Hypnoanalysis* (New York: Grune and Stratton, 1945).
2. Kline, *op. cit.,* p. 180.
3. *Ibid.,* pp. 179, 180.
4. Sears's investigations reported by Hull, *op. cit.,* pp. 256 ff.
5. Hull, *ibid.,* p. 264.
6. *Ibid.,* pp. 267, 269.
7. Brenman and Gill, *op. cit.,* p. 55.
8. Hull, *op. cit.,* p. 30.
9. Lawrence E. Cole, *Human Behavior: Psychology as a Bio-Social Science* (Yonkers, N.Y.: World Book Co., 1953), p. 655.
10. Hull, *op. cit.,* p. 272.
11. R. Heilig and H. Hoff, "Ueber psychogene Entstehung des Herpes

Labialis," *Medizinische Klinik,* no. 38, 1928, quoted by Hull, *ibid.,* pp. 272, 273.

12. Hull, *ibid.,* p. 274.
13. Heilig and Hoff, "Ueber hypnotische Beeinflussung der Nieren-funktion," *Deutsche Medizinische Wochenschrift,* 51: 1615–1616, 1925, quoted by Hull, *ibid.,* pp. 275, 276.
14. Cloquet, an eye-witness, in Hull, *ibid.,* p. 129.
15. James, *op. cit.,* p. 602.
16. Binet and Féré, in Hull, *op. cit.,* p. 130.
17. Moll, in Hull, *ibid.,* pp. 130, 131.
18. Hull, *ibid.,* p. 131.
19. Cole, *op. cit.,* p. 659.
20. Weitzenhoffer, *op. cit.,* p. 273.
21. Hull, *op. cit.,* pp. 391, 392.
22. S. H. Kraines, "The Therapy of the Neuroses and Psychoses," in Brenman and Gill, *op. cit.,* pp. 21, 22.
23. W. R. Wells, "Experiments in Waking Hypnosis for Instructional Purposes," Journal of Abnormal and Social Psychology, 18, 389–404, 1924, in Brenman and Gill, *ibid.,* pp. 37, 38.
24. Wells, in Brenman and Gill, *ibid.,* p. 40.
25. Brenman and Gill, *ibid.,* p. 100.
26. W. B. Carpenter, in his pioneer study: "On the Influence of Suggestion in Modifying and Directing Muscular Movements Independently of Volition," *Notices, Proceedings Royal Institute,* 1852, pp. 193, 194.
27. H. J. Eysenck, *Dimensions of Personality* (London: Routledge, 1947), p. 195.
28. *Ibid.,* p. 196.
29. Weitzenhoffer, *op. cit.,* p. 248.
30. Stedman's *Medical Dictionary,* definition of "tonicity."
31. Weitzenhoffer, *op. cit.,* p. 249.
32. Pierre Janet, "L'Automatisme psychologique" (1889), in Hull, *op. cit.,* p. 172.
33. Charles Theodore Burnett, "Splitting the Mind. An Experimental Study of Normal Men," Psychological Monograph, no. 34, no. 2 (Princeton, N.J.: Psychological Review Company, 1925).
34. Watkins, *op. cit.,* p. 93.
35. Hull, *op. cit.,* p. 176.
36. *Ibid.,* p. 176.
37. *Ibid.,* p. 191.
38. Cole, *op. cit.,* p. 675.
39. William James, *The Varieties of Religious Experience: A Study in Human Nature,* Being the Gifford Lectures on Natural Religion Delivered at Edinburgh in 1901–1902 (New York: The Modern Library, Random House, 1936), pp. 377, 378.

40. Lin Yutang (ed.) : "Hymns from the Rigveda," in *Wisdom of China and India, An Anthology* (New York: Random House, 1942), p. 12.
41. Philippe de Félice, "Poisons Sacrés, Ivresses Divines," in Aldous Huxley, *The Doors of Perception* (New York: Harper & Brothers, 1954), p. 68.
42. Huxley, *ibid.*, p. 67.
43. James, *The Varieties of Religious Experience, op. cit.*, p. 378.
44. Huxley, *op. cit.*, p. 9.
45. Weir Mitchell, in Aldous Huxley, *Heaven and Hell* (New York: Harper & Brothers, 1956), pp. 20, 21.
46. J. S. Slotkin, "Menominic Peyotism," in Huxley, *Doors of Perception, op. cit.*, p. 66.
47. Huxley, *Heaven and Hell, op. cit.*, p. 7.
48. Huxley, *Doors of Perception, op. cit.*, p. 12.
49. Huxley, *Heaven and Hell, op. cit.*, pp. 14, 15.
50. Huxley, *Doors of Perception, op. cit.*, p. 16. My italics.
51. *Ibid.*, p. 20.
52. Huxley, *Heaven and Hell, op. cit.*, p. 13. My italics.
53. Huxley, *Doors of Perception, op. cit.*, p. 54.
54. Renée's *Autobiography of a Schizophrenic Girl*, with an Analytic Interpretation by Marguerite Sechehaye, trans. by Grace Rubin-Rabson (New York: Grune and Stratton, 1951), pp. 4, 7, 8. See also Marguerite Sechehaye, *Symbolic Realization* (New York: International Universities Press, 1951).
55. Huxley, *Heaven and Hell, op. cit.*, p. 18.
56. J. A. Symonds, in James, *The Varieties of Religious Experience, op. cit.*, pp. 382, 383.

9. THE TAO OF THE EAST

1. See, for example: Eugen Herrigel, *Zen in the Art of Archery* (New York: Pantheon, 1953); Alan Watts, *The Way of Zen* (New York: Pantheon, 1957); C. G. Jung, Commentary on Richard Wilhelm's translation of *The Secret of the Golden Flower* (New York: Wehman Brothers, 1955).
2. Jung, in Wilhelm, *op. cit.*, p. 78.
3. Selected Sources: R. H. Blythe, *Haiku*, 4 vols. (Tokyo: Hokuseido, 1949–1952), and *Zen in English Literature and Oriental Classics* (Tokyo: Hokuseido, 1948); Herrigel, *op. cit.; I Ching*, or *Book of Changes*, see trans. by Richard Wilhelm rendered into English by Cary F. Baynes, 2 vols., Bollingen Series XIX (Washington: Bollingen, 1950); Lao-tzu, *The Way of Life According to Laotzu*, an American version according to Witter Bynner, 10th impression (New York: John Day, 1944); Lin Yutang, *The Wisdom of China*

and *India, An Anthology* (New York: Random House, 1942), Wilhelm, *The Secret of the Golden Flower, op. cit.;* R. Q. H. Siu, *The Tao of Science* (published jointly by Cambridge: Massachusetts Institute of Technology Press, and New York: Wiley, 1957); Daisetz T. Suzuki, *Essays in Zen Buddhism,* 3 vols. (London: Luzac, 1927; reprinted in London: Rider, 1949); Alan W. Watts, *The Way of Zen, op. cit.*

4. It is perhaps true that the bulk of printed Chinese "mysticism," as Lin Yutang called it in *The Wisdom of China and India,* is as large as the sacred Hindu-Buddhist books. Lin includes, in addition to Lao-tzu's *Tao Teh Ching* of 81 short verses, several writings in Chinese democracy (The Book of History, Mencius, Motze, The Aphorisms of Confucius, The Golden Mean of Tsesze), Chinese poetry, including some great ancient lyrics of Ch'ü Yüan, Li Po, the Tale of Meng Chiang, the Mortal Thoughts of a Nun, Chinese Tales, Six Chapters of a Floating Life, Parables of Ancient Philosophers, Family Letters of a Chinese Poet, and One Hundred Proverbs.

5. I have seen references to nine published versions of it. I have four in my own library. I have been guided here primarily by the tenth edition of Witter Bynner's particularly fine American version, *The Way of Life According to Lao-tzu, op. cit.*

6. Sheldon Cheney, *Men Who Have Walked With God, Being the Story of Mysticism Through the Ages Told in the Biographies of Representative Seers and Saints* (New York: Knopf, 1948), pp. 2-5, apocryphal conversations between Lao-tse and Confucius.

7. *Ibid.,* pp. 4, 5.

8. Herrigel, *op. cit.* See also Mrs. Gustie Herrigel, *Zen in the Art of Flower Arrangement,* trans. by R. F. C. Hull (Newton Center, Mass.: Charles T. Branford Co., 1958).

9. Herrigel, *Zen in the Art of Archery, op. cit.,* p. 65.

10. *Ibid.,* p. 64.

11. *Ibid.*

12. *Ibid.,* pp. 66, 70.

13. *Ibid.,* p. 61, 62.

14. *Ibid.,* p. 63.

15. *Ibid.,* p. 47.

16. *Ibid.,* pp. 34-37.

17. *Ibid.,* pp. 37, 38.

18. *Ibid.,* pp. 40, 41.

19. Daisetz T. Suzuki, in introduction to Herrigel, *ibid.,* p. 11.

20. Herrigel, *ibid.,* p. 48.

21. *Ibid.,* pp. 51, 52.

22. *Ibid.,* p. 82.

23. *Ibid.,* p. 76.

24. *Ibid.*, pp. 77, 78.
25. *Ibid.*, p. 88.
26. *Ibid.*, p. 91.
27. Here I follow Watts, *op. cit.*, p. 19.
28. *Ibid.*, pp. 24, 25.
29. *Ibid.*, pp. 25, 27.
30. Lao-tzu, in Watts, *ibid.*, p. 25.
31. Words of Chuang-tzu, from H. A. Giles, in Watts, *ibid.*, p. 28.
32. Jung, in Wilhelm, *op. cit.*, p. 90.
33. Lin Yutang, in *The Wisdom of China and India, op. cit.*, pp. 5, 6.
34. Behanan's judgment is that the most readable English translation is that of J. H. Woods, *The Yoga-System of Patanjali,* Harvard Oriental Series, vol. 17 (Cambridge: Harvard University Press, 1914).
35. Kovoor T. Behanan, *Yoga, A Scientific Evaluation* (New York: Macmillan, 1937), p. 29.
36. *Ibid.*, p. 166.
37. Vivekananda, "Raja Yoga," in William James, *The Varieties of Religious Experience: A Study in Human Nature* (New York: The Modern Library, Random House, 1936), pp. 391, 392. James recommends as "the completest source of information on Yoga" the work translated by Vihari Lala Mitra, *Yoga Vasishta Maha Ramayana,* 4 vols. (Calcutta: 1891–1899).
38. Behanan, *op. cit.*, pp. 30-32.
39. Geraldine Coster, *Yoga and Western Psychology* (New York: Oxford University Press, 1934), p. 79.
40. *Ibid.*, p. 159.
41. *Ibid.*, p. 186.
42. Lin Yutang, *op. cit.*, 116.
43. Coster, *op. cit.*, p. 199.
44. Lin Yutang, *op. cit.*, p. 116.
45. Coster, *op. cit.*, p. 187.
46. *Ibid.*, pp. 121-123.
47. James, *op. cit.*, pp. 392, 393.
48. Coster, *op. cit.*, p. 199.
49. *Ibid.*, p. 200.
50. *Ibid.*, p. 201.
51. *Ibid.*
52. See Sutras Book III, 10, 11, 12, in Coster, *ibid.*, p. 123.
53. Coster, *ibid.*, p. 205.
54. Behanan, *op. cit.*, pp. 245, 246.
55. *Ibid.*, p. 245.
56. William James, *The Energies of Men* (New York: Dodd, Mead, 1926), pp. 19-20.
57. James, *The Varieties of Religious Experience, op. cit.*, p. 392.

58. Behanan, *op. cit.*, p. 246.
59. *Ibid.*, pp. 248, 249.

10. THE TAO OF THE WEST

1. William James, *The Varieties of Religious Experience: A Study in Human Nature,* Gifford Lectures on Natural Religion delivered in Edinburgh in 1901–1902 (London: Longmans, 1902). I quote from the Modern Library edition (19th). Evelyn Underhill, *Mysticism: A Study in the Nature and Development of Man's Spiritual Consciousness* (New York: Noonday Press, 1955); (original ed., New York: Dutton, 1910), the 12th ed. to which I refer and from which I quote, pub. 1930. A long selection of the autobiographical account is given in the Appendix; magnificent digests, critical selections, and interpretations. Sheldon Cheney, *Men Who Have Walked With God: Being the Story of Mysticism Through the Ages Told in the Biographies of Representative Seers and Saints With Excerpts from Their Writings and Sayings* (New York: Knopf, 1945), 6th printing, 1948.
2. Underhill, *op. cit.*, p. 81 (all quotations in this paragraph).
3. *Ibid.*, pp. 232, 233.
4. *Ibid.*, pp. 236, 238.
5. *Ibid.*, p. 239.
6. *Ibid.*, p. 299.
7. *Ibid.*, p. 300.
8. *Ibid.*, pp. 301, 302.
9. Cheney, *op. cit.*, p. 366.
10. William Blake, in a letter to William Hayley, 23 October 1804, in *The Letters of William Blake,* ed. by Geoffrey Keynes (New York: Macmillan, 1956), p. 138.
11. Blake, "Auguries of Innocence" in *Blake,* Viking Portable Library, ed. by Alfred Kazin (New York: Viking, 1946), p. 150.
12. Blake, *ibid.*, p. 250.
13. Cheney, *op. cit.*, p. 309.
14. Arthur Symons, in Introduction of Samuel Taylor Coleridge, *Biographia Literaria,* Everyman's Library, no. 11 (New York: Dutton, 1947), pp. VII–IX.
15. John Livingston Lowes, *The Road to Xanadu, A Study in the Ways of the Imagination* (Boston: Houghton, Mifflin, 1927), pp. 483, 484.
16. Coleridge, in a letter to Thomas Poole, 23 March 1801, in I. A. Richards, *Coleridge on Imagination* (New York: Norton, 1950), p. 16.
17. Samuel Taylor Coleridge, *Biographia Literaria,* II, Shawcross Ed. (London: William Pickering, 1847), p. 87.

18. Coleridge, in Richards, *op. cit.*, pp. 68, 69.
19. Coleridge, *Biographia Literaria*, Everyman's Library Edition, *op. cit.*, p. 146.
20. Coleridge, in Richards, *op. cit.*, p. 66.
21. Richards, *ibid.*, p. 66.
22. Coleridge, in a letter to Robert Southey, August 7, 1803, in Richards, *ibid.*, p. 168.
23. Coleridge, *The Portable Coleridge*, ed. with an introduction by I. A. Richards (New York: Viking, 1950), p. 311.
24. Lowes, *op. cit.*, p. 4.
25. Coleridge, in Lowes, *ibid.*, p. 311.
26. Lowes, *ibid.*, p. 357.
27. *The Portable Coleridge*, *op. cit.*, p. 267.
28. Coleridge, in Lowes, *op. cit.*, p. 66.
29. Lowes, *ibid.*, p. 66.
30. Ben Jonson, in Lowes, *ibid.*, p. 66.
31. Lowes, *ibid.*, p. 67.
32. Coleridge, in Lowes, *ibid.*, p. 56.
33. Lowes, *ibid.*, pp. 60, 61.
34. Oliver Wendell Holmes, in Lowes, *ibid.*, p. 57.
35. Lowes, *ibid.*, pp. 57, 58.
36. Coleridge, in Lowes, *ibid.*, p. 72.
37. Lowes, in part quoting Coleridge, *ibid.*, p. 63.
38. Lowes, *ibid.*, p. 92.
39. *Ibid.*, p. 65.
40. Lowes, in part quoting Coleridge, *ibid.*, p. 432.
41. Lawrence Edwin Cole, *General Psychology* (New York: McGraw-Hill, 1939), p. 557.
42. Lowes, *op. cit.*, p. 55.
43. *Ibid.*, p. 54.
44. Goethe, in his conversations with Eckermann, March 18, 1831, in Lowes, *ibid.*, pp. 71, 72.
45. Epictetus, from his Discourses, in Lowes, *ibid.*, p. 72.
46. Lowes, *ibid.*, p. 72.
47. Poincaré, from *Science and Medicine*, in Lowes, *ibid.*, pp. 62, 63.
48. Lowes, *ibid.*, p. 54.
49. *Ibid.*, p. 431.
50. William James, letter quoted by Irwin Edman in his Foreword to Henri Bergson, *Creative Evolution*, trans. by Arthur Mitchell (New York: The Modern Library, Random House, 1944), p. ix.
51. Irwin Edman, in Foreword to Bergson, *ibid.*, pp. x, xi.
52. K. W. Wild, *Intuition* (Cambridge, Eng.: Cambridge University Press, 1938), p. 3.
53. Henri Bergson, *An Introduction to Metaphysics*, trans. by T. E. Hulme (London: Macmillan, 1913), pp. 76, 77.

54. *Ibid.*, pp. 12, 13.
55. *Ibid.*, pp. 15, 16.
56. *Ibid.*, pp. 55, 56.
57. *Ibid.*, pp. 6, 7.
58. *Ibid.*, p. 8.

11. OFF-CONSCIOUS FREEDOM TO CREATE

1. Lawrence Kubie, *Neurotic Distortion of the Creative Process*, Porter Lectures, series 22 (Lawrence, Kan.: University of Kansas Press, 1958), p. 38.
2. *Ibid.*, p. 14.
3. *Ibid.*, pp. 32, 33.
4. *Ibid.*, p. 33.
5. John Livingston Lowes, *The Road to Xanadu, A Study in the Ways of the Imagination* (Boston: Houghton Mifflin, 1927), pp. 429-434.
6. *Ibid.*, p. 431.
7. *Ibid.*, pp. 431, 432.
8. Jacques Hadamard, *An Essay on the Psychology of Invention in the Mathematical Field* (Princeton, N.J.: Princeton University Press, 1949), p. 29.
9. Kubie, *op. cit.*, pp. 50, 51.
10. *Ibid.*, p. 52.
11. See the following: Ralph W. Gerard, *The Body Functions* (New York: Wiley, 1941). Also his article, "The Biological Basis of Imagination," *Scientific Monthly*, June 1946. Lawrence S. Kubie, *Practical and Theoretical Aspects of Psychoanalysis* (New York: International Universities Press, 1957). Also his "On Preconscious Processes," paper read before American Academy of Neurology, April, 1957.
12. Sheldon Cheney, *Expressionism in Art* (New York: Liveright, 1934), pp. 58, 59.
13. Leo Stein, *The A-B-C of Aesthetics* (New York: Boni and Liveright, 1927), p. 122.
14. Henri Matisse in Stein, *ibid.*, p. 124.
15. Eugen Bleuler, "Autistic Thinking," in David Rapaport, *Organization and Pathology of Thought*, Selected Sources, Austin Riggs Foundation, Monograph no. 1 (New York: Columbia University Press, 1951), pp. 399-450.
16. Bleuler, in Rapaport, *op. cit.*, p. 401.
17. Bleuler, *ibid.*, p. 416.
18. *Ibid.*, p. 402.
19. *Ibid.*, p. 416.
20. Kubie, *op. cit.*, pp. 15, 16.
21. *Ibid.*, p. 27.

22. Peter McKellar, *Imagination and Thinking* (London: Cohen and West, 1957), p. 35.

23. These are reviewed in Gardner Murphy, *Personality: A Biosocial Approach to Origins and Structure* (New York: Harper & Brothers, 1947), pp. 365-374. For his theory of autism, see pp. 374-390.

24. Murphy, *ibid.,* p. 365.

25. *Ibid.,* p. 392.

26. *Ibid.,* p. 394.

27. Wilhelm Stekel, "The Psychology of Thought," in Rapaport, *op. cit.,* p. 314.

28. McKellar, *op. cit.,* p. 106.

29. Osmond, in McKellar, *ibid.,* p. 107.

30. McKellar, *ibid.,* quoting a patient, p. 38.

31. *Ibid.,* p. 67.

32. Howard C. Warren (ed.), *Dictionary of Psychology* (Boston: Houghton Mifflin, 1934).

33. McKellar, *op. cit.,* p. 60.

34. Gombrich, in McKellar, *ibid.,* p. 65.

35. McKellar, *ibid.,* pp. 55, 56.

36. *Ibid.,* reports of subjects, p. 56.

37. *Ibid.,* report of subject, p. 28.

38. *Ibid.,* report of patient, p. 68.

39. Galton, in McKellar, *ibid.,* report of subjects, p. 69.

40. *Ibid.,* report of subject, p. 36.

41. Selected References: Best over-all interpretation of experimental studies of isolation, by John Lilly: "Mental Effects of Reduction of Ordinary Levels of Physical Stimuli on Intact, Healthy Persons," *Psychiatric Research Reports 5*, American Psychiatric Association, June 1956; "Some Thoughts on Brain-Mind, and on Restraint and Isolation of Mentally Healthy Subjects," Scientific Staff Meeting, Philadelphia Psychiatric Hospital, 1955; "Some Considerations Regarding Basic Mechanisms of Positive and Negative Types of Motivations," *American Journal of Psychiatry*, vol. 115, no. 6, December 1958; "Illustrative Strategies for Research on Psychopathology in Mental Health," Group for the Advancement of Psychiatry, *Symposium No. 2, 1955.*

Autobiographical Statements of Solitaries on sea and land: Captain Joshua Slocum, *Sailing Alone Around the World* (London: Rupert Hart-Davis, 1948); Dr. Alain Bombard, *The Voyage of the Hérétique* (New York: Simon and Schuster, 1953); Jean Merrien, *Les Navigateurs Solitaires* (Paris: Editions Denoel, 1954); Walter Gibson, *The Boat* (Boston: Houghton Mifflin, 1953); Richard E. Byrd, *Alone* (New York: Putnam, 1938); Christiane Ritter, *A Woman in the Polar Night* (New York: Dutton, 1954).

All the short quotations in the remaining part of this chapter have been taken from Dr. Lilly's address of March 9, 1956, before the American Psychiatric Association. I shall give references only for the longer quotations.

42. Lilly, *ibid.*, p. 2.
43. *Ibid.*, p. 3.
44. *Ibid.*, pp. 4, 5.
45. *Ibid.*, p. 5.
46. *Ibid.*, p. 5.
47. *Ibid.*, pp. 7, 8.

13. AN APPROACH THROUGH BRAIN-MIND MODELING

1. The systematic publication of Kenneth Craik's theory was in *The Nature of Explanation* (Cambridge, Eng.: Cambridge University Press, 1943). He was killed shortly afterward in a motorcycle accident, thereby cutting off the contribution of one of the most promising speculative students in this multi-discipline field.
2. Craik, *ibid.*, p. 58.
3. *Ibid.*, p. 57.
4. *Ibid.*, p. 50.
5. *Ibid.*, p. 76 (my italics).
6. *Ibid.*, p. 53.
7. *Ibid.*, pp. 55, 56 (my italics).
8. Selected Sources: W. Ross Ashby, *Design for a Brain* (New York: Wiley, 1954), and *An Introduction to Cybernetics* (New York: Wiley, 1957); Craik, *op. cit.;* Warren S. McCulloch, *Finality and Form*, 15th James Arthur Lecture, New York Academy of Science, 1947 (Springfield, Ill.: Charles C. Thomas, 1952), and "Why the Mind is in the Head," in *Cerebral Mechanisms in Behavior*, Hixon Symposium, ed. by Lloyd A. Jeffress (New York: Wiley, 1951); Walter S. McCulloch and Walter Pitts, "The Statistical Organization of the Nervous System," *Journal American Statistical Association 4*, pp. 91-99, and "How We Know Universals: The Perfection of Auditory and Visual Forms," *Bulletin Mathematical Biophysics 9*, 1947, pp. 127-147; A. Rosenblueth, N. Wiener, and J. Bigelow, "Behavior, Purpose and Teleology," *Philosophy of Science, 10, 8,* 1943; W. Sluckin, *Minds and Machines* (London: Penguin, 1954), best popular treatment; Heinz von Foerster, *Cybernetics,* Ten Conferences 1944–1953, Symposia by Selected World Students, see especially McCulloch, pp. 15-19, 69-80, and W. Grey Walter, pp. 19-33 (6, 7, 8, 9, and 10 Symposia published: Macy Foundation); W. Grey Walter, "Activity Patterns in the Human Brain," in *Aspects of Form*, ed. by Lancelot Law Whyte (New York: Pellegrini and Cudahy, 1951), and *The Living Brain* (New York: Norton, 1953), basic treatment; Norbert Wiener, *Cybernetics or*

Control and Communication in the Animal and the Machine (New York: Wiley, 1948), technical and mathematical, and *The Human Use of Human Beings, Cybernetics and Society* (Boston: Houghton Mifflin, 1950), a popular treatment.

9. Norbert Wiener, *The Human Use of Human Beings, op. cit.,* p. 15.
10. Floyd H. Allport, *Theories of Perception and the Concept of Structure* (New York: Wiley, 1955), p. 493.
11. W. Ross Ashby, *Design for a Brain, op. cit.,* p. 29.
12. *Ibid.,* p. v.
13. Wiener, *The Human Use of Human Beings, op. cit.,* p. 12.
14. *Ibid.,* pp. 12, 14.
15. Wiener, *Cybernetics, op. cit.,* pp. 115, 116.
16. *Ibid.,* p. 135 (my italics).
17. Stanley Cobb, *Emotions and Clinical Medicine* (New York: Norton, 1950), pp. 48-49.
18. *Ibid.,* p. 52.
19. *Ibid.,* p. 57.
20. S.P.F. Humphreys-Owen, "Physical Principles Underlying Inorganic Form," in Whyte (ed.), *Aspects of Form, op. cit.,* pp. 20, 21.
21. Hadley Cantril, *The Why of Man's Experience* (New York: Macmillan, 1950), p. 72 (reporting on W. H. Ittelson, and A. Ames, "Accommodation, Convergence and Their Relation to Apparent Distance," *Journal of Psychology,* 1950, 50, pp. 43-63).
22. Cantril, *ibid.,* in part from Ittelson, p. 73.
23. D. O. Hebb, *The Organization of Behavior* (New York: Wiley, 1949), p. 17.
24. Cantril, *op. cit.,* p. 66.
25. See "Adaptation Level as Frame of Reference for Prediction of Psychological Data," *American Journal of Psychology,* XL, pp. 1-29, 1947.
26. F. H. Allport, *op. cit.,* pp. 254-256.
27. Konrad Z. Lorenz, "The Role of Gestalt Perception in Animal and Human Behavior," in *Aspects of Form, op. cit.,* all quotations in preceding two paragraphs, pp. 170-174.
28. *Ibid.,* pp. 176, 177.

14. Felt-thought through Gestural Symbol

1. Herbert Silberer, "Report on a Method of Eliciting and Observing Certain Symbolic Hallucination-Phenomena," in David Rapaport, *Organization and Pathology of Thought,* Selected Sources, Austin Riggs Foundation, Monograph no. 1 (New York: Columbia University Press, 1951), pp. 195, 196 (my italics).
2. Silberer, *ibid.,* p. 196.
3. Rapaport, *ibid.,* p. 196.

4. Silberer, *ibid.*, p. 233.
5. *Ibid.*, p. 218.
6. A. D. Ritchie, in Susanne Langer, *Philosophy in a New Key, A Study in the Symbolism of Reason, Rite and Art* (Cambridge, Harvard University Press, 1942), p. 27.
7. Susanne Langer, *ibid.*, p. 28.
8. Coleridge, from a letter to Thomas Poole, March 23, 1801, in I. E. Richards, *Coleridge on Imagination* (New York: Norton, 1950), p. 16.
9. R. G. Collingwood, *The Principles of Art* (Oxford, Eng.: Oxford University Press, 1950), pp. 157, 158, 159.
10. *Ibid.*, pp. 163, 164.
11. Gardner Murphy, *Personality: A Biosocial Approach to Origins and Structure* (New York: Harper & Brothers, 1947), p. 410.
12. Murphy, *ibid.*, pp. 410, 411.
13. *Ibid.*, p. 412.
14. Leo Stein, *The A-B-C of Aesthetics* (New York: Boni and Liveright, 1927), p. 36.
15. *Ibid.*, p. 39.
16. Walter B. Cannon, from his discussion at the Wittenberg Symposium, reported by M. L. Raynert (ed.), "Feelings and Emotions," and quoted in Stanley Cobb, *Emotions and Clinical Medicine* (New York: Norton, 1950), pp. 97, 98.
17. Stein, *op cit.*, pp. 35, 36.
18. *Ibid.*, pp. 37, 38.
19. Sheldon Cheney, *Expressionism in Art* (New York: Liveright, 1934), pp. 120, 121.
20. *Ibid.*, p. 160.
21. *Ibid.*, p. 158.
22. Rudolf Arnheim, *Art and Visual Perception* (Berkeley and Los Angeles, Calif.: University of California Press, 1954), p. 338.
23. Sergei Eisenstein, *Film Form*, ed. and trans. by Jay Leyda (New York: Harcourt, Brace, 1949), pp. 161 ff.
24. Alexander S. Pushkin, "The Bronze Horseman," in Oliver Eaton (ed.), *Verse from Pushkin and Others* (London: Edward Arnold, 1935), pp. 152-167.
25. John Marin, in E. M. Benson, *John Marin* (Washington, D.C.: The American Federation of Arts, 1935), pp. 36, 65.
26. John Marin, *Selected Writings of John Marin*, ed. with an Introduction by Dorothy Norman (New York: Pellegrini and Cudahy, 1949), pp. 4, 5.
27. William James, *Principles of Psychology* (New York: Holt, 1923), I, pp. 245, 246.
28. John B. Watson, *Behaviorism* (New York: Norton, 1930), p. 239.
29. *Ibid.*, p. 266.

30. E. Jacobson, "Electrical Measurements of Neuro-Muscular States During Mental Activities," in F. H. Allport, *Theories of Perception and the Concept of Structure* (New York: Wiley, 1955), p. 567; see also Jacobson, "Electro-Physiology of Mental Activities," *American Journal of Psychology*, 44, pp. 677-694.
31. William James, *Principles of Psychology, op. cit.*, II, chap. XX, pp. 134 ff.
32. *Ibid.*, II, pp. 134, 149, 189.
33. Margaret Floy Washburn, *Movement and Mental Imagery* (Boston: Houghton Mifflin, 1916).
34. *Ibid.*, pp. 152-155.
35. *Ibid.*, p. 153.
36. *Ibid.*, p. 161.
37. K. S. Lashley, "The Problem of Serial Order in Behavior," in *Cerebral Mechanisms in Behavior*, ed. by Lloyd A. Jeffress, The Hixon Symposium (New York: Wiley, 1951).
38. *Ibid.*, p. 119.
39. *Ibid.*, p. 122.
40. *Ibid.*, p. 123.
41. *Ibid.*, pp. 128, 129.
42. Helen Keller, *The Story of My Life* (New York: Doubleday), pp. 23, 24.
43. Susanne Langer, *op. cit.*, p. 63.
44. Ernst Cassirer, *Language and Myth*, trans. by Susanne K. Langer (New York: Dover, 1946), p. 87.
45. Langer, *op. cit.*, p. 139.
46. *Ibid.*, p. 147.
47. *Ibid.*, p. 145.
48. *Ibid.*, p. 145.

15. THE CREATIVE IMAGINATION

1. Alfred Einstein, in Max Wertheimer, *Productive Thinking* (New York: Harper & Brothers, 1945), pp. 183, 184.
2. Konrad Z. Lorenz, "The Role of Gestalt Perception in Animal and Human Behavior," in L. L. Whyte (ed.), *Aspects of Form, A Symposium on Form in Nature and Art* (New York: Pellegrini and Cudahy, 1951), p. 176.
3. S.P.F. Humphreys-Owen, "Physical Principles underlying Inorganic Form," in Whyte (ed.), *ibid.*, p. 21.
4. K. S. Lashley, "The Problem of Serial Order in Behavior," in *Cerebral Mechanisms in Behavior*, The Hixon Symposium, ed. by Lloyd A. Jeffress (New York: Wiley, 1951), p. 122.
5. Lancelot Law Whyte, *Accent on Form: An Anticipation of the*

Science of Tomorrow (New York: Harper & Brothers, 1954), p. 97.

6. H. J. Eysenck, *Dimensions of Personality* (London: Routledge, 1955), p. 196.

7. Susanne Langer, *Philosophy In a New Key, A Study in the Symbolism of Reason, Rite, and Art* (Cambridge: Harvard University Press, 1942), p. 139.

8. Ralph Gerard, "The Biological Basis of Imagination," *Scientific Monthly*, June 1946, p. 496.

9. Lawrence S. Kubie, *Neurotic Distortion of the Creative Process*, Porter Lectures, series 22 (Lawrence, Kan.: University of Kansas, 1958), p. 32.

Index of Subjects

343

Index of Persons and Works Cited